CHARLES AND RAY EAMES

Charles and Ray Eames
with model of
Mathematica exhibition,
1961.

CHARLES AND RAY EAMES

DESIGNERS OF THE TWENTIETH CENTURY

PAT KIRKHAM

The MIT Press

Cambridge, Massachusetts

London, England

Set in Garamond 3 and Stone sans serif.
Printed and bound in the United States of America.

Library of Congress Cataloging-in-Publication Data

Kirkham, Pat.
    Charles and Ray Eames : designers of the twentieth century / Pat Kirkham.
        p.   cm.
    Includes bibliographical references and index.
    ISBN 0-262-1119-3
    1. Eames, Charles.   2. Eames, Ray.   3. Designers—United States—Biography.   I. Title.
    NK1412.E18K57   1995
    745.4'4922--dc20
    [B]   94-24920
                                                                          CIP

Charles Eames was once described as a person with ideals, the courage to stand up for them, and the ability to live up to them. This book is dedicated to my daughters, Alex, Kate, and Sarah, in the hope that they will always find the necessary courage and abilities, and to Beverley and Johanna for their friendship, courage, and ideals.

CONTENTS

ACKNOWLEDGMENTS

So many people have helped me during this project that it is difficult to know where to begin my expressions of gratitude. Ray Eames gave the project her "blessing," and since her death Eames Demetrios, Marilyn and John Neuhart, and the Eames Office have been exceptionally generous with their time and knowledge. Stanton Stephens assisted with the early part of the research. Linda Folland, archivist to the Herman Miller Furniture Company, has been helpful beyond the call of duty—as have Laurent Torno Jr. and Andrew Raimist of St. Louis, who helped me sort out the work of Charles Eames in that city. Andy Hoogenboom enthused over the sculptures of Ray Eames and advised on illustrations, as did Shelley Mills of the Eames Office, who also liaised with the Library of Congress over archive material. Charlotte Benton, Jim Cook, Eames Demetrios, Janet Myles, Beverley Skeggs, Elizabeth Smith, Lynne Walker, Judith Weschler, and Christopher Wilk read the manuscript, in full or in part, and made valuable comments. I am extremely grateful to everyone mentioned above and will not forget that several of them also gave support and encouragement when I most needed it.

Many people who knew the Eameses were generous with their time, knowledge, and contacts. Speaking with them was one of the great pleasures of my research, and I want particularly to thank Deborah Sussman, Jeannine Oppewall, Elaine Sewell Jones, Ralph Caplan, Don Albinson, Jehane Burns, Richard Donges, Paul Schrader, Billy Wilder, Julius Shulman, Judith Weschler, and Alison and Peter Smithson. The following people helped in a variety of ways, and I am glad to offer my thanks in print: Viv Andrews, Judy Attfield, Jeremy Aynsley, Mary Banham, Jim Benjamin, Tony Benn, Ralph Birkenhead, Pam Birley, Judith Brauner, Rhoda Brawne, Bob Brenner, Aaron Brenner, Floris van der Broecke, Ella Calver, Bob Carter, Ashoke Chatterjee, Mary Cortiss, Alan Crawford, Barry Curtis, David Curtis, Martha Deese, Susanne Donges, Simon Field, Christopher Frayling, Ken Garland, Steve Gamble, Alice Gerdine, Joseph Giovannini, Peter Groschl, Jennifer González, Samira Haj, Esley Hamilton, Michael Harvey, Janice Helland, Wendy Kaplan, Kevin Jackson, David James, David Lane, Michael Large, Alan

Love, Serge Mauduit, Dan McLoughlin, Louise Marshal-Nicols, Andrew Meschanivov, Anne Massey, Craig Miller, Leslie Miller, Steve McIntyre, Gillian Naylor, Molly Noyes, Margaret O'Brien, Michael O'Shaughnessy, Derek Ostergard, Paul Overy, J. A. Panchal, James Part, Ford Peatross, David Rau, Pamela Robertson, Charles Silver, Judith Smith, Peter Smith, Virginia Stith, Diane Taylor, Lou Taylor, Roger Towe, Tise Vahimagi, Clive Wainwright, Cynthia Weese, Paul Wells, Mary Weston, Audrey Wilder, Bob Winter, Noel Witts, and John Wyver.

My final thanks are of the "without whom this would not have been possible" variety. It gives me great pleasure to thank the Trustees of the South Square Trust for funding a fellowship at the Royal College of Art, London, which enabled me to complete my research and, for the first time in almost twenty years, take a sustained length of time away from teaching to write. I would also like to thank my own institution for allowing me to take up the fellowship, my colleagues in the School of Arts, particularly David Thoms, Stephen Knight, and Wray Vamplen, for their support and those many students who, over the years, have shared my enthusiasm for the work of Charles and Ray Eames. Last but by no means least, my thanks to my editors, Paul Bethge and Roger Conover, for their patience, pleasantness, and professionalism.

CHARLES AND RAY EAMES

Panel detailing work of
Eames Office, 1957.

Charles Eames and his wife and collaborator Ray Eames (née Kaiser) oc-
cupy a central position in the history of postwar American design and are
considered by many to be among the most, if not *the* most, important
American designers of the twentieth century. It is as furniture designers
whose work was both technologically and aesthetically innovative that
they are most famous. Their 1946 bent plywood chair, their 1950 fiberglass chair, and their 1956 lounge chair and ottoman quickly became regarded as classics of mid-century modernism.[1] Their architecture and
exhibition design brought them international acclaim, as did their films
and their multi-media presentations. Their home became internationally
known as a warm and "human" solution to standardized prefabricated domestic building. Their many short films (more than eighty) brought
them awards at film festivals in the United States, Europe, and Australia.
In addition, they received an Emmy Award, and they were part of the
team that produced (in 1953) the first American multi-media presentation. Their exhibitions, films, and multi-screen shows testify to their role
as educators and their dedication to communicating ideas.

In view of the wide range of their work and the numerous magazine articles about it, and in view of their reputation, it is surprising that
no book on them was published during their lifetimes. This was partly because Charles hated the idea that such a book might be done while they
were still active as designers. He felt that to be "written up" implied that
one's work was done, and he joked about "memorial monographs." In
1960 Charles and Ray were honored with the first Kaufmann International Design Award, which involved the writing of a book about the re-
cipients. Charles was as uncooperative as Edgar Kaufmann jr. was
persistent, and the two men stopped speaking. Had I known this in
1983, I would have been terrified to approach Ray Eames with the idea of
writing a book such as this one. As it was, she was delighted (possibly
even a little flattered) at my scholarly interest and sufficiently proud of
their achievements to take pleasure in their continued public acknowledgment to give me every encouragement. Realistic enough to accept that
someday the memorial monographs would be written, she saw my project

as complementary to the "book without adjectives" which she was then compiling with Marilyn and John Neuhart. That book—*Eames Design: The Work of the Office of Charles and Ray Eames*—was not published until after Ray's death (ten years to the day after that of Charles), but it was worth waiting for.[2] An excellent *catalogue raisonné* of the output of the office headed by Charles and Ray Eames between 1941 and 1978, detailing each piece of work in chronological order, it is an essential starting point for any study of the Eameses' work.

In the present book, I analyze the Eameses' output in each of their main areas of activity, pursue common threads, and highlight differences. I examine Charles and Ray's early careers, before they moved to California (chapter 1), as well as their later joint work, which I consider in its wider historical and cultural context.

Much of the existing writing about the Eameses comes from a pro-modernist position and reveals a bias toward new materials and technology at the expense of aesthetics and other matters—a prejudice that is more readily visible in these "postmodern" days than before the hegemony of modernism was seriously undermined. It also overprivileges the contribution of Charles in relation to Ray, who, like so many female designers before her, has not always been given due recognition for her many and considerable achievements. To give Ray full credit, however, is not to deny the titanic achievements of Charles but rather to reassess their partnership. This is done throughout the book, but in the greatest detail in chapter 2.

My second chapter also touches on the collaborative nature of the Eames Office. It is clear that but for the abilities and dedication of the staff the products of the Eames Office would have been different. Gregory Ain, Don Albinson, Harry Bertoia, Jehane Burns, John Neuhart, Deborah Sussman, and many other talented individuals played important roles which deserve recognition; indeed, the Eameses would not have hired or retained them had they not been brimming with energy, ability, and ideas. *Eames Design* lists the staff members year by year and (whenever possible) credits individuals with particular contributions, but more research needs to be completed before a full picture can be obtained of who did what on each particular project. Meanwhile, it needs to be acknowledged that a book such as this, which aims to reassess Charles and Ray's partnership and to give a broad overview of the main areas of their work, cannot hope to do justice to the many individuals who worked for them.

The Eameses' contribution to architecture is detailed in chapter 3. They designed very few buildings, and their fame as architects mainly rests on one building: their own house in Pacific Palisades, California (1945–1949). Charles's most prolific period as an architect was c. 1933–1938, before he met Ray, when he was influenced by the Colonial Revival and by Scandinavian modernism as well as by the ideas of Frank Lloyd Wright. His buildings of those years have been virtually ignored by historians and critics because they were not designed in the approved International Style of the modern movement, yet through an understanding of these earlier projects the Eameses' particular contribution to modernism can be better understood.

Most publications on the Eameses have concentrated on their furniture, which is indeed central to any consideration of their work. Chapter 5 covers Charles's work with Eero Saarinen and then discusses Charles and Ray's plywood, plastic, and metal furniture and the associated stylistic developments. But furniture design was only one part of their product output. Their toys, games, and masks constitute a small but significant part of their product-design output, although their furniture was regarded as more "serious" and was more successful commercially. These items are discussed in chapter 4, which focuses on the Eameses' love of objects and on how they used them in "functioning decoration" (another neglected area of their work).

Their work as communicators and educators was of equal importance to their design and architecture. Indeed, it was their desire to transmit to others their passion for ideas and objects that led them into film, multi-media presentations, and exhibition design. The exhibitions are examined in chapter 6, which contextualizes the Eameses' contribution to exhibition design and also discusses in detail certain features they introduced or emphasized. That chapter considers early arrangements of Eames furniture within commercial and museum spaces before looking at theme exhibitions, particularly those focused on important historical characters and events and on science, mathematics, and computers. (In the 1950s and the 1960s the Eameses managed to give computers a more human and user-friendly image—an aspect of their work that has not been sufficiently appreciated.)

Chapter 7 focuses on films and on multi-media and multi-screen presentations, contextualizing them within postwar developments in experimental and business filmmaking and "communications theory." The films and the exhibitions reflected some of the Eameses' many interests, including science, mathematics, computing, history, philosophy, objects (especially toys), the circus, and the environment.

Interviewing Ray Eames and some of the people who knew her and Charles was extremely rewarding but also somewhat problematic (as oral history always is, because human memory is partial, biased, selective, and sometimes simply inaccurate). Oral evidence was weighed against that obtained from written and visual sources, but it should be noted that there is relatively little written documentation related to the Eameses or the Eames Office. Communications were mainly conducted in person or by telephone. (Ray used to joke that she wanted to frame a brief note sent by Charles to a mutual friend about a business matter because it was a rare object.[3]) Furthermore, since a great deal of the preparatory design work was done by talking ideas through, making models and prototypes, using a camera, or moving pieces of paper around a board, there are few drawings. For the most part, the archive of the Eames Office consists of images, mainly slide transparencies. These, together with the drawings, were transferred to the Library of Congress after Ray's death.[4]

I used still images to reinforce and supplement my viewing of the Eameses' products (including their films), and also to "read" their styles of dress and to evaluate their relationship. No one who studies Eames photographs can but be aware that all photographs are constructions; nevertheless, the consistency of the images presented over a very large number of photographs proved informative, especially when considered in tandem with other information.[5]

This study has been informed by feminist scholarship, particularly within history, art and design history, and cultural studies. The retrieval of Ray Eames from the margins of history forms part of a wider feminist project of studying the lives and work of women formerly "hidden from history."[6] However, in addition to analyzing and celebrating the achievements of female designers, it is important to go beyond this and understand the marginalization of women in design. In Ray's case I hope to indicate some of the ways in which, at particular times and in particular ways, her talents were given the space and opportunity to flourish, as well as suggest the more obvious ways in which they were and remain underappreciated.

Today the work of the Eameses is admired not only by architects and designers who work within the modernist tradition (including

Norman Foster and Richard Rogers) but also by "postmodernists" (such as Robert Venturi and Charles Moore). This study has been informed by recent debates on the history, contents, and contexts of modernism and "postmodernism" and on the relationship between the two. Contemporary material culture is the product of a particular phase of late capitalism and, as such, takes on particular forms.[7] Like David Harvey, I consider the major cultural changes that have occurred since the late 1960s to be not without significance in relation to contemporary ways of viewing the world; however, I agree with Peter Wollen that much of what is now claimed as "postmodernism" is, in fact, aspects of modernism that have always been there.[8] I would not call myself a "postmodernist," but it is clear that our histories and understandings of modernism have been too exclusive.

Ten years ago a book such as this would have devoted much less attention to the aspects of the Eameses' work that relate to decoration, fantasy, fragmentation, and addition or to those that can be regarded as prototypically "postmodern." If nothing else, the debates have led to a greater recognition of the pluralism of modernism (or modernisms, as the "postmodernists" would have it)—something which the work of the Eameses illustrates better than that of any other mid-twentieth-century designer-filmmakers. Charles and Ray Eames thought of themselves as modernists and belonged to a generation of designers who, immediately before, during, and after World War II, aimed to use new materials and industrial processes to produce quality everyday goods at prices affordable to most people. The problem was to make them popular, and this book considers the ways in which Eames products appealed to those who wanted contemporary styles and imagery but found much modernist design cold and impersonal.

Aspects of modern architecture and design had been viewed as cold and impersonal ever since the 1920s, even by many supporters of modernism who stopped short of going all the way with Bauhaus design or International Style architecture. Behind the jokes about furniture more suitable for operating theaters than for living rooms and the difficulty of finding Bauhaus-style food to match rigidly geometric plates, cutlery, tables, and chairs lay serious questions about semiotics, "functionalism," the relationship between object and user, and a world ruled by machinery. By the late 1920s the eminent and influential design reformer and critic

William Lethaby could be dismissed as old fashioned for questioning the proposition that style would disappear when form truly followed function.[9] In the 1930s and the 1940s, however, it became increasingly difficult for "machine aesthetic" modernists to refute dissenters who had once been in their ranks. Alvar Aalto, Eva Zeisel, and others reacted to what they considered the denial of aesthetic variety and autonomy and questioned the logic that when form followed function the inevitable result was a building or object in "compass and ruler" forms.[10] The attack of those who developed what is now known as organic modernism[11] on the formulaic "functionalist" myth and on geometric form was not a rejection of a rationalist approach to solving the problems of life or design but rather a plea for the recognition of intuitive, emotional, psychological, and non-rational elements (what Aalto called "human quality") in design.[12] This book aims to illustrate how and to what extent the Eameses combined the rigors of rationalism with more openly expressive and affective qualities of design. It indicates how they drew on modernist fine art, on two major strands of modernist design (the "machine aesthetic" and organic modernism) that were in certain respects mutually contradictory, and on a variety of other sources to produce some of the most visually appealing and technologically "progressive" products of the mid twentieth century.

The horrors of World War II left many architects and designers more convinced than ever that there was no alternative but to address wider social questions—and the early work of the Eameses did just that. Technological development had increased rapidly during the war and continued to do so after 1945, when the reorganized American economy seemed finally able to deliver the low-cost but high-quality mass-produced goods that design reformers had aimed at for half a century. For the most part, progress seemed inevitable and the possibilities of the application of new technologies to the peaceful pursuit of happiness through the enjoyment of beautiful homes and domestic objects seemed endless. However, the politics of progressivism meant that most designers (and many other people) never challenged the fundamental questions of whether technological change was a good thing per se and whether design reform could effect social reform.

Charles and Ray Eames had a vision of life made better through design and technology. Their belief in the inevitability of progress and in the essential role of technology never wavered, and they played a central role in making modernism acceptable to the American bourgeoisie in the postwar years. Their work was rooted in European as well as American traditions; however, in common with much of postwar art and design in the United States, there is no sense of the inferiority complex with respect to European styles that had characterized much of America's cultural production in the nineteenth and the early twentieth centuries. Their pronouncements on design emphasized the centrality of function and the use of the technologies of mass production to make quality goods cheaper and more widely available—as did those of most designers at the time. They commented less on aesthetic matters and on the affective and sensual qualities of products, but this did not mean they cared less about them. Their work reveals a dynamic fusion of aesthetic and technical concerns—and, at times, intellectual concerns. Although they were almost obsessive about visual form, they found it difficult to accept that it had any autonomy, even though their own practice proved that it did.

I have consistently argued against the general tendency within history to focus on individuals at the expense of wider developments. In this book I place considerable emphasis on contextualization in order to depict the Eameses' work as the product of a particular moment and a particular outlook rather than as "timeless classics" created by individual "geniuses"[13] without historical roots. However, I have never been against monographs as such, believing that detailed studies often highlight the inadequacies of existing historical interpretations and help refine the stories and analyzes we call history. I make no apologies, therefore, for focusing on two immensely talented and creative individuals or for studying in detail objects, exhibitions, and films that have been used, admired, and appreciated by millions.

My contextualizing does not seek to deny that the Eameses were regarded as outstanding and inspirational in their own day. Many of those who knew Charles referred and continue to refer to him as a "genius." Although the label embarrassed and sometimes irritated him (he believed that, given the right opportunities and teaching, everyone has enormous potential), the fact that he was so regarded by contemporaries of the stature of R. Buckminster Fuller, Philip Morrison, and Paul Schrader cannot be ignored any more than the fact that much of what they admired was his joint work with Ray.

The Eameses believed in hard work rather than inspiration. They directly experienced what Ruskin called "joy in labor," and they believed that one of life's main objectives was "to get as many of the rewards of life from the work that you do."[14] The products of their work form the basis of chapters 3–7, which I hope will also convey a further sense of Charles and Ray Eames as people as well as what it was like to work in what has been described as "a Renaissance workshop" and "a designer's heaven."[15]

Charles and Ray Eames met in 1940 at the Cranbrook Academy of Art, in Michigan, where she had gone to study and he had recently been placed in charge of what would later become the Department of Industrial Design. Born in 1907, the same year as Ray's brother Maurice, Charles was older than Ray by five years. From the moment they met, she looked up to him as mentor, big brother, father figure, and ideal romantic partner all rolled into one. They shared many interests, yet they had arrived at Cranbrook by very different routes. Each was the younger of two children in a middle-class family, and each showed an early interest in visual matters, but other aspects of their childhoods and early years differed quite considerably.

CHARLES ORMAND EAMES (1907–1978)

Charles Eames was brought up in St. Louis and liked to describe himself as a "real Midwesterner."[1] His father, likewise named Charles Ormand Eames, a New Englander of English Methodist origins who brought up his son according to the Protestant ethic, had fought in the Civil War and settled in St. Louis afterward. In 1901, at the age of 52, he married the beautiful and much younger Celine Lambert, who came from a respectable and well-established local French Catholic family.[2] Life was in good in St. Louis for the young Charles, whose earliest memories included his parents' playing duets for piano and flute and who later described his family as "super middle-class respectable" but not at all puritanical.[3] His mother was the "most motherly of all motherly types,"[4] but there was a certain formality and distance in his relationship with his father, partly because the elder Eames was already 58 by the time the younger was born and partly because his job guarding trains for Pinkerton involved many absences from home. The elder Eames enjoyed a sense of the dramatic and added to the air of mystery surrounding his work (according to Charles he was also a secret agent working for Scotland Yard[5]) by signing the letters he wrote to his son when away on assignments with the pseudonym

Victor Samuels.[6] He sometimes took Charles with him on the trains he guarded. After he was shot in the course of duty, the elder Eames was able to devote a great deal of time to his hobbies of painting and photography, both of which were to greatly interest his son in later years. He also published adventure stories in *The American Weekly*.[7] Some of his creative energy probably rubbed off on his son, but it was only after his father's death in 1921 that Charles began to use the antiquated photographic equipment in the house, making wet-plate pictures and mixing emulsions for more than a year before he found out that film had been invented.[8] Fascinated from the start, he became hooked on photography for the rest of his life.

After his father's death, Charles noted, "what had been the family fortune that kept us in reasonable state . . . disappeared" and the family was left with only a Civil War widow's pension of $30 per month to live on—plus whatever the son could earn.[9] Charles, his mother, and his sister Adele moved in with two aunts. Later Charles often commented on the "strong-minded" women who had brought him up, always speaking of them with great affection and respect.[10] He enjoyed female company and was greatly at ease in it, unlike many men of his generation. Out of necessity and obligation he worked to help support the household, taking a wide variety of jobs while he was at school and college. (His first regular after-school and summer job was in a printing shop, around the age of 10; later he worked in a grocery store and in a drugstore.[11])

In 1921, the year he entered Yeatman High School in North St. Louis at the age of 14, Charles went to work as a laborer (part-time during school and full-time during vacations) at the Laclede Steel Company in nearby Venice, Illinois. His drawing and practical skills were such that he was soon promoted to the engineering shop as a draftsman. A quick learner, he enjoyed the work and was soon entrusted with small jobs which so impressed a rival firm, the Aitkens Mill Company, that it offered him a scholarship to study engineering.[12] By then, however, Charles had already decided that he wanted to become an architect.[13]

Some of Charles's later ideas about education can be related to his school days. His kindergarten experience was based on the Froebel system (which also informed the early days of one of Charles's later heroes, Frank Lloyd Wright,[14] and which was regarded as extremely progressive). Charles later described it as "to do with elementary blocks of spheres and

cones and pyramids and different kinds of exercises,"[15] and it may well account for his abiding interest in structure. Recalling his days in elementary school, he said "I have never had any negative feelings about my education . . . there was always a teacher on the scene who took the subject seriously and took their pleasures seriously."[16] This man, remembered by many as a brilliant teacher, also commented on the "little affectionate attentions" that were given by certain teachers.[17] He played down any notion that he might have been especially talented at art at school—though he did admit to drawing a lot. He also modestly pointed out that his early aptitude for mathematics and science should be placed in the context of North St. Louis High School, which he described as socially a "mixed bag" of respectable and "pretty seamy elements" of the white community.[18] He also noted that "between the mathematics teacher (a woman) and the physics teacher (a man) you realized there was . . . something there that had a basis of pleasure to it"[19]—a pleasure he was to convey to thousands of others through the exhibitions, films, and multi-image shows he created with Ray.

His high school career was distinguished; he was president of the class, a track star (he did especially well at the 200 meters), and captain of football in his graduation year of 1925.[20] The class yearbook described him as "a man with ideals, courage to stand up for them and ability to live up to them."[21] He never lost the ideals, the ability, or the courage, although they got him into trouble from time to time, particularly when he was an architecture student.

In the summer of 1925, immediately before entering Washington University, Charles worked at the Edwin F. Guth Fixture Company designing lighting fixtures—a job which proved "an interesting transition from steel mill to architecture."[22] At the university, his self-confidence, his qualities of leadership, and what people later described as his charisma got him elected president of the first-year class.[23] Although he was awarded two first prizes for "ultra-modern" designs,[24] he was asked to leave in 1928 because of his general non-conformity, his "premature enthusiasm for Frank Lloyd Wright" (who was arguing for an American architecture free from the trappings of European historicism), and the time he spent working for one of St. Louis's busiest architectural firms, Trueblood and Graf.[25] Ray told me that Charles found the Beaux-Arts curriculum narrow and constraining, with its emphasis on a "correct" manner of drawing plans, elevations, and ornamentation as well as on the symmetry, solidity, and monumentality of classical architecture.[26] Yet Charles always insisted that the discipline imposed by the course had stood him in good stead, discipline being a quality he felt essential in any good designer.[27] Although Wright's autobiography had made a great impression on Charles, he did not see his enthusiasm for the man as necessarily incompatible with a Beaux-Arts training—not least because his new hero knew his history of architecture.[28] Eames simply did not understand why the School could or would not embrace new ideas such as those of Wright. One member of the staff did (Paul Valenti, an Italian whom Charles admired), but the "patron" (this was a French school in more ways than one), Gabriel Ferrand, was "absolutely rabid on the subject."[29] Ferrand also told Charles's prospective father-in-law that he would never amount to anything as an architect. Not surprisingly, Charles took some pleasure in the "poetic justice" of Ferrand's later public defense of International Style architecture in a debate during which he "demonstrated . . . he knew neither the modern nor the classical side of the argument."[30] The two men who most impressed Charles as teachers were Lawrence Hill, who taught "history and elements," and Valenti, who "enters into a plot with the students and gets them to do interesting things" and who could make the Italian Renaissance "come to life."[31]

Between 1928 and 1930 Eames continued to work for Trueblood and Graf, a firm with "a pretty good tradition,"[32] but now on a full-time basis. He learned enough there to open an office with a colleague, Charles Gray, in 1930. There was a lively cultural and artistic scene in St. Louis, and Eames flourished in it. His introduction to "a part of St. Louis society where the mother had a certain social standing but was also a political activist" came through a student colleague, George Sansone, whose father was a doctor and whose mother Charles greatly admired.[33] There was a strong and determined group of women, including Edna and Martha Gelhorn, who campaigned for equal rights,[34] and the university had a better reputation than most as far as the training of women architects was concerned.[35] Indeed, Catherine Woermann, whom Eames married in 1929, was one of the few women training to be an architect at that time (she had already obtained her bachelor's degree from Vassar).[36] Eames learned a great deal about printmaking, lithography, and engraving, and about Jewish culture, from Dr. Albert Auer, the father of another classmate, Jimmy Auer, and he had several very "positive" Jewish friends, through whom he was "introduced to an aspect of world culture I would otherwise have missed."[37] He belonged to the Paint and Potter Club where the local artistic intelligentsia met to drink and to discuss art, design, and life,[38] and he was able to turn his hand to a wide range of activities, including lithography, etching, weaving, pottery, stage design, and product design as well as photography, engineering design, and architecture.[39] His horizons were further broadened when he traveled to Europe in 1929 on a honeymoon financed by his father-in-law. The newlyweds visited France, Germany, and England, sketching buildings old and new, and saw the work of the "pioneers" of the International Style, particularly Mies van der Rohe, Gropius, and Le Corbusier, at the Weissenhof Siedlung in Stuttgart—an exhilarating experience which Eames later compared to "having a cold hose turned on you."[40] Stimulated he may have been, but it was a decade and a half before Eames designed a building in that style.

Eames's architectural work in the intervening years was eclectic, drawing on the Colonial Revival and Moderne styles as well as on Scandinavian influences (particularly the work of Eliel Saarinen, who fused a re-strained, stripped-down classicism with Arts and Crafts ideals and Scandinavian National Romanticism). This eclecticism and lack of "purity" made, and still makes, his work of this period unpalatable to hard-line International Style modernists, and once he had left St. Louis it was never discussed by architectural or design critics and commentators. Nor was it foregrounded by Charles; it was almost as if he and Ray did not want to draw attention to work that appeared "traditional" and old fashioned by the standards of their joint work from 1941 onward.[41]

On his return from Europe, Charles Eames went into partnership with Charles Gray; they were later joined by Walter Pauley.[42] Work was hard to come by during the Depression and little is known of what they did apart from a "fairly simple house with reasonably nice Colonial detailing"[43] for Ernest Sweetser, Professor of Engineering at Washington University (figure 1.2). It may have been Charles's interest in engineering that won the firm the commission, although it may have come to him through the Woermann Construction Company (headed by his father-in-law, Frederick Woermann), which eventually built the house.[44] The influence of British Domestic Revival architecture had led to a renewed interest in American colonial architecture of the seventeenth and eighteenth centuries, and the Sweetser House, with its massive chimney in decorated brickwork, refers back to the British Domestic Revival more directly than many American Colonial Style houses of the 1930s. But this red brick structure (blue bricks were also used on the chimney), with its white-painted wooden gable, windows, and shutters, also stood in the American tradition of "modernized colonial."[45] Photographs of the house in the 1930s show ceilings at a fashionably low "modern" height as well as classical style covings, oak floors, and bookcases in arched alcoves with wood keystones and moldings in the living room. The firm also worked on the restoration of the lightning-damaged St. Louis Pilgrim Congregational Church on North Union Boulevard, restoring the spire and the west door in 1933.[46] Eames also designed the stained glass windows and mosaics (in collaboration with Emil Frei, a well-known glass designer and maker whose firm had supplied mosaics for the internationally famous Stockholm Town Hall).[47]

The Depression devastated the architectural and building trades; between 1924 and 1933 employment in the building industry fell by 63

1.2 Sweetser House, St. Louis, 1931. Eames & Gray.

percent and in New York 85 percent of architects were unemployed in 1932.[48] Charles Eames "could not avoid seeing how thin the glitter, how insubstantial the values" of the world he had previously inhabited.[49] The Depression hit hard many whom Charles knew well and who had hitherto enjoyed a lifestyle heavily based on consumption. He himself found it difficult to scrape a living, but it was the concomitant psychological depression that finally made him leave the city and reassess his life.[50] He found others as disillusioned as he who agreed that life should be "based on doing rather than having."[51] Later he painted a not unsympathetic picture of the world from which he increasingly felt the need to escape—particularly the heavy drinking which he, his friends and other "victims" of the Depression were caught up in. "You'd want to get drunk every night," he recalled. "It got to be so much I finally thought to hell with it and paid off all the debts I could, took what was left, and took off for Mexico."[52]

In the autumn of 1933 Charles Eames left his home, wife, and young daughter Lucia and set off on an eight-month visit to Mexico—a trip which he later referred to as his "On The Road tour" and which gives a glimpse of the "wild streak" in him at that date.[53] He spent most of his time in Mexico painting—each picture "a personal memento recalling a fiesta, a fine dinner or a night in jail."[54] The *St. Louis Post-Dispatch* featured his colorful story, and three of his watercolors, after his return, commenting thus:

> The architect confined his travels to the northern states of Coahuila, Nuevo Leon and San Luis Potosi. Part of the time he lived with people of the peon class, eating and sleeping in their lowly homes, often repaying their hospitality by making pictures of them. Once he was the honored guest of a mountain village, having won the friendship of the villager [*sic*] by repainting a statue of St. Peter in their chapel. A fiesta was held in celebration of the event and solid-faced [*sic*] peons thanked him with tears running down their cheeks. [55]

Charles, who spoke no Spanish, was arrested twice. The most dramatic incident occurred in Linaras, Nuevo Léon, where he was arrested for having in his possession a book on Mexican antiquities which local officials thought showed their country in a bad light. He spent two nights in jail

1.3 "A Market Place in
Monterrey, Mexico,"
watercolor, 1933–34.
Charles Eames.

and was only released after the intervention of the American consular office. Mexico introduced him to an immensely rich craft tradition, and he returned home with a small collection of objects which he considered of both artistic and archaeological value, including a wand used in the rituals of the ancient Toltecs.[56] This admiration for "ethnic" objects was to form an important aspect of the Eameses' later work.

The oil and watercolor paintings produced by Charles in Mexico were technically skilled (he regularly produced prints of St. Louis on his own press) but showed little artistic adventurousness. Influenced by the Spanish Impressionist painter Joaquin Sorolla, who was popular in the United States in the early twentieth century and whose work hung in the Washington University Gallery of Art, they proved of sufficient interest to get him at least one exhibition outside his home town.[57] But, once again, there was no foretaste of the geometric and abstract forms of contemporary modernism which were to later emerge in his design work.

Either before or shortly after the Mexican trip he found some work with the Historic American Buildings Survey, a Works Progress Administration initiative, in St. Louis, Ste. Genevieve, and New Orleans.[58] In 1934 he set up a partnership with another old colleague from Trueblood and Graf, Robert Walsh—a collaboration which was to prove his most productive to date. They took what work they could get during those lean years and between 1935 and 1938 managed to design at least six buildings, including two churches in Arkansas—a small one in Paragould and a larger one in Helena. Built to a traditional church plan and topped by a wooden spire, the impressive Roman Catholic church of St. Mary, in Helena (1935–36), was designed "with the manifest intention of making the most simple and extensive use of brick surfaces," in the manner of the Scandinavian National Romantic Movement.[59] In an area noted for the high quality of its brickwork,[60] the builder, a local man, was extremely impressed with Charles's detailed blueprints for the brickwork, and by his professionalism in general.[61] Eames and Walsh were involved with every aspect of the design, from the construction of the building to the design of the interior fittings, vestments, and vessels in an attempt to provide a *Gesamtkunstwerk* in the best Cranbrook tradition. They supervised the women of this Roman Catholic community ("in redneck Ku Klux Klan Arkansas"[62]), whose skills resulted in "marvelous things" for their church. Eames and Walsh's interior light fixtures (figure 1.5) are particularly notable. The brasswork that encloses the white circular globes

1.4 St. Mary's, Helena,
Ark., 1935–36. Eames &
Walsh.

1.5 Interior, St. Mary's.

1.6 Dinsmoor House, Webster Groves, Mo., 1936. Eames & Walsh.

features crescent-moon and "star" shapes as one walks down the nave to the altar and "sun" shapes on the reverse. The whole project so impressed Eliel Saarinen when he saw illustrations of it in *Architectural Forum*[63] that he contacted the designers and inquired about their forthcoming project. This proved to be an important moment in the career of Charles Eames.

Of the three houses known to have been designed by Charles Eames and Robert Walsh, the Dinsmoor House (335 Bristol Road, Webster Groves, Missouri) was much more traditional in style than the others. Relatively modest in scale, this two-story brick house was designed in the "Colonial Williamsburg" style, which became popular in the United States after the reconstruction of that town in 1932. Indeed, it drew directly on a building which was seminal to that style—Carter's Grove, a mid-eighteenth-century plantation house and the only one remaining in the Williamsburg area—particularly the fine brickwork, pedimented doorways, classical details, and sash windows.[64] Although the Dinsmoor House was on a smaller scale, the front doorway was more dramatic.

1.7 Door of Dinsmoor
House.

EARLY LIVES AND WORK

Eames and Walsh chose to break the white-painted pediment of their doorway to provide further contrast to the surrounding brick. No furniture or fittings were designed for this house which was furnished with genuine (or what was thought to be genuine) eighteenth-century American furniture.

The Dean House (101 Mason Avenue) was more "modern." It retained some classical elements, such as dentils and corner quoins, which, together with the belt course, created a solid base and a horizontal feel. The corner quoins rather wittily echoed the "advanced" corner windows (made possible by modern technology). Like the Dinsmoor House, it was built of brick. However, the white paint, the clean lines, the restrained use of ornament, the low pitched roof, the Art Deco west porch stairs, the metal-framed corner windows, and the chevron-paneled door made it much less traditional.[65]

The Meyer House (1936–1938), in Huntleigh Village, Missouri, was the largest and most assured of the house designs and was the major achievement of Charles's St. Louis period.[66] Built in brick, this substantial residence, with five bedrooms, servants' quarters, library, nursery, wine cellars, and formal gardens, drew on Swedish modernism of the 1920s, as exemplified by Gunnar Asplund's Stockholm City Library (1920–1928), and had some similarities to Saarinen's own house at Cranbrook (1928–1930). Eames visited Cranbrook during the period of design and construction to obtain advice from his new mentor and to liaise with Cranbrook staff members who produced stained glass, rugs, and metalwork designed by Eames and Walsh.[67] The classicism was as stripped down as anything in Scandinavia, but occasionally it was played for wit as well as visual impact—for example, the rear terrace door (figure 1.10) echoed the broken pediment of the more elaborate door of the Dinsmoor House and more directly referenced the simpler doorways of Carter's Grove.

The Meyers wanted a house that looked up-to-date, and they got an assured piece of Scandinavian modernism to grace their five-acre site. Alice Meyer (now Gerdine) recalled: "We had met Charles Eames through his first wife, Catherine Woermann, who had been a classmate of mine. We knew we wanted a contemporary house, we'd seen the houses that Charles had designed, and decided to give him the commission."[68] It was

1.8 Dean House, Webster
Groves, Mo. 1936.
Eames & Walsh.

1.9 Meyer House,
Huntleigh Village, Mo.,
1936–1938. Eames &
Walsh.

1.10 Door of Meyer
House.

one of the first air-conditioned houses and, according to Eames, the first to use aluminum sash windows.[69] Alice Meyer described the steel-framed house, with its brick infill and concrete, as "like a fortress."[70] It combined new and traditional materials as well as classical and contemporary elements. For example, the arrangement and decoration of the interior spaces referred back to the Federal period (c. 1788–1825), but the balustrade of the main marble staircase was made of aluminum, a very "new" material in the 1930s. The first set of drawings took 9 months to prepare but were rejected by the clients ("I can't remember why, now, but they just weren't what we wanted").[71] After the second scheme was accepted Charles went to Cranbrook to discuss it with Saarinen, who suggested that certain details—such as the niches in the dining room, which were based on an eighteenth-century prototype—be changed to something less traditional.[72]

The interior of the Meyer House can best be described as a combination of Georgian Revival, Scandinavian National Romanticism, Swedish modernism, Vienna Secession, and Art Deco styles, the latter two of which already drew heavily on eighteenth-century neo-classical sources. The entrance hall had an elaborate maple parquet floor based on eighteenth-century French examples and a rich color scheme of terra-cotta walls and silver-leaf ceiling (which was thought to have an eighteenth-century precedent). The two most important interiors were the *en suite* living room and dining room, for which Eames also designed some furniture. The former, a long rectangular space with a coffered ceiling, had as its central focus a large marble fireplace, flanked by two grey niches, on which was placed a bust designed by the Cranbrook sculptor Carl Milles. The color scheme was fashionable: the walls were pink, the drapes (designed by Loja Saarinen) grey, the furniture upholstered in grey and terra-cotta, and the rugs terra-cotta-colored.[73] The geometric forms of the curtains and rugs added a "modern" feel to the interiors, but the classical theme of the living room was emphasized by the use of coordinated motifs based on the acanthus leaf and the clam shell, the former on light fittings and the latter on door pulls and fire irons. The furniture designed by Charles Eames included a veneered card table and four armchairs (figure 1.11),[74] the general proportions and elegant restrained classicism of which drew on Eliel Saarinen's veneered table and chairs of

1929–1931 (figure 1.12), which had been influenced by Viennese furniture of the early twentieth century, particularly that of Koloman Moser. However, Eames's chairs owed a great deal more to the French "Art Deco" style of the mid 1920s than did his more obviously Classical Revival table.

The dining room of the Meyer House was even more classical in spirit than the living room. The furniture was in the Classical Revival style, but, as in the living room, the color scheme reflected contemporary tastes. The plaster grey of the walls was offset by pale yellow draperies with a coral and silver pattern, coral brocaded upholstery, a white rug (made by V'Soske), an inlaid sideboard, and an acanthus-leafed chandelier—the last three all designed by Charles Eames.[75] Eames also designed a sectional sofa to fit a bay window in the library—the first of several fitted seating areas he was to design, including one in his own home in the late 1940s. The house had odd witty and whimsical touches to it, such as bars of music (figure 1.13) and a dachshund carved in the bricks,[76] which also functioned to personalize and humanize it, thus predating a strong element in the joint work of Charles and Ray. (In later years the "whimsy" noted in certain Eames designs was attributed mainly to Ray, because critics could not accept that Charles could be so frivolous.) The Meyer House confirmed Eames and Walsh as a "hot" firm.[77] It so impressed Saarinen that he offered Charles a fellowship to study at the Cranbrook Academy of Art, which he entered in the autumn of 1938.[78]

The three houses discussed above were interesting buildings, particularly the Meyer House, but they were hardly at the "cutting edge" of design practice. The 1932 Modern Architecture exhibition at the Museum of Modern Art had featured International Style buildings, and considerable time had passed since the completion of Rudolph Schindler's "Co-operative" House (1921–22) and Lovell Beach House (1925–26) and Richard Neutra's Lovell Health House (1928–29). Charles Eames is on record as saying that in the Depression one had to take what work there was[79]; however, since in later years he never took on any work with which he did not feel entirely happy, there is nothing to suggest that, at this date, he had any objection to designing in an eclectic or revivalist manner.

1.11 Bridge table and
chairs, Meyer House,
1937–38. Charles Eames.

1.12 Occasional table,
Saarinen House,
Cranbrook, 1929–1931.
Eliel Saarinen.

1.13 Brick sculpture,
Meyer House. Eames &
Walsh.

Little is known of the early years of Ray Eames, who was remarkably guarded when discussing that period. Her defensiveness on the issue went beyond an extreme reluctance to reveal her age, which seemed to me a grand old lady's prerogative but which others regarded as perverse, if not paranoid, in one so apparently keen on accurately documenting the work of herself and Charles. Although *Eames Design* revealed her to have been at least four years older than most of us had guessed, there is no sense in that publication of her trying to trace roots or explain how she or Charles each arrived at the positions they occupied by 1941. It is difficult to say why this was. She had a somewhat ahistorical view of the world, felt that Charles's early career outshone hers, and undervalued the quality and innovation of her own early work, including graphic design, yet she was happy to reminisce about her student days as a painter. Although almost 28, she was still a student when she met Charles in 1940, and so powerful was the pull of her relationship with him, both personally and professionally, that, in many ways, she regarded her life as only fully starting when they met.

Bernice Alexandra Kaiser was born on December 15, 1912, in Sacramento, the daughter of Alexander and Edna Burr Kaiser. She was known as "Ray Ray" and later simply Ray.[80] Her mother was a housewife; her father had been a jeweler and the manager of a variety theater before finding more secure employment as an insurance salesman for the Californian State Life Company in the 1920s.[81] Ray came from a loving but overprotective home. Her elder sister died a few months after Ray was born and her parents thereafter lived in fear that they would lose her too.[82] The overprotectiveness was further fueled by Ray's mother's anxiety that her short, squat child might be deformed.[83] Despite and because of this, Ray was very close to her mother, living with her in California and New York until her death in 1940, and also to her elder brother Maurice.

Although Sacramento was the capital of California, it was something of a cultural backwater compared to San Francisco and Los Angeles. Nevertheless, the general ease of Californian life made other states seem stuffy and conservative by comparison. How far the California lifestyle's emphasis on the new affected the attitudes of the young Ray Kaiser is impossible to ascertain, but she later developed a passionate interest in new forms of art, design, film, and dance.[84] She showed a very early aptitude

for art—she remembered drawing from the age of 3. At Sacramento High School she belonged to the Art Association[85] and enjoyed French and English. Her talents as a decorator revealed themselves even then, and she chaired the decoration committee for the school's annual football dance. (One cannot help but reflect on the gender-stereotypical division of labor and leisure interests here: He was captain of football—the active outdoor male—whereas she excelled in what was seen as the womanly sphere of decoration.)

After graduating in 1931, Ray spent a term at Sacramento Junior College before she and her widowed mother moved to New York to be near her brother, who was a cadet at West Point. She attended the May Friend Bennet School in Millbrook, which was something of a "finishing school" for young ladies,[86] leaving in 1933. By that time she knew that she wanted to further develop her interest in modern art.

New York in the early 1930s was an exciting place to be for a young artist. Ray enrolled at the Art Students League, where she studied with the avant-garde German émigré Hans Hofmann.[87] Regarded by Clement Greenberg as "the most important art teacher of our time,"[88] Hofmann so inspired Ray and her fellow students that they followed him when he left the Art Students League and established his own institution in 1933. Ray attended his Manhattan school and his summer schools on Cape Cod. Later she recalled not only the countless naturalistic drawings Hofmann made his students execute but also his insistence on understanding structure[89]—an element central to her joint work with Charles. Hofmann's work of this period, while abstract in form, often dealt with recognizable genres (mainly portraits, still lifes, interior scenes, and landscapes) and employed expressionistic brush strokes with bright primary colors.[90] He was concerned with creating the illusion of volume while retaining the integrity of the flat canvas—in other words, translating three dimensions into two. To achieve this Hofmann animated his pictures with what he called "push and pull," whereby the visual movement of one plane forward was counteracted by the movement back of another to give a feeling of depth yet emphasize the two-dimensional nature of the canvas.[91] These ideas were established by the mid 1930s (see figure 1.17), when Ray studied with him (although they found more sustained expression in his organically influenced abstractions of the mid to late 1940s), and later they informed the design of the Eames DCM chair (see chapter

1.15 A 1933 drawing by
Ray Kaiser.

1.16 Students of Hans Hofmann, mid 1930s. Ray Kaiser is seated third from left.

5). Hofmann owned works by Miró, Arp, and Kandinsky, all of whom influenced the painting and graphic design of Ray in the early 1940s (though, interestingly, the biomorphic shapes of Miró and Arp are more apparent in Hofmann's own work in the years immediately after World War II than when Ray was his student).[92]

A popular figure affectionately known as "Buddha,"[93] Ray attended modern dance classes led by Martha Graham and Hanya Holm[94] and was also very keen on the new art form of the twentieth century, film.[95] From 1936 on she devoted a great deal of her time to American Abstract Artists (AAA),[96] a militant group that fought for the right to exhibit non-representational art, picketing galleries that refused to do so and organizing petitions and meetings around the issue. It held its own exhibitions at Manhattan's Municipal Art Galleries, and Ray showed work in the very first show.[97] The group tended to look for inspiration to foreign painters, including Picasso, the Bauhaus abstractionists, and Mondrian.[98] (Mondrian's geometric rigor appealed to a whole generation of American artists trying to come to terms with abstraction.) In the late 1930s AAA members turned to more organic forms derived from Arp, Miró, Picasso, and Kandinsky. Ray had already used such forms in some

CHAPTER 1

1.17 "Table with Tea
Kettle, Green Vase, and
Red Flowers," oil on
canvas, 1936. Hans
Hofmann.

1.18 Plate XXXIII,
Barcelona Series, 1944.
Joan Miró.

of her abstract studies of about 1935 (which predate the formation of the AAA),[99] and they later appeared in her graphic designs of 1942–1947.[100]

After her brief stint at Cranbrook (see below) and her move to California with Charles in 1941, Ray continued to paint. The romantically titled "For C in Limited Palette," which explored "the rediscovery of form through movement and balance and depth and light," was illustrated in *California Arts & Architecture* in 1943, and in the following year she exhibited "Composition with Yellow" at the Los Angeles Museum, but thereafter she produced mainly sculpture and graphics.[101] After her death, copper cut-out sculptures from her days with Hofmann in New York were found among her personal possessions.[102] Similar to but predating the plywood sculptures made in California in the early to mid 1940s, they reinforce the argument that Ray made a major contribution to the forms of Eames furniture. Some of her best graphics, produced (often at great speed) for the magazine *California Arts & Architecture,* reflect the influences of Arp, Miró, Picasso, Gabo, and Calder. The April 1942 cover, for example, with its two curving black lines snaking across a lighter biomorphic shape set off against a dark background, relates to the work of Arp, as do those of February and May 1943. The influence of Hofmann is seen in the overlapping shapes of the December 1942 and February 1944 covers (which compare well with anything Hofmann had produced by that date), and the ink splashes on the December 1943 cover suggest the influence of Surrealism. The "naive" script references Picasso and Miró (whose influence is also seen in the August 1944 cover); the influences of Calder and Miró can be seen in Ray's cut-paper collages.

Ray's graphics were also influenced by Herbert Matter, a Swiss photographer and artist who worked for *Arts & Architecture* and for the Eameses from 1943 to 1946. He encouraged Ray to find new ways to juxtapose images with a total disregard for scale, and some of her work for the magazine used this approach to great effect. The November 1942 cover, for example, included an out-of-scale aircraft wing which almost seemed to grow out of a piece of graph paper on which was explained a mathematical equation. Her collage of September 1943 (figure 1.23), which comprised wildly out-of-scale images of an airplane, an early car, an Eames/Saarinen chair, an electricity pylon, automobile shock mounts, an army helmet, parachutes, Picasso's "Guernica," and Le Corbusier's Ministry of Education and Health building at Rio de Janeiro, also owed a

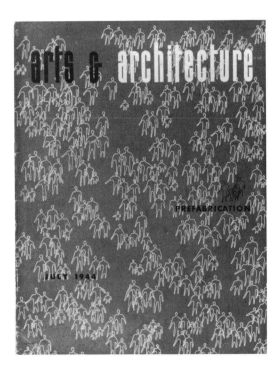

LINE AND
COLOR DEFINE
VOLUME
THAT VOLUME
CAN BE TANGIBLE
OR NOT BUT THE
SPACE BETWEEN
TWO TANGIBLE
VOLUMES IS
NEVERTHELESS
        A VOLUME

ray eames

it is impossible to talk about painting without bringing up the whole weary subject of aesthetics   philosophy   and metaphysics.

the fact is that without any talk we are influenced by the world in which we live and by the synthesis of the experiences of the world by all creators ● the engineer   mathematician   sculptor   physicist   chemist   architect   doctor   musician   writer   dancer   teacher   baker   actor   editor   the man on the job.   the woman in the home   home   and painters

for the past many years the western world has been working back through the maze of surface decoration and meaningless gloss to the fundamentals of form ● sometimes this has been an economic necessity as in the present war years   other times it comes from an aesthetic demand ● where the people through the sensibilities of the creators find it necessary to rediscover values and to cast aside the non-essentials ● hindrances of the past

why is it that today we are more concerned with the materials and design of a chair than with its covering or ornament?   why are we more concerned with the quality of the music than with the personal idiosyncrasies of the conductor?   why are the uniforms . the word itself becomes strange   so varied and differ so radically from those of former wars?   why are our houses being designed from the inside out   rather than fitting the living to a predetermined style on the outside?   why indeed do we not only accept but also admire and feel intensely proud of the jeep?   a superb example of a healthy direction of thinking and feeling

in spite of prejudice and confusion we are becoming aware slowly of true and good and vital and therefore beautiful form.

my interest in painting is the rediscovery of form through movement and balance and depth and light ● using this medium to recreate in a satisfying order my experiences of this world   with a desire to increase our pleasure   expand our perceptions   enrich our lives

debt to the Austrian artist and designer Herbert Bayer (particularly his catalog cover for the exhibition Wunder des Leben, held in Berlin in 1935).[103] In the case of Ray and Alvin Lustig, an immensely talented graphic designer who also contributed covers to *Arts & Architecture,* it is difficult to ascertain who influenced who. Lustig's witty and inventive design for the inside cover of Mel Scott's book *Cities Are for People* (1942), with its cut-out silhouettes of people with cut-out hearts and carrying flowers (figure 1.24), may well have influenced the Eames child's chair (1945, chapter 5) and the flowers and hearts that appear in Eames films (chapter 7). But cut-out art and handicrafts were popular in the interwar years, and Ray was well versed in cut-out paper and metal work from at least the late 1930s and certainly before she went to Cranbrook[104]; thus, Lustig may have derived some of his ideas from her. At any rate, there is a strong similarity between Lustig's silhouettes and those on Ray's cover for the July 1944 issue of *Arts & Architecture* (figure 1.22), which were probably also influenced by the drawings and sculpture of Henry Moore and Barbara Hepworth. The same issue contained a diagram by Charles, relating to family housing needs in the postwar period, which included silhouette figures almost certainly drawn by Ray. (Virtually identical to those on the cover, they contrast starkly with Charles's less sophisticated but more humorous illustrations in the same article.) That from the mid 1940s Ray chose not to continue with her graphic design and dedicated herself to joint projects with Charles which were largely related to product design is seen as a great loss by those of us who have a high regard for her *Arts & Architecture* work and her textile designs of 1945 and 1947.[105]

By 1940, when she enrolled at Cranbrook, Ray Eames had been firmly committed to modernism for several years and was in touch with all the latest developments in painting and sculpture. That she was more avant-garde than Charles when he entered Cranbrook in 1938 has been overlooked by most writers on the Eameses—including, ironically, those who privilege the avant-garde. The histories that foreground Charles as the main force behind their modernist products designed from 1941 onward, therefore, need some qualification in order to give Ray full credit for her part in them.

CITIES
ARE FOR
PEOPLE
BY MEL SCOTT

THE LOS ANGELES REGION PLANS FOR LIVING

1.24 Inside cover design for Mel Scott's book *Cities Are for People*, 1942. Alvin Lustig.

1.25 Lead page of "What Is a House?" *Arts & Architecture*, July 1944. Charles and Ray Eames.

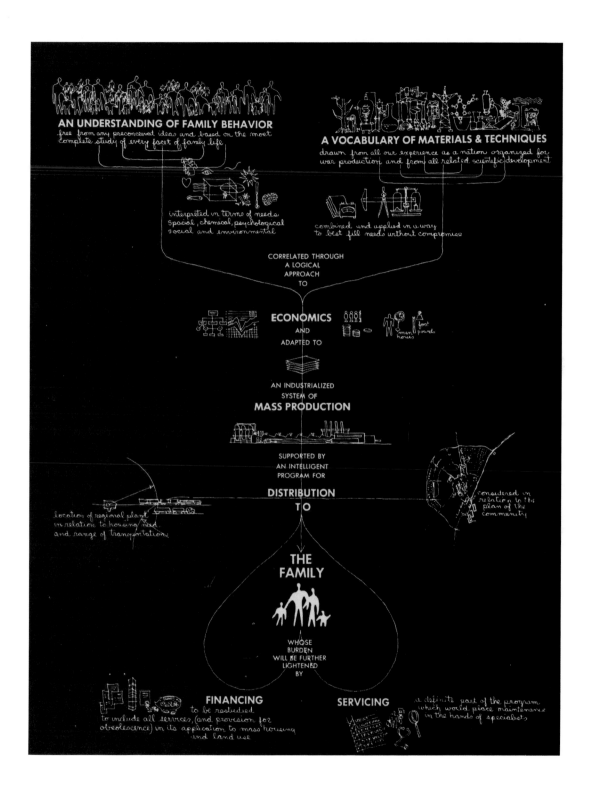

AN UNDERSTANDING OF FAMILY BEHAVIOR
free from any preconceived ideas and based on the most
complete study of every facet of family life

A VOCABULARY OF MATERIALS & TECHNIQUES
drawn from all our experience as a nation organized for
war production, and from all related scientific development

interpreted in terms of needs
spacial, chemical, psychological
social and environmental

combined and applied in a way
to best fill needs without compromise

CORRELATED THROUGH
A LOGICAL
APPROACH
TO

ECONOMICS
AND
ADAPTED TO

man
hours

foot
pound

AN INDUSTRIALIZED
SYSTEM OF
MASS PRODUCTION

SUPPORTED BY
AN INTELLIGENT
PROGRAM FOR

DISTRIBUTION
TO

location of regional plant
in relation to housing need
and range of transportation

considered in
relation to the
plan of the
community

THE
FAMILY

WHOSE
BURDEN
WILL BE FURTHER
LIGHTENED
BY

FINANCING
to be restudied
to include all services, (and provision for
obsolescence) in its application to mass housing
and land use

SERVICING

a definite part of the program
which would place maintenance
in the hands of specialists

1.26 Illustration in "What
Is a House?" Charles
Eames.

After her mother's death, in 1940, Ray was encouraged by Benjamin Baldwin, another Hofmann pupil, to study at the Cranbrook Academy of Art, to which she moved in the autumn of 1940. It was there that Ray Kaiser and Charles Eames met and, immediately after Charles left there, formed one of the most creative and productive design partnerships of the twentieth century.

Charles's work had changed somewhat since his arrival at Cranbrook. Just over 30, he had considerable artistic flair and exceptional practical skills, but he had worked within more traditional parameters than some of his fellow students—although he could not by any stretch of the imagination be called a traditionalist. It was not just that he turned to a more purist modern aesthetic at Cranbrook; rather, his whole way of thinking was transformed.

The Cranbrook community, of which the Cranbrook Academy of Art was part, was established by the Detroit newspaper tycoon George C. Booth. Inspired by the ideals of the Arts and Crafts movement, which spread rapidly across the United States at the turn of the century,[106] Booth was concerned about the standard of design in Detroit. In the tradition of design reformers from Henry Cole onward, he decided that the root of the problem lay in the lack of contact between designers and manufacturers. Booth searched for models to help him promote design reform. After visiting the American Academy in Rome in 1922, he became convinced of the need for an experimental educational community. Eliel Saarinen, then Visiting Professor of Architecture at the University of Michigan, was asked to prepare a plan for such a community.[107] Work was slow, however, because of the Depression. It was not until 1932 that the Academy of Art finally opened, with Saarinen as director.

The debate on design reform in America was rooted in the ideas of the Arts and Crafts Movement and was not dissimilar from the debates that took place in Britain, Austria, and Germany before, during, and after World War I.[108] There had been a growing consciousness of the threat to the American economy posed by well-designed, high-quality German goods before the war and after 1918 there was a renewed determination that German economic competition should not threaten America's world leadership. From the earliest years of the twentieth century, after the realization that the Arts and Crafts movement could or would not in itself provide the impetus for design reform at a commercial level, certain colleges of art and design in Germany, Austria, and Britain had aimed at linking art and design projects with local manufacturers.[109] Such ideas led to the foundation of the Deutsche Werkbund (1907), the Austrian Werkbund (1910), the Swiss Werkbund (1913), the British Design and Industries Association (1915), and the Norwegian Brukskunst (1918). These organizations brought designers, manufacturers, and retailers together and stressed that design reform was central to the advancement of national economies. The idea that good design improved sales and profits was embraced elsewhere—not least in the United States, where there was something of a shift in emphasis within the Arts and Crafts movement toward a greater concern with the production of commercially viable objects of everyday use, whether made by hand or by machine.[110] The depressed economy of the 1930s added to the necessity for the constituent parts of Cranbrook to be self-financing, and Booth emphasized the importance of designing and making saleable products. The ideas of truth to materials, honesty of construction, learning from established and tested traditions, and joy in labor and the concern for quality, utility, and beauty in all aspects of life remained but were now guided by a determination to produce affordable objects for everyday use.

Cranbrook soon became highly regarded within American design education, and the time during which Charles and Ray were there is considered the "vintage" period of the institution.[111] Cranbrook's success was due in no small part to Eliel Saarinen, who was open to ideas and who encouraged his students to experiment with form, materials, and techniques. At a time when Scandinavian architecture and design were increasing in popularity in the United States and offering an alternative to International Style modernism and to traditional styles,[112] Saarinen kept in touch with all the latest developments.[113] Besides making regular trips to Europe, he kept abreast of new developments through magazines and through his friend and compatriot Alvar Aalto.[114]

Of paramount importance in this narrative is Aalto's influence on the work of Charles Eames and Eero Saarinen and later on that of Charles and Ray Eames. In the 1930s Aalto, who was a friend of Arp and who was extremely knowledgeable about abstract painting and sculpture, experimented with free plastic shapes for buildings and objects in the hope of avoiding the dangers implicit in strict standardization.[115] This and his belief that wood and the wood-processing industry were capable of reconciling humanism and the industrial present[116] influenced the Eameses, who, while never committed to wood as strongly as Aalto, were greatly concerned with organic plastic form and, as will be argued throughout this book, were at great pains to humanize the industrialized world in which they lived.

There was a constant stream of stimulating visitors to Cranbrook, and Eliel Saarinen's international reputation meant that talented designers and teachers were eager to work for him. The staff, too, was impressive. Both Charles Eames and Ray Kaiser learned a great deal from Loja Saarinen, Marianne Strengell, Carl Milles, Zoltan Sepeshy, Marshall Fredericks, and Wallace Mitchell. It is to the great credit of the institution that several tutors and students from the late 1930s were to make names for themselves in the postwar design world, the best-known (aside from the Eameses) being Florence Schust (later Knoll), Don Albinson, Harry Bertoia, Benjamin Baldwin, and Harry Weese.[117]

The Cranbrook emphasis on workshop activities and learning by doing greatly appealed to Charles Eames, as did the interchange of ideas and the debates about the future of design. Ray Kaiser's four-month stay reinforced her Arts and Crafts notions of quality handwork and joy in labor. In her weaving classes, under the direction of Marianne Strengell, she designed and wove rugs, one of which later took pride of place in the Eames House in Los Angeles. In later years she occasionally designed textiles,[118] something to which she was introduced at Cranbrook.

Charles, by contrast, came to Cranbrook better versed in Arts and Crafts ideas, which he retained and developed while becoming more fully acquainted with International Style architecture and with Organic Modernism. He accepted the Cranbrook fellowship because it offered him time to read and reflect on his own work without the pressures of having to make a living. His plan was to read for a year—"to live for a year in a library." "In a sense," he said, "it was an attempt to make up what I had lost in the academic world."[119] He managed to read for about three months before getting involved in projects. One of the first of these projects was the Meeting of the Waters fountain, commissioned in 1931 for Charles's home town of St. Louis and designed by the Swedish sculptor Carl Milles.[120] Work began in 1938 and the newly arrived Eames assisted with the design of the fountain basin and prepared the scale models, in the Cranbrook tradition of involving students with projects related to their home communities and of fellows and students learning in the time-honored mode of working with experienced "masters."[121] Eames greatly admired Milles, whom he described as "the last of the Renaissance sculptors" and "a great Romantic," and the two men became such friends that Charles entrusted Milles with cutting his hair.[122]

Eliel Saarinen was so impressed with Eames that at the end of the year he appointed him Instructor of Design in the Intermediate School of Design, which prepared students for the full Cranbrook curriculum. Eames did so well at that job that after only a year he was put in charge of what later became the Department of Industrial Design, sometimes referred to by Charles as the Department of Experimental Design or simply the Design Department.[123] He also worked in the architectural and design practice run by Saarinen and his son Eero, learning an enormous amount in the process and acknowledging that it was not until he started working with them that he had "any concept of what a 'concept' was."[124]

It was while working in the Saarinens' office in 1939–40 that Eames undertook three important projects with Eero Saarinen, who was to become an extremely close and lifelong friend. Few people could stretch Charles Eames, but Eero Saarinen was one of them. The "chemistry" between the two was remarkable,[125] and even in later years the "somber and solid" Eero became quite a different person when in the presence of his more "bubbly" friend.[126] Three years younger than Charles, Eero—a child prodigy carefully nurtured by his gifted parents—was a well-rounded artist and architect ("a real star," according to Charles[127]) by the time the two men first met. He had studied sculpture in Paris for a year and had been trained in architecture at Yale, graduating in 1934 and winning a traveling scholarship to Europe for two years before returning to the United States to work with Walter Gropius and later for his father. After an initial period of mutual suspicion, Charles and Eero realized they had a great deal in common besides a Beaux-Arts architectural training and a burning desire to find design solutions appropriate to the contemporary world. Not least was the powerful influence of the elder Saarinen, the son of a Lutheran minister, whose belief that work was the central focus of life was accepted by both young men. Although Charles's views on work were rooted in his childhood and adolescent experiences, they were reinforced by Eliel Saarinen's insistence that "work is the key to creative growth of mind" and that "as long as man is compelled to find his own way, his mind is bound to increase in inventiveness."[128] This attitude colored the future thinking of Charles and Ray Eames, as did Eliel Saarinen's view that careful research lay at the root of good design. In the postwar period, both the Eames Office and Eero Saarinen's architectural practice were noted for carrying out enormous amounts of research.[129] The younger Saarinen had been trained by his father to look beyond the project at hand to wider implications, and Charles learned this through working with them both.[130] Beyond that, the elder Saarinen drummed into him a particular way of working, which was to take the given brief, consider the detailed issues within it, and then work out to the next stage, and then the one beyond that, and so on, until one attained a "total view." Charles later acknowledged that the notion that "one can't look at a project without thinking of the next smaller or larger thing" influenced him thereafter.[131] Both Charles and Eero were idealists, and both were fascinated by ideas and possessed what in Finland is known as *sisu,* namely the capacity to keep going even beyond the limits of your energies and the expectations of your resources[132]—a capacity they also expected of their employees.

It was largely through Eero that Charles became a full-fledged modernist, determined to research every aspect of a project and to use the techniques of mass production to improve the human environment for the population at large. Through Eero, Charles also increased his appreciation of the fine arts. Charles loved sculpture, and it is important to note that before he worked collaboratively with Ray he had extended his interest in and his knowledge of sculpture through his work and friendship with both Milles and Saarinen. (To assert that sculpture was important to Charles before he met Ray Kaiser is not to deny that she had an enormous amount to offer him in that area; but, rather, to indicate that he was in a position to appreciate her considerable talents.)

Charles Eames and Eero Saarinen's first collaboration, an exhibition of faculty work at Cranbrook in 1939, was a forerunner of later Eames exhibitions. The Cranbrook exhibition reflected the avant-garde ideas of Herbert Bayer[133]—particularly in the use of strings and wires to suspend display stands and to define and organize space. This work not only reveals the pair's awareness of European ideas about exhibition design but also illustrates how much Charles's outlook had changed since his arrival at Cranbrook. The second collaborative project was the furniture for the Klienhans Music Hall in Buffalo (1939–40).[134] The building was designed by the Saarinens; Charles assisted with the seating, including an armchair that reveals the influences of Alvar Aalto and the American designer Gilbert Rohde,[135] and while Eliel and Eero Saarinen were in Europe he was left to draw all the furniture, including details and specifications.[136] The third and most important collaboration of these years came when Charles and Eero entered the Museum of Modern Art's 1940 Organic Design in Home Furnishings competition and won major prizes in the seating and case furniture categories (see chapter 5).

Detroit offered Charles a magnificent opportunity for studying the prefabricated automobile factories designed by Albert Kahn, who had close connections with Cranbrook.[137] He also visited László Moholy-Nagy, the former Bauhaus teacher who had established the New Bauhaus in Chicago in 1937 and who encouraged Charles's interest in new materials, technology, and forms.[138] It must be stressed, however, that in no way did Charles leap headlong into New Bauhaus-style modernism. Under the watchful eye of Eliel Saarinen, Cranbrook staff members and students stood back and looked at many manifestations of design. Alvar Aalto and Frank Lloyd Wright were considered as important as Le Corbusier, Gropius, and Mies van der Rohe, Arts and Crafts ideals as worthy as modernist ones, and sculpture and the decorative arts as important as architecture.

Certain Cranbrook students were later to favor the "Machine Aesthetic," and others "Organic Modernism"; some, like the Eameses, were to work in both. But the issues debated at Cranbrook went beyond style to a consideration of how best to retain human values while using new materials and technologies to produce better living environments. In the period of great optimism and determination to build a better future that followed World War II, those who had been to Cranbrook knew that there were no simple solutions. The Eameses offered particular solutions to the questions of how people might be seated and housed and of how they might live. Those solutions developed and took on many different manifestations in the years after they left Cranbrook; however, by and large, they all involved the personalizing and humanizing of modernism, an approach to design to which they had been exposed at Cranbrook. Charles Eames was far from dogmatic about design issues when he went to Cranbrook, where he was taught to eschew dogma as such. Ray was more narrowly focused when she arrived there, but she too learned that dogma stood in the way of clear thinking and the full flowering of creativity.

Howard Myers, in the foreword to George Nelson and Henry Wright's 1945 book *Tomorrow's House,* adopted a position that, in its attack on modernist dogma, comes close to that espoused by the Eameses (and many others at Cranbrook), who were unrelentingly modernist but not tied to any one style, medium, or material:

> We should not let sentimental ties with the past stand in the way of getting the best house present technology and design can produce. The notion that the contemporary approach to design involves flat roofs and corner windows and the exclusion of the rambler rose is one kind of nonsense this book aims to expose. Perhaps the greatest virtue of tomorrow's house is that it frees the plan—and therefore the family—from arbitrary concepts which have gotten in the way of gracious living these many years.[139]

Myers's mention of the rose in relation to modern design is reminiscent of an earlier debate in Britain around the concept of "fitness for purpose" within the Design and Industries Association. The poet T. Sturge Moore pointed out in 1918 that roses protested against reason, economy, and order with "raptures of quite useless beauty."[140] William Lethaby disagreed with this approach to the debate but was adamant that the way forward was not a new dogmatism. A pedantic adherence to the "no-style style" of the Bauhaus would, he argued, hold back the development of true rationalism in architecture and design. In their openness and lack of dogmatism, Myers and the Eameses stood in the Lethaby tradition, but there was also more than a touch of the poet in them. Like Sturge Moore and Myers, they loved flowers—including the rose, which they used to humanize new technological wizardry such as the computer. For them the rose represented not only singular beauty but also the human qualities of love and caring, which were outside the remit of the machine. Their personalizing and humanizing of modernist architecture, interiors, and technology helped what Myers called "gracious living" to flourish in the postwar period.

In 1941 the Eameses moved to California. In the postwar years, Californian modernism, with its connotations of easy, comfortable, gracious living in an economy of plenty, came to symbolize not only the "good life" but also the popular acceptance of modernism in the United States. Los Angeles was an exciting place to be after World War II—especially in the early 1950s, when it became something of a Mecca for young artists and designers.[141] The Eameses played a major part in shaping Californian modernism in the thirty-odd years they worked there—and California (Los Angeles in particular) was not without its influence on them.

In order to better understand the design context in which the Eameses worked, and the specific influences upon them, it is necessary to consider the architectural traditions and preoccupations of Southern California. However, it must be remembered that the Eameses decided to move to Los Angeles not because they saw it as a hotbed of modernism but rather because they felt "the need to get away from the community life at Cranbrook and to work on their own."[142] They considered that they could dedicate themselves to their work more easily in California than in New York, the other place they considered living, where they had "too many" friends and acquaintances.[143] They wanted somewhere pleasant yet stimulating to live and work and the casual Californian lifestyle suited their preference for the simple. Above all, they wanted to pursue their own projects without too many distractions.

This is not to say that particularities of place are not important, especially with regard to a city like Los Angeles, or that early Californian modernism did not make a greater impact upon them because they experienced it directly—literally in the case of the Neutra apartment, in which they lived until they built their own home. I would argue, however, that reductionist positions which claim that the work of the Eameses was archetypical of California or that it could not have been produced outside California neglect the extent of non-Californian influences on their work and just how many of their commissions and business connections came from outside the "Golden State." The Eameses' Venice workshop undoubtedly reflected something of the informality of certain aspects of Californian life, but it also epitomized the Protestant ethic. Most of the "California reductionism" is based on the modernist myth of Los Angeles, which, as Mike Davis has so brilliantly shown in his book *City of*

Quartz,[144] was only one part of a far more complex myth and only one strand of its reality. Furthermore, whatever the myth or reality of Los Angeles itself, the Eameses always stood slightly apart from the city in which they lived, just as they stood slightly apart from each of the social, cultural, and artistic circles in which they moved. They spent most of their time at 901 Washington Boulevard, and most of it working; sometimes it seemed that the Eames Office could be anywhere, so hermetically sealed off was it from the outside world.

Nevertheless, the creative cultural environment of California, and particularly Los Angeles, offered the Eameses a conducive climate in which their talents flourished. Their architecture drew on certain Southern Californian traditions that privileged the new and the individual, but they repudiated the worst results of commercialism, uncontrolled growth, and an obsession with novelty and "showiness" which they considered had turned Los Angeles into an "aesthetic nightmare."[145]

If the single-family domestic residence is taken as a yardstick of the "American dream," then Los Angeles epitomized that dream more than any other city, with a staggering 94 percent of all dwellings falling into this category by 1930.[146] The architectural language used to express that ideal in the early twentieth century was rooted in the Arts and Crafts Movement, in the Hispanic Revival, and, increasingly, in varieties of the "modern," all of which played a part in the broader architectural and design background against which Charles and Ray Eames developed as artists and designers. In the late 1940s and the 1950s they offered modernist versions of the high-quality single home. If the large timber-framed houses with overhanging roofs designed by Charles and Henry Greene in Pasadena in the early twentieth century (see figure 1.27) represent the high point of the Californian Arts and Crafts movement,[147] the low-cost single-family Californian bungalow was its most democratic manifestation.[148] The Eameses were influenced by Arts and Crafts ideas before they settled in California, but it is interesting to note that their friend John Entenza, organizer of the Case Study House Program (see chapter 3), greatly admired the Greenes' houses for their "simple beautiful modesty" and "elegance, at once innocent and enormously sophisticated"[149]—qualities he also found in the work of the Eameses. To the extent that the Eameses set their goal as low-cost housing for "ordinary people," their architecture stood in the "craftsman" bungalow tradition;

1.27 Gamble House,
Pasadena, 1908. Greene
and Greene.

their projects, however, had more in common with the elegant one-offs built for the Pasadena haute bourgeoisie.

Closely linked with the Arts and Crafts Movement's concern for the vernacular was the Hispanic Revival, which focused on California's "Spanish" past. So popular was this somewhat Romantic concern for "old" California that Mission Revival architecture and design had long been used to "sell" Los Angeles as a desirable place to live.[150] An influential architect who believed that Spanish Colonial architecture expressed "traditions, history and romance" but felt it should inform the search for contemporary form was Irving Gill, whose Allen House (1907), described as "the first anti-ornament architect designed building," predates the work of Adolf (*Ornament and Crime*) Loos in Vienna and whose cubistic volumes and abstracted forms resemble the later International Style.[151] Gill's increasing use of concrete, his interest in low-cost and low-density workers' housing, and his commitment to minimalism all marked him as distinctly "modern," yet his work also reflected Arts and Crafts ideals in its insistence on simplicity and the vernacular. His Dodge House (1914–1916) in West Hollywood illustrates his "modern" aesthetic together with an Arts and Crafts concern for quality craftwork and the integration of house and landscape as well as a respect for individuality and place "that characterized Californian modernism and set it apart from that of Europe."[152]

Before discussing other avant-garde elements of Californian modernism, it is worth reflecting on the powerful impact of the various manifestations of the Hispanic Revival, which came to be regarded as the "natural" and "normal" way of building in Southern California.[153] So appropriate did the style feel that when the Eameses first planned to build a house in Los Angeles they decided on a "Spanish" one—not least because Charles wanted to follow the tradition of building the front of the house out to the street, thereby creating more space for a private garden inside.[154] Charles and Ray both liked the idea of an "anonymous location right in the heart of the city" and a modest exterior with high walls and a small door; only after entering the latter would one experience the space "expand[ing] out to the sky."[155] The very fact that they could consider such a house confirms that they were not committed to design in the International Style of the modern movement in the early 1940s, a fact too little appreciated by those who wrote (and write) about their later architectural work.

Frank Lloyd Wright, the architect whom Charles Eames had most admired as a student, was responsible for several houses in Los Angeles: the Barnsdall (Hollyhock) House (1920) and the Millard (La Miniatura), Ennis, Freeman, and Storer Houses (1923–1925). Although an excessive admiration for Wright was the ostensible cause of Charles's being asked to leave Washington University, Wright's influence on him was broad rather than particular. Wright rejected "dead" architecture of the past more emphatically than his young admirer, especially the "Spanish" styles ("dead things that we have sentimentally taken as live traditions")[156] that had spread like wildfire over the richer suburbs of Los Angeles. He looked, rather, to the Mayan, Aztec, and Toltec architecture of Mexico and Central America and the Pueblo forms of the southwestern United States for representative native building styles. All American postwar architects interested in new materials and techniques were influenced to some degree by Frank Lloyd Wright; his use of concrete blocks in his Los Angeles houses of the 1920s could not have but impressed the technologically minded Charles Eames. Yet in later years Charles emphasized that what had most impressed him about Frank Lloyd Wright was the "schmalzy stuff about the fields and the earth . . . and materials."[157] Charles loved the grand concepts about the relationship of architecture to nature in Wright's autobiography, commenting "really great stuff . . . boy, that really got to me,"[158] just as he later responded to Aalto's ("such an earthy guy"[159]) emphasis on the relationship between nature and materials. Wright, who spoke of shelter "not only as a quality of space but of spirit" and of "poetic tranquility instead of a more deadly 'efficiency,'"[160] touched Charles's spiritual, romantic side. Charles developed greatly after the late 1920s and the early 1930s, the period of Wright's greatest influence upon him, but he never forgot those grander ideas about what architecture and design might be.

There were some similarities between Frank Lloyd Wright and Charles Eames. Both questioned their Beaux-Arts "pseudo training" of imitation and "superficial eclecticism" (as Wright put it).[161] Wright's intense individualism struck a chord with Charles, who was also steeped in the American tradition (or myth, depending on one's viewpoint) of individual freedom. Natural forms and a belief that there were "laws of procedure inherent in all natural growths" informed Wright's architecture[162] and, together with his strong emphases on organic architecture rooted in indigenous culture and on the need to humanize the standardization that accompanied machine production, influenced a whole generation of younger architects and designers.

It was the Viennese émigrés Rudolph Schindler and Richard Neutra, both of whom had been influenced by Adolf Loos (a great admirer of America and American technology), who most extended the terms of modernism in Los Angeles.[163] Schindler, who had been trained as an engineer before studying architecture under Otto Wagner, was sent by his employer, Frank Lloyd Wright, to supervise the building of the Barnsdall House. After setting up on his own in 1921, Schindler produced some highly original designs, including one for a two-family communal house in West Hollywood with separate living quarters (1921–22) that combined the concerns for simplicity and for outdoor living in what Schindler called a marriage between a "solid permanent cave and an open light-weight tent."[164] His most famous work was commissioned by Dr. Philip Lovell, well known for a health column in the *Los Angeles Times* in which he extolled vegetarianism, physical exercise, natural remedies, nude sunbathing, and open-mindedness toward sexuality. Lovell moved in the avant-garde circle that centered around Schindler and was so impressed with Schindler's home that he commissioned a house at Newport Beach. Influenced by De Stijl, it had five free-standing concrete frames supporting the large two-story living area, with its balconies leading off to flexible bed-*cum*-dressing rooms.[165] Now recognized as an important modernist building the Lovell Beach House was given little recognition at the time by critics; they saw it as unorthodox[166] and favored Neutra's Lovell Health House (figure 1.28). Nevertheless, as Wendy Kaplan points out, Schindler's "concrete slab level with the garden, flat roofs, sliding doors, the clerestories and movable non-bearing partitions" all "became part of the vocabulary of Californian Modern architecture."[167]

Far grander than the later Case Study houses, many of which it influenced, the Health House was similar in that it was built as a demonstration house. All "progressive" architects and designers of the 1930s and the 1940s knew it well. With its large areas of glass, its open plan, its lightweight steel frame, its curtain wall, and its dramatic cantilever, this "European's dream come true"[168] was the most exemplary piece of International Style architecture in Los Angeles and the only California building included in the 1932 Modern Architecture exhibition at the Museum of Modern Art.[169] As in the Eames House, completed 20 years later,

1.28 Lovell Health House,
Griffith Park, Los Angeles,
1928–29. Richard Neutra.

a prefabricated steel frame was used. In both houses, light poured through large sections of glass and the flexible internal spaces were broken up by partitions. Furthermore, each house featured a built-in sofa in an intimate "alcove," soft light-diffusing curtains, and plants in a double-height living room. The Eameses had great respect for Neutra as an architect, and until they built their own home they lived in an apartment designed by him—an experience they greatly enjoyed.[170] Neutra shared their passion for mass production; indeed, he seems to have been even more addicted than the Eameses to mail-order catalogs of industrial and standardized items. While Neutra dominated Modern Movement architecture in California in the 1930s, other slightly younger California-based architects—most notably Harwell Hamilton Harris, Gregory Ain, Raphael Soriano, Whitney Smith, Wayne Williams, and William Lescaze—also worked in the International Style, their buildings illustrating the tremendous flexibility of interior planning offered by steel-frame architecture as well as the notion that outdoor space was a valid concern for architects.[171]

Any consideration of modernist architecture in Los Angeles, or the United States in general, must acknowledge the continuing popularity of historical styles. The majority of people felt more comfortable in a house designed in a historically recognizable style or in a style that referred back to the past. When the Eameses went to Los Angeles, in 1941, they found an architecturally eclectic city where the Colonial and Hispanic Revivals competed for supremacy with Art Deco.[172] The popularity of historical styles continued after World War II, but modernism began to make greater inroads than ever before. The Eameses offered their architecture and design as part and parcel of a postwar movement to build a better world in which to live, and, for a period, Californian modernism seemed to offer just that.

When asked about the Eameses, many people comment on their lifestyle of studied simplicity and on their distinctive appearance. That they were not outwardly concerned with a conspicuous display of wealth can be seen in their approach to clothes and products. Once they were satisfied with an item they saw no reason to change it; the only appliance that was changed in their house in almost 40 years was the refrigerator, which they were forced to replace when it ceased to function. Fabric samples were kept so that faded or rotting drapes could be replaced with closely matching ones. At a time when many American designers drove foreign cars, Charles and Ray favored black Fords, symbols of the "American System" of mass production, which they kept for a long time—one as long as 18 years. In 1972, however, he got a grey Mercedes and she a black Jaguar, both of which had connotations of quality finish and sound European engineering and stood out in Los Angeles as smart yet not too ostentatious.[1]

They bought or had specially made high-quality clothing, chosen, like the cars, for reasons of utility as well as beauty and never ostentatious. In clothes, as in other areas of design, the Eameses were sticklers for detail and quality—particularly Ray. In 1984 she had me hunting all over London for a particular cotton velvet, in a specified width and colors, which she liked to use for her famous bows. Many of her friends recount similar stories; for the Neuharts it was a whole day spent on a short visit to London looking for a particular grey-blue braid.[2] Charles and Ray each found a style of dressing with which they felt comfortable and stuck to it for the rest of their lives. It was not that they thought dress unimportant: no one spent longer obtaining the correct "look," be it for an interior, an informal dinner party, or a bowl of flowers, than these two, particularly Ray. It was rather that they considered it *too* important to be subject to the vagaries and dictates of fashion.

Both adopted dress styles which were essentially informal, as was their lifestyle. Ray favored simply cut blouses, jackets, and plain full skirts or pinafore dresses. During the 1940s, the 1950s, and much of the 1960s, when rigid dress codes (particularly for women) demanded specific outfits for different times of the day or different areas of life (such as

2.1 Charles and Ray
Eames with Richard
Donges during production
of the film *Merlin and the
Time Mobile*, 1978.

work, home, and leisure), the Eameses—and Ray especially—were notable for a style of dress that saw them through all their daily routines and social activities. It was, of course, easier for them than for many others, because their work, domestic, and social lifestyles were highly integrated and because casual dress was more acceptable at that time in California than in other areas of the United States. They did not need glamorous evening clothes, because their lifestyle did not call for them—and they did not like them anyway. The most formal occasions they attended were exhibition openings, public lectures, and business meetings, to which they simply wore more formal versions of their basic outfits. Charles would wear a jacket and often a bow tie, while Ray might wear her best blouse, a jacket, and a little more jewelry. On very formal occasions Charles translated a "black tie" invitation as strictly that, complying with the color of the tie but nothing else. Audrey Wilder recalls that when she, Billy Wilder, and the Eameses went out to eat in restaurants, "dressing up" meant little more than Charles's wearing a favorite bow tie or bandanna and Ray's adding a small scarf—"always extremely 'artistic'—just like her—and always beautiful, sometimes with tiny gold threads running through."[3]

Their dress styles were rooted in the movement for simpler and more rational clothes that flourished among the American cultural intelligentsia in the interwar years. The middle-class love affair with "the simple life" dated back to the Arts and Crafts movement, some adherents of which adopted "reform dress" which, in more or less "alternative" versions of contemporary fashions, emphasized comfort, utility, and the natural and traditional in terms of materials, colors, and decoration.[4] This "arty-crafty" dress represented an approach to life as much as a style, but nevertheless there was a distinct look to it. In the early twentieth century, art schools and arts-and-crafts societies all over America housed people whose garments set them apart from their more conventional neighbors. Charles and Ray Eames stood in this tradition—imbibed by them at Cranbrook, if not earlier.

The move toward more rational dress was linked to the search for a distinctive American dress style that would stand in contradistinction to Paris fashion—a search that was equivalent to the search for a distinctive American style in architecture and design. The Wall Street crash of 1929 and higher taxes on imported clothes accelerated this development.

Designers such as Claire McCardell used "traditional American" and hard-wearing materials such as denim, calico, seersucker, and wool jersey for comfortable, casual, unpretentious clothes.[5] It was both patriotic and "arty" to wear such dress. It was also politically "progressive" to wear clothes that referenced work clothes in type, fabric, and style—in New Deal America it was "politically correct" to dress down. While essentially easy to wear and sensible by haute couture fashion standards, this "simple" dress was rational for ideological as well as practical reasons. The delight taken by "thinking" Americans of the 1930s in the plain and simple verged on the nostalgic, as in the case of the folksy ethnic look of the late 1930s (the peasant-style pinafores of which were one source for the pinafore dress that became such a distinguishing feature of Ray Eames's wardrobe).[6] At the other polarity was the preppy "coed" look, which combined traditional qualities of WASP tailoring with an updating and subversion by the young of various conservative middle-class items of clothing. Photographs of both Charles and Ray in the 1930s and the early 1940s show them to have been influenced by this trend.[7]

Ray's dress style echoed but did not copy Charles's. She wore blouses with skirts or pinafores; he wore shirts and trousers. The blouses were worn casually and often open-necked, like Charles's shirts, or more formally with a bow—a small, soft, "feminine" bow, usually in velvet and clearly differentiated from Charles's bow tie. When she wore suits she often chose tweeds and corduroys, as he did, but in softer textures, and her high-necked jackets, which had small rounded collars or none at all, were cut short and fitted at the waist. In short, she evolved a uniform for work and leisure, conceived of in terms of utility and beauty, which clearly emphasized her femininity. The adoption by women executives in the 1980s of a male "uniform," complete with certain signifiers of masculinity such as the suit, the tie, and the briefcase, helped to confirm and assert their position in the male world of commerce and business yet did so without arousing fears that they had lost their femininity and were therefore threatening to men in other ways. "Femininity" was affirmed by the wearing of a skirt with the suit and by the transformation of the tie to a floppy neck bow. Although there are many differences between the position of Ray Eames and that of 1980s "power dressers," her dress can be considered that of an artistic woman negotiating a world of work dominated by men and established in a period when society frowned upon any

woman who did not foreground her femininity. It must have been difficult for Ray Eames to know exactly where to pitch her image. Had she
been too fashionable, she might have been labeled frivolous. Too "arty"
would have meant that she was insufficiently concerned with practicalities, while too conservative might have suggested that her design work
was dull. Had she dressed in garb too "sensible," severe, or "masculine,"
her femininity or her sexual orientation might have been in question. As
it was, the degree of "prettiness" (to borrow a word used in relation to the
Eameses' design work) in her dress counterbalanced its rational and work-
aday qualities, thereby making it acceptably "feminine."

Ray's image was as complex as it was contradictory—sensible yet
soft, modern yet nostalgic. She is best remembered for her small, soft
bows and her pinafore dresses. The pinafore dress has associations with
the world of work, but it is mainly remembered as a utilitarian garment
worn by late-nineteenth and early-twentieth-century schoolgirls and dis-
carded by adolescents in favor of adult dress. As such it seems a curiously
girlish choice for a grown woman whose diminutive stature already encouraged a patronizing view of her (one TV program referred to her as
"like a delicious dumpling in a doll's dress"[8]). Yet this adult Pollyanna
was a capable, talented, and independent avant-garde artist turned successful designer who sometimes tempered the more obvious references to

a "little girl" image by adopting very unchildlike colors, such as black and brown. Ray eschewed high heels (even though she was only about 5 feet tall) and often wore light slipper-style shoes or espadrilles. She also stood aside from those women who before, during and after the war, wore trousers. Ray never wore trousers (even in the early 1940s, when she worked day and night on war-related plywood experiments), mainly because she felt her body shape did not look good in them. They certainly would have been less restrictive than her skirts and pinafore dresses, but it needs to be remembered that trousers were still minority wear, even during the war, and that her full skirts, which came exactly to the knee and offered modesty without undue restriction, provided considerably more freedom than the longer very full or pencil slim skirts of the late 1940s and the 1950s.

Ray brought to mind some of the great characters of American girls' literature. These, and other images which reverberated in my mind when I met her (and still do when I study photographs of her), mainly refer to mid-to-late-nineteenth-century or early-twentieth-century America. If Ray's dress reminds one of characters from this period featured in Hollywood films and book illustrations from the early 1930s to the 1950s, it is because she had a somewhat nostalgic view of America's not-so-distant past similar to the view of their creators. Ray reminded me not only of Jo March in Louisa May Alcott's *Little Women* (first published in 1868) and related novels but also of the illustrations of the March sisters in the editions I read as a girl. It was more than the fact that here was a literal little woman who, even in her seventies and at her most matriarchal, retained something of the adolescent, if not the child. Like Jo, she had a "merry sort of face, that never seemed to have forgotten certain childish ways and looks, any more than her voice and manner had."[9] She also shared Jo's enthusiasm and energy.

Ray's dress reflected the ambiguities and changes between girlhood and womanhood addressed in *Little Women* as well as those faced by American women in the middle of the twentieth century. It also evoked memories of other fictional energetic young girls—particularly "tomboy" heroines whose rites of passage into adulthood included adopting more feminized clothes and putting up their hair. Their clothes, like Ray's, were always more rational and "sensible" than mainstream fashion yet never left in any doubt the newly enhanced femininity of the wearer. Ray put up her hair around 1941, signifying that she had passed into womanhood, yet she retained the girlish bow and other signifiers of pre-adult femininity.

The college-girl look of Ray's early womanhood[10] was replaced by a look more influenced by the Romanticism that crept into women's dress in the late 1930s. The most extreme versions of this—Vivien Leigh's costumes in the 1939 film *Gone With The Wind*—might seem a far cry from Ray Eames's apparel of the 1940s and the 1950s, but the narrow waist, the full skirt, and the nostalgic references were all present. In Ray's case, however, they were used in conjunction with a modest utilitarian dress type (pinafore or suit) and length (always at knee level). In that her image offered one resolution of the contradiction of being a working woman, creative artist and designer, wife, lover, and stepmother in mid-twentieth-century America, it could be seen as the thinking, working, artistic, modern woman's answer to Scarlett O'Hara—or at least to Dior.

One source of the nostalgic, the utilitarian, and the "little girl" elements of Ray's image was Judy Garland, who wore a short pinafore dress with nipped-in waist and a soft, high-necked, short-sleeved blouse in *The Wizard of Oz*. Other films of the 1930s, the 1940s, and the early 1950s idealized late-nineteenth-century and turn-of-the-century America, recreating a past at once pre-adult, prewar, pre-industrial, and preoccupied with women's place being in the home and subordinate to men yet offering audiences vivacious and capable young women whose independence, while contained within an acceptable femininity, was signaled by the rationality of their dress. The combination of rationality and a femininity without undue fussiness was as essential an ingredient in the style adopted by Ray Eames as it was in those favored by Hollywood's celluloid heroines.

There was a certain contradiction between Ray Eames the avant-garde artist and designer and Ray Eames the woman who, as she searched for an individual dress style, looked to images of the past and to popular culture from a particularly poignant moment in a woman's development, namely the transition from child to adult. Many women were influenced by similar trends and experienced similar contradictions, but few resisted the force of postwar fashion to the same degree as Ray. It was more acceptable in artistic and intellectual circles to adopt an apparently unchanging mode of dress (although it was more acceptable for men to stand aside from fashion than for women), but even in those circles her tenacity was as remarkable as the individuality of her style. Her shape meant that it was extremely difficult (and frustrating) for her to buy anything "off the peg," and therefore her clothes were custom-made. She found a mode of dress that suited her small, squarish frame, that was comfortable for workshop, domestic, and leisure activities, and that allowed her to retain an aura of femininity, and she stuck to it. How much she was influenced by Charles in her dress style (and vice versa) is not clear, but Ray always tried to please Charles in whatever she did, and it seems likely that his approval of her dress style was a major factor in her retaining it for so long.

If Ray resembled Jo March in *Little Women,* the young Charles Eames resembled the high-minded architect Howard Roark in Ayn Rand's 1943 novel *The Fountainhead.* Although based on Frank Lloyd Wright and Ely Jacques Kahn, Howard Roark also had much in common with Charles Eames. The book opens with Roark studying architecture at the Beaux-Arts-influenced Stanton Institute of Technology at the same time when Eames was at Washington University and feeling frustrated with a similar course. Roark had a casual approach to dress, wearing "old denim trousers, sandals and a shirt with short sleeves," and, also like Eames, had previously worked at a variety of jobs, including a steel mill, and excelled at engineering. His refusal to toe the Beaux-Arts line and his admiration for the unorthodox Henry Cameron (supposedly based on Louis Sullivan) led the dean to expel the "gifted" Roark, whose final words to the dean suggest what Eames may have thought when he left Washington University: "I came here to learn about building. When I was given a project, its only value to me was to learn to solve it as I would solve a real one in the future. I did them the way I'll build them. I've learned all I could learn here—in the structural sciences of which you don't approve. One more year of drawing Italian postcards would give me nothing."[11]

Charles dressed very informally for the Venice workshop-*cum*-office and also at home, usually wearing "casual" trousers and a shirt. His style was studiously non-bourgeois but not without contradictions. His shoes may have been mail-order from the Sears catalog, but some of his tweed and corduroy jackets and suits were made by London tailors.[12] What people remember most about his clothes are the beautiful fabrics, the handmade shirts worn open-necked or with a bow tie or a bandanna, the cuffed trousers, the woollen cardigans and corduroy vests worn as alternatives to the traditional jacket, and the turned shirt collars. Charles was "very careful not to be modish or arty about clothes,"[13] but, although he was never modish in the sense of slavishly following fashion or wearing exaggerated styles, his clothes signified a degree of artistic sensibility and "otherness" that set him aside from the dominant images of white middle-class men in grey-suited America.

His bow ties and bandannas signified this difference but in different ways. The bow tie was "safer" within contemporary fashion codes in that it at least was a tie, if not a conventional one. It had a small but established following in the United States, especially among architects and designers, but still it carried some connotations of caddish behavior and effeminacy. Charles, however, with his charismatic, confident, overtly heterosexual persona, was well able to negotiate the ambiguities and complexities of the image. If the bow tie signified the more formal, urban, indoor world, the bandanna conjured up the rugged outdoor values of the American West. As worn by Charles, they both referred back to the neck bow worn by male artists and designers in the late nineteenth and the early twentieth centuries and represented worlds a million miles away from the world of business, let alone big business and the major institutions with which the Eameses were increasingly associated.

The casual Charles of the 1940s and the 1950s looked as much like a movie star as like a designer. Firmly in the Robert Ryan/Glenn Ford/Henry Fonda mold, and well versed in Hollywood culture, he played (consciously or unconsciously) with images of the supposedly honest and free pre-industrial America and of true-grit, salt-of-the-earth proletarian unpretentiousness, which Hollywood portrayed so convincingly though inauthentically. To certain artists and theatre people Charles's dress appeared somewhat sober, even old fashioned, in its materials and its "crafty" nature, but to businessmen and government officials he appeared casually dressed and the epitome of the designer. The image was arty but not too arty, sensible but never dull, radical but never outrageous. The Eameses' clothes were, rather like their wearers, a complex mixture of rationalism and romanticism—as was their whole lifestyle of studied simplicity.

The individual contributions of each person in any creative partnership are often difficult to assess,[14] and this is certainly so in the case of

Charles and Ray Eames. Each of them brought different areas of expertise to their joint work, Charles from architecture and design and Ray from painting and sculpture, but their contributions never simply divided along these lines. Their personal and design relationship was extremely close, and the situation is further complicated by the fact that they worked closely with a dedicated group of employees. With certain projects it is extremely difficult to penetrate the complexities of life in a busy design office and itemize who thought of and executed what; with other commissions the individual contributions of each partner and those of the key staff members are easier to ascertain. Talking with Ray Eames and former employees sometimes clarified these issues; at other times it confirmed the rich and complex nature of collaboration in one of the most exciting design practices in the United States.

When trying to estimate or illustrate the importance of each person in a lifelong collaboration, one needs to be clear that the aim is not necessarily to establish that input was equal in every part of every project. As anyone is aware who has ever worked collaboratively on anything over a length of time, let alone in something as complex as a design partnership with someone who is also a sexual partner, it is often difficult to explain exactly how an idea or a concept develops, so speedy are the interactions when the adrenaline is high and ideas are flowing freely and when one person is picking up ideas from another before she or he has begun to express them. When discussing her own close working relationship with her husband, the architect and designer Alison Smithson used the word "telepathic" to describe the understanding that develops between two individuals who live and work together.[15] The cumulative effect of interaction between partners is also important. What might have appeared a decision of Charles's could well have been based on ideas exchanged with Ray a day, a week, a month, a year, or several years earlier.

In the complex set of developments that make up the design process, with its dialectic between ideas and practical experimentation and between function and aesthetics, one small input can be crucial to the conception, development, or final appearance of a project, be it a piece of furniture or an exhibition design. While attempting to give due credit to Ray and to temper the previous overprivileging of Charles's role without diminishing his achievements, it is worth reiterating that the aim is not to quantify creative input in the hope of occasionally coming up with a

50:50 division between Charles and Ray. Rather it is to convey some of the workings of a close and complex relationship which was personal as well as professional and which changed in each of these spheres over a long period of time.

The discussion of the personal relationship between Charles and Ray Eames which follows is not to add "romantic interest" but to better understand their partnership and work. The sense of coupling, bonding, "togetherness"—call it what you will—between Charles and Ray was extremely strong and frequently remarked upon. They were often photographed with Charles's arm around Ray, smiling at each other with hands touching or both touching the same object.[16] This happened more in the first 20 or so years of their relationship, but even that is a long time to sustain such an intense closeness. In the early years they sometimes deliberately matched or contrasted their clothes to emphasize their connectedness (figure 2.3). Their 1944 Christmas card (figure 2.4) shows them in matching black T shirts and similar poses, and a 1947 photograph features them in matching gingham shirts, posed in similar positions and holding hands (figure 2.5). Photographic poses of the later years involved less physical contact and less obvious matching of clothes, but even so the sense of them as a couple remained strong. People who knew them only in the 1970s remark on how they appeared very much a "couple" and how their shared sense of humor, friends, family, and visual pleasures were obviously sources of mutual joy. Michael Glickman, who worked in the Eames Office in the early 1970s, recalls seeing them for the first time (on a campus where they were screening some of their films): ". . . in the courtyard of the architecture department I saw Charles, who was then in his late 60s, walking around the narrow edge of a low planter, arms outstretched like a tightrope walker. Ray, giggling, in one of her full . . . skirts . . . pirouetted by his side. Her hand was outstretched, simultaneously—it seemed—to present him and to be there if he had to check his balance."[17] They both enjoyed what others might classify as childish pursuits and enjoyed discovering new things together as well as the spontaneity of each other's reactions to them for nearly 40 years.

For Ray, the coupling with Charles was absolute. He was the center of her world till the day she died. There is abundant evidence of Charles's devotion to Ray, but he was brought up to operate in a man's world and to prioritize work over emotional and personal commitments.

2.3 Charles and Ray
Eames photographed
against a blue background
and wearing blue clothes,
1949.

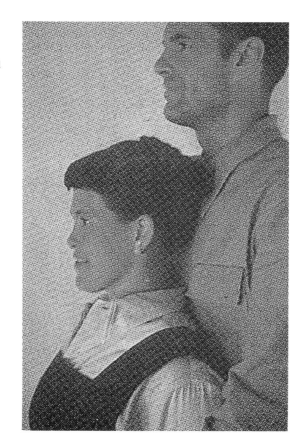

2.4 Charles and Ray Eames,
Christmas 1944, with
plywood sculpture by Ray.

A LIFELONG COLLABORATION

2.5 Charles and Ray
Eames wearing matching
gingham shirts and posing
with metal bases for DCM
chairs, 1947.

2.6 Ray Eames preparing design for Eames room in Exhibition for Modern Living, 1949.

2.7 Charles and Ray Eames working on an idea for upholstering the Aluminum Chair, 1958.

2.8 Ray Eames meeting
staff and students on her
last visit to National
Institute of Design,
Ahmedabad, India, 1987.

However, one senses that at certain times and in certain ways he needed
Ray as much as she needed him; their dependencies within and rewards
from their relationship were mutual but different. Ray gave Charles what
he thought most important in the wife of a designer—someone who
could fully understand his work and provide an effective support structure for it—and that resulted in a stability hitherto lacking in his life.

Charles had more than one serious extra-marital relationship.
The extent, if any, to which this affected his working relationship with
Ray is not clear, and there was some disagreement on this point among
the people I interviewed.[18] Most of those who knew them well or worked
with them consider that, although Ray at times seemed somewhat tense
and although either she or Charles occasionally spent a little more time
away from 901 Washington Boulevard, work went on pretty much as
usual, with both putting their not inconsiderable energies into the tasks
ahead of them. So well established was their working relationship in the
early years and so deep and continual the influence of the one on the other

over the years, that it is difficult to imagine Ray as peripheral at any stage. Even when he was working without her alongside him, Charles's approach to what he was doing was the result of a long and complex dialogue with Ray, and vice versa.

The image of Charles that Ray carried with her was that of a knight in shining armor, and during the early years (and maybe most or all of their years together) this was how she experienced him. He was charismatic for her, just as he was for others. He was handsome, and there is no doubt that many women, and men too, found him "enormously seductive,"[19] both physically and intellectually. Charles's self-centeredness, to which the Neuharts[20] and others (including members of his family) attest, ensured that he never did anything he did not wish to; it was his choice to leave his first wife and their child for Ray and to spend the rest of his life in close personal and professional proximity to her. He never chose to alter that, even if, in later years, they were at times apparently less close than before. But even if one concludes that Ray was more devoted to Charles than he to her, in absolute terms Charles's caring for and

2.9 Charles Eames talks to staff and students on his last visit to National Institute of Design, 1978.

A LIFELONG COLLABORATION

devotion to Ray was very considerable. No one will ever know the full details of the personal life of these two remarkable individuals or of how they regarded and related to each other. What the actual texture of their relationship was like—and it must have changed many times over many years—only they really knew. Even if it had its sticky moments, they managed to sustain a remarkable closeness in working and living together over a great many years—a closeness that went far beyond the bounds of the "togetherness" extolled and promoted in postwar America.

There is insufficient evidence around which to construct convincing psychoanalytic case studies of Charles and Ray. Charles was not expansive about the details of his early years, although in the last months of his life he commented on a growing desire to return to his roots and mentioned "early memories that were flooding him."[21] Ray rarely talked about her early life, even to her closest friends; therefore, what she said to them about her overprotected childhood seems especially significant. The reasons for and the degrees to which women desire and find protection through men are far from clear but Ray's need for protection was commented upon by many of the women who knew her (not all of whom necessarily thought it such a bad thing). All-embracing theories of patriarchy tend to pose women as victims without agency or ability to negotiate complex situations to their own advantage or satisfaction, at least in part, and some of those to whom I spoke saw Ray mainly as victim to Charles's selfishness, self-centeredness, and propensity for extra-marital relationships. This may have been the case, but psychoanalytic theories that focus on pre-Oedipal periods of development or articulate the pleasures of masochism suggest that subordination has its compensations.[22] But one may not have to delve so deep to account for Ray's many investments in remaining with Charles. After all, he was enormously charming, prodigiously intelligent, handsome, sexually attractive, and adored by many other than Ray. He gave Ray a great deal, not least an enormous amount of care. He recognized her talents—probably more than anyone else—and encouraged her to develop them. Consequently, she flourished creatively, enjoying an immensely satisfying career as a partner in what was probably the most exciting design practice in the United States at the time.

It is tempting to link Charles's later life to an Oedipal narrative—the absent (and subsequently dead) father and the close relationship to and championing of the mother are there—but too little is

2.10, 2.11 Charles Eames
at National Institute of
Design, 1978.

known of the details of his early years. Whatever the root causes, Charles was remarkably self-focused. Other adapted to his interests, ideals, and ambitions, rather than he to theirs, but it was usually easy to do so because he and they were so fascinating and rewarding. Ray was not the only person willing to subordinate her interests to those of Charles and go on to make them her own. She welcomed the direction; he enjoyed the control.

Part of Ray enjoyed playing the wife behind the great man, but another part craved recognition in her own right—a recognition she deserved. To the extent that the Eames style of the 1940s and the 1950s was "progressive" and "avant-garde," Ray was certainly as responsible as Charles. Deborah Sussman and many other Eames Office employees claim that Ray played an extremely important part in refining shapes and insist that the final forms of the artifacts produced must be seen as the joint work of Ray and Charles. Discussing the wartime plywood work, Gregory Ain stated that Ray was able to "bring things into relation with one another" and to "find the inner order in whatever she touched,"[23] and the final form of the famous DCM chair owes a great deal to her interest in abstract art. While Ray insisted that Charles's sense of form was "perfect," he made similar claims about her; for example:

> She has a very good sense of what gives an idea, or form, or piece of sculpture its character, of how its relationships are formed. She can see when there is a wrong mix of ideas or materials, where the division between two ideas isn't clear. If this sounds like a structural or architectural idea, it is. But it comes to Ray through her painting . . . any student of Hans's has a sense of this kind of structure.[24]

There are parallels between the way Charles and Ray Eames have been viewed and the way another famous pair of designers, Charles Rennie Mackintosh and Margaret Macdonald Mackintosh, have been evaluated since the 1930s. In both cases, the man (trained in architecture) has been hailed as a genius in the field of modern architecture and design. The talents of both men are undisputed; however, in view of the intensity of the admiration for Charles Eames and C. R. Mackintosh, it is all the more surprising to find that the women designers they not only greatly admired but chose to live and collaborate with have been relegated to the margins of history.[25] How the role of women has been "hidden from history" in general and why the contributions of so many female artists and designers have not been given the credit they deserve are well debated elsewhere.[26] The comparison with the Macdonald-Mackintosh collaboration helps place that of the Eameses in perspective and forces the realization that wider historical and historiographical issues are involved in evaluating their partnership. It also reveals the extent to which, in the hierarchy of the arts, architecture (largely male) was (and still is to a great degree) more highly regarded than the "decorative arts" (largely female). This, coupled with a pro-modernist and patriarchal view of the world, has, in my opinion, led to willful ignoring of evidence and serious distortions of history, particularly where male-female and husband-wife collaborations are concerned. As Alison Smithson told me,

> It was and is extremely hard for anyone to stomach the fact that there can be two people of equal talent in a partnership. Someone always says that one must be being carried. And—if it is a woman—then she must really be tired to the kitchen sink, that they wouldn't be working with her were they not married and all that sort of thing. . . . People still can't face the fact of women being equal, of women being good designers. . . . If there are male partners no one nit-picks over the issues of who did what or who thought of what. If there is a woman involved the assumptions are that the male is the leading partner.[27]

It is no coincidence that reevaluations of Ray Eames, Margaret Macdonald Mackintosh, and other female designers have taken place against the background of the development of the women's movement, gender studies, a massive questioning of modernism, and a more widespread appreciation of decoration and cross-cultural references in architecture and design. Despite C. R. Mackintosh's declaration that "Margaret has genius; I have only talent,"[28] her work was later denigrated because it was "decorative" rather than structural and her design preferences for decoration and symbolism have been blamed for holding back her husband from a bolder, purer form of modernism.[29] Similarly, those who would have preferred the work of the Eameses to have been less concerned with "prettiness" blamed Ray for what was regarded as a deviation from the strait and narrow path of orthodox modernist concerns.

Like Mackintosh, Charles Eames constantly emphasized the part played by his wife, almost as if embarrassed by the lack of understanding shown by critics and commentators. He knew the extent and the value of Ray's contribution better than anyone, because he was the other half of the partnership, and he freely acknowledged that his fame was the product of their joint endeavors. It was he who claimed "anything I can do, she can do better," opened a major presentation on design with "Ray can really do it," and insisted "she is equally responsible with me for everything."[30] In a 1969 television interview, Charles corrected the view that Ray's contribution to the partnership was restricted to aspects of color and juxtaposing images (marginalized then but given much more credit today by architects, designers, and critics) and insisted that her contribution usually had to do with "the consistency of structure."[31] He comprehended something of the way in which Ray was being marginalized, and he tried to correct matters. This notwithstanding, Charles had the high public profile. Many long-standing admirers of the Eameses' work, let alone others, did not begin to fully appreciate the extent of Ray's contribution until the exhibition Connections: The Work of Charles and Ray Eames opened in Los Angeles at the end of 1976, shortly after which Ray was named "Woman of the Year" by the California Museum of Science and Industry. Despite that exhibition and 20 years of a women's movement, most of the assessments of her work in the obituaries of 1988 were less than generous.

Since then there has been little reassessment of Ray's role, let alone within the context of broader factors which affected the position of women at the time or a comprehension of the gender roles and types of masculinity and femininity absorbed and lived out by her and Charles. Ray was acutely aware of her deficiencies with regard to practical and technical skills and scientific knowledge, the lack of training in which was a feature of women's education in the United States in the first half of the twentieth century (and beyond).[32] Like thousands of other young girls, she received an education inclined toward the arts. Charles, by contrast, had enormous practical skills and an intense interest in technology and science.

After World War II, Ray had to negotiate being a talented, white, middle-class, working woman without children at a time when there was enormous pressure for such women to stay at home as part of postwar "refeminization." Having established herself as an independent artist before she met Charles, and having worked jointly with him on aesthetically and technologically innovative design ventures during the war, Ray combined the roles of wife and working woman at a time when there were considerable tensions and contradictions between the two. When she married Charles, in 1941, Ray made the transition from artist to designer and also from single woman to wife. There were few role models for a woman working as a full partner with her husband in a design practice. Cranbrook offered the Saarinens, but they were less a husband-wife team than separate but mutually supportive designers who prioritized the career of the male. Some of the few married women who managed to find work as architects or designers in the interwar years were married to fellow architects or designers and worked in partnership or group practice with them, but they were not personally known to the Eameses.[33]

Throughout their years together Charles was the public face of the partnership, and this reinforced the marginalization of Ray's contribution. In postwar middle-class America the public world of work was largely a male sphere, with women playing the supportive wife. In the Eameses' first television appearance, on NBC's "Today" show in 1956, Arlene Francis introduced Ray as follows: "Almost always when there is a very successful man there is an interesting and able woman behind him. This is Mrs. Eames and she is going to tell us how she helps Charles design these chairs." Charles squirmed, while Ray seemed less anxious about the introduction or at least more comfortable dealing with it. It is not surprising that the "common-sense" notions about women's role and a "woman's place" that pervaded (and still pervade) Western society should affect how Ray was viewed and, indeed, how she viewed herself. To a large degree her situation was historical and generational. She was the victim of particular circumstances, as were her friend Lee Krasner and other women artists, designers, collectors, and patrons who are only now emerging from the shadows of their husbands' achievements and public profiles. Yet not all women of similar age and circumstances behaved the same as Ray, whose early social and psychic development led her to need and desire a considerable degree of protection, just as Charles's encouraged him to offer it to women.

Ray's overprotected childhood has already been referred to. She married shortly after her mother's death, and Charles offered her the care and comfort previously provided by her family—and more. Charles was extremely protective of Ray because he loved her, because it appealed to chivalrous elements within him, and because she desired it. So blanket-like was the protection, however, that Ray never had to face up to doing things she did not like or do well. This meant that she never came to grips with certain matters in which she was not as skilled as Charles, particularly business dealings, most things practical, and speaking in public. Some friends and colleagues consider that this was ultimately at the expense of her self-development, but I, and they, suspect that Charles and Ray saw it differently.

Ray was far from weak in many aspects of her character, yet she based her life on what was initially Charles's work, eventually (in the late 1940s) abandoning painting and graphic design. But the fact that she made Charles's ambitions her ambitions is not to be scorned out of hand. It was one of the ways in which a woman of talent and ambition but naive in the ways of the world and of business could at that time combine the roles of wife and designer. Although Charles had relatively enlightened ideas on women's equality for a man born in the United States in 1907 and spoke admiringly of the strong women who had raised him, he subscribed to the notion of the "supportive" wife.[34] It informed his conception of the perfect wife—a role he thought was epitomized by Loja Saarinen who combined being an artist in her own right with providing a strong support structure within which Eliel Saarinen could pursue his career.[35] Ray gave Charles much of what Loja gave Eliel, including entertaining important visitors and clients and stimulating him creatively, and he loved and admired her for it.

One problem involved in assessing Ray's role in the Eames partnership is that, besides a strong feel for structure, her strengths included an extraordinary sense of color and form and a remarkable ability to arrange groups of objects and "decorate" interiors, be they domestic or exhibition spaces. There is no doubt that these talents contributed significantly to the products that emerged from the Eames Office, as did Ray's sense of structure, but their designation as concerned with decoration and "prettiness" meant that they were viewed (partly correctly) as part of women's traditional concerns with beautifying and decorating the home and consequently marginalized by those who saw them as less important than structure and technology. Paradoxically, those who could not accept that Ray might play a significant role in the "male" spheres of architecture and furniture design acknowledged, albeit patronizingly, her abilities as a "decorator" and her brilliance with color because these supposedly less "important" areas were ones in which it was deemed acceptable and respectable for women's design talents to flourish.[36] While I can appreciate Charles's desire to counter the ghettoization of Ray by associating her with aspects of design that were regarded as "serious," it is important to emphasize that color, the arrangement of objects, and the composition, framing and juxtaposition of images and objects are significant in their own right and that they were central rather than peripheral to the work of the Eameses. Some recognized this at the time, including Alison Smithson, who wrote in *Architectural Design* in 1966: "I can see the part played by Ray Eames in all that they do: the attention to the last detail of the collected material, the perseverance in finding exactly what is wanted. . . . The prettiness of our lives now I attribute to Ray even more than Charles."[37]

By and large, the Eameses did not differ on matters of content, direction, or aesthetics. They had their own ways of presenting their points of view, however. Neither Charles nor Ray was particularly easy to understand, as new employees found to their cost.[38] To newcomers they appeared unclear about what they wanted and how they wanted it done. Some simply fled; others stayed and learned new ways of working. Iconoclastic and analytical, Charles seemed to think in images (as did Ray). He used language sparingly and often found it difficult to articulate visual and other ideas. He spoke slowly, in a deep voice, and often in phrases rather than fully coherent sentences, and thus it was not always easy to understand what he was getting at.[39] However, his use of simple phrases, understatement, and double negatives could be powerful, particularly when accompanied by visual references. Though an excellent teacher, he was uncomfortable with large audiences and with public speaking, often showing slides or films to communicate his ideas.

Ray was more chatty than Charles in everyday life but extraordinarily shy when it came to public appearances of any sort. In a 1968 television interview Charles noted how interviews paralyzed Ray yet transformed him "into a monster full of great wisdom—the know-it-all of the century . . . running off at the mouth."[40] He attributed her lack of words and his plethora of them to the same cause—nervousness— expressed in different ways. Ray rarely spoke in public when Charles was there to do it for the two of them, although she managed to do so after his death at events honoring their work. Aside from occasional appearances on panels, Ray undertook no solo public engagements until after the Connections exhibition of 1977, which enhanced her public profile. Charles, in contrast, lectured frequently and sat on numerous panels and juries.[41] In 1978, however, in the six or seven months before Charles's death, Ray went to Italy to attend a meeting of the American Academy in Rome, sat on the jury for the Boston Art Directors' Club's Silver Anniversary awards in visual communications, attended a meeting of the National Institute of Education in Washington, sat on the Rockefeller Panel at the Annual National Art Association Convention, and participated in a symposium in Tokyo.[42] It was as if she realized that she needed to forge more of a public profile and an independent persona for herself, and to know that she could do things without Charles.

Ray preferred to express herself through artistic "intuitions." These, of course, derived from a keenly trained visual sensibility, from strongly held convictions about the role of art and design in modern society, and from experience. The Eameses learned from each other, from their workers, and from the many outside "experts" who were brought in as advisers or collaborators on specific projects. They both valued trial and error, and their "hands-on" approach involved continually testing ideas by building models and prototypes or shifting around pieces of paper or photographs in ever-changing collages. They were willing to learn from mistakes, even accidents, and from others as well as from each other.

Charles was always the "boss" of the firm, dealing with clients, attending to financial matters, and generally acting as entrepreneurial head, while Ray played the "Japanese wife"[43] and was largely responsible for providing a conducive environment for staff members, visitors, and clients. Charles did not see his role as more important than Ray's. He recognized that her abilities were greater than his in certain areas, just as she applauded his ability to deal with the top managements of major corporations and with government officials. Both were vital to the well-being of the firm, but the fact remained that his role involved more interface with the outside world while hers was the more "wifely." This replicated the dominant gender division between the public (male) sphere and the domestic and private (female); it also reflected traditional business practice within small-scale private companies, with the owner (generally male) acting as managing director. As far as Ray was concerned, the normal sexual division of labor within husband-wife business partnerships applied in the Eames Office, and she saw no reason to challenge it. Running a firm was accepted as a man's job, and Charles had previous experience of it whereas she had none. Nor was it something Ray ever wanted or enjoyed doing. She was not good at it and was happy to leave meeting clients, finalizing deals, and organizing new projects to the more "worldly" Charles, who had made his own way since an early age.

Though it is clear that Charles was firmly "in charge" of the business, one should not fall into the trap of thinking that, because she had a lower public profile and was noted for her slowness to come to a decision, Ray played no part in running the firm or in making decisions. Charles discussed major decisions and a great many minor ones with her. Furthermore, it was not always Ray who was the indecisive one. Ken Garland, a British designer, tells how in 1965 Charles was extremely worried about how to deal with an issue concerning the manufacture of the lounge chair and ottoman in Britain. He became increasingly agitated over the matter during a weekend he spent with Garland. Only after an extremely long transatlantic telephone conversation with Ray, "from which he emerged looking vastly relieved, as if the decision had been made for him," was he able to relax.[44]

Opinion is somewhat divided on Ray's indecisiveness and on how far it affected the work of the firm. Her general reluctance to finally decide upon a color, a fabric, a shape, or a course of action undoubtedly meant that some projects were not completed as quickly as they might have been, but her search for perfection contributed enormously to the success of those projects and should be viewed positively as well as negatively. Furthermore, it should be remembered that Charles never rushed decisions and that his search for perfection was only slightly less manic than Ray's.

There is also some disagreement as to whether or not Ray was a good organizer. Pupul Jayakar, who worked closely with the Eameses on a film, a report, and an exhibition, attributed the concretization of Charles's "creative vision" to Ray's discipline and organizational abilities.[45] Billy

Wilder saw Ray as "a very good organizer . . . much less of a dreamer than Charles . . . she sort of holds things together."[46] By contrast, Deborah Sussman, who knew Ray well, does not feel that organization was Ray's forte. She tells how, when she and Ray were in India preparing the Nehru exhibition (1965), progress almost ground to a halt and she felt obliged to send a note to Charles saying "We need a giant to pull things together. Know anybody?"[47] There is, of course, no disagreement that both Charles and Ray were terrific at pulling things together visually. One aspect of Ray's talents which is related to an ability to organize material, yet is often ignored, is her editorial skill. Jehane Burns, a key Eames Office researcher noted for her rigorous and meticulous approach, who was in many ways the opposite of the "intuitive" and often indecisive Ray, drew very considerably on Ray's skills as an editor in the 1970s when producing texts for exhibitions, books, and catalogs and feels that Ray's talents in this area have not been sufficiently appreciated. Although some considered Ray "scatty," Burns insists that she "had a brilliant mind and was one of the best editors I ever met."[48] Burns was referring to written texts, but the same could be said of Ray's work on films.

The Eameses never delegated major managerial tasks to their staff. They usually spent only short periods of time away from the office, and when away they kept in constant touch by telephone. Certain long-term employees were entrusted with communicating information to other staff members during projects, but the only managerial task delegated was the particularly unpleasant one of "letting people go."[49] Otherwise, Charles was happy to deal with business matters on his own—and this was not due entirely to Ray's disinclination to deal with them. He enjoyed that aspect of the work, particularly the control and the freedom to do as he pleased.[50] Even at the busiest times, senior staff members never met with clients or substituted for the boss, as they might have done in other design practices.

Just as their employees learned a great deal from the Eameses, they learned a great deal from those who worked for them. But for the abilities and dedication of their staff members, whom Ray and Charles expected to be as innovative as they were dedicated, the products of the Eames Office would have been different. There is no doubt that working at the "huge warehouse workshop . . . making furniture, making films, making slide shows, making toys" was an exciting experience.[51] A "truly

Renaissance environment,"[52] it was "part museum, part funhouse, and part design and film studio."[53] The intense enthusiasm of the team members and their dedication to the enrichment of human life and experience through design offered the perfect situation for young idealistic designers: "It was the greatest school you could go to. Things could be crazy but it was a pivotal experience where intellect and good design came together with a soft sell."[54] For the young Deborah Sussman it was "like visiting another planet," so different was it from her college experience of designing. Richard Donges recalls that it seemed too magical to be real when he first arrived, and he still remembers it as "fairyland but real . . . a true designer's heaven."[55]

The firm was run on the belief that everyone possessed myriad talents which could be developed given the right opportunities. Everybody was expected to handle a wide variety of jobs, and Charles and Ray welcomed enthusiastic "novices" who did not realize that many of the tasks asked of them were well nigh impossible.[56] With no training or professional experience in photography, Don Albinson was given charge of the darkroom for a year after Herbert Matter.[57] Deborah Sussman had no previous experience with film when she went to Mexico to help make *Day of the Dead*.[58] It was customary to take people from design projects to help out on film production at vital moments when extra hands were needed. Each day in the Eames Office brought new challenges which required employees to be inventive and draw upon their own resources. It is the only job in Jeannine Oppewall's career that she feels has drawn on each and every part of her Bryn Mawr liberal arts training—and more.[59] She is a good example of how the Eames Office encouraged personal development. After leaving teaching in 1970 to work there, she first had responsibility for the visual library and film distribution but ended up researching and scripting exhibitions. Today she works as a production designer in the film industry, but she has never once been asked to show a portfolio. The fact that she worked in the Eames Office for several years is taken as a guarantee that her work will be of the highest quality (Charles's parting words to her were "remember the standards here . . . don't let them down") and that she will be enterprising, flexible, and able to undertake a wide variety of tasks.[60] One of the great abilities of the Eameses was to recognize talent, nurture it, and allow it to flourish and develop in new directions.

Both Charles and Ray commanded considerable personal loyalty and affection from their staff members, some of whom stayed with them for long periods of time. Gregory Ain and Don Albinson each stayed for 13 years, Sam Passalacqua for 12 (22 if one counts—as he does—the decade he stayed on after Charles's death), Alex Funke for 11, Jehane Burns for 9, John Neuhart for 5 in the first instance and 7 in later years and Deborah Sussman for 4 in the first instance followed by 6. Richard Donges joined the office immediately after graduating in design from the University of Southern California and stayed there for 20 years, until after the death of Charles. It was he who lovingly made the beautiful casket to contain Charles's remains—and another a decade later when Ray died—and today he and his partners John and Marilyn Neuhart keep alive something of the spirit of the Eames Office in their own Los Angeles design firm. So too do others, each in his or her own way. Deborah Sussman readily and warmly acknowledges debts to the Eames Office, which are evident in her design philosophy as well as her visual style. For Jeannine Oppewall, the continuing influence of the Eames Office comes more from an overall approach to work than from what she learned about filmmaking (which was never a major part of her work there). She recognizes that her method of working within relatively modest limits comes from the Eameses' philosophy of "choose your corner, pick away at it carefully, intensely and to the best of your ability and that way you might change the world."[61] Don Albinson's careful and thoughtful approach to design and product development was learned from Charles at Cranbrook and later in Los Angeles. Alex Funke, winner of an Oscar for special effects in *Total Recall,* regards the period he spent in the Eames Office as important to his subsequent success.[62]

In the early 1940s the Eameses' relationship with staff members (such as Gregory Ain and Harry Bertoia) who joined the team as established designers in their own right was more that of equals working together, although it was always clear, in the last analysis, who were the employers and who the employees. With other employees the relationship was more paternalistic. On occasions it was that of master and pupil at its best, in the sense that everyone was encouraged to develop and grow. Don Albinson and Charles Eames had enjoyed a close teacher-pupil relationship at Cranbrook, where Albinson attended Charles's class in industrial and product design and showed such exceptional abilities with his hands and expertise with power tools that, in 1946, he was invited to join the small team put together by the Eameses. Albinson remembers this as an extremely "lucky break" and recounts how the Eameses treated him like a son when he lived with them in their Neutra apartment for nearly 6 months.[63] The three got on well together despite living and working in close proximity. They traveled to work together, shared long workshop hours, ate and relaxed together, and sometimes collapsed in front of a television set after a 12- or 14-hour working day to catch the end of a movie.[64]

If Albinson was treated like a son, Deborah Sussman was treated like a daughter. Recommended by Konrad Wachsman, an engineer and architect who was a close friend of the Eameses, she arrived in California in 1953, full of enthusiasm and trepidation, after completing her studies ("in sculptural form with some graphics") at the Chicago Institute of Design.[65] Charles and Ray were extremely kind to her. When they left on their first-ever trip to Europe, in 1955, they offered her the use of their house, a gesture which she regarded as a great honor. She remained close to the Eameses after leaving in 1957 to travel and work in Europe, and she worked for them again from 1961 to 1967. Deborah and Ray, who were in many ways similar, were extremely close for 20 years. In some ways Deborah was the daughter Ray never had. Both were small, energetic, vital, witty, amusing, and formidably talented, with a remarkable and apparently intuitive sense of color and form.

Talent, energy, and drive, especially in the young, always attracted the Eameses. They were generous with their time to visiting students, designers, and architects—and sometimes also with their money. In 1958 they were "exceptionally kind" to the young Peter Smithson, paying his traveling costs from Chicago to Los Angeles so that he could visit them.[66] Paul Schrader, a filmmaker and critic who has written of the "great patience and diligence" shown by Charles in explaining his notions of how visual images can convey ideas, recently commented: "Today, occasionally, when I talk with students I grow impatient with their questions and with the repetitious things they're saying. Whenever that happens I remember Charles and think, 'Jesus, here was a man telling me what to him must have been the most prosaic and mundane truth imaginable, being a designer and architect, and yet he took the time to explain it to me patiently and make me understand it. If he could take that time, as busy and important as he was, then who am I to think I'm too superior to pass on that kind of simple information to the next person?'"[67]

Yet Charles Eames never praised or thanked his employees, no matter how hard they worked or how magnificent the results. He used suggestion and criticism rather than praise. Because his own pleasures and rewards came from the satisfaction offered by the work itself, he thought that this should suffice—as, for the most part, it did, so energized were employees by the "buzz" of the workshop and the passion for design apparent in every aspect of the Eameses' lives. Some have described this inability to praise, thank or give credit to employees as a psychic "block."[68] However, Charles had no block about bestowing public credit upon Ray.

Although the designs of the early years owed a great deal to Ray and to the small band of employees, until 1947 work was submitted to clients or competitions in the name of Charles Eames alone. There was considerable dissatisfaction on the part of some staff members with this, particularly in relation to the highly successful plywood furniture, so much so that some resigned.[69] From 1947 on the firm was known as the Eames Office. Credit for a project was sometimes given to every individual who had worked on it, but after internal squabbles about the "pecking order" attribution was simply given to the Eames Office as a whole.[70] The logic was that the work of the office was collaborative and therefore "Eames Office" sufficed as a credit. The exception was the films. It was almost as if, having had their fingers burned once over attribution, Charles and Ray were determined to make it clear from the outset that the films were their creations. Each film cited them as directors. Sometimes her name preceded his in an attempt to suggest an equality within the mutuality of the activity,[71] but their names were always separate from any general reference to the Eames Office. Major contributions by individual staff members were credited, and this system seems to have worked at least as well as the more general "Eames Office" credit for all other projects.

Some of the Eameses' employees managed to cope with the lack of thanks and public acknowledgment. However, at least three key figures involved with furniture design left feeling that their contributions had not been sufficiently acknowledged: Gregory Ain, the architect and plywood "expert" who worked for 13 years under the title of "chief engineer" and who played a crucial role in the development of the plywood furniture, Harry Bertoia, who also worked on the plywood projects, and Don Albinson, whose "understanding of production processes and engineering" led to many of the "technical and design innovations in Eames furniture."[72] Their degrees of frustration differed at the times they left, as did their later thoughts on what had happened, but the lack of public acknowledgment and thanks affected how all three of these men felt about working in the Eames Office.

The difficulty of determining exactly who did what in the Eames Office intensifies from the late 1960s because of the large number of employees and the variety of projects undertaken. The amount of time that Charles and Ray had to devote to each of these projects was limited, but they remained dedicated to (many would say "obsessed with") working ideas through and seeing them into production.

Few who met Charles and Ray Eames were not captivated by their enthusiasm and charisma. "Inspiring" is a word frequently used about them, their work, and the beautifully illustrated lectures which Charles gave with increasing frequency in later years. Paul Schrader was "knocked . . . out" and "changed permanently" in 1970 by just such a lecture and by his subsequent meeting with Charles.[73] Schrader described Charles's personal magnetism and ability to make one rethink issues thus: "He was one of those men—Rossellini is another—whose presence in a room makes it feel bigger. You walk in and because he is there, the room gets bigger. He goes and opens the shutters and says 'Look, the world could be like this' and then moves to some other window and says 'But it could also be this way.' You walk out of the room and think 'Yes, my God, it could really be like that.'"[74] Similar language was used by the Neuharts to describe their experience and that of fellow students in the UCLA Art Department 20 years earlier on hearing Charles lecture and on first seeing Eames designs. The designs were, to the Neuharts, "like bolts from the sky" and a "kind of Bible."[75]

Inspiring they may have been, but the Eameses were not always easy to work for. They were hard taskmasters. As Marilyn and John Neuhart so succinctly expressed it, "you were always expected to give more than you thought you had."[76] And it was not just their own employees who were driven to distraction by the insistence on perfection; several middle managers at IBM wished that Eliot Noyes had chosen less exacting people with whom to work.[77] However, for the Eameses there was no other way to operate, regardless of the pressures it put on staff members or clients.[78] Today they would be called workaholics. Their working day usually started at 8 or 9 in the morning and often lasted till about 10 P.M. (and frequently all through the night), at least six and sometimes seven days a week. They had a cook and a well-equipped kitchen at their office-*cum*-workshop so that they did not need to go home to eat.

Although there was an atmosphere of informality and equality in the Office, there was never any doubt that the Eameses stood apart from everybody else. Charles's charm was such that generally he could persuade people to do what he wanted, as and how he wanted it. He was so charismatic that it was not so much a case of his manipulating situations, though he was capable of that, as of people being swept along by his enthusiasm and dedication and by the brilliance of his ideas. But his "snake-charming skills" should not blind one to the fact that he had a temper and could be intimidating.[79] He had no time for people who were not as serious as he about all they did. He is reminiscent of William Morris in this, as well as in his concern for quality in every aspect of life and in his passionate hatred of "the cheap and the shallow."[80] When he vehemently attacked lack of quality or tore into some other issue dear to his heart, he sometimes surprised those who knew him as a quiet and patient man.[81] Charles's anger and "righteous indignation," when forcefully expressed, could be devastating. Jeannine Oppewall believes that one of the reasons for her succeeding in the cutthroat world of film production design is that no one can ever again intimidate her as much as did Charles Eames when she was in her twenties.[82] Standing up to any father figure is difficult, and standing up to one as immensely talented and (usually) benevolent as Charles was doubly so. Young employees did not always find it easy to define and assert their own identity when that of Charles was so powerful, and it was particularly difficult for younger women.[83] Ray offered a model of women acting as supportive agents for Charles, but by the early 1970s, when the ideas of the women's movement had taken root, there were certain female employees who would have preferred a less deferential role model.

Charles's enthusiasm, charm, and general ease helped smooth his day-to-day relations with the staff, but most knew that, if necessary, he would ride roughshod over them to get what he wanted. Ray could also be charming, and was generally easy to work with, but she could be "difficult," particularly in later years. Charles had a stronger sense of himself as the boss, but on an everyday basis at work he had an easier and more open manner than Ray. The more trying aspects of Ray's office persona should always be set against the many more pleasant ones. Bouncy, enthusiastic, and generous, she was exceptionally good company socially. She gave freely of her talents and advice, but there is no getting away from the fact that, from time to time, she was not the easiest person with whom to work. Described as "something of a snob" and "autocratic" or "aristocratic" in her approach to work relationships, Ray was less skilled than Charles at handling people and problems in the day-to-day running of what came to be a fairly large firm.[84] Sometimes she acted as if she expected deference, and friction ensued. However, many people worked easily and amicably with her for many years and remember her with the deepest affection. Staff members who were less tolerant of what they saw as Ray's "feudal" manner felt frustrated because they could not deal openly with the issue.[85] It was never discussed. Charles would brook no criticism of Ray (and vice versa), and many employees tolerated Ray's occasional difficult behavior out of a desire to please Charles, get on with the job, and not rock the boat. Ray did not hold grudges and always made it easy for someone with whom she had had a falling out to resume working with her. Staffers usually found it easy to forgive her, not least because of her "generous advice," "brilliant insights," "rare visual eye," and "sense of fun."[86]

The Eameses took on only jobs which they felt were morally worthy. In later years Charles was fond of quoting the Bhagavad Gita when explaining their attitudes toward work: "Work done with anxiety about results is far inferior to work done without such anxiety, in the calm of self-surrender."[87] The calm of self-surrender might not be exactly how former employees remember the atmosphere of the Eames Office, but the integrity of the projects was always supreme.

So much attention has been focused on the Eameses' house in Pacific Palisades that other buildings have not been paid the attention they deserve. Although they were much more involved in product design and other activities after 1950, the Eameses retained a great interest in architecture. Indeed, one of the reasons they went into filmmaking was to communicate large amounts of information to professional architects.

Charles continued to refer to himself as an architect rather than a designer. He always claimed that he did so in order to emphasize his concern with structure, and there is no reason to doubt that, but it was also something of an affectation (forgivable enough in a man thrown out of architecture school) in a world where the profession of architect had more cachet than that of industrial designer. The point is not that Charles did not have every right to describe himself as an architect (his work warranted it, and he knew a great deal about the technicalities and practicalities of construction) but rather that he chose not to describe himself as a designer—a choice that perturbed certain fellow designers anxious to see their field regarded more seriously. When asked if he had an objection to the word "designer," Charles replied: "It is not that I'm embarrassed about 'designer' so much as the degree to which I prefer the word 'architect' and what it implies. It implies structure, a kind of analysis, as well as a kind of tradition behind it."[1]

According to Charles, Ray had as strong an understanding of structure as he (though, of course, she did not have his technical knowledge). She, however, tried to avoid labeling herself. When the tag of the fine-arts-trained wife who worked with her more famous husband was imposed on her, she partly resisted it and partly colluded in it. Her role in relation to interior decoration has been more widely acknowledged than her role in the joint architectural work.

The Eameses' architecture and interiors made space within modernism for a more personal view of house and home. Geoffrey Holroyd has suggested that a better term for what in the 1950s was called "communications theory" is "signification,"[2] and it is no surprise that two people fascinated by "communications theory" adopted a clear set of signals that translated "house" into "home." The Eameses were "orthodox" modernists in that they used standardized parts for prefabricated buildings; however, what they added to the frame and what they did to the interior raised issues related to signification and decoration, even though it was rarely discussed in those terms. Their "functioning decoration" reintroduced arrangements of decorative objects to interiors from which they had largely been banished—a move that was welcomed by many as refreshing.

THE CASE STUDY HOUSE PROGRAM

The Eames House was built as part of the Case Study House Program, a postwar experiment to develop high-quality homes which was organized by John Entenza and publicized in *Arts & Architecture.* During the war the question of the nature of housing was an important part of wider debates on postwar reconstruction. The Case Study House Program was one outcome of those debates, and one of the most technologically and aesthetically (though not socially) advanced.[3] Most architects agreed that use should be made of new materials and technology, but to some this meant little more than air conditioning, easy-to-clean surfaces, and so-called labor-saving devices in traditional-style homes. One of the most commercially successful of the postwar house models was Levitt and Sons' "Cape Codder" (figure 3.1). Another was the ranch house, which sprang up all over Southern California in the late 1940s. Derived from a design by Cliff May and Chris Choate, the California "ranches" were timber-frame, one-story, open-plan houses with floor-to-ceiling windows and sliding glass patio doors. Sheathed in stucco, board, or shingle, this single-family house type, which was promoted as a "free-flowing, beautifully functionalized house born of our nineteenth-century West,"[4] had enough historical references to meet the desires of those who wanted a modern home with a traditional feel. The white "blue-collar workers" who were the typical owner-occupiers of the postwar years preferred "heritage" overtones, and certainly did not favor the Case Study houses.[5]

The basic Levitt house sold for as little as $5000, and California ranch houses started at approximately $7500 for a two-bedroom with carport and $10,000 for a three-bedroom, two-bath model.[6] When the Eameses designed a low-cost prefabricated house for a family with two

3.1 House at Levittown,
N.Y., 1950. Levitt and
Sons.

children in 1951—a project that, unfortunately, never came to fruition—they worked to an estimated cost of $8000. It is difficult to estimate the cost of comparable-size Case Study houses, because the project paid little attention to the working class or the lower middle class. As Dolores Hayden puts it, "Many of the [Case Study] designers simply assumed that they could generalize about 'the American family' from their own, and their clients', elite vantage point."[7]

Although the Case Study Program appealed mainly to affluent members of the intelligentsia with an interest in contemporary art and design, not all modernist house design focused so exclusively on wealthy clients or on single-family dwellings. Early modernist architecture was intensely concerned with social conditions and with the lot of ordinary people, the greatest manifestation of which was the model workers' housing shown at numerous exhibitions in Europe during the interwar years. Many American architects, including Charles Eames, were aware of these developments, but this utopian aspect of modernism was considerably weaker in the United States, partly because of the comparative underdevelopment of the American labor and socialist movements and partly because of a campaign against "un-American" state-funded mass housing.[8] Nevertheless, there was in the United States an honorable history of public and collective housing for low-income families, a concern which took on greater urgency during the Depression of the 1930s and continued into the 1940s.[9] However, much of the financing came from private sources.

Los Angeles was not without its attempts at social housing, from the short-lived Llano del Rio socialist settlement (1914–1918) to the involvement of modernists such as Richard Neutra (a European socialist) and Gregory Ain (who had spent part of his childhood at Llano del Rio) in cooperative housing schemes in the 1940s.[10] By 1941 Los Angeles had twelve public housing projects, the most important of which was Neutra's federally funded Channel Heights Project, in San Pedro, which consisted of 222 redwood-and-stucco residential houses providing accommodation and communal facilities for 600 families.[11]

Despite these and other examples, communal and/or state-funded housing continued to be seen as the antithesis of the "American dream" in which every family owned its own home—the dream on the basis of which Los Angeles was developed and promoted.[12] Those who argued the case for mass low-income housing with good communal facilities and a decent public transport system had their hopes dashed when the 25-year development plan of the Los Angeles Regional Planning Commission categorically stated in 1941 that the privately owned single-family home was the way to house citizens.[13] In that the Case Study House Program looked to the privately owned single-family unit, it accorded not only with the federal government's policy but also with that of the city of Los Angeles (which, since the late nineteenth century, had been the creation of real-estate developers). It is somewhat ironic that, as modernism became increasingly accepted in the United States and particularly in California, public housing disappeared from the political and architectural agendas.

One of the main means by which modernism was popularized in the immediate postwar years was through magazines such as *Progressive Architecture, Architectural Forum, Interiors,* and *Industrial Design.* One of the magazines most influential in suggesting what the postwar home should be like was *California Arts & Architecture* (later simply *Arts & Architecture*), to which both Charles and Ray Eames contributed.[14] John Entenza had acquired this regional arts magazine in 1938, and under his direction it became more "modern" and national (later international) in outlook, dropping *California* from its title in January 1944. During the 1940s many members of the Los Angeles avant-garde contributed to its columns, including Neutra, Ain, Alvin Lustig, Julius Shulman (a photographer), and Esther McCoy (a writer and design critic). In 1942 Charles Eames became an editorial associate and Ray joined the advisory board; he contributed articles and photographs, and she wrote one article and designed a series of covers (see chapter 1 above).[15] *Arts & Architecture* became the mouthpiece for modernist ideas and a platform for the California avant-garde. It took a liberal stance on issues of race, human rights, and child care, and it advocated equality among the arts, regularly featuring painting, sculpture, architecture, design, photography, dance, and film.[16]

The magazine found an appreciative audience in Los Angeles, as well as other parts of the United States and abroad. Although attacked by some intellectuals as philistine, Los Angeles had had a thriving cultural and creative intelligentsia ever since the 1920s, when the film and oil industries had brought unprecedented prosperity.[17] The home of Aline Barnsdall was the center of an avant-garde circle which was particularly concerned with theatre, dance, and painting,[18] while the Echo Park home of the bookseller Jack Zeitlen provided a meeting place for the photographer Edward Weston, the artist Rockwell Kent, the young Frank Lloyd Wright, and others.[19] A more politically radical group centered around the architect Rudolph Schindler.[20] The same decade saw the first exhibition of the Group of Independent Artists of Los Angeles (1923), a "varied front for the 'New Form'" in art.[21] European émigrés (pre- and post-Hitler) including Josef von Sternberg, Oskar Fischinger, Igor Stravinsky, Thomas Mann, Arnold Schoenberg, Theodor Adorno, Man Ray, Christopher Isherwood, Aldous Huxley, and Billy Wilder (who was to become a great friend of the Eameses) brought new dimensions, horizons, and energies to the cultural life of Los Angeles.[22] Wilder had been a supporter of modernism before fleeing Germany in the mid 1930s, leaving behind his collection of modernist paintings and Bauhaus furniture.[23] Other patrons of the arts who worked in the film industry included Vincent Price and Edward G. Robinson, both of whom were involved in establishing the short-lived Modern Art Institute in Beverly Hills in the mid 1930s.[24] John Entenza himself had worked under Paul Bern and Irving Pitchel in an experimental film unit at MGM.[25]

The "cosmopolitan perspective and sense of community with the avant-garde"[26] of Entenza and his associates was reflected in *Arts & Architecture,* which was read by the cultural intelligentsia described above, by museum curators, by gallery owners, by collectors, and by the owners and managers of certain firms committed to modernism. Entenza's magazine promoted "progressive" architecture long before the Case Study House Program, starting in 1938 with a series of articles about low-cost, prefabricated "small homes of the west."[27] In 1943 Entenza organized the Design For Post War Living competition, which was to draw on the Californian tradition of light, airy, comfortable, and relatively inexpensive modern houses (a tradition already sufficiently distinctive for the San Francisco Museum to devote an exhibition to it in 1942). This competition confirmed to Entenza, and to Charles Eames (one of the judges), that there was still a great deal of work to be done:

> To the magazine this has been a hectic and stimulating experience, and it is our hope that we will soon be able to announce a

continuing series of such competitions, believing that American designer-architects will welcome an opportunity to send further trial balloons into the modern air.[28]

Those balloons came to be known as the Case Study houses.

The Case Study House Program, which began in 1945,[29] aimed to produce contemporary solutions to house design and to offer prototypes from which low- and medium-cost housing could be developed. The magazine commissioned architects to design and build houses, which were illustrated in the magazine, opened as show houses, and finally sold. These demonstration dwellings, which stand in the tradition of Prince Albert's Model Cottages at the Great Exhibition of 1851 and the Weissenhof Siedlung of 1927,[30] proved popular; however, the project was not about universal solutions:

> While these houses are not to be considered as solutions of typical living problems; through meeting specific and rather special needs, some contribution to the need of the typical might be developed. The whole solution proceeds from an attempt to use space in direct relation to the personal and professional needs of the individuals revolving around and within the living units inasmuch as the greater part of work or preparation for work will originate here. These houses must function as an integral part of the living pattern of the occupants and will therefore be completely "used" in a very full and real sense. "House" in these cases means center of productive activities.[31]

Eight houses were originally commissioned from Richard Neutra, J. R. Davidson, William Wurster, Sumner Spalding, Ralph Rapson, Whitney Smith, Thorton Abell, and Charles Eames.[32] Those built before 1949 were simple wood-frame pavilion forms with infill panels of glass, plywood, concrete, and even adobe brick. Wood was used partly because of immediate postwar restrictions and shortages and partly because it was considered an economically viable alternative to steel.

Although the steel-frame Eames House first won fame because of its prefabricated industrial components, its greater novelty lay in its insistent modesty, its detailing, and its colorful facade.[33] It was welcomed as an extremely habitable piece of Machine Aesthetic architecture and as part of a modernist project to develop prototypes for cheap mass housing. In the United States in the 1930s a great deal of experimentation had taken place with timber, concrete, glass, and steel. Neutra had used standardized wood chassis construction for the Hollyridge Estate in 1932,[34] and sheet steel had been used for floors in the 1931 Aluminaire House (designed by Kocher and Frey, who also experimented with wood-frame structures in the mid 1930s).[35] Some of the larger American steel producers had backed research on prefabrication, and about a dozen models of wholly or partly prefabricated houses had been displayed at the 1933 Chicago World's Fair.[36] General Houses Incorporated, of Chicago, had produced a pressed-steel house in several models based on standardized parts designed by the architect-engineer Howard Fisher in 1933.[37] Neutra had produced a model plywood house in 1936,[38] and Gregory Ain (who had worked with Neutra) had designed a prefabricated plywood cabin just before going to work for the Eameses in 1942, the year in which Walter Gropius and Konrad Wachsmann's "Packaged House" was patented.[39] Other important developments in prefabrication included complete "factory fabricated" kitchens and bathrooms such as those with which Case Study architects William Wurster and Ralph Rapson were associated.[40]

CASE STUDY HOUSES 8 AND 9

Charles Eames was involved in designing two Case Study houses: his own and that of John Entenza, which share a site in Pacific Palisades. The Eames House was designed in collaboration with Ray Eames, the Entenza House in collaboration with Eero Saarinen. Less than 200 yards apart, they are separated by a plant-covered mound created to form a "natural" barrier for the sake of privacy. Although the houses share a site and an architect, and although both are steel-framed, they differ in form. The Eames House is an open structure with infill panels; the Entenza House conceals its structure and emphasizes the horizontal. They have been called "technological twins but architectural opposites . . . a tenuous web [and] . . . a solid shell": "Where the Eames House is a tall construction through which space is permitted to flow in three dimensions, the Entenza House is a flat metal box with a distinctly horizontal flow of space inside, strictly controlled by free-standing screens and partitions."[41] Many

3.2 Charles Eames, Ray
Eames, and John Entenza
at site of Eames and
Entenza Houses, Pacific
Palisades, 1945.

3.3 Briefs and first designs
for Eames House and
Entenza House. *Arts &
Architecture*, December
1945. Charles Eames and
Eero Saarinen, with Ray
Eames.

of the differences are attributable to the fact that in one case Charles
Eames worked with Eero Saarinen for a client whereas the other building
was designed in collaboration with his wife and was their own home.

The Eames House

Ever since their arrival in Los Angeles the Eameses had wanted to create
their own ideal home. They knew they liked the intimate relationship of
indoors to outdoors, the privacy of an enclosed living space, and the comfort and ease of maintenance their apartment offered.[42] Although they
were modernists, they were not ideologically tied to the International
Style.[43] They originally planned to build a "Spanish Style" town house,
flush with the road and centered around a garden, in Santa Monica.[44]
What changed the form was the change of location. Yet, even after they
had decided on an International Style house, they radically altered their
ideas at a rather late stage.

Although the first design for the Eames House (figure 3.3) is generally attributed to Charles Eames and Eero Saarinen, the catalog compiled by the Neuharts with Ray Eames states that the 1945 design was
by "the Eames Office, working with Eero Saarinen," thus giving Ray
some credit from the earliest stage.[45] The idea of separate living and working spaces came from the Eameses themselves and was retained when the
house was completely redesigned by Charles and Ray between 1947 and
1949 (figures 3.4–3.6). It was not until Charles worked in collaboration
with Ray that the plywood furniture he had developed with Saarinen
took on lighter and more harmonious forms,[46] and a comparison of the
two versions of the Eames House with the Entenza House leaves no doubt
that, despite the massive talents of Eero Saarinen as an architect and designer, Charles and Ray proved a more creative partnership in the Case
Study House Program than Charles and Eero.

Charles, the architect, was generally cited as the designer of the
Eames House as built, but this was a joint effort. This is not to say that
there was fifty-fifty collaboration at every stage. Charles's expertise in architecture and his interest in engineering and in steel structures meant
that he took the main responsibility for the constructional elements, and
Ray stated that Charles's concern that the design did not justify the cost
of the steel was the main impetus behind the redesigning of the house

CASE STUDY HOUSES
8 AND 9

BY CHARLES EAMES AND EERO SAARINEN, ARCHITECTS

This is ground in meadow and hill, protected on all sides from intrusive developments free of the usual surrounding clutter, safe from urban clatter; not, however, removed from the necessary conveniences and the reassurances of city living.

Two houses for people of different occupations but parallel interests. Both, however, determinedly agreed on the necessity of privacy, or the right to choose privacy from one another and anyone else.

While these houses are not to be considered as solutions of typical living problems; through meeting specific and rather special needs, some contribution to the need of the typical might be developed. The whole solution proceeds from an attempt to use space in direct relation to the personal and professional needs of the individuals revolving around and within the living units inasmuch as the greater part of work or preparation for work will originate here. These houses must function as an integral part of the living pattern of the occupants and will therefore be completely "used" in a very full and real sense. "House" in these cases means center of productive activities.

For a married couple both occupied professionally with mechanical experiment and graphic presentation. Work and recreation are involved in general activities: Day and night, work and play, concentration, relaxation with friend and foe, all intermingled personally and professionally with mutual interest. Basically apartment dwellers, there is a conscious effort made to be free of complications relating to maintenance. The house must make no insistent demands for itself, but rather aid as background for life in work. This house—in its free relation to ground, the trees, the sea—with constant proximity to the whole vast order of nature acts as re-orientor and "shock absorber" and should provide the needed relaxations from the daily complications arising within problems.

In this house activities will be of a more general nature to be shared with more people and more things. It will also be used as a returning place for relaxation and recreation through reading and music and work—a place of reviving and refilling, a place to be alone for preparation of work, and with matters and concerns of personal choosing. A place for the kind of relaxed privacy necessary for the development and preparatoion of ideas to be continued in professional work centers. The occupant will need space used elastically where many or few people can be accommodated within the areas appropriate to such needs. Intimate conversation, groups in discussion, the use of a projection machine for amusement and education, and facilities for self-indulgent hobbies, i.e., cooking and the entertainment of very close friends.

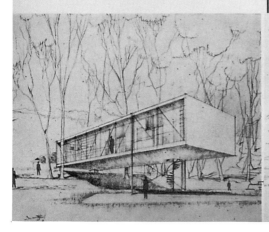 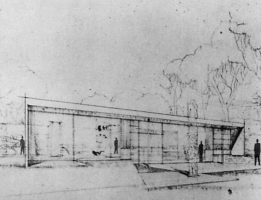

3.4 Revised plan of Eames
House, 1947. Charles and
Ray Eames.

3.5 Drawings of Eames
House by Ray Eames, c. 1949.

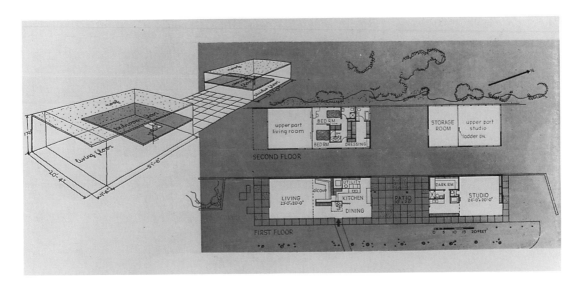

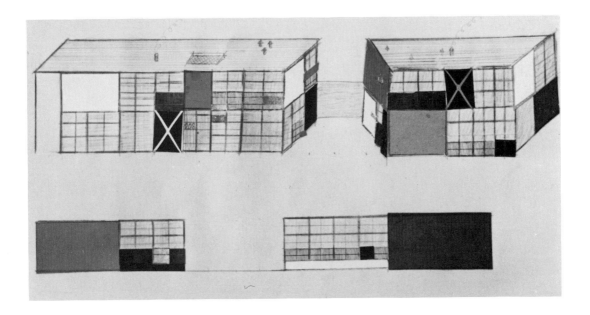

3.6 Exterior of Eames
House.

after the materials had been delivered to the site.[47] Charles had a wider repertoire of architectural forms and references to bring to their discussions, but he greatly valued Ray's sense of structure and form. Furthermore, their dialogue in all matters pertaining to design was so intense at that time, and the references to fine-art sources in the building are so obvious, that one cannot even say that the decision about the basic forms of the house came solely from Charles. It is inconceivable that a woman of such strong opinions on design and aesthetics as Ray, who was used to talking through every design issue with her husband and had collaborated with him for several years through all the experimental and production stages of their plywood products, would not play a significant part in the design of her own home. Forceful in her own way, and obsessed with the appearance and the details of objects of all sizes and shapes, Ray would have wanted a say in how her home would look, externally and internally, as well as how it would function for her as working designer, a wife, and a stepmother.

The brief the Eameses set for their house succinctly states what they wanted as well as telling us something about how they viewed themselves:

> For a married couple both occupied professionally with mechanical experiment and graphic presentation. Work and recreation are involved in general activities: Day and night, work and play, concentration, relaxation with friend and foe, all intermingled personally and professionally with mutual interest. Basically apartment dwellers, there is a conscious effort made to be free of complications relating to maintenance. The house must make no insistent demands for itself, but rather aid as background for life in work. This house—in its free relation to the ground, the trees, the sea—with constant proximity to the whole vast order of nature acts as re-orientator and 'shock absorber' and should provide the needed relaxations from the daily complications arising within problems.[48]

Ray recalled having many discussions with Charles about their "dream home." As built, it differed considerably not only from many of the schemes they had discussed but also from the original (1945) design developed by Charles and Eero Saarinen. The first design was for two separate steel-frame structures made up of prefabricated industrial parts. One was to be a workshop and studio equipped for power tools and photography and set into the side of a hill at one end of the site. The other, a living block, was to be raised up from the ground on steel supports and cantilevered out over the field at a right angle to the studio, "bridging" the meadow from the hill and offering views of the Pacific. The cantilever, an established feature of European International Style architecture, had gained popularity in California after Neutra's dramatic use of it in the Lovell Health House (1929). The 1945 Eames House design drew heavily on Mies van der Rohe's designs for a cantilevered glass house on a hillside (c. 1934; figure 3.7) and for the Resor House in Jackson Hole, Wyoming (1937–38).[49] Edgardo Contini, the engineer who assisted with the working out of the cantilever structure in the original design, recently pointed out how closely the design resembled a house designed by Eero Saarinen only four years earlier and suggested that the original

3.7 Sketch for glass house on a hillside, c. 1934. Ludwig Mies van der Rohe.

Eames House design may have been abandoned because the designs were too similar. The reasons Charles and Ray always gave to explain the abandoning of the "bridge" design in favor of two simple yet sophisticated pavilions were an increasing interest in Mies van der Rohe's 1930s steel-frame pavilion forms[50] and an increase in the price of steel (which made Charles question the economy of the overall design in relation to the amount of space enclosed).[51] Whatever the reason, Saarinen and the cantilever both disappeared from the project, which suggests that the new design was more the work of Charles and Ray.

3.8 Front entrance of Eames House.

3.9 Reflections of trees
through glass walls of
Eames House.

Whereas the original design was "a minimum house which used a lot of steel," the new version aimed at maximum volume from minimum materials.[52] Space was a key consideration for the Eameses, who regarded it as more important than a swimming pool or a garage (neither of which they ever built for themselves). Steel was chosen for its relative cheapness as well as its lightness and strength. Although steel initially cost more than wood, and although it was expensive to transport, labor costs were reduced to about 33 percent of the cost of materials as against about 50 percent in a traditional wood-frame house. The structural shell of the Eames House was raised by five men in 16 hours, and the roof deck was completed by one man in three days.[53]

It was the site that finally dictated the position of the house. The Eameses could not believe their luck when Entenza first offered them a share of the splendid site in Pacific Palisades: "We hocked all we had to get it."[54] They surveyed the plot themselves and got to know it well. The large expanse of meadow, one boundary of which overlooked the ocean, offered privacy and tranquility in one of the world's largest and noisiest cities and was conveniently located for their Venice workshop as well as their friends in Hollywood and Santa Monica. It was, and is, an idyllic spot. Wildflowers fill the grassy field, in which eucalyptus trees grow and mockingbirds sing. Charles and Ray grew increasingly fond of the meadow and, consequently, less inclined to encroach upon it. The retention of the open meadow was to be one of the great features and pleasures of the location. As Ray later put it: "It is wonderful to see all the changing seasons in it—even in Southern California. . . . In July it is yellow and dry whereas in spring it is high and full of flowers. We cut it only once a year, in late May or June."[55]

The sensitive location of the house within the landscape places it in the Arts and Crafts tradition. The change from having the house dominate the site to letting the site dictate the house's location resulted in a solution that now appears so natural and inevitable that it is difficult to imagine any other location. The Eameses capitalized on one of the most striking natural features of the site—a row of ten eucalyptus trees near one boundary—and located the house and studio behind it. This cost them dearly. The flat area behind the trees was not sufficiently large, and it proved necessary to dig into a hillside and build a retaining wall some 8 feet high and 175 feet long. Any saving attained by using steel for the house was swallowed up by the $5000 expenditure for the wall,[56] but without doubt the result was worth every cent. The location is as stunning as the house.

A modest walkway made from old railway sleepers provided a path to the house from the road entrance, and there were patios adjacent to the house and studio, but the large area beyond the eucalyptus line was left "natural." By contrast, the plots of other Case Study houses were tamed by the professional landscapist Garrett Eckbo, who used concrete slabs, wood boards, and small stones to create sharply angled walkways, walls, and patios in well-ordered environments in which plants and flowers in bright clashing colors provided more than a dash of contrast to the neutral, mainly natural tones and textures of the other materials. The landscaped sites were, in a way, outdoor extensions of modernist interiors. This makes the decision of the Eameses to retain some wildness in their site all the more interesting. Once again, they were the ones to break the mold and stretch the definition of informality and casualness. The surroundings of the Eames House were, like the interior decoration, easy to emulate, in that the initial costs and the upkeep were minimal; however, in the main, those people who chose modernist statements for their homes, let alone less "progressive" middle-class American owner-occupiers, preferred something more ordered and reflective of their social status than a simple meadow.

As built, the house consisted of two rectangular steel cages, each about 20 feet wide, connected by a brick-paved patio. The larger cage (51 feet long) was the living quarters; the smaller (37 feet) was the studio. Together they provided about 2500 square feet of space. The overall effect is reminiscent of traditional Japanese architecture in its emphasis on lightness, elegance, minimalism, and rectilinear geometric form. The light steel frame, painted dark grey, was left exposed, and the effect of the slim 12-inch rods (some spanning 20 feet or more) and the 4-inch columns (some rising 17 feet without support) was that of delicate tracery, elegant in its minimalism. It was "as light and airy as a suspension bridge—as skeletal as an airplane fuselage"[57]; "poetry expressed with high-tec vocabulary."[58] The steel structure dominates the form, and the various infill panels (some translucent, others opaque) emphasize rather than disguise it. The sliding glass doors and windows produced an intimate relationship between outdoors and indoors, as in traditional Japanese architecture, and the large amount of glass, some of it wired "to make people realize it is there,"[59] gave the house a very open feel, although a sense of enclosure could be obtained by drawing the lightly textured rayon and linen drapes.

A powerful visual effect not usually given sufficient emphasis is the overall composition of the front facade. Here is a Mondrian-style composition in a Los Angeles meadow. Once the shell of the house was complete, the Eameses experimented with the colors of the stucco, cemesto, asbestos, and plywood exterior panels. Several schemes were considered before the final painting was undertaken. Ordinary house paint from the local Sears, Roebuck department store was used, so that if the Eameses did not like a color it could easily be changed, but the scheme as originally completed remains unchanged today.[60] To students and devotees of modern architecture brought up on black-and-white illustrations of the Eames House, which tend to emphasize its prefabricated and standardized nature and its Japanese references, the first viewing of one of the most colorful house facades of mid-century modernism is a great visual treat.

Two aspects of the "machine aesthetic" are brought together in this house: the use of mass-produced parts and the geometric forms and abstraction of De Stijl. With its vibrant exterior coloring and its "additive" aesthetic, the facade of the Eames House stepped outside what had become the dominant tradition of modernist architecture, but it did so with reference to revered early modernist heroes. The result was both startling and novel. Ray was certainly influenced by Piet Mondrian, and a great deal of the credit for the final appearance of the building (particularly the front facade) must go to her. But it would be too simplistic to attribute the "factory" aesthetic solely to Charles and the De Stijl-style front to Ray. Although Ray greatly admired Mondrian, so did Charles, and the two would have been in agreement before making such a major decision.

Besides the Mondrian-style abstraction and the Miesian aesthetic, there was a third strong aesthetic influence at work in the Eames House: traditional Japanese architecture (which had, of course, influenced the modern movement). After 1945, and particularly in the 1950s, there was a renewed interest in Japanese culture in the United States.[61] The Eameses' interests ranged from the ritualistic design and dressing of Japanese Sumo wrestlers' hair to tea ceremonies which they held in their home.[62] The house makes many references to the lightness, the elegance, the minimalism, and the rectilinear geometric forms of Japanese architecture. The Eameses' flexible interior partitions, lanterns, and pottery enhanced the overall Japanese "feel" of their house, as did the intimate relationship between exterior and interior.

The harmonious relationship between the house and its surroundings does not reach beyond the patios and the eucalyptus trees. The sensitivity displayed in locating the house within the particular landscape should not detract from the fact that the placing of a three-dimensional Mondrianesque composition in an uncultivated Californian field (or what has been described as a brightly colored Chinese kite in an American meadow[63]) is essentially unharmonious and out of keeping with both Arts and Crafts and Japanese traditions. A brightly colored geometric industrial box does not blend with the natural tones of the Californian landscape but stands in direct contrast to them. Rather than see the house as part of the landscape, as in the orthodox readings, it is possible to see house and setting as yet another Eamesian juxtaposition of disparate images, as strong and powerful as any in an Eames film, multi-screen presentation, exhibition, or eclectic assemblage of objects. Though I would not go so far as to argue that it was a proto-postmodern statement or conceptual art form, deliberately contrasting the artificial nature of art with the wild "natural" meadow beyond, I do wish to indicate the incongruity of such a house in such a landscape and question the commonly accepted notion that it is somehow inevitably and self-evidently harmonious and edifying for fine-art objects to be sited in the natural environment. Perhaps the saving grace of the Eames House, when viewed in these terms, is the way the trees filter the view of the house from the meadow and soften its starkness and brightness. Above all it needs to be emphasized that, while the "Mondrianesque," "Miesian," and "Japanese" aesthetics had a common concern for abstraction, and at times fused together in the Eames house in a coherent minimalist elegance that was more than the sum of the parts, part of the attraction of the house and its surroundings lay in the ways in which the various aesthetic references played off and against one another.

The interior of the Eames House is spacious, light, and flexible. The main living area (23 by 20 feet) utilizes all 17 feet of the two-story structure. Where the living and dining areas divide, there is an overhanging sleeping gallery (which can be closed off by sliding panels) and, below it, an intimate alcove with built-in sofa, storage cabinets, and radio (figure 3.10). The ceiling is light and skeleton-like, revealing the steel frame. The lighting is simple and does not detract from the delicate structural pattern of the ceiling, which is so high that a visitor might lose it were the eye not drawn down by objects suspended there (a piece of Native American sculpture, a Hofmann painting, or a paper butterfly). The back wall is lined with vertical panels of birch, providing a warm contrast to the "industrial" finish evident elsewhere.[64]

The original brief for the living room was set out thus: "For music, reading, watching the fire, talking, leaving large unbroken area for

pure enjoyment of space in which objects can be placed and taken away."[65] With the exception of watching the fire, this is precisely how the space was used, with Ray, in particular, making a special art out of the placing of objects, either on their own or in groups. The Eameses included a fireplace (to warm the house on chilly winter mornings and evenings) in the first plan,[66] but according to Ray they abandoned the idea after Eero Saarinen told them they were "absurdly romantic"[67] in wanting a fireplace—an item which for Frank Lloyd Wright and his followers was the main focus of a room (a symbol of "home") and which had been used in the Entenza House.

The small "front door" is probably the most modest one in any widely acclaimed building of this or any century. In most photographs of the front facade it is barely visible, and even in full-frontal ones it is overshadowed. This was a deliberate statement by the Eameses, but it can be argued that they overplayed it to the extent that the door appears insignificant. It is rescued by a small but significant addition: the simple "folk art" bell, which catches the attention of the visitor (see figure 3.8). Only a few steps inside the door, one is faced with a modest compact spiral staircase set in a small space. Described as a "cagey masterpiece of space economy,"[68] it can feel slightly cramped. The staircase itself consists of triangular plywood treads secured to an I beam mounted to a pipe pole, with a circular skylight overhead. Ordered (like the other standard parts) from an industrial catalog, it is quite stark, but once again the "high-tech" elements are offset by "art" objects (figure 3.11). The north of the living block is taken up by the kitchen and dining area, which was fitted with simple units and the latest equipment.[69]

The two levels of the studio were connected by a metal staircase. The lower level housed a darkroom and a bathroom, the upper level a sleeping area and a work space. With the expansion of the Eameses' film and exhibition projects in the 1950s, the space became too cramped and most work was done in the Venice Office, the studio being used mainly as extra living space. Molly Noyes recalls how, when she and her late husband Eliot Noyes, stayed in the house, Charles and Ray would kindly vacate their bedroom and "decamp" to the studio so that the Noyeses might enjoy the pleasures of the main living block in privacy.[70] The Eames House was a joy to behold and to live in (Charles and Ray thought so, at least), but it was also quite small—something that continues to surprise the first-time visitor.

The Entenza House

In 1937 Charles Eames collaborated with Eero Saarinen on a house for
John Entenza, who had previously commissioned a house by Harwell
Hamilton Harris—"the only Harris house that had any relation to the In-
ternational Style."[71] By 1945 the Harris-designed house seemed out of
date, and Entenza became one of the first clients of his own Case Study
House Program. Eames and Saarinen worked to the following brief:

> In this house activities will be of a more general nature to be
> shared with more people and more things. It will also be used as
> a returning place for relaxation and recreation through reading
> and music and work—a place of reviving and refilling, a place to
> be alone for preparation of work, and with matters and concerns
> of personal choosing. A place for the kind of relaxed privacy nec-
> essary for the development and preparation of ideas to be contin-
> ued in professional work centers. The occupant will need space
> used elastically where many or few people can be accommodated
> within the areas appropriate to such needs. Intimate conversa-
> tion, groups in discussion, the use of a projection machine for
> amusement and education, and facilities for self-indulgent hob-
> bies, i.e. cooking and the entertainment of very close friends.[72]

They used the same structural elements as in the Eames House; however,
they did not achieve the same aesthetic inventiveness:

> Next to this ineffably blithe, elegant, and original architecture
> [Eames House], the low, flat box of the Entenza House can only
> invite invidious comparisons, though it is neat enough, the pat-
> terns of louvers and fixed panels in the glass area are handsome,
> and there is some nice applied decoration. . . . The light steel
> truss frame of the Entenza House is perhaps even more of an engi-
> neering triumph than that of the Eames House, but the eye is
> not permitted to enjoy it; a thick steel and concrete covering and
> a lining of wood prevent even a suspicion of its existence. The
> structure has no more steel skeleton in its character than an
> abode hut. In fact it has very little character at all until one gets
> inside. . . . The shell is merely weather protection for the
> interior—but *what* an interior![73]

3.12 Exterior of Entenza
House, with Eames House
to left.

3.13 Exterior of Entenza
House, showing service
entrance.

The exact nature of the collaboration between Charles and Eero is not clear. In later years Ray Eames claimed that most of the ideas were Charles's,[74] but it must have been a far more equal collaboration. Many of its features first appeared in the Pre-Assembled Compact (PAC) House, designed by Eero Saarinen and Oliver Lundquist for the 1943 Designs For Post War Living competition.[75] Both houses were square in plan, with three sides closed by infills of plywood, stone, and concrete while the fourth was glass. Each house was dominated by a large open-plan living room, each with smaller private enclosed rooms off it, a sunken seating area, and an open fireplace (figure 3.14). The extensive use of wood in the Entenza House, particularly for the ceiling, was probably Saarinen's idea, but it must be remembered that the collaboration between these two men was always extremely close.

The structure of the Entenza House was ingenious. The weight of the frame was supported on twelve steel columns. Most of the weight was carried by the four internal columns, only one of which was exposed, the others being hidden behind plaster-covered walls. New materials were in evidence; the roof was covered with a single slab of insulating concrete pierced by the chimney, the side walls were formed of building blocks covered in ferroboard, and the service entrance was through a steel-frame canopy with ferroboard panels arranged in geometric forms reminiscent of the Eames House. Natural light poured in through the huge glass windows and a skylight.

Entenza, who lived on his own, wanted a refuge from the pressures of work and a place to entertain friends. The interior layout reflected those wishes, with over a third of the space given to a 36-foot-wide open-plan living room surrounded by a series of smaller spaces, including a kitchen, a dining room, two bedrooms, a bathroom, and a completely enclosed study. The most imposing room in the house was the living room, which occupied the whole front of the house. The sensation of occupying that space has been compared to "looking out of a broad-mouthed cave."[76] In contrast to the Eames House, all the glass was translucent, providing a magnificent panoramic view of the tree-dotted meadow and the ocean beyond. The floor was on two levels, separated by two steps. The upper part was carpeted and contained the partly partitioned dining area and an area for displaying art objects; the lower and larger level contained a seating area, the central focus of which was a

3.14 View of living area of
Entenza House showing
DCM chair, plastic
armchair, and ETR table.

brightly painted fireplace. There the floor was tiled, and its continuation outdoors expressed the contemporary concern with breaking down barriers between indoor and outdoor living.

In comparison to the large living area, the other rooms were extremely small. The main bedroom provided just enough room for a double bed, although its panel walls could be pulled back to afford views across the living room and beyond. The guest room was even smaller and shared the only bathroom. Much greater priority in terms of space was given to the two-car garage than to guests. Separated from the living room by a corrugated glass wall, in terms of a prototype for mass housing it brought the Entenza House closer to the American ideal than its neighbor. The most unusual room of all was the small, womb-like study. Soundproofed (the occupant was accessible only on an intercom system), and designed without windows in the belief that more work would be done without the distractions of natural light and sound, it provided a complete contrast with the open plan of the rest of the house.

The Entenza House was seen by some as an excellent solution to the problem of adapting standardized buildings to personal needs: "To those who hold that there is no freedom of design within standardized building systems, this plan—a portrait, almost, of its owner—is about as good an answer as anyone could find."[77] However, Esther McCoy, who knew Entenza well, suggests that the house proved too geared toward large-scale entertaining.[78] This and other reasons, including a "falling out" with the Eameses,[79] led Entenza to sell the house only five years after moving in. Since then a great many interior alterations have taken place. At the time of this writing little remains visible of the modernist exterior under the thick coverage of creepers, although I have recently been informed that the new owners are planning to restore the house to its former glory. In later years Ray Eames could hardly bear to let anyone so much as catch a glimpse of it, let alone consider looking inside, so different was it from the original design.

THE HERMAN MILLER FURNITURE SHOWROOM

In 1948, shortly after the Herman Miller Furniture Company began to manufacture Eames furniture, the Eameses designed the firm's first showroom on the West Coast. It was located at 8806 Beverly Boulevard, in

3.15 Herman Miller
Furniture Company
showroom, 8806 Beverly
Boulevard, Los Angeles,
1949. Charles and Ray
Eames.

West Hollywood, then the center of the Los Angeles's fast-growing trade in the manufacture and distribution of furnishings.[80] The Eameses aimed at a "minimum of architecture," claiming that the building was important only to the extent that and in the way in which it served its main commercial purpose: the display and sale of furniture.[81] The steel-frame showroom was rectangular in shape, with the two brick side walls painted white on the interior and fronted by a steel frame fitted with sash windows and opaque decorative panels of plaster and composition. The Mondrianesque quality of this distinctive facade relates it to the Eames House. Depending on the arrangement of the panels on the front, the showroom could either be a "giant shop window" or be closed off, completely or in part. The open-plan floor (some 5000 square feet) was divided into separate areas by a grid which allowed for an almost infinite number of positionings of display panels, supported on poles which fitted into holes in the floor and the ceiling. The space provided showroom, office, and reception space. Artificial light supplemented the natural light from three large circular skylights. In this building, as in their own home, the Eameses showed that modern architecture need not mean dull uniformity and that it was possible to create unique, attractive, highly flexible solutions to particular briefs using standardized and/or industrial components.

After their own house and the Herman Miller showroom were completed, the Eameses concentrated more on furniture design, filmmaking and exhibitions than on architecture and interiors. Charles now claimed that he preferred design work over architecture, because smaller-scale projects allowed more direct control over the final product, but the Eameses did not lose all interest in architecture. Charles had been involved with it since 1925, some of their closest friends were architects, and architecture was featured in several of their films—and they designed a few new buildings, some realized, others not.

THE MAX DE PREE HOUSE, ZEELAND, MICHIGAN (1954)

Designed for the son of the president of the Herman Miller Furniture Company, this simple open-plan timber-frame house, influenced by post-war Scandinavian modernism and by the local vernacular, offered a contemporary, bourgeoisified version of an early settler dwelling. The brief stipulated that local artisans, many of whom had been trained in Holland, should be used, and consequently the quality of finish on this substantial wooden building was very high indeed.[82] The Eameses drew on the cultural heritage of the area for inspiration and tempered the radical modern design with what they hoped was the spirit and feel of the vernacular design of the area while avoiding the pastiche Dutch Colonial that was common there. The house, a two-story pavilion with a flat overhanging roof echoed on the front by an overhanging deck and on the back by a balcony, was pleasing in its simplicity and its regularity.[83] The strong vertical emphasis of the uniform panels was countered by equally strong horizontal lines, resulting in a neat rectangle firmly rooted to the ground. There was some variation in the amounts of wood and glass used in the infill panels, but the overall impression was of uniformity and regularity. There were no large expanses of glass, because of the severely cold Michigan winters, and there was none of the colorful infilling or the excitement of the Eames House. The latter was due in part to the brief and in part to the fact that the Eameses themselves were less involved in working out the detailed structure, plan and the interior of this house than they had been with their own home. Don Albinson was responsible for much of the main structure, and he and other Eames Office staff members worked

3.16 Max De Pree House,
Zeeland, Michigan, 1954,
under construction.

on the interior.[84] To state this, however, is not to absolve the Eameses of responsibility for a house that is not regarded as highly as their other work. It was their choice to fuse modernism with the traditions of Zeeland in that particular way, and they always approved all designs before any work went ahead. Furthermore, it should be noted that the design of this house allowed rooms to be added without destroying the overall aesthetic effect—a factor that many of the Case Study architects failed to take into consideration, only to find their designs desecrated by insensitive additions and alterations in later years.

THE GRIFFITH PARK RAILROAD (1957)

Griffith Park, one of the main parks in Los Angeles, used to include a miniature railroad (one-fifth life size). In 1957, the year in which the Eameses made the film *Toccata for Toy Trains,* Sam Bernstein, who leased the railroad, asked them to redesign the station. The project fascinated them (particularly Charles, whose love of trains went back to his childhood), and the whole office soon became involved in redesigning not only the station but also the tickets, the posters, and the signs.[85] The willingness to take on such a project says a great deal about the Eameses, who were already designers of international standing. To them, this was just as important as an office block or a private house. Charles and Ray oversaw the entire project, with Don Albinson and Dale Breuer responsible for designing the station and the railway yard, Deborah Sussman in charge of signs and tickets, and John Neuhart responsible for the poster.

The designs drew on the nostalgia surrounding trains, particularly older trains. In 1957 the great American railroad system was already something of an anachronism. This was certainly the case in Los Angeles, the city of seemingly endless freeways, in the age of the automobile and jet plane. Yet the railroad system symbolized a great deal of the American myth. It had helped open California to white settlers from the Midwest, and it was associated with the "frontier spirit" (whatever that was and however it was interpreted). The Griffith Park trains had been modeled on the railroads of the late nineteenth and the early twentieth century, and the Eames Office's scheme continued the evocation of that period. The station resembled a toy one in the Eameses own collection, and the graphics drew on typography associated with turn-of-the-century circuses

3.17 Station on Griffith
Park Railroad, Los
Angeles, 1957.

3.18 Design for a City
Hall prepared at invitation
of *Architectural Forum* for
1943 issue "New
Buildings for 194?"
Charles Eames and John
Entenza with assistance
from Ray Eames.

and carnivals. This populist style was thought vulgar by some,[86] and in a way it was, but it had vitality, immediacy, and an ability to conjure up the past—real or mythical. In this project, and particularly in the graphics, American populism met American modernism head on and won easily.

UNREALIZED ARCHITECTURAL PROJECTS

In 1943 Charles Eames (encouraged by John Entenza, who considered him the brightest prospect on the American architectural scene) accepted the invitation of *Architectural Forum* to submit designs for public buildings suitable for the postwar period. The submission for a City Hall complex shown here in figure 3.18 is cited in *Eames Design* as the joint work of Charles Eames and John Entenza, although it was published under Charles's name alone.[87] The brilliant sketches and the lucid texts were completed within a few days,[88] and this, together with Ray's heavy involvement in the plywood work for the U.S. Navy and her lack of experience with architectural projects, probably accounts for her relatively small input. Her influence can be seen in some of the shapes on at least one plan, and it is unlikely that her comments and assistance were not sought. This project was a magnificent opportunity to move away from the monumental historical styles that still dominated public architecture, but the entry went even further and developed what was the first of many proposed "information centers."[89] The design also indicates that Charles's deep concern with communications, normally said to begin around 1950, dates back at least as far as this project.

The scheme reflected Entenza's strong belief in the social role of architecture—a belief that, for Charles, reinforced ideas and values learned at Cranbrook, if not before. A desire for greater communication between local government and "the people" was articulated in the accompanying text, which began by pointing out that in 1943 in a typical small American community only a small percentage of those registered actually bothered to vote in a municipal election and argued that government should be seen as something more than a group of administrators. The text went on to suggest that government buildings include facilities for "the expression of the idea of government" as well as "the administration of rules and regulation." The design brought together various depart-

CITY HALL   *CHARLES EAMES, LOS ANGELES, CALIF.*

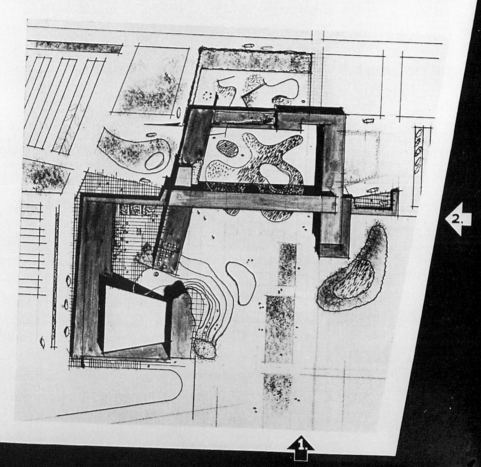

auditorium
concert hall
theatre   stage

the "bridge" houses the
machinery of municipal
planning and government   upper part of
                                                 val

EW 1.

ments of local government in an attempt to link them for the better functioning of society: ". . . it should be impossible to think in terms of the juvenile court without thinking in terms of the children's clinic, without thinking in terms of a Board of Education."[90] The scheme was rooted in the belief that there was a solution for every problem, and a rationalist approach to building was seen to have a role to play in a broader enlightened system of welfare provision. Within that framework, the importance of the image of local government was emphasized. A cinema, a theater, and an exhibition space were included because Eames and Entenza wanted such pleasurable and cultural activities to be associated with an institution all too often viewed as worthily utilitarian and dreadfully dull.

Four years later, in 1947, Charles and Ray entered the Jefferson National Expansion Memorial Competition, sponsored by Charles's native city of St. Louis, which wanted to build a monument to celebrate the city's role as the "Gateway to the West."[91] Once again the entry was submitted under Charles's name, but it was in fact a joint venture by him and Ray, both of whom had admired Thomas Jefferson since childhood, assisted by John Entenza. As modernists, the Eameses wanted to move away from traditional memorials such as statues or classical arches and find a contemporary mode of expression. They also wanted to convey Jefferson's philosophy and ideas to a twentieth-century audience. Their design, which owed a great deal to Charles's thinking about public architecture and communications, included a public park with an amphitheater, a memorial mound, a museum, a "living memorial" housing a library, design laboratories, a printing plant, and accommodations for visitors and researchers. A walkway lined with abstract sculptures symbolizing the life and ideas of Jefferson (the design of which probably owed a great deal to Ray, and models of which were made) linked the two main parts of the memorial. The Eameses' entry did not win, partly because it would have been extremely expensive to build and maintain and partly because the city authorities wanted something more obviously like a monument. The 590-foot stainless-steel parabolic arch designed by Eero Saarinen that now stands on the banks of the Mississippi was finally chosen, not least because it conveyed in symbolic form something of the philosophical ideas which the Eameses had hoped to convey in their massive and massively ambitious project.

One of the most important buildings designed by the Eameses, shortly after the completion of their own home, was a house for the recently married Billy and Audrey Wilder. Despite his wealth, Wilder lived in what has been called "spartan splendor"[92] and "unostentatious reserve."[93] He liked his twelfth-floor apartment in a high-rise building in West Los Angeles, but it had began to feel a little cramped—largely because Wilder was continually adding to his impressive art collection.[94] The Wilders admired the Eameses' new house, and in 1950 a proposal (which reveals a great deal of Ray's hand as well as Charles's) was drawn up for an extended version of the Eames House to be built on Sunset Boulevard and Foothills Drive. Like the Eames and Entenza houses and the Herman Miller showroom, the design was based on a prefabricated steel structure with infills of glass and a mixture of opaque panels, although less of the "guts" of the building was revealed than in the Eames House. Ray told me that the building was conceived as a simple enclosure to house the art collection and that the idea was to produce a dynamic space in which no single architectural feature was allowed to dominate[95]— although the main entrance was signified by a large entrance porch-*cum*-carport, in direct contrast to the Eames House. The rectangular and modular Wilder House, similar in plan to Mies van der Rohe's Tugendhat House,[96] incorporated into an open-plan interior a two-story living space (with a sunken seating area and a free-standing storage wall and a fireplace), a dining area, study, three bedrooms, three bathrooms, dressing rooms, and a large utility area. One side of the roof extended into the garden to form a verandah, and concrete-slab patios connected the house to the garden (which, with its flower beds, was more formal than that of the Eameses). It has been said that "Brunelleschi would have envied the sleekly thin wall planes that followed modular lines to enclose a regular, clearly organized volume,"[97] which "would have rivaled the Irwin Miler house in its sumptuousness had it been executed."[98] That this project went unbuilt has been called as great a loss to American domestic architecture as Frank Lloyd Wright's McCormick House of 1907.[99]

The next project concerned mass housing. In 1951 the Kwikset Lock Company of Anaheim, which had produced much of the hardware for the Case Study houses, commissioned the Eameses to design a low-cost prefabricated house to be manufactured in quantity and sold as a kit.[100] Encouraged by their success with low-cost mass-produced furniture, they eagerly took up the challenge of low-cost mass-produced housing. Their approach to this project was similar to that taken toward their

3.19 Model of Wilder
House, 1950.

3.20 Model of Kwikset
House, 1951.

own house. They prioritized the enclosing of as much space as possible within a specified budget (in this case $8000), and by using a wooden shell of posts carrying a curved plywood roof they obtained twice as much space as in a masonry house of the same price.[101] Only the frame of the main facade, into which panels of translucent and opaque glass could be inserted, was made from metal—an admission that wood was cheaper than the steel framing they had used in their home and proposed for the Wilder House. As in the Eames House, the structural elements were exposed. Only after the exterior was fully resolved did the Eameses turn their attention to the interior, which was divided by movable partitions and units into living and dining areas, a kitchen, a bathroom, and two bedrooms, thereby offering suitable accommodations for two adults and two children. Although there were certain similarities between this and the Eames House (notably in the infill panels, the exposed structure, and the flexible interior), the conception and the development of this project owed a great deal to Richard Neutra's plywood model demonstration house (1936),[102] to Gregory Ain's knowledge and enthusiasm about the design and construction of plywood buildings, and to Don Albinson's experience of living in a prefabricated house developed by Walter Gropius and Konrad Wachsmann (a friend of the Eameses).[103] Despite the enormous amount of work poured into the project, it never came to fruition. Models were made of the house, complete with miniature Eames furniture, but the project ended when a change in the ownership of Kwikset caused the flow of development money to be halted before the Eameses were happy with the proposed production methods.[104] Although the aim was to make good, inexpensive modern architecture available to the majority of the population, the new management of Kwikset considered the severe modernist aesthetic a handicap in terms of sales at a time when the general public was thought to hanker for California ranch-style houses.

Prefabricated frame construction and modernist aesthetics were given further expression in a dollhouse designed for the Revell Toy Company in 1959.[105] Like many Eames designs, this project involved updating a traditional object by giving it contemporary form. The design was based on injection-molded plastic modular frames and infill panels from which different houses could be constructed, ranging from a simple pavilion shape to more complex structures. A set of miniature Eames furniture, including GRP and Aluminum Group chairs, a sofa, and a pedestal

3.21 Model of Revell Toy
House, 1959.

3.22 Model of "Birthday
House," 1959.

table, graced the interiors, along with small-scale rugs and flowers, and it was intended that the structures could also be used by the Herman Miller Furniture Company for display and marketing purposes. The Eameses' relationship with the Revell company proved the least harmonious of their client relationships, and this project was never brought to fruition.

One of the Eameses' most unusual projects was a "Birthday House" for Hallmark Cards (1959), designed in the form of a bandstand-*cum*-carousel (figure 3.22).[106] The idea of a special space in which to celebrate birthdays (as they always did) appealed to them greatly; however, this was another case where they felt they did not have the full backing of the client, and they abandoned this delightful project. Seven years later they were involved in a project related to a historic carousel. The History and Technology Division of the Smithsonian Institution wanted to operate a nineteenth-century carousel from its collection on the National Mall in Washington and commissioned a shelter to protect it from the elements.[107] The cover had to be in keeping with the carousel but also with the Mall, noted mainly for the overriding seriousness of its monuments, museums, and government buildings. The Eameses loved the carousel on the Santa Monica pier, near their workshop, and they decided that the covering for the Smithsonian carousel should be as unobtrusive as the one at Santa Monica. Their solution was a glass "skin" that would reveal the glories of the nineteenth-century object within. The doors of the faceted glass pavilion would be open during the day (weather permitting) to allow access; at night, when they would be closed, the pavilion would be illuminated so that the carousel could still be seen. This novel architectural solution was considered too costly.

The Eameses undertook no major architectural commissions after 1951, partly because their interests were diversifying but also because they were frustrated by their lack of control over projects involving contractors, subcontractors, engineers, and large sums of money.

The Eameses went far beyond what was normally expected of designers; they "shaped not only things but the way people think about things."[1] They changed the way people thought about objects, largely by presenting them in new ways and by encouraging different ways of perceiving, grouping, and displaying them. In particular, they used toys and everyday objects to illustrate design principles and craft skills, and they emphasized the need to understand the contexts in which material culture was produced and used. Yet in what they called "functioning decoration" (though not in their exhibitions) objects were taken out of their usual contexts for visual effect and "extra-cultural surprise."[2]

Throughout their years together, Charles and Ray shared a delight in and an insistent curiosity about objects. Pleasure from objects was one of their main joys in life—be it the arrangement of colorful glasses on a tray, a display of machine tools in a department store, a nicely shaped piece of bread, or a finely woven and embroidered sari—and one which they communicated to others through still and moving images and exhibitions. Even before they went into filmmaking, they experimented with using slides (hundreds of them) to convey the many, varied, and complex pleasures that one could get from the simplest of objects by studying them in detail and by juxtaposing them with others. In short, they had what Esther McCoy called "an affection for objects."[3]

The Eameses' respect for objects was rooted in the Arts and Crafts ideals of truth to materials, honesty of construction, joy in labor, and the dialectical relationship of beauty and utility. Charles scorned items self-consciously designed for "shelf-appeal"[4]; he admired those that revealed love and care in their making. He and Ray considered that many objects, particularly old objects, to have an integrity in and of themselves which related to the materials, the processes of production, the care, and the skill with which they were made. When I asked Ray about their fascination with toys, she stated that toys were simply one of the most important types of objects they admired, reminded me that Charles had been passionately interested in "real" trains and railways since his boyhood, and referred me back to the "toy" movies.[5]

4.1 "Functioning decoration." Display on gold table in living room of Eames House, 1949.

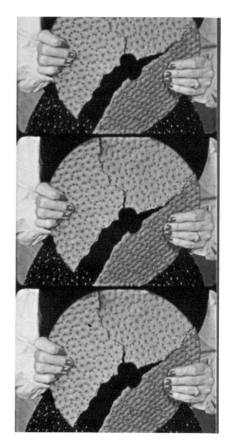

4.2 Sequence from *Bread* (1953).

The Eameses always discussed objects within the framework of the functionalism that then dominated the discourse of design. When I admired a Hopi kachina in the lobby of the Eames Office, Ray stated that its design was clearly related to its function of informing Hopi children about their history and their gods and pointed to the headdress as an example of the constraints within which a designer has to work.[6] Yet, although Charles and Ray insisted that these remarkable objects—the spirit essences of things and customs in the real world—could be understood only in the context of Hopi history and culture, the example we were discussing was mainly used for decorative effect on a sofa.

At the height of modernism's hegemony it was difficult to admit simply liking the look of something, especially an object that could be classified as non-industrial, decorative, and trivial. The Eameses' insistence on stressing the processes of design and manufacture helped validate their delight in the appearances of particular objects (and some of the objects they collected were extremely beautiful), as did the insistence on their instructional qualities. However, the contextualizing and the emphasis on process avoided any discussion of the visual per se. Although I felt somewhat frustrated when Ray referred me back to the films for an answer to my question about the fascination with objects, perhaps she was

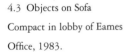

4.3 Objects on Sofa Compact in lobby of Eames Office, 1983.

FUNCTIONING DECORATION

correct to do so. The films convey something for which, at the time they were made, there was little or no language. The discourse of design excluded the non-functional or trivialized it as whimsy. The films, however, articulated in non-verbal and often non-narrative and/or emotive ways issues related to memory, nostalgia, texture, color, movement, excitement, and joy—all of which, it seems to me, were elements in Charles and Ray's love of objects. Film gave them a means of expressing their sheer and utter joy in objects, their reveling in detail, color, and texture, and their respect for craft traditions.

Tops (1969), like *Toccata for Toy Trains,* used toys to explain principles of design. Respect for ordinary, everyday objects is foregrounded in many of the slide shows and in the films *Blacktop* (1952), *Bread* (1953), *SX-70* (1972), and *Something About Photography* (1976). The last two of these films pointed out that art and inspiration always lay near at hand and suggested the most familiar objects of everyday life as subject matter for aspiring photographers.

Many of the objects used by the Eameses in their films and in their "functioning decoration" were toys from their own collection, gathered from all over the world. Toys were treated as seriously as any other object by the Eameses, whose delight in them related to their own sense of fun and to a belief in learning through play as well as to visual appreciation. Toys were vehicles for creative and expansive play that not only recalled memories of childhood but also offered adults opportunities to recreate their childhood and/or behave as children. Some of the toys the Eameses designed grew out of existing projects; for example, the plywood animals were designed at the same time as the plywood furniture, and the Revell Toy House grew out of domestic housing projects. Others filled a gap in the market for educationally progressive and visually stimulating toys. Fascinated by play and by pleasurable ways of learning, and great givers of presents, the Eameses found it hard to find suitable gifts for children and so decided to try their hand at toy design.[7] They made no attempt to replicate the older toys which they so admired and collected—they respected them far too much to do that. Rather, they produced up-to-date versions of "traditional" toys, such as blocks, cards, masks, coloring toys, and play houses.

The Eameses' toys encouraged the expansion of the child's mental and imaginative powers and/or practical skills. This serious approach to "fun" activities, which aimed to make creative development pleasurable, relates to other aspects of the Eameses' work, particularly their exhibitions and films. It has roots in two related developments of the late nineteenth and the early twentieth centuries: the Arts and Craft Movement and new educational theories related to creative play. The Arts and Crafts movement, which admired the material culture of "simpler" pre-industrial (and frequently pre-capitalist) societies, promoted handicrafts as character-building as well as utilitarian. At a time when hand processes were fast disappearing from many areas of work, values related to the morally uplifting nature of labor were reallocated to other areas, particularly adult leisure handicrafts and children's "play."[8] Activities that involved creativity or learning a skill were sanctioned; those that did not, such as watching movies, were regarded as unproductive and frowned upon. Parents, design theorists, reformers, and educationalists who wanted children to grow into worthy citizens who would know quality craft work when they saw it and would aspire to and maintain standards of quality in whatever sphere of life they later inhabited encouraged a pedagogy based on practical and creative exercises and equating work, art, and play.[9]

Children's craft work developed apace after World War I with the acceptance of new educational philosophies based on the belief that children are innately artistic if given freedom of expression. The roots of the movement can be traced back to Rousseau, Froebel, and Pestalozzi as well as to B. Stanley Hall, James Sully, and John Dewey.[10] To what extent Froebel's occupations or gifts were responsible for the staggering self-expression of Frank Lloyd Wright (or even Charles Eames) is not certain,[11] but the ideas that children were naturally artistic and that art was a healthy means of self-expression were well established in the United States by the interwar period. One of the most enthusiastic and internationally known of the new breed of design teacher/child educators was Franz Cizek. Influenced by both Rousseau and Froebel, a teacher at Vienna's Kunstgewerbeschule whose books on cut-paper work for and by children[12] were almost certainly known to Ray in her later years at high school or when she was an art student. John Dewey's commitment to the integration of mind and body and his enthusiasm for "learning by doing" were redolent of the ideas of William Lethaby, the grand old man of the Arts and Crafts movement, who argued the centrality of workshop practice to design and craft teaching.[13] This "hands-on" approach to learning by doing, and a belief that children and adults could do many more tasks than they or society deemed them capable of if only given a conducive environment and sufficient stimulation, formed the basis of the Eameses' own workshop practice. Geoffrey Holroyd noted a parallel between Dewey's notion of the school as a miniature workshop and community, teaching through practice, trial, and error, and the Eameses' understanding of a laboratory workshop.[14]

The earliest and some of the most beautiful "toys" designed by the Eameses were masks for children and adults. These reflected an interest in ritual, performance, and play as well as in "primitive" and modern art. They grew out of the Eameses' desire to facilitate free expression in children and to encourage it in the activities of adults. Charles and Ray's fascination with masks, masking, and masquerade relates particularly to their love and appreciation of popular play traditions, the entertainment and celebratory aspects of which foregrounded the visual (and often also the spectacular and the comic) rather than the verbal. It suggests a sensitivity toward sensory stimulation and the psychological complexities of identity, transformation, and disguise. The Eameses enjoyed performances that featured non-verbal expression, spectacle, and pleasure.

4.4 Staff members wearing cardboard mock-ups of toy masks, 1950.

4.5 Ray Eames with
printed cat face from
magazine, 1971.

4.6 Charles Eames with
printed face from
magazine, 1971.

One of Charles' most enduring love affairs was with the circus, an arena in which so many problems of communication seem to dissolve or be irrelevant. He was fascinated by the energy, discipline, and spectacle of what he saw as a well-orchestrated ensemble of disparate parts[15] (rather like "functioning decoration"). Ray also became an enthusiast. Indeed, in the mid 1940s they were about to audition as a clown act when a financial deal related to the production of their plywood furniture eased their financial worries enough to allow them to continue as designers.[16]

In contrast to the circus, where the viewer takes pleasure from watching performers such as clowns in disguise, the carnival directly involves participants in acts of disguise and transformation which open up possibilities for behaving differently. The Eameses referred to such magical transformations in a note to children using The Coloring Toy: "Imagine yourself a magician who can change a girl into a mermaid, a butterfly into a swan, a boy into a monkey, who can make a bird swim and a fish fly."[17]

The Eameses had their own collection of masks and were also interested in face painting. Masks and painting, traditional methods of transforming the face, had been used in modernist theater and opera to suggest differences between the outer and the inner person and the complexities of identify.[18] These issues interested the Eameses, who before they embarked upon mask design had experimented with more obviously avant-garde devices in relation to transformative images and to composing images which themselves suggested the constructed nature of images.

The Eameses' selfconsciousness about construction is fascinating. They often posed for photographs or photographed themselves and others in the act of photography or constructing images to be photographed. Their interest in the process of image making is clearly revealed in three photographs involving reflections. The first (1946, figure 4.8) is of them reflected in the shiny surface of a Christmas bauble (one of their favorite objects). The second (1947, figure 4.9) includes a superimposition of two "ghostly" images of Charles on a photograph of a display of plywood furniture. The third (1950, figure 4.10) is of them posed and photographing their own reflections in the large glass windows of their house. By 1950 they were experimenting with photographing an image of a person's head and upper body on 35-millimeter color transparency film, projecting that image onto a human subject, and then rephotographing the subject's

4.7 Ray Eames and
Konrad Wachsman
wearing Chinese masks at
Eames Office, 1950.

4.8 Christmas card, 1946.

Charles and Ray Eames.

4.9 Superimposition of
images of Charles Eames
over photograph of
plywood furniture, 1947.

4.10 Charles and Ray
Eames photographing their
reflections in windows of
Eames House, 1950.

4.11 Drawing by Saul
Steinberg, 1950. Color
transparency taken by
Charles Eames.

FUNCTIONING DECORATION

4.12 Photograph by
Charles Eames of color
transparency in figure 4.11
projected onto head and
body of Hedda Sterne (Saul
Steinberg's wife), 1950. A
similar photograph was
taken of Ray Eames.

head and body as veiled and transformed by the transparency (figures 4.11, 4.12). The distortion caused by the play of a transparent two-dimensional image on a solid three-dimensional form produced a frozen, ghost-like appearance. Unlike the recognizable but ethereal superpositions of Charles in the 1947 photograph, the identity of the person was altered and transformed.

Painting was a simpler and more direct way of transforming the human face. Once again an old tradition was given new form by the Eameses, usually on the faces of visiting children. Charles had been interested in clown makeup since the 1940s if not earlier,[19] and in 1971 he and Ray made a film (*Clown Face*) on that very subject. The symmetry of classical clown makeup was one of the things that interested them about it; however, when Charles had his face painted by Ray for a rare party appearance (in 1953) the image was distinctly modern (figure 4.14).

Deborah Sussman, whose invitation to a nearby Halloween party which she had organized with friends encouraged the Eameses to attend, remembers the design as Ray's, and Ray certainly executed it. It was devised about an hour before the event when Charles, whose dislike of parties was well known, suddenly announced his intention to go by asking "Where's my costume?"[20] The face design incorporated the traditional white background of the clown face but transformed it into an asymmetrical, uneven, fractured grid, the cracks suggesting a spider's web. Restricted to the space between eyebrow and chin, this fractured Mondrianesque composition fused orthodox modernist theatrical references to psychological complexity with "postmodern" complexity and contradiction. Ray wore a black outfit, Charles a white one. He wore on his head a large but plain structure with long, thin elements radiating from a circular band, rather like the light fixture displayed in the Eames room at An Exhibition for Modern Living[21]; she wore a small, decorative hat (though what it was made of no one can now recall). Rather than have her face painted, Ray disguised herself behind a piece of exquisite black Japanese oshibori dyed fabric.[22] Deborah Sussman recently commented that "the whole thing was most un-Eames, it was spontaneous and party."[23]

In 1950, the year in which they made their first toy film, the Eameses set aside their experiments with reflection and superimposition for a project that dealt with changing identity in a more direct and concrete way: the design of masks. Intended for mass production, these cardboard head and body masks with paper additions were, like some items of

4.14 Deborah Sussman,
Charles Eames, and Ray
Eames at Halloween party,
1953. Charles's face
painted by Ray.

Eames furniture, up-to-date models of traditional products. The Eameses owned some highly decorated Chinese masks of the sort admired by Gordon Craig and Bertolt Brecht, and some homemade ones, and sometimes used them for home performances with friends such as Konrad Wachsmann and John Entenza. Ray, who was keen on contemporary dance and performance, particularly enjoyed these events, which she described as "impromptu."[24] She first began to draw, paint, and model masks for use at home,[25] and she probably drew on her earlier experience with the design of cut-out dolls[26] when she and Charles decided to develop masks for mass production.

A Tennessee toy firm, Tigrett Enterprises, showed an interest in manufacturing the cut-out masks, to be colored and assembled at home. However, the project never got beyond the vibrantly colored cardboard prototypes, which included a frog, a rooster, a giraffe, a cat, an eagle, an owl, a turtle, some unspecified birds and fishes, a dragon, and a giant clown face. That the masks were not produced commercially did not dampen the interest of either Tigrett Enterprises or the Eameses; another self-assembly project, The Toy (1951), went into production and was sold through the Sears catalog.[27] More modern in concept and form than the masks, this constructional toy was aimed mainly but not exclusively at children. The kit comprised dowels, pipe cleaners, and brightly colored panels (four squares and four triangles) of plastic-coated, moisture-resistant stiff paper, which could be used to make a variety of structures, including play houses and puppet theaters. This and other constructional toys designed by the Eameses required active participation—it was the child who decided the final shape and form.

The idea of play environments had already received some attention from the Eameses: they had suggested that the large shipping cartons used for the ESU storage units be accompanied by instructions for transforming them into play houses.[28] Related to the modularity and formalism of the facade of the Eames House and the ESU storage units, The Toy was modern art translated into toy form. The advertising stressed that it could be used at various stages of childhood and adult life. It sold well—particularly after a representative of Sears, Roebuck suggested reducing the size of the flat package, which was then redesigned as an eye-catching hexagonal tube. The Little Toy, designed in 1952, had perforated and silk-screened panels as well as solid ones.[29]

4.15 Ray Eames with early
prototype of The Toy,
1951.

4.16 Room setting: child's
room with Hang-It-All
(1953), Little Toy (1952),
and House of Cards
("pattern deck," 1952).

Also developed for Tigrett Enterprises was another modular constructional toy, House of Cards (1952), which used a pack of 52 cards, each 4¼ by 6½ inches and each with six slots so that one could fit into another. On one side of the "pattern deck" was an assortment of patterns and textures; on the other was a black asterisk. Printed by American Playing Card and distributed by Tigrett Enterprises, the House of Cards was popular among adults. So successful was it that Tigrett Enterprises undertook production and distribution of a giant version and a standard-size "picture deck" or "miniaturized encyclopaedia of everyday objects."[30] The latter was a do-it-yourself "Eames aesthetic" kit with which people could make their own juxtapositions of images and learn the skills of "functioning decoration" and the fast-cutting of images, a technique favored by the Eameses in certain of their films. In production for almost a decade, House of Cards is the toy that relates most closely to the Eames aesthetic of addition, juxtaposition, and "extra-cultural surprise" (discussed later in this chapter).

The next project did not involve the interlocking of shapes into complex structures so much as the positioning of right-angled partitions to divide up space and create small environments for toys to reside in or pass through. Known in the Eames Office as "blocks," the component parts were, in the main, two panels joined at right angles, although there were some free-standing blocks.[31] This project, which never got beyond the prototype stage, indicates a radical rethinking of both blocks and environments for toys.

Another idea developed for Tigrett Enterprises at the same time, the Hang-It-All, went into production, and several thousands were sold before the firm went out of business in 1961. This was yet another product developed out of previous work—in this case, the Eameses' bent-metal furniture (discussed in the following chapter). A "fun and playful" hanging device comprising a white-painted metal frame and a set of colorful wooden balls, it was intended for a child's room.[32] The Eameses were more delighted than anyone when, like the House of Cards, it proved to have a wider appeal. Drawing on the growing fashion for "scientific" imagery (it suggested the diagram of an atom), it was a friendly use of what could be an ambiguous image.[33] The Hang-It-All was sufficiently distant from the molecular models used in classrooms and laboratories not to emphasize connections with the "real" world of science, let alone the atomic bomb, but to still appear novel and progressive. For a photo session, Ray hung on it a roller skate, a kachina doll, a petticoat, and a bow of ribbon. It proved, like a pegboard, to be an excellent structural setting for an arrangement of diverse objects. In other words, like the House of Cards, it was a piece of "functioning decoration."

Five years after the cut-out coloring masks did not progress beyond prototypes, the Coloring Toy was developed. It combined elements of the traditional coloring book and cut-out dolls and animals. Ray's interest in cut-out dolls would seem to be crucial to this product, which consisted of eight sheets of card, 49 die-cut shapes, 16 crayons, 32 butterfly clips, and an instruction sheet. What was new was that each shape could be colored to make different things and that the shapes could be combined in many different ways. The "notes to parents" said that one of the ideas behind this project was to "provide a sort of jet assist into a world of color, drawing, shapes and play,"[34] stressed that the toy was not intended to transform children into artists or teach them how to play, and expressed the hope that it would stimulate further creativity and discoveries about materials.

4.17 Box for The Coloring Toy, 1955.

With the exception of the Revell Toy House (1959), which was an offshoot of thinking about industrial housing, no more toys were designed in the Eames Office. More and more, the concentration was on exhibitions and on films. However, a very special type of "toy," the Solar Do-Nothing Machine,[35] was designed for Alcoa, which in 1957 set aside $3 million to promote aluminum and commissioned several leading designers to design products that would illustrate the diversity and potential of the material. Alexander Girard designed shelving, Isamu Noguchi a table, and Jean Deoze an aluminum crepe ball gown.[36] The Eameses, who were already well known for their toy designs, were asked to produce a toy, but they interpreted the brief very liberally. The Solar Do-Nothing Machine was an extremely serious piece of equipment that resembled more a piece of abstract art than any of the toys they designed. It consisted of a platform on which stood a multitude of poles and pedestals with cut-out pinwheels and stars worked by a series of shafts, pulleys, and pistons using solar energy generated by photovoltaic cells, thus linking aluminum with the very latest and ecologically progressive technology. It made a statement about the potential of aluminum and solar power in an amusing and interesting way; at the same time, it allowed Charles the "Yankee mechanic,"[37] Ray the sculptor, and some of their employees to express their talents.

The Eameses' decorative talents found expression through "functioning decoration." They used this term to describe their carefully composed arrangements of disparate objects, some of which were quite small, within interior spaces. The aesthetic was one of addition, juxtaposition, composition, changing scales, and "extra-cultural surprise." The word "functional" validated "decoration," which was usually regarded as non-functional, while entering into a dialectic with it. Functionalism was a difficult concept to avoid in the architecture and design discourses of the postwar years, and had been since the early years of the century; "decoration" had become a pejorative in "progressive" architectural and design circles. Eliel Saarinen tried using the term "spiritual function" to refer to what others labeled non-functional aspects of design, such as the symbolic, the associative, the affective, and the decorative.[38] This had the virtue of acknowledging that architecture and design involved non-rational elements, whereas "functioning decoration" could be taken to imply that there were other types of decoration which were not functional. The

4.18 Solar Do-Nothing

Machine, 1957.

Eameses' decoration was no more "functional" than any other sort, but referencing it as such enhanced its chances of acceptance by modernists (even, perhaps, by the Eameses). To refer to it as the use of "fresh, pretty, colorful ephemera," as did Alison Smithson, may have been more honest and certainly focused attention on the embrace of elements of design previously outside the canons of "good design" (including "the Woolworth's plastic Christmas decoration and . . . the cheap Mexicana and candles available to American tourists").[39] Alison and Peter Smithson described the Eames House as a "cultural gift parcel" whose bright wrapper "made most people—especially Americans—throw the contents away as not sustaining!"[40] Yet the contents formed one of the best examples of one of the Eameses' most significant contributions to twentieth-century design—a contribution that stands well within Frank Lloyd Wright's understanding of decoration as something that "makes use more charming and comfort more appropriate."[41]

The designer George Nelson was one of the first to comment on Eames "functioning decoration," stating in 1949 that Eames room settings were more artistic statements about new ways of viewing objects than concrete suggestions for placing furniture.[42] Nelson was referring to the display at An Exhibition for Modern Living; however, the point held true for the Carson Pirie Scott window display of 1950. Though these room settings were at the forefront of new developments in using cut-out shapes, blown-up photographs, and a variety of objects to produce decorative compositions within which to display commercial goods, they were not unique. For example, the Saarinen furniture shown at the Carson Pirie Scott store was displayed within an equally abstract assemblage of objects designed by Saarinen himself, Herbert Matter, and Florence Knoll.[43] The influence of Matter on the Eameses has been mentioned in chapter 1 and is referenced below, but it was the Eameses rather than Saarinen or Matter who went on to develop this decorative approach to the display of objects.

Esther McCoy pointed to certain Herman Miller Furniture Company advertisements of the 1950s for Eames furniture (advertisements over which Charles and Ray had considerable control) as another early manifestation of these developments.[44] She commented on the light and mobile qualities of the Eames pieces in the firm's 1952 sales catalog ("They played Klee to Nelson's Braque") and on how they were presented as "fragmented, wrenched out of context," and she argued that all the objects chosen to accompany them either confused any sense of scale or "purposely introduced an alien object which diverted attention from the furniture, as for instance the large paper butterfly dropped prettily on the floor of an aisle between rows of storage cabinets; the rock on top of one case in the foreground." She continued: "It was a technique out of cinema and one which they were to use later in films—odd juxtapositions that shocked the eye into seeing. What is more haunting, for instance, than the black paper bird poised on one frame of a calculated jumble of shells of wire chairs? Yet it suggested the similarities of the centers of gravity of two very different doubly-curved objects, animate and inanimate. Tough conceptions surrounded with prettiness."[45]

In 1966 a group of British designers and writers produced a special issue of *Architectural Design* that drew attention to the extent to which the Eameses had altered the aesthetic ground rules of modernism: "In the 1950s the Eames' [*sic*] moved design away from the machine aesthetic and bicycle technology, on which it had lived since the 1920s, into the world of the cinema-eye and the technology of the production aircraft; from the world of the painters into the world of the layout-men."[46] The new aesthetic was as "high-tech" as any other, in that it celebrated mass-produced everyday objects, but it was less homogeneous and less dull. It was design seen through the eye of a camera or, rather, design by those whose eyes were used to composing or picking out images to be captured on film. It relied on carefully selected juxtapositions of objects or groups of objects to produce "extra-cultural surprise" and a "wide-eyed wonder of seeing the culturally disparate together and so happy with each other."[47]

Robert Venturi, architect, designer, and high priest of postmodernism, also noted in the 1960s the degree to which the Eameses placed large numbers of objects in interiors and exhibitions. Applauding their reintroduction of "good old Victorian clutter,"[48] he recognized far more than they ever did that this aesthetic of accretion and proliferation was the antithesis of minimalist modernism.[49] For Venturi, the wonderful thing about the Eameses was that "modern architects wanted everything neat and clean and they came along and spread eclectic assemblages over an interior."[50] The implication was that the wheel had turned full circle, but no one knew better than Venturi the difference between the grouping of objects in an Eames interior, composed by the joint effort of an abstract artist turned designer (Ray) and a designer/photographer/architect (Charles), and that in a nineteenth-century bourgeois interior. But Venturi had a valid point, and in terms of interior design modernism was never the same again.

"Functioning decoration" drew on a broad range of sources relating to decoration, design, representation, and collecting. The Smithsons' references to objects from wildly different cultures sitting happily with one another and to "wide eyed wonder" today read as somewhat naive and as portentously postmodern. It is easy to forget that the use of objects from different cultures and periods to decorate interiors has a long history, dating back at least to the sixteenth century in Europe (where it became established practice in the Romantic interiors of the early nineteenth century).[51] The use of antiques and objets d'art in interior design was a well-established element of Western culture by the middle of the twentieth century, and Eames interiors are nothing if not part of the grand Romantic tradition. The Romantic interior, defined as including objects of aesthetic or historic interest from earlier periods, began to flourish in the early nineteenth century, when the emergent antiques trade catered to the needs of antiquarians and "nicknackitarians" alike. Some of what was collected in the hundred-odd years before the Eames House was rare and expensive. At the 1823 sale of William Beckford's famous eclectic collection, for instance, King George IV and the Marquis of Westminster were both outbid for the famous "Borghese Table"[52]; however, in remote places (and in early-nineteenth-century Europe and America "remote" was a relative term) "quaint" items could be picked up for a song. There was a growing market in Britain for old, commonplace items from the 1820s, and the fashion spread to Europe and the United States. Sir Walter Scott, an important influence on the Romantic interior, complained that all one needed to set up as an antiquary was "a bag or two of hobnails, a few odd shoe buckles, cashiered kail pots, and fire-irons declared incapable of service . . . a sheaf or two of penny ballads and broadsides"[53]—all commonplace objects of the sort admired by the Eameses. Not all the objects in the Eameses' "functioning decoration" were commonplace or old—but many were, and nostalgia formed part of their appeal, just as it did for Sir Walter Scott and the less sophisticated collectors to whom he felt so superior.

One of the individuals most responsible for popularizing the Romantic interior in the United States was Washington Irving, who visited Sir Walter Scott and wrote about his house and collection. Irving also wrote about the house of George Lucy at Charlecote, Warwickshire, the historical and literary associations of which furnished him with "food for curious and amusing speculation."[54] Irving's own interiors at Sunnyside, the Tarrytown house he furnished in the 1830s, were less grand and featured simple but old objects,[55] the interest in which increased immensely after celebrations of the American centennial promoted Colonial Revival styles in architecture and design.[56] And from the 1890s on Edith Wharton and her decorator, Ogden Codman, did much to promote the collection of "well-chosen" objects, which they thought gave a room its crowning glory.[57]

The room in which the "best" objects were displayed was the parlor, described in 1888 as a shrine "into which is placed all that is most precious."[58] Surely this is the room Venturi had in mind when he referred to the Eameses' bringing back "good old Victorian clutter." In these "memory palaces," domesticity and culture fused, or at least met, in varying degrees of comfort.[59] The parlor was the place for visitors to take tea and engage in conversation or amateur theatre—just as in the Eames House. It housed objects that delighted the knowledgeable eye in terms of the technical skills involved in their making, visual puns, memories, and other associations which transformed even the most ordinary things into potent symbols.[60] Katherine Grier notes that in Victorian culture "ordinary people used objects to create dense webs of connections to their culture and to society."[61] The Eameses did something similar with their interiors. If pianos, music corners, and items brought back from travels signified culture and cosmopolitanism in late-nineteenth-century America, the Eamesian equivalents included African stools, Chinese masks, Japanese pottery, Indian chairs, and the almost-obligatory Thonet bentwood chair. The Victorian parlor's precious collections of shells, minerals, insects, butterflies, coins, or miniature paintings, which signified learning and culture, also had equivalents in the Eameses' Japanese combs, Chinese masks, toys from all over the world, and stones. More personal parlor mementos opened the way for expressions of identity and explorations of nostalgia; so did "functioning decoration," which took objects from earlier periods of American history, from other countries,

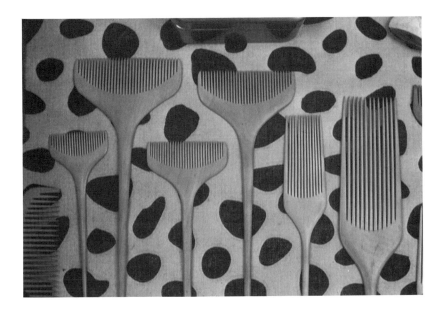

and from non-modernist contemporary design practice and, in the Eames House and the Herman Miller showrooms, mixed them with "found objects" and contemporary furnishings. That this was regarded as not unacceptable, and even as visually attractive and indicative of a certain desirable cultural capital, testifies to the strength of eclecticism and Romanticism within American interior design.

The Eameses' "functioning decoration" was also firmly rooted in the Arts and Craft movement and in those tendencies within modern art and design that opposed strict functionalism and never wholly adopted minimalism as an all-embracing aesthetic or philosophy. The romanticism and the radicalism of the Arts and Craft movement encouraged looking to past societies for examples of preferred ways of living. Eileen Boris has pointed out that in early-twentieth-century America seventeenth-century New Mexico and fourteenth-century England offered "primitivists" and medievalists examples of societies where craft work was supposedly integrated with the whole of life[62]—a position that underpinned every activity in the Eames Office. The Arts and Crafts impulse was to offer something different to the contemporary urban dweller, to provide a sanctuary in the harsh new industrial world. Charles Keeler, the California poet-naturalist, went so far as to recommend the elimination of all factory-made accessories, "in order that your dwelling may not be typical of American commercial supremacy but rather of your own fondness for things that have been created as a response to your love of that which is good and simple and fit for daily companionship."[63] The "functioning decoration" of Arts and Craft interiors might reference the past, but it also had to relate to present needs. Frank Lloyd Wright's studio, for example, was admired because the objects therein—"a choice bit of plaster, an apt motto, or a floral arrangement"—provided the "right sort of inspiration, which recognizes the wondrous beauty of the works of the past, while at the same time it lives in the world of to-day and cares for its simplest flowers."[64] Eames interiors did much the same in mid-century America.

The Arts and Crafts emphasis on life's "simplest flowers" was extended by Lethaby (the movement's figurehead after Morris's death in 1896) into a persuasive philosophy of fitness for use and an insistence that the very essence of civilization lay in caring about simple, everyday things. The admiration of the commonplace led to the fetishization of the everyday object and to expansive and democratic definitions of "art," both of which informed the Eameses' attitudes toward their work. Lethaby insisted that a work of art was simply "a well made thing," "all worthy handicrafts," and the "well doing of what needs doing" and argued that the shaping of a loaf of bread was "art," as was "laying the table nicely."[65] No one else in the history of twentieth-century design gave more prominence to such apparently simple tasks than Lethaby—except perhaps the Eameses (as anyone who has eaten a meal at a table prepared by Ray can testify). Indeed, it could be argued that if anyone carried on the Lethaby tradition in the United States it was Charles and Ray Eames. Such activities had, of course, been undertaken by women for years and years without being considered art, and Lethaby realized that modern society was too concerned with notions of "genius" and "great performers" to appreciate the common things of life designed and executed by common people. There was no overnight transformation in attitudes toward "women's" crafts, but Lethaby's insistence on equating them with oil painting or marble statuary encouraged new conceptions of them, as did his belief that they were of central importance in any civilized society.[66]

At the turn of the century, the ever-modest Lethaby probably knew more about handicrafts than anyone in the Western world. The movement was steeped in admiration for craft work; Eileen Boris astutely

4.20 Eames plywood
chairs and table, with table
setting by Ray Eames, c.
1949. Used in Herman
Miller Furniture Company
advertisements in the
1950s.

remarks that by decorating in an Arts and Crafts manner members of the American artistic intelligentsia could "become part of a historic tradition of craftsmanship."[67] It is my contention that the Eameses also brought something of this reaching across time and across cultures to their interiors—and to films such as *Tops*, which features tops from a variety of places and periods. Collections and the practice of collection varied enormously, but in early-twentieth-century America craft ideals were generally regarded as residing in medieval European artifacts, in the products of the colonial settlers, in European peasant crafts, in Native American items, and in the products of the Mission era.

Arts and Crafts interiors were as eclectic as more orthodoxly "bourgeois" ones. A list of items that might be found within the same American "simple life" interior is striking in terms of difference—difference of style, of period, of country of origin—to say nothing of signification; for example, a fifteenth-century Italian majolica plate, a wicker chair, a reproduction Greek or Renaissance statue, a Hispano-Moresque jug, an antique Persian bowl, contemporary American "art" pottery, blue and white oriental pottery, old Delft, an oriental rug, a Native American rug, and a stag's head might all be included in one interior.[68] There was considerable emphasis on things local, on the vernacular. While looking to the traditions of the indigenous peoples to evoke simplicity and harmony in the home, Gustav Stickley, Charles Keeler, and others prominent in the movement recommended the peculiarly American versions of European peasant design traditions, including patchwork quilts from the Appalachian mountains, hand-braided rugs from Massachusetts, and Pequot rugs from Norwich Town, Connecticut, which referenced America's white settler past and the values represented by Teddy Roosevelt (a political folk hero to many in the Arts and Crafts movement). The keen interest in Native American products evoked a pre-industrial world at one with nature and the outdoors. These items appealed to the strong masculinist element within the "simple life" movement, but there was also considerable admiration (much of it from white middle-class women) of the decorative work of "women of the red race of America."[69] In general, baskets, bowls, and blankets were regarded as particularly worthy of attention,[70] an opinion still held by the Eameses and others in the middle of the twentieth century. The tastes of the American craft revivalists were catholic, and they saw no contradiction in looking to Europe and the Orient as well as to indigenous sources for inspiration in the creation of a distinctly American lifestyle.[71]

As the Arts and Crafts movement grew and extended its scope in the early twentieth century, a worldwide network was established of designers, design reformers, teachers, craft workers, anthropologists, ethnographers, museum curators, missionaries, and sundry philanthropists who took a serious and scholarly interest in the commonplace and ceremonial objects of "peasant" or "primitive" societies, from Bosnia to Borneo and from Latvia to Latin America.[72] There was a growing appreciation of "primitive art"—especially by modern artists, psychologists, and educationalists who saw in it the same "untutored" qualities as in children's art. What had hitherto been perceived as crude in both children's and "primitive" art came to be regarded as expressive. A flood of scholarly studies illustrated a variety of artifacts, drawings, and paintings from so-called uncivilized societies and equated the qualities revealed in them with those expressed in children's artistic endeavors. While the interest produced more scholarship than ever before and removed some of the mystique surrounding concepts of the professional and the genius, it extended the myth of the child-like primitive.[73] In the interwar years, private and museum collections of such items grew apace; the postwar collecting activities of Alexander and Susan Girard and many other modern artists, designers, and intellectuals relate to this often-forgotten earlier tradition.[74]

What is surprising about the items the Eameses used in their interiors is just how many were craft items of the sort admired in the years 1890–1930. The fact that the Eameses collected, preserved, and displayed some objects "that normally escape preservation"[75] was not new in itself; they simply found more and different objects (new "others," if you like) to preserve and to fetishize. Their use of desert weeds to decorate exhibitions of furniture and their own home was new, but there were cultural equivalents in other periods; it could be argued that the desert weed was to an Eameses interior what the peacock feather was to an Aesthetic interior of the late nineteenth century.

But collecting the "primitive" was (and is) not unproblematic, partly because it was viewed as exotic. Edward Said has shown that the scholarly study of peoples and objects within colonial and imperialist cultures enforces rather than redeems the colonialism or imperialism and that the study of difference or "otherness" validates feelings of superiority, no matter that some of the individuals involved in the "scientific" study and aesthetic appreciation of those cultures might be deemed radical within their own culture and not unsympathetic to the plight of the "natives."[76] In the United States, whole cultures were viewed as "other" and as exotic. Opinions are divided on Charles Lummis's attitudes toward Native American and Hispanic cultures, but even Eileen Boris, who manages to say more nice things about Lummis than other radical historians, admits that he was no different from those other folklorists and preservationists whose collections of indigenous artifacts ironically transformed such cultures into phenomena romanticized by urban elites.[77] The Eameses, the Girards, and other "artistic" collectors of the third quarter of the twentieth century did not see themselves in this role any more than did Lummis, yet they were part of the same process of transformation. Today it is more acceptable that the "others" should speak for themselves.[78] But what of the objects? Can they really "speak for themselves," let alone for the cultures that produced them? Do they have they what Charles and Ray Eames called a "timeless appropriateness"[79] (an ahistorical concept, much beloved by modernists and designers, of which I am skeptical, though I recognize that objects can and do carry and take on myriad meanings)?

It could be argued that the Eameses differed from the Arts and Crafts supporters of the early twentieth century in being firmly committed to the cause of industrial design and production and at the same time valuing craft work, but two points need to be borne in mind here. First, in the interwar years several prominent supporters of Arts and Craft ideals and design reform—including George C. Booth, the founder of the Cranbrook Academy—held positions similar to that of the Eameses. William Lethaby himself was favorable to new materials and not hostile to machine production. One of Lethaby's disciples, Harry Peach, personally collected more than 3000 craft objects from all over the world between 1918 and 1936, and his collection would have sent the Eameses into ecstasy so "matter of fact" yet beautiful were the objects; yet Peach was also one of Britain's leading advocates of the mass machine production of quality everyday goods at prices affordable to the vast majority of the population.[80] Second, the similarities between the Eameses and Lethaby, Peach, Booth, and others aside, the fact that the Eameses were industrial designers does not mean that their attitudes toward "folk" and "primitive" crafts were any less romantic than those held by people completely antagonistic to the machine.

I am constantly struck by similarities between the objects collected by Harry Peach and those in the Eameses' collection. Charles and Ray would have admired the beaded bamboo hat from Borneo, the German peasant pottery (made near Jena at a workshop used by the Bauhaus when it was at Weimar), the combs from Nyassa, the grass fans from Australia, and the basketwork from all over the world. Above all they would have loved the papier-mâché work and textiles from India and the toys, marionettes, puppets, and dolls of every description.[81]

"Mexicana," which the Eameses sometimes used in their "functioning decoration," gained popularity in the United States through the Arts and Crafts movement. The Eameses and the Girards (particularly the latter) stand in the tradition established by Lummis and other white middle-class seekers of the "simple life" who established the Southwest Museum in Pasadena and who contributed to archaeological scholarship and architectural preservation at the turn of the century.[82] The interest in the "folk art" of the American Southwest developed at the height of the Arts and Crafts movement, when local vernacular architecture and design were seen as authentic, honest, rational, and appropriate to local needs and conditions. It was, as I have already suggested, extremely romantic and, particularly in the case of the revival of interest in the indigenous peoples of the American Southwest, highly selective and inconsistent. There was a marked shift in the 1880s from an early interest in "Indian" rights and education among "simple life" enthusiasts and do-gooders to a romanticization of the "Spanish" past (which focused on the supposedly halcyon days of the powerful Spanish Dons rather than on the Mexican peasants).[83] The mythmaking was as spectacular as its chosen subject matter; however, it hid ugly truths, including the fact that Los Angeles's first fiesta (in 1894) was organized to divert attention from serious labor unrest.[84] By 1900 the "Mission Revival," which instituted in the United States a new but supposedly old institution, the "Spanish Fiesta," was in full swing.[85] Offering the plain and simple life and also the decorative and the exotic (the best of all Arts and Crafts worlds), it remained a strong design influence in the interwar years.

Radical critics tend to focus on the lack of authenticity in cultural revivalist policies. But the question of cultural authenticity is a tricky one.[86] Who is to say what is authentic? Certainly not liberal (even radical) outsiders, whose own critiques imply that outsiders cannot know what is authentic. When does an invented or reconstituted "fiesta" take on its own energies, become "owned" or even "subverted" by its participants rather than organized by the city fathers, and begin to make it own distinctive contribution to the popular culture of urban America? Such questioning allows a less censorious view of the appropriation of ethnic arts and crafts by outsiders for reuse in alien environments than would have been held even a decade ago; however, there is no disputing the fact that the Eameses, the Girards, and thousands of others took objects from their environments and transferred them to others.

Aesthetic influences from Mexican and Chicano popular culture also touched the Eameses via another route. Recent writing on women, memory, identity, and designed objects within these cultures—particularly on household altars—has emphasized excess, display, ornamentation, elaboration, textures, sensuous surfaces, and patterns and has noted that such an excessive aesthetic is disruptive of the symbolic order.[87] It is certainly the antithesis of minimalist and spartan versions of modernism—and all the qualities listed as contributing to it exist in the Eameses' "functioning decoration." Another description of the latter might be "[the] process of collecting and creatively assembling odd or seemingly disparate objects into a functional integrated whole," which Melissa Meyer and Miriam Schapiro call "femmage," and which is evident in many traditional women's arts and crafts.[88] As Meyer and Schapiro define it, 'femmage' is simply a variant on 'collage' ("pictures assembled from assorted materials"), a high-art term "invented in the twentieth century to describe an activity with an ancient history."[89] Thus, in her modernist collages as well as in her "functioning decoration," Ray Eames could draw, consciously or unconsciously (mainly the latter, I suspect), on rich, well-established decorative traditions in "women's art" that celebrate the disparate, the personal, the fragment, and the found item in an aesthetic of addition and composition.

Jennifer González has recently illustrated the importance in representations of memory and identity of objects and arrangements of objects that "reflect private identification and projected desires" within physical sites, often domestic spaces.[90] The Eameses' "functioning decoration" was also a vehicle for such representations, and it is no coincidence that the Eameses (Ray in particular) used private objects—souvenirs in the original meaning of the term[91]—not only in their small domestic arrangements of objects but also on tackboards and in their exhibitions (see chapter 6). "Functioning decoration" was quickly established as a popular mode of interior decoration, not simply because it was a cheap way of decorating an anonymous interior but also because it offered an accessible process of personalization. What were seen by some in the 1950s and the 1960s as unimportant and sentimental gestures—a pressed flower, a letter, a pottery vase purchased on holiday, a heart-shaped object, a child's drawing, a greeting card—can also be seen as significant bearers of memory and nostalgia.

Contemporary artwork was also an influence on "functioning decoration." Surrealism, which had a considerable impact in the United States in the 1930s, deliberately juxtaposed apparently incongruous objects in an attempt to indicate unconscious and contradictory dreams and desires. The Surrealists and those who would later be known as Abstract Expressionists were fascinated by Native American art as they searched for material expressions of the primitivist myth.[92] Jackson Pollock was especially intrigued by Navajo sand paintings, and in the late 1930s he researched them by reading ethnographic reports prepared for the Smithsonian Institution in the nineteenth century, thus taking on the role of a scholar as well as an artist.[93] In the 1930s and the early 1940s there were several exhibitions of Native American Art in the United States, and other exhibitions that concentrated on other "primitivisms" (including African, Aztec, Mayan, and Inca art and design).[94] It seems highly unlikely that Charles and Ray were not reasonably well informed about various aspects of "primitive" art by the time they met. Charles had visited Mexico and collected some craft objects there, but Ray appears to have been more interested in avant-garde painting and sculpture than in craftwork before she went to Cranbrook, although she had a long-standing interest in small decorative objects and dolls.[95]

Collages and three-dimensional assemblages bear the most obvious relation to "functioning decoration" in the nature of their construction, but certain Miró paintings that consist of colorful compositions of extremely disparate objects and shapes decoratively arranged across the

canvas with little regard for scale also relate to "functioning decoration."
Miró's *Carnival D'Arlequi* (1924–25), for example, is rather like the
Eameses' film *Parade* (1952) in that it depicts a colorful procession of objects celebrating in carnival spirit.[96] P*aisatge Català (El Cacador)* (1923–
24) and *Une Étoile Caresse Le Sein D'Une Négresse* (1938) are both
assemblages of shapes with handwriting (which, since it is not normally
found in painting, adds "extra-cultural surprise").[97] The graphic design of
Herbert Matter, which involved juxtaposing objects with an eye to their
decorative effect and to contrasts in scale and space,[98] was a direct influence on "functioning decoration." In 1946 Matter, who had worked in the
Eames Office since 1943, prepared an assemblage of photographs and
three-dimensional objects illustrating plywood forms and some panels explaining the production of Eames molded plywood furniture, some of
which were assemblages of different parts of that furniture. The 1946 article in *Arts & Architecture* that featured the furniture included photographs of Matter's collages; Matter also designed the article and the cover
(another collage). His influence on Ray's work for *Arts & Architecture* has
been discussed in chapter 1, but of particular relevance to "functioning
decoration" is his ability to let objects speak as decoration—something
Ray was also able to do.

The Eameses used a wide but particular range of objects in their
"functioning decoration," items they had collected for a variety of reasons
and from all over the world. However, like many others who took a serious interest in craftwork and worried about its survival in a period of intense technological development, the Eameses did not regard themselves
as collectors. They claimed that much of what they collected was not of
monetary value in the art market (although that was never true of their
Hofmann paintings and several other pieces). But even collectors or accu-
mulators of seemingly valueless, trivial, and extremely personal objects
are subject to complex regulations related to taste, desire, and broader
socio-political considerations, and the Eameses were no exception.[99] They
were connoisseurs in the best sense of the word, i.e., people who know.
They knew an enormous amount about objects, and each had a keen sense
of critical judgement, although Charles once joked that he might not always know "good" but "I sure know terrible."[100] At the end of the day,
however, they were collectors.

4.21 Assemblage of photographs and objects, New Furniture Designed by Charles Eames exhibition, Museum of Modern Art, New York, 1946. Herbert Matter for Eames Office.

Not all the objects the Eameses collected fell outside the established categories of museum classification systems ("fine," "decorative," "ethnic," "folk"), but many did. Although fewer of them would escape the attention of auction houses and museums today, the feathers, chalks, marbles, nicely packaged candies, fresh flowers and plants, wrapping paper, ribbons, and other such items were, by and large, of little monetary value and generally regarded as of little "cultural" value. What the Eameses did was give each and every one of them "added value" from the ways they were wrapped, filled, decorated, or positioned—very often next or near to items more obviously "collectable," or placed in series for more impact.

In their interior arrangements the Eameses often used objects they regarded as "special"—a Kandinsky painting or a piece of African sculpture, for example—and which most viewers would also recognize as "special" and as of high artistic quality. However (and more interesting in terms of "extra-cultural surprise"), they also used objects, such as a glass crystal chandelier or candelabrum, that at the time did not have high status as "art" in America. Nor were these objects exotic in any of the accepted senses of the word, being mainly associated with the design

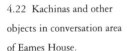
4.22 Kachinas and other objects in conversation area of Eames House.

4.23 Living area of Eames
House, c. 1976.

repertoire of white bourgeois taste. I can still remember my own surprise and unease when I first saw the candelabrum in the interior of the Eames House. I was surprised partly because, in my ignorance, I knew the Eameses mainly as the designers of "modernist" buildings and furniture, but the unease came from my own cultural predilections and preoccupations at the time. I thought I had wider views of and interests in the history of taste than many people, and fairly eclectic personal tastes—yet here was an object—a glass crystal candelabrum—that made me feel strangely uncomfortable. The Eameses were saying "Look at this object anew!" I was not sure I wanted to, but look again I did.

Alexander Girard undoubtedly influenced the activities of the Eameses as serious collectors of quality craftwork, particularly from India, Mexico, and New Mexico. Extremely well informed about handicrafts, Girard, together with Dorothy Liebes and Jim Thompson, played a crucial role in the revival of interest in handicrafts in 1950s modernist America and in "infusing American culture with the spice of exotic expansiveness."[101] The discerning tourist met the discerning modernist, and tasteful interiors full of "color" and gaiety were the order of the day. India, Thailand, Nepal, and remote parts of South America entered the living rooms of the design-conscious through the courtesy of people such as

4.24 Sofa in living area of Eames House, 1983. Arrangement by Ray Eames.

Girard. This architect-designer-showman-scholar was an important influence on the Eameses, encouraging their decorative and flamboyant tendencies.[102]

In 1949, when the Eameses took part in An Exhibition for Modern Living (designed and curated by Girard), they were already using disparate objects as decorative items—in this case a homemade paper kite, paper flowers, plants and real flowers, a Mexican mask, Japanese tea bowls, a pottery vase, and a photographic mural featuring a close-up of a piece of bark.[103] In other words, they were mixing "old" objects with new ones and items from different cultures with commonplace and novel items from their own. There were to be other collaborations with Girard, including the exhibition and film Textiles and Ornamental Arts of India (1955), the Nehru exhibition (1965),[104] and the film *Day of the Dead* (made in Mexico in 1957). Girard's enthusiasm for Mexican "folk art," particularly that made every year for All Souls' Day, provided not only the inspiration for *Day of the Dead* but also the money—he managed to persuade the Museum of International Folk Art in Santa Fe, where he lived, to fund a research and collecting trip and the making of the film.[105]

The Eameses' continued contact with Alexander Girard and their increasing familiarity with the collection built up by Girard and his wife Susan and beautifully displayed in their Santa Fe home extended the Eameses' acquaintance with "folk" and "ethnic" art and design and encouraged Ray's already exuberant use of color and her penchant for using objects decoratively. Illustrations of the Girards' adobe house show many groupings of small objects in decorative patterns and compositions in the manner so loved by Ray.[106] The Girards' functioning decoration informed that of the Eameses and suggested to Ray ways in which the decorative and compositional talents she showed in her graphic and textile design could be applied to interior design.[107]

There is no doubt that the Eameses foraged other cultures for objects to use in decoration. Against such acts of cultural appropriation, however, we should set the fact that objects removed from their larger schemes of meaning take on other meanings as they are redefined within different (often private or more local) schemes. Rarely does an object have a single, specific identity, and one of functioning decoration's strengths was its responsiveness to individual interpretation. In this there are parallels between the large number of objects (and written texts) in an Eames exhibition and the large number of objects in a domestic interior.

It was through displays of objects (some very personal) and the intimate scale of the decoration that the Eameses personalized their prefabricated house and transformed it into a home. This personalizing element in the Eames aesthetic is little different in essence from the personalizing or "customizing" of one of the main mass-produced icons of the twentieth century: the automobile. The culture of customized cars, which eventually gained the status of folk art, began in Southern California in the 1940s and was part of a more widespread attempt to deal with the problems of anonymity raised by much of contemporary design.[108] The question was what to make individual and how to do it. The Eameses were never remotely interested in personalizing automobiles—indeed, they celebrated their anonymity.

In general, the Eameses did not customize an individual object, such as a table or a chair, by adding decoration.[109] The personalizing of the exterior of the prefabricated Eames House by the addition of a unique composition of colored infill and glass panels was an exception to what appears to have been their rule of not adding to, altering, or personalizing existing individual objects (if a domestic residence can be classified as an object). Another exception was the customizing of one of the eucalyptus trees outside the house. The Eameses were never afraid to add other objects to existing ones; thus, although they did not customize in the sense of altering a piece or decorating its surfaces, they sometimes so transformed an item that it was unrecognizable. For example, they used the sofa in their house and the one in their office as canvases on which to make patterns and compositions. Both sofas were personalized, but the one in the house was transformed. Other examples of customizing objects include the addition of objects to the Hang-It-All and the witty addition of an ostrich plume to a whale sculpture.

The glass panels on the exterior of the Eames House formed a series of decorative variations on the idea of translucency.[110] The transparent, opaque, and semi-opaque panels of glass (and, in the studio, wired glass) formed a pattern in relation to one another and the solid infill panels. An outline of a tree was etched on the panels above the living room's sliding doors, and additional patterns came from the play of light and shadows of the trees on the glass. According to Geoffrey Holroyd, the effect of the interplay of light and shade, of changing patterns, and of representations of trees and real trees was to "destroy an articulated glass

4.25 Decorated eucalyptus tree, Eames House, 1950.

volume and to create out of it a context sympathetic to the many objects placed inside."[111] In other words, this interplay mediated between the contrasting aesthetic elements—the minimalist structure clad with panels and the rich decorative detail of a host of small objects. To a degree, structure, space, and content blend in the Eames House; however, the house and its contents also work against each other, offering the viewer another version, or other versions, of "extra-cultural surprise."

The Eameses wrote the display of objects into the brief for their house in 1945, specifying a "large unbroken area for pure enjoyment of space in which objects can be placed and taken away . . . driftwood, sculpture, mobiles, plants, constructions, etc."[112] As happens in many homes, more objects were added than taken away over the years. Photographs taken in 1950, shortly after they moved in, reveal (as one might expect of people moving from an apartment to a house) less furniture and fewer objects than in later years, when they actively "collected"; however, it is important to note that the aesthetic of collage and addition in their work was already established by that date and that the accretion was rapid. The film *House After Five Years of Living* (1955) illustrates just how many objects entered the house in the early years. In 1956 Charles stated that it had "gotten to be like an old cave to us."[113] To visitors, Edward Carpenter noted, it seemed like Aladdin's cave, full of "lovingly positioned collections of shells, baskets, blankets, mats, candles, pillows, pots, plants, sculpture, chairs . . . which add texture, form space, play with the light that comes subtly, with constant change, through the house's transparent and translucent shell."[114]

"Object overload," like the "information overload" of their films and exhibitions, came to be an essential part of the Eameses' approach to interior design, not a whimsical adjunct. Photographs taken in 1950 show Japanese mats and paper lanterns, plants, rugs, two Hofmann paintings, and an abstract stabile of sheet steel by Alexander Calder. The paintings, the sculpture, and the Japanese simplicity suggest the house of an art lover, as do the desert weeds. Although the latter were indigenous and therefore appropriate in an Arts and Crafts sense, they were not within the accepted repertoire of 1950s "good design," and therefore they came as something of an "extra-cultural surprise" to visitors. Also unexpected in a minimalist steel frame was the bright Chinese paper butterfly hovering high over the living area, drawing the eye up that large space and adding a focal point. When they moved in (on Christmas Eve, 1949), Charles and Ray placed other oriental paper decorations in the house, suspending some of these from the ceiling to decorate the space above the traditional Christmas tree.[115] The tree (dressed by Ray) stood on Japanese mats, and near it were placed white candles in candlesticks and an arrangement of old toys, including a toy train. This hinted at the richness of displays to come. In contrast to the light paper decorations and the light desert weeds, a simple but solid terra-cotta pot was suspended from the ceiling. Hanging near some Hofmann paintings, and filled with flowers, it offered a simple, "homely," traditional image in contrast to the internationalism and modernism of the bold abstract art. Small decorative objects were displayed on the shelving in the seating alcove, an intimate

space with a magical ceiling lit by a multitude of tiny lights. In 1950 the
seating had only a few pillows and one small rug for adornment, whereas
by the late 1950s both sections were covered with "ethnic" blankets. In
1950 the furniture included a Saarinen Womb Chair, later to be replaced
by an Eames Lounge Chair and Ottoman and two carved and painted Indian chairs. Later the small, low Eames plywood table with wooden legs
was replaced by one with metal legs, and the small wood unit from the
Eames case goods system by an antique wooden trunk on a stand. The
DCM chairs placed there in 1949 were joined by a Sofa Compact, some
African stools (two of which came from the Wilders, who had "swopped"
them for the Calder stabile[116]), and a host of decorative items, including
candlesticks and masks. Flowers also featured in Eames "functioning
decoration"; indeed, every individual floral arrangement was "functioning
decoration" in miniature in the sense that it was a composition of objects, often quite disparate in size, shape, color, smell, degree of maturity,
and texture.

Every arrangement was extremely carefully thought out, down to
the last detail, and many variations were tried before Charles and Ray felt
satisfied with the composition. The smaller objects were easier to move
around, and Ray was constantly shifting them until they looked just
right.[117] The effect of the individual placing of objects may have looked
informal, but every object was placed with great precision. The casualness
was carefully constructed; this was artifice under the guise of artlessness.
Audrey Wilder remembers admiring the many beautiful objects in the
house of these "two very special people," but her overriding memory of it
is how neat and precise everything was[118]—hardly surprising, since before an informal evening at home with the Wilders the Eameses sent
members of their staff to ensure that the candles had burned down to an
appropriate length and that every pillow and each plant was in the proper
place.[119]

The simplest of objects were often used as "functioning decoration," sometimes in combination for added effect. The pillows' main purpose was decorative; they formed small compositions and were, at the
same time, part of larger ones. Figure 4.26 shows three pillows of the
same size placed on top of one another, on a rug on the floor, offering contrasts in color and tone. At other times, more pillows were used and the
grouping was placed slightly differently on the rug and in relation to the

other objects. On the Sofa Compact in the late 1960s and for much of the 1970s, two patchwork pillows complemented each other and contrasted with a larger striped one.

The African stools in the Eames House provided contrasts in themselves, as did the large and small Indian chairs. The juxtapositions with most immediate impact in terms of mediating between structure and contents include the objects hanging from the staircase, which was made from industrial parts. In the early days a wooden sculpture was hung from it to offset its standardized nature; later this was replaced by a plump cherub (figure 4.27). Both are startling juxtapositions, and the latter still offers "extra-cultural surprise" to visitors. The bell by the front door (figure 4.28) works in a similar way, the "folk art" object at once signaling entrance and personalizing an anonymous place and object, as does the Native American sculpture from the Northwest that hangs from the ceiling in the main living area (figure 4.29). The latter draws the eye up and holds it more firmly than the floating butterflies of earlier years, and its pre-industrial and "ethnic" references contrast with the modern corrugated industrial roofing material, the ribs of which run at right angles to the sculpture. The right angle is repeated where the long, thin ladder running from floor to ceiling meets the horizontal roof span and where the glass wall cuts across the roofing which extends to cover a patio. Together these elements form a complex composition based on linearity and on contrasts between horizontals and verticals, between craft and industrial products, and between elements integral to and those independent of the house's structure.

The floor acted as a canvas. In the later years even the rugs—Navaho, Chinese, and Berber—were layered one upon another, providing contrasts in color, size, and shape. Candlesticks were placed directly on rugs in the 1950s, but later trays or tiles were used as bases for assemblages of objects (which, particularly when they included candlesticks, were reminiscent of a shrine—something which, again, refers to domestic and "female" art forms). Geoffrey Holroyd saw the Eames House as a place wherein "magic totems" defined space and created meanings as well as a conducive environment for the playing out of rituals.[120] The stage-set feel created by some of the Eameses' "functioning decoration" certainly enhances the sense that the space is one in which rituals are observed, and the self-consciousness of the constructed image draws attention to the

4.27 Cherubs hanging
from staircase in Eames
House.

4.28 Bell by front door of
Eames House.

4.29 Native American sculpture suspended from ceiling of Eames House.

role of the objects in establishing structures of meaning. Holroyd noted that the Eameses' functionalist language and discourses did not allow them to articulate the complexities of their creations, and he criticized Charles for describing the house and its contents as "matter-of-fact" because it denied rich and complex relationships between rich and complex objects and also between them and the building.[121] Likening the house to ancient cathedrals and temples, Holroyd went on to draw parallels between their secondary structures, wherein "shrines or tombs combine with furniture and equipment to create another system," and the relationship of items in the Eames House.[122] Robert Venturi's association of Eames assemblages with Victorian interior decoration also references the Eames House as a shrine. Whatever its roots, the Eameses' "functioning decoration" not only made it respectable for modernists to like pretty things[123] but also offered personal memory, identity, cultural, and cross-cultural ensembles that self-consciously carried complex webs of meaning as dense as those of any Victorian parlor.

The Eames House seems to beg comparison with Mies van der Rohe's Farnsworth House (1950), which was planned, built, and furnished around the same time.[124] Both were light, minimalist steel-frame pavilions filled with glass, but there the comparison ends. "Mies," Holroyd wrote, "wants all glass and no clutter; Eames wants clutter; 'functioning decoration.'"[125] One was an aesthetic of reduction, the other of seduction; one an aesthetic of subtraction, the other of addition. If less was more for Mies, *more* was more for the Eameses: "functioning decoration" was much more than the sum of the parts.

While they were considering how to furnish their new home, the Eameses worked on displays for the Herman Miller Furniture Company's new showroom in Los Angeles. Although no attempt was made to create room settings as such, partitions were used to create spaces in which to group furniture. Flowers, plants, magazines, and even a stove were used to suggest how the furniture might look in domestic situations. The old-fashioned stove was a point of visual interest and nostalgia, as was the antique American weathervane lent by Billy Wilder (who also lent his African leopard stool, later to end up in the Eames House).[126] John Entenza lent a Herbert Matter photograph and a Hans Hofmann painting, and the designer John Follis lent a wire sculpture and some bottles from his collection.[127] A Kandinsky painting from the Stendahl Art Galleries vied for dominance with a huge photomural composed of various images of trees. There were also displays of desert weeds and starfish (both much favored by the Eameses) and, in a bedroom, a panel featuring a full sun, a thin crescent moon, and assorted stars. Exactly what two paper butterflies were doing on the "sun and moon" panel I do not know—but that was probably the point; they certainly added surprise.

The office interior that the Eameses designed for the screenwriter Philip Dunne in 1952 contained two walls of "functioning decoration."[128] The first utilized a system of pegs to display a changing array of photographs by Dunne's wife Amanda; the second was a tackboard for family photographs and other mementos. Also in the office were a Saarinen womb chair, a built-in seating unit like the one in the Eames House, a paper kite, some "found" objects (including a large shell and a stone), and the obligatory plants and flowers.[129] In the same year the collage principle was extended to completely covering partition walls in the Herman Miller showrooms with assorted seed packets and pages from the Herman Miller catalog.

4.30 "Functioning decoration" in setting for George Nelson furniture, Herman Miller Furniture Company showroom, 1950.

The range of items used by the Eameses was enormous: buttons, pebbles, stones, matches, pencils, scissors, marbles, fruit, flowers, glass bottles and carboys, terra-cotta plant pots, kachina dolls, English pillboxes, Mexican masks, Chinese kites, Japanese toy cars, Japanese and Belgian wooden combs, Indian fabrics. . . . Some of the objects appeared exotic in Los Angeles or other parts of the United States but were commonplace elsewhere. Some of the juxtapositions were highly novel; others depended for their impact on contrasts of color, shape, size, decoration, or material.

In 1952 the Eameses put a wooden sculpture of a whale from the Pacific Northwest in the Herman Miller showroom. Later they added an orange ostrich plume in lieu of spouting water (figure 4.32). This juxtaposition of two differently exotic objects also brought a dramatic juxtaposition of color—a factor often forgotten in discussions of juxtaposition and extra-cultural surprise. Other combinations of colors and unusual juxtapositions of objects included a large mauve powder puff placed in a Japanese

4.31 Philip Dunne's office
at Twentieth Century Fox,
1952.

ceramic bowl in the Herman Miller showroom and a Mexican glass box filled with balls of colored tissue paper and tied up with gold ribbons.[130]

In 1959, in a display designed for the new Aluminum Group furniture, a papier-mâché tree (complete with birds) was installed in the Herman Miller showroom, along with five shrubs in planters and a mural made from torn-paper collages of trees, to suggest an outdoor atmosphere and reaffirm the appropriateness of the furniture for outdoor living.[131] In contrast, the Eameses used a crystal chandelier—a recent "find"—to symbolize the domestic and to confirm the suitability of the furniture for indoor use.

For the 1963 launch of Tandem Sling Seating, the Eameses tried to create a sense of public space in which to display the new airport seating. However, the most impressive image they used was an enormous photographic mural of the glass-and-iron roof of a German railway station.[132] A café-like ambience was created using La Fonda chairs and tables,[133] the tables beautifully set by Ray to coordinate with different types of food from around the world. This, perhaps more than any other Eames showroom display, attained something of the atmosphere of an Eames exhibition.

The Eameses' last involvement with a showroom interior for Herman Miller came in 1966, when the firm moved its showroom to larger premises in New York. George Nelson was in charge of the overall architecture of the showroom, Alexander Girard arranged the textiles, and the Eameses concentrated on the larger display areas. Olga Gueft remarked that the designers seemed to have turned comedians in their old age and described the showroom as "both poetic and hilariously funny," with "photo murals, pop art and op column sheathings play[ing] one visual pun after another on the amused spectator."[134] The Eameses gave Deborah Sussman and the visiting English designer Rusell Frears a considerable amount of freedom on this project, which involved a series of witty displays. Among the most distinctive features were the coverings of the internal columns, which ranged from cracked mirror glass to a column made up of a stack of chairs.[135] The mirrors in a *trompe l'oeil* photomural reflected other unusual objects, and Sussman and Frears followed the pattern established by the Eameses in 1949 in introducing "special" objects into their display. Karl Gerstner's blue "Light Box," which emitted dots of light, was situated near the very "serious" area displaying educational seating (one of the best-sellers in the contract trade); Roy Lichtenstein's *Shopping Bag* and Robert Watts's *Fish Dinner* also graced the showroom, adding a distinctively up-to-date and "fun" image.[136] Although the Eameses continued to act as consultants on matters related to Herman Miller's Los Angeles showroom for another decade, they did not undertake any other showroom design, restricting their interior design work and "functioning decoration" to exhibitions and their own home.

Many admirers of Charles Eames have been reluctant to accept his role in "functioning decoration" and have sought to absolve him of accusations of clutter and "object overload." But, although there is no doubt that Ray was more of a "decorator," Charles did play a part in the development and the practice of "functioning decoration."

Ray, who had shown an interest in decoration ever since high school, had more flair for composition, collage, and color, and visual excess—all qualities that Charles admired in her work. It is important to

4.33 Herman Miller
Furniture Company
showroom, Los Angeles,
1959.

remember, however, that Charles reveled in celebratory decoration before he met Ray, just as he appreciated Mexican handicrafts before he met her or Alexander Girard. In the early 1930s, he and other "arty" friends in St. Louis once decorated a room for an Easter party by hanging 132 dozen blown and decorated eggs from the ceiling.[137]

Although Ray was more involved with and more skilled at the practice of "functioning decoration," Charles was as obsessed with objects, images, and details as she was. After his death, Ray was fond of quoting him on details: "The details are not details—they make the product. It is, in the end, these details that give the product its life."[138] Charles's interest in the grouping of objects in his photography dates back at least as far as 1942. He certainly loved photographing the Eames House and its "functioning decoration." Although in later years he might have occasionally commented that there were too many objects in the house (though not, of course, to Ray),[139] there can be no question that he was wholeheartedly in favor of an additive aesthetic. This can be seen in both the exterior and the interior of the Eames House. Ray and Charles drew up the brief for the living area (which included space for the display and contemplation of objects) jointly, and those who knew them commented on their shared enthusiasm for the design.[140]

Much of the resistance to accepting that Charles had much of a part to play in "functioning decoration" comes from the fact that decoration was and is seen to be extraneous to modernism and to belong to the woman's sphere of activities: the domestic, the private, the trivial. Certain areas of design were, and continue to be, privileged over others—the public world of exhibitions and learning, for example, over the domestic world of interiors, decoration, and "homemaking." The interior decoration of her home allowed Ray an opportunity to express her femininity in a time-honored tradition and through time-honored skills. It also gave her a large, ongoing project that developed her decorative skills enormously. To state this is not to imply that Charles played no part; it is simply to say that Ray had more input than Charles into what was their longest collaborative project.

Between 1945 and 1978 more than forty major designs or ranges of designs for furniture from the Eames Office went into commercial production. Whether in plywood, plastic, or metal, they all grew out of an
intense concern with new materials and technology and a search for perfect form which took note of elementary ergonomics. A major theme of
these designs is the development of plastic form, from the earliest plywood pieces of the mid 1940s to the fiberglass and wire mesh shells of the
early 1950s and on to the flowing aluminum shapes of 1958, which broke
from the shell form while retaining some plasticity.

More than twenty projects went into production between 1945
and 1955, after which date films and exhibitions took up more of the
Eameses' time and that of their staff. Nevertheless, the period 1956–
1966 saw eleven major furniture projects go into production, including
the Lounge Chair and Ottoman and the Aluminum Group. Though only
six major projects went through to production in the years 1967–1977, it
should be remembered that research and development was extremely important in the Eames Office and that even six projects represented considerable amounts of time, money, and energy.

PLYWOOD FURNITURE

The story of Eames furniture begins with Charles Eames and Eero Saarinen at Cranbrook in 1938. By that date a considerable amount of plywood furniture was being commercially produced in the United States.
There had been more than a decade of sustained and systematic experimentation with and production of plywood furniture, both molded and
cut out, by many of the leading designers of the day, including Gerrit
Rietveld, Marcel Breuer, and Alvar Aalto.

The successful commercial production of molded-plywood furni-
ture dates back to the 1850s, when Henry Belter, a German émigré to the
United States, used heat to bend plywood in three dimensions.[1] However,
Belter's sophisticated technique, which produced up to eight pieces at a

time, does not appear to have been known to the avant-garde designers of the early twentieth century. Molded-plywood chairs were patented in the United States in the late 1860s and the 1870s by Isaac Cole and by the Gardner Company of New York,[2] which went on to manufacture these "genuine American veneer seats" in considerable numbers for the domestic and foreign markets. The Austrian firm of Thonet experimented with bent laminated wood in the 1880s but did not pursue the project.[3] Before World War I plywood was mainly used as a cheap substitute for solid wood and was rarely visible when used in furniture; it was often used in drawers or on the backs of cabinets and wardrobes.[4] However, plywood technology improved during the war, and by the 1920s a considerable amount of plywood furniture was available. Some of the best-known plywood pieces in the United States were the Gardner chairs, or ones similar to them, and the "Lutherma" seats used in tram cars and public waiting rooms.[5]

In the 1920s avant-garde designers recognized the potential of using this "new" material to produce cheap furniture for the masses. The avant-garde's interest in plywood was part of a broader movement to democratize design which had flourished in several countries (particularly Austria, Germany, and Britain) ever since the early years of the twentieth century and which had roots in the Arts and Crafts movement's appreciation of commonplace objects. A host of designers and architects, including Josef Hoffmann, Peter Behrens, Henry Van de Velde, Richard Riemerschmid, Karl Schmidt,[6] Benjamin Fletcher, and J. H. Cuypers, tried bentwood, cane, and even fiberboard in an effort to produce cheap but well-designed everyday objects.[7] Since the late 1920s there had been a concerted drive by modernists to produce commercially viable products in "new" materials, including plywood and tubular steel.

The plywood furniture designed by the architect Heinz Rasch and produced in prototype by the German metal furniture company of L & C Arnold and exhibited in Stuttgart in 1927 and 1928 included a lounge chair with a seat made from a single piece of molded plywood.[8] And in 1927 the architect Gerrit Rietveld designed a fiberboard chair with a one-piece seat; this was later commercially produced in quantity for the Dutch firm of Metz using the much lighter plywood.[9] In both of the aforementioned chairs the plywood seat was screwed to a metal frame, whereas Alvar Aalto, in some of his designs of the early 1930s, suspended

5.1 Chair with one-piece
seat in perforated, molded,
and laminated wood,
manufactured by Gardner
and Company, New York,
from about 1870 to 1920.

a one-piece seat within a frame, thus utilizing the resilience as well as the strength of the material. Rietveld and Rasch continued to experiment in the late 1920s, as did Bauhaus members Per Bücking and Josef Albers,[10] but it was the furniture of Aalto that was to most influence Charles Eames and Eero Saarinen—and, later, Charles and Ray Eames.

In the vanguard of a shift away from "machine aesthetic" modernism, Aalto influenced a new generation of designers in Europe and the United States. He recognized the need for rationality and standardization, but he thought that an exclusive focus on these matters denied the expressive nature of the human imagination. Aalto experimented with various materials (including tubular steel) in his search for appropriate "modern" products, but he came to favor wood, with its long cultural associations with furniture making, for the following reasons:

> The tubular steel chair is surely rational from technical and constructive points of view. It is light, suitable for mass production, and so on. But steel and chromium surfaces are not satisfactory from the human point of view. Steel is too good a conductor of heat. The chromium surface gives too bright reflections of light, and even acoustically is not suitable for a room. The rational methods of creating this furniture style have been on the right track, but the result will be good only if rationalization is exercised in the selection of materials which are most suitable for human use.[11]

The close connections between Alvar Aalto and Eliel Saarinen leave no doubt that Eero Saarinen and Charles Eames were well acquainted with Aalto's plywood furniture. Indeed, the younger Saarinen is known to have owned at least one Aalto chair in the 1930s.[12] In 1938 the Museum of Modern Art held an exhibition of Aalto's furniture, which then toured the United States. His furniture was also shown at the 1939 New York World's Fair in the Aalto-designed Finnish Pavilion.[13] By 1940 Aalto's furniture was greatly admired by design-conscious Americans, who could buy it from at least three outlets in their own country.[14] The Cranbrook pair almost certainly knew the plywood furniture of Marcel Breuer, whose lounge chair for the British firm of Isokon (1936) drew heavily on Aalto and whose side chairs and tables (1935 and 1936)

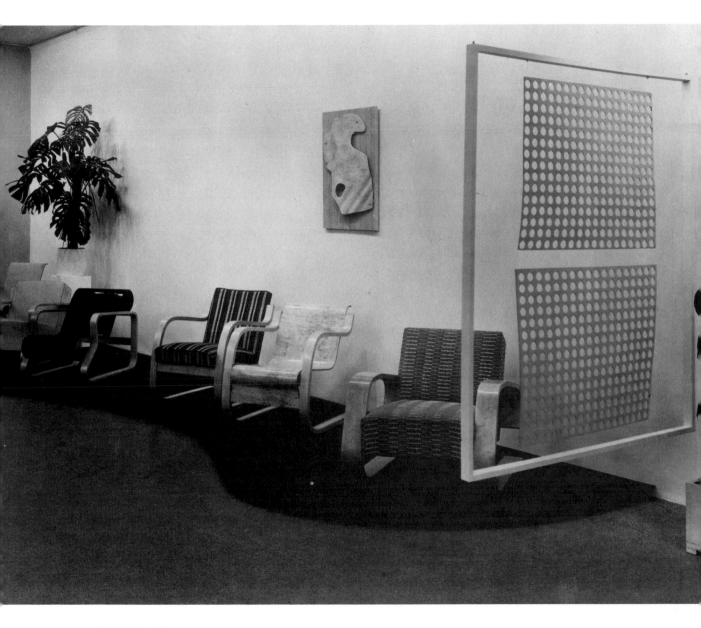

5.2 Chairs designed by
Alvar Aalto. Alvar Aalto:
Architecture and
Furniture, Museum of
Modern Art, New York,
1938.

5.3 Molded plywood
tables, 1936. Marcel
Breuer for Isokon
(England).

influenced the work of the Eameses in the mid 1940s (figures 5.3, 5.10).[15] Charles Eames learned a great deal about the interplay of technology and modernist form from László Moholy-Nagy, whose New Bauhaus he visited on several occasions in the late 1930s when Kenneth Eversten, Nathan Lerner, and other students were bending and cutting plywood into complex forms.[16]

But it was the challenge of shaping plywood in more than one dimension, as opposed to more than one direction, that excited Charles Eames and Eero Saarinen. Aalto had done it with a compound molded armchair (1931–32), which had been advertised in *Domus* in 1932 and shown at the Nordic Building Congress in the same year but which was never exhibited again or manufactured (probably because the process was time consuming and riddled with technical difficulties).[17] The British designer and furniture manufacturer Gerald Summers, some of whose plywood furniture was sold in American department stores in the 1930s, produced two multi-dimensional plywood chairs, seemingly with more success than Aalto,[18] but it was not until 1946 that the Eameses, their team, and their manufacturer produced a commercially successful version.

The idea of a comfortable molded-plywood chair without upholstery was well established, therefore, by the time Charles Eames and Eero Saarinen set about taking compound molding through to the mass-production stage. This they did in response to a competition, organized in 1940 by the Museum of Modern Art, that guaranteed the manufacture of the winning entries. In 1938–39, when working in the Saarinen Office, Charles Eames had been involved with the making of a prototype, and possibly with the design, of a molded-plywood armchair with a one-piece upholstered seat for the Klienhans Music Hall in Buffalo,[19] and his collaboration with the younger Saarinen continued when they decided to submit entries for seat and case furniture to the Museum of Modern Art's Organic Design in Home Furnishings competition (1940–41).[20] Eames and Saarinen won first prize in each category. The seat furniture (figure 5.5) looked radically different from what had gone before—a point that Christopher Wilk emphasized in an effort to obtain for these plywood shells the aesthetic recognition they deserve.[21] In their enthusiasm for the potential of molded plywood, Eames and Saarinen gave little thought to the problems.[22] When the engineers at the Grand Rapids branch of the Haskelite Manufacturing Corporation of Chicago, with their experience

5.4 Molded plywood
chairs and plywood table,
1934. Gerald Summers
for Makers of Simple
Furniture (England).

5.5 Molded plywood
chairs and storage cabinets
on benches (Charles Eames
and Eero Saarinen),
Organic Design in Home
Furnishings, Museum of
Modern Art, New York,
1940.

in the mass production of plywood stadium seating, encountered difficulties, Charles realized that the production of compound curves was "no snap."[23] He went to the plant to work on the molds. Despite heroic efforts by all, it proved difficult to produce smooth, clean shells. Upholstery was added to all but one of the chairs by the Heywood-Wakefield Company of Gardner, Massachusetts. Nevertheless, the seat furniture was greatly admired because it proposed to bring to furniture making the most up-to-date technology of the automobile industry. Eames and Saarinen wanted to use rubber shock mounts and a technique of electronic cycle welding developed by Chrysler to join the aluminum legs to the wooden seat without protruding bolts or screws.[24] However, when the time came to prepare prototypes, both aluminum and cycle welding were reserved for military use; thus, the furniture shown at the Museum of Modern Art in 1941 had wooden legs fastened to the seats from within by means of metal flanges. The moratorium on the use of the latest technology of the automobile industry did not hurt the reputation of Eames and Saarinen. Fortunately for Eames and Saarinen, the war delayed the realization that the seat furniture was not the major advance in furniture technology that it was claimed to be; the technique was problematic and remained so for many years to come, plaguing those who manufactured Eames furniture. [25]

The MoMA competition entry consisted of drawings accompanied by photographs of models in room settings complete with miniature rugs and drapes made by Cranbrook's weaving department. According to Don Albinson, the models were so realistic that the judges thought the photographs were of full-size prototypes. Later Albinson did build prototypes; however, that was as far as this scheme went toward realization.[26] In terms of influence, however, the story is quite different. As has often been noted, the 1940 Eames-Saarinen side chair was developed by Charles and Ray Eames into the plastic shell (1950), the wire shell (1952), the La Fonda chair (1961), and the Soft Pad chair (1969), and also influenced the Aluminum Group (1958). The 1940 armchair directly influenced the plastic and La Fonda armchairs (1950 and 1961 respectively) and the Loose Cushion chair (1971). The 1940 lounge design influenced the Eameses' 1956 version as well as the 1948 chaise.

As with other collaborations, it is difficult to separate Charles Eameses' input to the MoMA competition entry from Eero Saarinen's.

Ralph Rapson, a Cranbrook student at the time, recalled that Eero had plenty of ideas about how the chairs should look but knew very little about construction and technology, whereas Charles knew a great deal about the latter.[27] Charles certainly worked with the Haskelite staff, but the collaboration was more than simply a matter of Eero's taking care of the aesthetics while Charles sorted out the technology.[28] Eero Saarinen's later designs certainly put aesthetics before technology (in the case of his Tulip Chair of 1955–1957 he was prepared to put a plastic seat on a metal base and disguise the fact to achieve a unified visual form), but both men were influenced by the trend toward sculptural and organic forms in design. Charles Eames was too interested in aesthetics in general and in sculpture in particular to leave the overall form to his collaborator.

By the time Charles and Ray Eames left Cranbrook for California, it was clear that much work remained to be done before the successful mass production of non-upholstered compound-curved plywood furniture at relatively low prices would be possible. This was to be the goal to which the Charles and Ray would devote much of their energy in the next five years. Ray had become involved with the MoMA competition entry at a fairly late stage, but she had helped with the presentation drawings and was familiar with the main aspects of the work. As soon as they had settled into their new apartment, they established a workshop in the spare room and began to experiment in earnest. They had very little money, and their equipment was makeshift, assembled from parts and materials smuggled in under cover of dark lest the landlord discover their activities[29]; nonetheless, they managed to experiment with many different forms, using a variety of woods and glues obtained from the MGM lot where Charles worked. Charles's job meant that Ray could devote more time to this project than he—and the sculptural pieces produced at this time, which tested the limits of the technology and suggested a variety of aesthetic solutions, owed a great deal to Ray.

Charles and Ray eventually produced an unflawed one-piece compound-curved chair using their homemade "Kazam" machine, in which a membrane inflated by a bicycle pump pushed glued plies against an electrically heated plaster mold. Although the results were often good, the process took from 4 to 6 hours and hand finishing was still required.[30] The Eameses were tantalizingly close to their goal, but they were not able to progress further until John Entenza entered into partnership with

5.6 "Kazam!" machine in "workshop" of Eames apartment, Strathmore Avenue, Westwood, Los Angeles, 1941. The molded-plywood mobile is by Ray Eames (1941).

them, investing enough capital for the establishment of a workshop (at 10946 Santa Monica Boulevard) and making it possible for Charles to give up his MGM job in the summer of 1942.[31]

The first of the Eameses' plywood pieces to be mass produced were not furniture but splints made for the Navy (figure 5.7).[32] The idea for lightweight molded-plywood splints designed for comfort and easy transportation came after a medical friend of the Eameses detailed some of the problems caused by unhygienic metal splints. The military contract gave Charles and Ray access to classified information, including the latest Allied developments in synthetic glues and plywood production. Almost as important was the experience brought to the project by Gregory Ain, an architect known for his prefabricated-plywood cabin and fitment designs, whom the Eameses hired in 1942 to work for what was known as the Plyformed Wood Company.[33] The exigencies of war and problems of mass production meant that the compound curving of the original design (which was shaped to the contours of an "ideal" soldier based on Charles) was abandoned for a simpler form molded in only one plane, but even that required some hand finishing. Made of Douglas fir veneered in mahogany or birch, with the plies varying in number according to the support needed at various points, the splint proved effective. Its contribution to the war effort was later officially acknowledged.

As production expanded, the firm moved to new premises at 558 Rose Avenue, Venice, in January 1943. The work force increased to 22, including Herbert Matter and Harry Bertoia. However, the newly expanded enterprise was almost immediately threatened by a severe cash-flow problem caused by delays in payment by the Navy after a trial run of 5000 splints. The Eameses sold out to the Evans Products Company, a Detroit-based component manufacturing firm with interests in timber and in the West Coast plywood industry,[34] in October 1943, just 3 weeks before the Navy placed an order for 200,000 splints.[35] Thus the Eames team became the Molded Plywood Products Division of the Evans Products Company,

5.7 Molded-plywood leg splints (Eames Office, 1942–1944) and sculpture (Ray Eames, 1942–1944).

5.8 View of Design For
Use exhibition (Museum of
Modern Art, New York,
1944) showing molded-
plywood parts for aircraft
(Eames Office, 1943–44)
and molded plywood
sculpture (Ray Eames,
1943).

with Charles as Director of Research and Development. The manufacture of the splints continued at 555 Rose Avenue, but the Eameses and part of their team moved to 901 Washington Boulevard to develop a stretcher (which never went beyond the prototype stage) and plywood parts for aircraft. The manufacture of such large items as stabilizers and nose cones for aircraft tested the ingenuity and skills of the team as never before. Gregory Ain developed a special "Kazam" machine to cope with nose-cone sections up to 11 feet long and 7 feet wide. The team also experimented with plywood pilot seats and fuel tanks, using new synthetic glues. By the end of the war the Eameses had produced about 150,000 splints and had learned a great deal about the mass manufacture of plywood objects.[36]

While working on the military contract, Ray (and to a lesser extent Charles) used the improved glues and molding machinery to produce sculptures in complex shapes, ranging from coils and springs to highly abstract forms. In 1944 one of these (shown at far left in figure 5.8) was included, together with examples of the war work, in the Museum of Modern Art's Design For Use exhibition as an example of "the principle of organic integration of function, technology and form . . . and the similarity . . . between the tasks of the artist and engineer both of whom endeavor to find the most adequate formulation of specific human demands within universal principles of order."[37]

The experimentation with plastic form and the experience gained from the large-scale production of the splints stood the Eameses in good stead for their postwar ventures into mass-produced plywood objects. By 1944 they were convinced that the shapes Charles and Eero had developed were not the most suitable ones for mass production in molded plywood, and they began to favor separate seats and backs.[38] The children's furniture of 1945 (discussed below) involved subtle curving of plywood, but it was not a commercial success; the plywood furniture for adults proved to be the major breakthrough in the mass production of complex molded-plywood furniture. A storage system developed at the same time was not mass produced, but the radio housings developed for it led to contracts to produce radio cases for some of the leading radio manufacturers. About 200,000 were sold between 1946 and 1952; however, they received very little attention in the design press, where they were overshadowed by the plywood furniture.[39]

sculpture by Ray Komai, Los Angeles, Cal.

BUILT IN USA

The Eameses' stackable plywood chairs, tables, desks, and stools for children, produced and distributed by the Evans Products Company beginning in the middle of 1945, were the first such pieces designed by them to be mass produced; the first and only production run was 5000.[40] Brightly stained in red, yellow, blue, and magenta, this furniture was promoted as easily cleaned, able to withstand the rigors of classroom use, and suitable for outdoor as well as indoor use. The deceptively simple table, formed from one piece of molded plywood, was similar to a table designed by Marcel Breuer in 1936 (figures 5.3, 5.9).[41] The chairs, developed from earlier experimental ones, were formed out of two pieces of molded plywood, one serving as the legs and seat and the other as the back (figures 5.9, 5.10). An interesting feature was the cut-out heart motif. Arthur Drexler and other purists were impressed with the technology of the chair but disturbed by what they regarded as a sentimental and "absurdly romantic" symbol.[42] Recent critiques of modernism have addressed its failure to recognize that architecture and design could and perhaps should be "romantic," symbolic, and evocative of feelings and sentiments,

5.9 Molded-plywood children's chairs, stools, and table, 1945. Eames Office.

5.10 View of Connections: The Work of Charles and Ray Eames (Sainsbury Centre, Norwich, England, 1978) showing molded-plywood children's chairs (Eames Office, 1945).

and indeed it is easy to be amused by Drexler's attitude. With hindsight, it appears just as absurdly romantic to praise an object that drew its imagery from a machine, an airplane, or some other "modern" icon as it was to use the heart motif. If one is looking for an example of modernism's insensitivity to the human dimensions of design, here it is. The Eameses' work paid attention to but was never constrained by "rationality" and "functionalism," even though they worked within a tradition that venerated those concepts.

The cut-out heart shape was a well-known folk motif that linked the chairs to the past; it was also a tried and tested handhole for lifting. Although there is no firm evidence that its use was Ray's choice rather than Charles's, it is sometimes attributed to her whimsicality. Alvin Lustig had used a heart in 1942 on the inside cover of Mel Scott's book *Cities Are for People* (figure 1.25), and both Ray and Charles would have known this; however, whimsy and childish forms were more acceptable in graphic design than in the more "serious" area of product design, and it was a bold move to transfer the motif to a chair. Ray had no monopoly on whimsy within the partnership, and critics' "blaming" her for the heart seems to have been a case of their not wanting to accept that Charles—their "hero" of industrial design—could so flagrantly transgress the canons of modernism and use what appeared to be decorative and traditional. But the heart motif was more than whimsy; it effectively humanized the product, making it more attractive and accessible to children[43] and (perhaps more important) to "young-at-heart" adult purchasers. Having decided to include a "functional" handhole, the Eameses deliberately chose to use a heart rather than a more obviously "modern" shape, such as a circle or a rectangle, just as they later chose to use the heart elsewhere—most notably in films about information systems and computers. They consistently used the heart symbol to denote the human aspects of life in the machine age and to signify that most vital aspect of life, love. Despite being distributed to shops that specialized in "modern" design. The furniture did not prove popular, a fact which the Eameses felt had less to do with the heart motif than with the overall form's being "too modern" in appearance.[44]

The Eameses also designed plywood frogs, seals, horses, bears, and elephants, all large enough for a child to sit on, but only the elephant and the horse were even prototyped. The elephant was similar in form to

some of the experimental chairs of the mid 1940s in that the legs and
the seat were made out of one piece of molded plywood. Even though its
subtle undulations marked it as technologically and aesthetically advanced, it was considered by those who promoted modernist design in
the United States to be lacking in seriousness and even more sentimental
than the chair with the heart.[45]

In 1946 the Museum of Modern Art hosted its first "one-man"
furniture exhibition, New Furniture Designed by Charles Eames, which
featured the plywood pieces designed and developed jointly by Charles
and Ray between 1941 and 1946. This show premiered the DCM (Dining Chair Metal) and the DCW (Dining Chair Wood), which Eliot Noyes
described as "the finest chairs of modern design."[46] The presence of the
Eameses' furniture in this and other MoMA exhibitions, notably the
Good Design shows of the 1950s, was an important factor in their increasing popularity—there is no doubt that the MoMA "seal of approval"
helped sell products, particularly those that were radically new in terms
of design and construction.[47] This particular exhibition was the first of
many that would focus attention on Charles at the expense of Ray and the
staff. While Ray, as a partner in the firm and as Charles's wife, found

5.12 View of Connections:
The Work of Charles and
Ray Eames (Sainsbury
Centre, Norwich, England,
1978) showing
experimental chairs in
molded plywood and metal
(Eames Office, 1945).

ways of accommodating this and reassurance in Charles's public statements about her contributions, some of the staff members who had put a tremendous amount of energy into the project found the lack of recognition difficult to accept. After the exhibition and the publication of articles related to it, Gregory Ain, Harry Bertoia, Herbert Matter, and Griswald Raetze resigned. The end of this particularly fertile period of the Eameses' careers was also marked by the dissolution of the Molded Plywood Division of the Evans Products Company and the beginning of a long and mutually beneficial association between the Eameses and the Herman Miller Furniture Company.

THE HERMAN MILLER FURNITURE COMPANY

The remarkable firm that manufactured, marketed, and distributed the Eameses' furniture was based in Zeeland, Michigan. Founded in 1905, it had been producing traditional "period" furniture of good quality but uninspired design.[48] Michigan had led the United States in furniture production in 1900, but in the 1920s its position was threatened by Chicago, North Carolina, and California, and the situation worsened after the Wall Street crash of 1929.[49] During the Depression some of the major firms went out of business and economic necessity forced others to reconsider their production methods and turn their attention to more "modern" styles.[50] By 1930 Herman Miller's devout Dutch Reform Calvinist president, Dirk Jan De Pree, was praying for guidance because his firm was close to bankruptcy.[51]

It seemed providential that an energetic designer with positive ideas about the importance of "modern" design should walk into his office. Gilbert Rohde, who had visited the Paris Exhibition of 1925 and whose work revealed the influence of Art Deco and the rationalism and simplicity generally associated with the Bauhaus, persuaded De Pree that the smaller houses then being built needed furniture more appropriate than the historicist pieces Herman Miller was producing. In a courageous move born out of conviction as well as desperation, De Pree's firm commissioned two bedroom suites to be exhibited at the 1933 Chicago World's Fair. On the strength of their success Rohde designed "total home groupings" for dining and living rooms, and these further increased

Herman Miller's sales in the domestic market.[52] In the late 1930s Rohde turned his attention to modular office furniture and Herman Miller began to make inroads into the lucrative contract market. It appeared that De Pree's prayers had been answered. Freda Diamond was hired to improve the "period" range (including the "Shaker" pieces), but Rohde's furniture was so successful that by 1937 many of the "period" items had been phased out.[53]

De Pree decided the solution to the problem of persuading retailers and the general public to consider "modern" furniture as an alternative to "period" pieces was to show it in attractive room settings. In 1939, the Herman Miller firm opened a showroom in Chicago's Merchandise Mart. Here specially trained assistants encouraged customers to rethink their lifestyles and "go modern."[54]

That both Eric Mendelsohn (a high priest of European modernism) and Russel Wright (a well-known American designer) were considered as successors to Rohde after his death in 1944 indicates that the Herman Miller firm was committed to high-quality furniture of contemporary design before its association with the Eameses began and was determined to use the very best designers available.[55] In the end, the position went to George Nelson, editor of the magazine *Architectural Forum,* who recommended developing a corporate identity, standardizing lines, placing more emphasis on showrooms, introducing catalogs, and targeting architects.[56] Nelson designed many of the items in the Herman Miller furniture range, and in his capacity as director of design he brought in Isamu Noguchi and Charles Eames as consultant designers. (Nelson joked that his title was something of a misnomer in relationship to the latter "because nobody was going to direct Charlie."[57]) Although it was Charles who was given the consultancy (in 1947), Ray and the staff contributed to the designs.[58] Those designs, together with those of Noguchi and Nelson, ensured that Herman Miller retained its position as a leader of modernist furniture design in the United States. It was precisely because Nelson knew so much about design that he immediately recognized the importance of the Eameses' work when he and James Eppinger, sales manager at Herman Miller, first saw it at the Museum of Modern Art in 1946. Pronouncing it "years ahead" of anything he had even thought of, Nelson managed to persuade D. J. De Pree of the importance of this molded-plywood furniture, although De Pree's father-in-law, Herman Miller, needed more persuasion as to its commercial potential.[59]

Herman Miller was not the only furniture company to court the Eameses as their work became better known. Florence Knoll, a contemporary of the Eameses at Cranbrook, was considering asking them to work for Knoll Associates when they joined forces with the Evans Products Company.[60] The Eameses' agreement with Herman Miller stipulated that the Evans company would manufacture the furniture at a plant in Michigan and would leave the marketing and distribution to Herman Miller, which by then had the experience and contacts to sell such radically "different" items. In 1949, however, Evans severed its connections with the Eameses when it sold the production rights to Herman Miller, which went on to make an enormous amount of money from the venture.

Herman Miller began to market Eames plywood furniture in 1946. Billed as "not only the most advanced part of the Herman Miller collection, but the most advanced furniture being produced in the world today," it was featured prominently in the 1948 catalog. The plywood pieces, faced with walnut, rosewood, birch, or ash and occasionally with zebra and other exotic woods (sometimes left plain and sometimes stained with aniline dyes), were aimed at middle-class American families that wanted an up-to-date image. The prices could be kept low because, although there remained some hand finishing, the molding process had been reduced to about 10 minutes.[61]

The range was based on items shown at the Museum of Modern Art in 1946 and included the DCM, which, with its fusion of technical virtuosity, plastic elegance, and lightness, delighted those who set the standards of "good design" and also appealed to more popular tastes. Widely imitated, it became both a best seller and a cult object. It differed radically from the Eames-Saarinen forms of 1940 in that the seat and the back were separated in the minimalist manner of early Modern Movement design. The separation of these parts simplified the molding process by dramatically reducing the depth of the forming required. However, the design of the DCM was not dictated solely by practical concerns. Like Mart Stam's, Marcel Breuer's, and Ludwig Mies van der Rohe's cantilever chairs of the late 1920s and the 1930s, it was an attempt to make a chair's seat appear to float in the air (although the floating rhomboidal elements attached to one another by thin metal strips referred more to the mobiles and paintings of Joan Miró, Alexander Calder, and Hans Hofmann). Ray Eames played a considerable part in the development of

5.13 View of New
Furniture Designed by
Charles Eames exhibition,
Museum of Modern Art,
New York, 1946.

5.14 Herman Miller
Furniture Co.
advertisement for
molded-plywood furniture,
1948. Ray Eames and
Charles Kratka for Eames
Office.

this chair but, as Craig Miller has recently noted, has not been given sufficient credit for its subtle sculptural forms.[62]

While she was experimenting with the sculptural molding of plywood, Ray kept in touch with Hans Hofmann and Lee Krasner and abreast of developments on the New York art scene.[63] Her splendid covers for *Arts & Architecture* show the influences of Miró, Arp, Calder, and Hofmann in their primary palettes, biomorphic shapes, ink splashes, irregular washes, and use of line. Her paintings, one of which was exhibited at the Los Angeles County Museum of Art in 1944, explored space and volume, defining the latter by line and color as in some of the magazine covers. Later, however, she concentrated almost exclusively on the plywood furniture, translating the ideas and forms of abstract art (especially the work of Hofmann, and particularly the "push and pull" element) into three-dimensional plastic form in the DCM.

According to Irving Sandler, Hans Hofmann was one of the first to "loosen [painting] by opening its closed planes and by using color in itself to determine structure . . . pulling receding areas up to the surface and pushing back areas that protruded, in order to flatten the picture plane. The sense of the push and pull turns a picture into a dynamic field

5.15 DCM chairs, lounge and dining heights. Eames Office, 1946.

5.16 DCM. Eames Office, 1946.

of forces."[64] That the pleasing harmony of the DCM comes from the resolution of two conflicting forms, an ovoid and a rectangle, has often been remarked—for instance, Arthur Drexler commented that

> Part of the elegance of this design must be attributed to the contours of the seat and, even more, the back panel. Eames himself cites the hundreds of studies discarded because the contours of these two elements somehow attracted undue attention. The back panel might be described as a rectangle about to turn into an oval, the transformation being arrested at a point midway between the two shapes. Ambiguous but not bland, the shape is instantly seen as a whole, with no part of its contour catching the eye. The curve of the seat flares more emphatically and from certain angles gives the chair a curiously animated look.[65]

Drexler's remarks about the transformation of shapes in the DCM could be equally applied to a Hofmann painting. Others have commented on the chair's "animated" look. Christopher Wilk sees it as resembling a "living organism with spine, head, pelvis and four legs" and argues that its "insistent zoomorphism" imbues it "with a symbolic aspect that has been frequently overlooked in favor of . . . structural and technical qualities."[66] The extent to which the DCM was more directly "human" than the 1940 organic designs of Charles Eames and Eero Saarinen again indicates the significance of Ray's contribution to the Eames partnership at that date.

The DCM was an enormous success. By 1951 the rate of sales was an astonishing 2000 per month. This chair came to epitomize the Eameses' plywood furniture, yet it was only one of a group sharing a similar aesthetic and mode of manufacture. Dining and lounge chairs with wood legs were produced, but these were never as successful (perhaps because the legs and the joining piece were thicker than the seat and the back, making the chair look more squat and solid than the elegant DCM). A group of multi-purpose tables complemented the chairs. The coffee table, which came with either wood or metal legs, was a development of a 1940 Eames-Saarinen design (figures 5.5, 5.14). Rectangular folding dining,[67] card, and children's tables were derived from a prototype shown at the 1946 MoMA exhibition. The most unusual piece in the group was the folding screen, made from U-shaped plywood pieces. This was influenced by a very similar screen designed by Arthur Mack in Finland around 1937–1939 and marketed by Artek, the firm founded in 1935 by Alvar Aalto and others to sell Aalto furniture.[68] The Eameses originally envisaged joining the U-shaped plywood strips by means of canvas hinges, as in the Mack piece; however, for greater stability they used canvas strips running the entire length of the plywood. The screens differed from the other items in the range in that they were entirely handmade and therefore expensive to manufacture.

With the plywood group the Eameses achieved what had been their central ambition since they left Cranbrook: to see through to mass production well-designed and relatively inexpensive molded furniture with compound curves. By 1948 they had turned their attention to the new challenges of metal and fiberglass furniture, but the lessons of the years of intensive work on plywood were not forgotten. They returned to that material in the mid 1950s, developing one of their best-known pieces, the Lounge Chair and Ottoman, in 1956.

In 1940 Charles Eames and Eero Saarinen had discussed designing a chair as comfortable as a traditional upholstered armchair, and the large shell shape of the 1956 chair resembles the 1940 Eames-Saarinen design for relaxation chairs. But the idea of a three-piece molded-plywood shell was mainly derived from an experimental lounger designed by Charles and Ray in 1946 (although in the 1956 version the spaces between the pieces were less apparent and the whole assumed a more unified form). The ottoman, when used in conjunction with the chair, added to the unity of effect.

It was not unusual for the Eameses to refer back to earlier projects when looking for solutions to a particular problem. Nor were they averse to looking to history for models. The Eameses saw it as a challenge to produce a modern and American equivalent to the comfortable leather armchair found in English gentlemen's clubs (which had been given canonical status within modernism by Le Corbusier and Adolf Loos). Charles used all-American terminology when he stated that the chair should have the "warm receptive look of a well-used first baseman's mitt."[69] Once again, the impulse was to make the product culturally acceptable to large numbers of people. The Lounge Chair and Ottoman offered modernism with a human face and a comfortable bottom. No shell was molded through more than two planes; the most novel technical fea-

5.17 Lounge Chair and
Ottoman, molded plywood
and leather. Eames Office,
1956.

ture of the chair was probably the "spider" mechanism on which it rotated. The rosewood veneer on the seven-ply shell gave a more distinguished and sophisticated appearance than the earlier furniture had, as did the buttoned black leather upholstery filled with down, duck feathers, and foam. The chair was also available in other colors. The automobile designer Harley Earl ordered one in orange leather, and white leather ones achieved a degree of popularity in the early 1970s. But the black leather version was and remains the favorite. Despite the high price ($404 in 1956 and approximately $2500 today—nearly $3500 with the ottoman), 100,000 were sold by 1975, bringing the Herman Miller Furniture Company an estimated $100 million in retail sales. The Eameses had produced a "best-seller" that offered a new direction for furniture design. But not everyone sang the praises of this chair. It was the antithesis of light, elegant, minimalist, low-cost furniture, and some saw it as relatively dull, conventional, too solid, opulent, ugly, awkward to move and control, not particularly easy to clean, and far too expensive. In an interview in 1977, Charles Eames commented that it had "a sort of ugliness to it" and noted that he had never considered it as good a solution as the 1946 plywood chairs, "although it has apparently given a lot of pleasure to people."[70]

PLASTIC FURNITURE

Once the plywood project of the mid 1940s had been seen through to a successful conclusion, Charles Eames decided that the time was ripe to pursue other materials and methods of mass producing furniture. He considered metal stamping to be "the technique synonymous with mass production," and he hoped to develop products that would "free metal furniture of the negative bias from which it has suffered."[71] Under the terms of the International Competition for Low-Cost Furniture Design, held at the Museum of Modern Art in 1948, Charles and Ray were funded to work with a research team from the UCLA Department of Engineering to develop stamped steel and aluminum chairs. However, because the estimated production prices (between $5 and $11) were not as low as they had hoped and because manufacture proved somewhat difficult, the Eameses realized that these chairs were not likely to be the ones to significantly break down customers' resistance to metal furniture. Thus, they

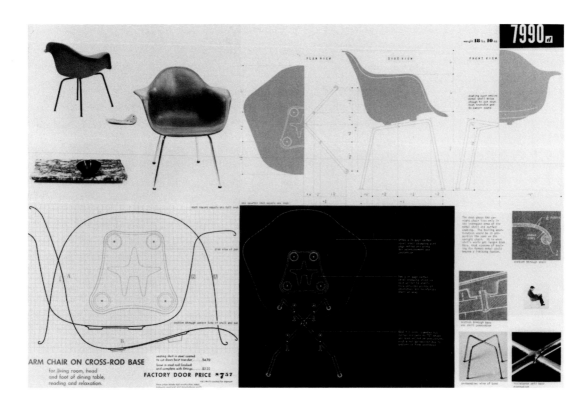

5.18 Specification panel
for stamped-metal chair,
International Competition
for Low-Cost Furniture
Design, Museum of
Modern Art, New York,
1948. Eames Office and
UCLA Department of
Engineering.

reconsidered the use of plastics, which were much lighter than steel or aluminum and more malleable than plywood.

Although the Eameses were not the first furniture designers to work in plastic, their designs proved among the most popular in this medium. Polyester plastic reinforced with fiberglass, developed during the war by the U.S. Air Force, was perceived as a wonder material that "could do damn near anything."[72] It was recognized by many designers, including Eero Saarinen, Isamu Noguchi, and George Nelson. Nelson later claimed to have suggested the use of fiberglass to the Eameses in 1949—an assertion that made Charles Eames extremely angry.[73] Nelson attributed this reaction to Charles's massive ego, but Charles probably had good cause to be angry with Nelson. Both Charles and Ray were well aware of developments in plastic resin and fiberglass furniture before 1949. Mies's Conchoidal Chair designs of 1941, which show a shift in his work away from a geometric to an organic aesthetic, influenced the designs for molded-plastic chairs published in 1946 by Ralph Rapson and Eero Saarinen.[74] Through Saarinen the Eameses knew that Knoll Associates was developing the designs of Rapson and Saarinen, and they were well acquainted with Saarinen's Womb Chair (from its design in 1946 to

5.19 View of Connections: The Work of Charles and Ray Eames (Sainsbury Centre, Norwich, England, 1978) showing plastic armchairs (one with drawing by Saul Steinberg) (1950), plastic side chair (1950), and Sofa Compact (1954).

its manufacture in 1948).[75] Both the Womb Chair and the Eameses' plastic chairs of 1950 drew on the shell forms developed by Charles Eames and Eero Saarinen in 1940. However, the Saarinen chair was upholstered, whereas the Eameses' chairs were the first to reveal the marble-like effect of the fiberglass that was used to reinforce the polyester.

The Eameses had found fiberglass cloth and plastic resin material in military-surplus shops, and they had used it for screens in their house (c. 1948–49) and in their proposal for a chaise longue with a shell of resin and fiberglass cloth, filled with a core of hard rubber and styrene foam bricks, which formed been part of their submission to the 1948 MoMA competition for low-cost furniture.[76] "La Chaise" [77] had more in common with the Eames-Saarinen single-shell designs of 1940 than with the Eameses' plywood furniture, and it was certainly the most formalist of the Eameses' furniture designs, drawing inspiration from the sculptures of Barbara Hepworth and Henry Moore. A full-scale model was made, and factory costs were estimated at $15 for the shell and $12 for what was one of the most complex of Eames bases—a large wooden star supporting two different types of metal supports.[78] Although the chaise was and is much admired as an art object, the Eameses always stressed its "work-in-progress" aspect (it did "not pretend to clearly anticipate the variety of needs it is to fill . . . needs . . . as yet indefinite") and the fact that the solution of the form was largely "intuitive."[79] The "intuitive" shell, which probably owed more to Ray than to Charles, appeared in Ray's color proposal for the 1949 Exhibition for Modern Living and was featured prominently in the exhibition. "La Chaise" entered the Museum of Modern Art's collection,[80] but it did not go into commercial production until 1990. The 1948 designs for metal side and arm chairs, rather than the chaise, were chosen to be developed for a cheap plastic chair.

Zenith Plastics (now Century Plastics) of Gardena, California, which had used fiberglass during the war, worked in conjunction with the Eameses and with the Herman Miller Furniture Company on the new project. Even though the eventual development costs were four times as great as estimated,[81] Herman Miller's investment remains one of the best ever made in the American furniture industry. The chairs were first made by laying on the material by hand, but later the most sophisticated hydraulic dies available in boat manufacture were used. With the side chair (figure 5.20) retailing at $32,[82] the Eameses had achieved their ambition

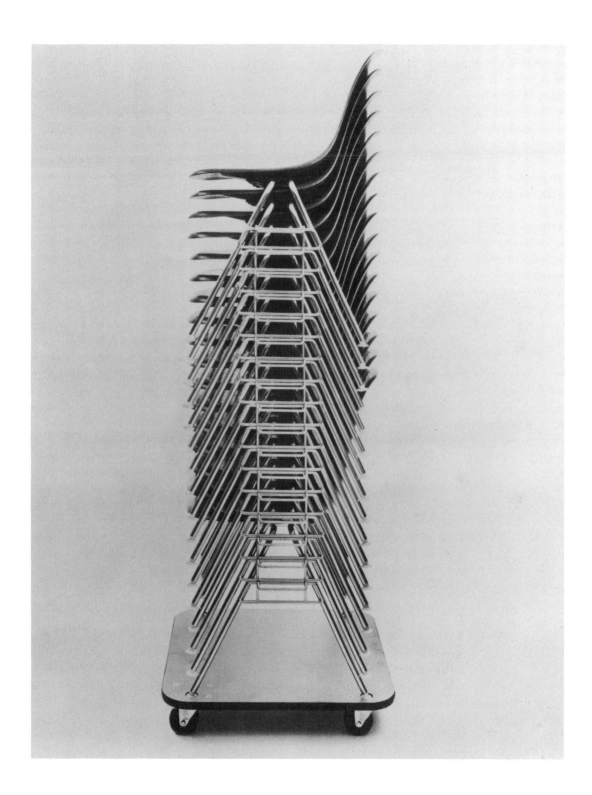

5.21 Tandem Shell Seating
(1963), plastic shells
(1950), La Fonda
shells (1961), and base
for Tandem Sling
Seating (1962). Eames
Office.

of bringing the benefits of a sophisticated military development to "ordinary people . . . at non military prices."[83]

The chairs were first offered in grey, beige, or parchment; brighter colors, including red, yellow, and green, were added to the line later. The side chair came in similar colors. In 1951 upholstered versions were produced in a strong and cheap hopsack fabric, which was available in a variety of colors and in a "harlequin" mix.[84] A variety of bases was soon offered besides the original metal rod legs, which were attached to the shell by the same rubber shock mounts the Eameses had used in 1946 to give extra resilience to the DCM. That the bases were not changed and were used on other pieces has been taken to illustrate how, once they had settled on a design, the Eameses used it again and again; however, in later years the Eameses regretted not having had more time to devote to the bases of these chairs.[85]

The armchair, the first to be manufactured, was immediately validated as "good design," obtaining the Museum of Modern Art's seal of approval when it entered the permanent collection in 1950 (its first year of production). The side chair, which soon followed, was used extensively in public spaces, so much so that it took on a certain invisibility and was taken for granted by many who used it, day in and day out, in restaurants, schools, and office buildings. Thus, this chair was at once highly "visible" in design-conscious circles and somewhat invisible in the ordinary world. The high aesthetic and technical standards which the Eameses achieved with this chair were acknowledged by many—not least by the British furniture designer Robin Day, who, when asked by the firm of Hille to produce a fiberglass chair, refused to do so because he thought the Eameses had produced the definitive design in that material.[86]

The chairs also came in rocker, bar, and stacking versions. In 1954 the shells were used for Stadium Seating (the first project developed expressly for the growing contract market, into which the 1950 chairs had so successfully tapped), Tandem Shell Seating (1963) and School Seating (1964), all of which involved attaching the shells to metal bars. They were also adapted and modified, as in the La Fonda chairs (1961) and the Loose Cushion Armchair (1971).[87]

5.22 Educational Seating,
1964: upholstered plastic
stacking shells with tablet
arms. Eames Office.

5.23 La Fonda Chair and
Table, 1961. Eames Office.

The Eameses successfully adapted the shell form to another material: bent wire. They were not the first furniture designers to work in this light, airy "fabric," but their designs were among the first to be successfully mass produced. Sol Bloom's woven steel mesh Lounge Chair and Ottoman and Catch All were both produced in 1950, the year before the Eameses' chair, and Harry Bertoia's wire mesh series was produced the year after.[88] The popular Hardoy or "Butterfly" chair (1938) had a bent-metal frame,[89] and metal rod bases had been used on Eames chairs since 1946 and tables since 1950, but the development of a wire chair was an altogether different project.

Charles and Ray were fascinated by the proliferation of ordinary objects produced in wire in the late 1940s and the early 1950s: "If you looked around you found these fantastic things being made of wire— trays, baskets, rat traps, using a wire fabricating technique perfected over a period of many years. We looked into it and found that it was a good production technique and also a good use of material."[90] Open woven wire proved popular because it was light and airy as well as appearing "modern." In this its appeal was similar to that of wicker, a material that made a comeback in the 1950s.

Produced by Banner Metals of Compton, California, and marketed through the Herman Miller Furniture Company, the Eames wire mesh chair was aimed at the domestic consumer who wanted quality modern furniture at a relatively low price (it originally retailed at $21).[91] Also sold in the contract market, it found its way into offices, hotels, and restaurants across the United States and abroad. Developed while the fiberglass chair was being refined, it is similar in form. In many contemporary pieces the mesh was cut like a fabric and hung on a heavy frame, but in the Eameses' chair it had cross-weaving only where strength was required and the rim was kept as light as possible. This chair's double wire edging received the first American mechanical patent for design.[92] The wire mesh chair, an exemplary essay on the minimal use of a "new" material, had a tremendous impact. According to Alison and Peter Smithson, it "hit us like a bombshell. It was very different . . . rather like the Eiffel Tower. You hadn't seen anything like it. It was extraordinary. . . . It was light yet it was metal. It was like a message of hope from another planet."[93]

5.24 Wire Mesh Chairs
(1951) and wooden decoy
from the Eames collection.
(Photograph by Charles
Eames, used in
advertisements for the
chairs.)

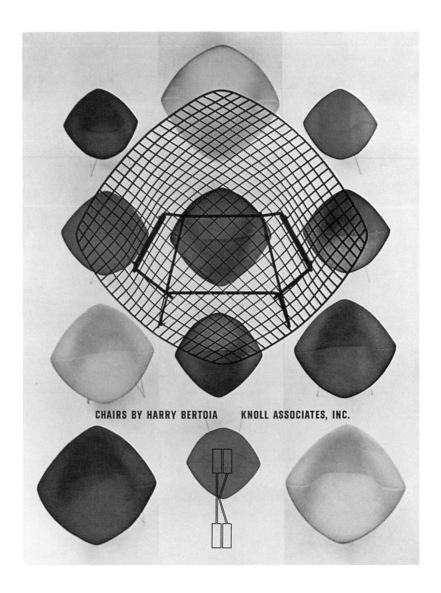

The wire chair's similarity to Harry Bertoia's 1952 series of
chairs, Bertoia's employment in the Eames Office from 1942 to 1946, and
the fact that small models similar to the Bertoia chair were found in the
Venice workshop after Ray's death raise questions about authorship and
influence in regard to both the Eames and the Bertoia designs. The question of who first developed the edging technique was legally settled in
1955 in favor of the Herman Miller Furniture Company after a dispute

between that firm and Knoll Associates, which produced the Bertoia chair.[94] In the end, Knoll was granted a license by Herman Miller to use the bent-wire technique patented under the name of Eames. However, legal niceties do not always reflect all the relevant facts or acknowledge that often more than one designer pursues an idea at the same time, and the question of attribution becomes even more complicated in the case of design. Ray and Charles Eames and Harry Bertoia knew one another well from Cranbrook and were all conversant with similar sculptural concepts and forms. Bertoia played an important part in the development of the plywood group; however, he left the Eames Office in 1946—five years before the Eames wire mesh chair and six years before his own chair was produced, and also before the development of the metal and plastic chairs whose form influenced that of the Eames wire chair. There is no reason not to believe Bertoia's claim that it was while he was devoting his energies to bending plywood in the Eames Office that he realized his preference for bent metal, which took more readily to plastic form.[95] Bertoia was paid by the Eameses to develop ideas and products, but it must be remembered that the Eameses were also experimenting with bending and shaping metal in those years. To see the Eames chair as Bertoia's design is to miss its similarity to the fiberglass shell and to miss the fact that Charles Eames and Eero Saarinen had developed shell forms in 1940. The Eameses' chair postdates Bertoia's employment in the Eames Office, and it owed as much to the ideas of the Eameses and to the extensive development work of Don Albinson, Fred Usher, and Dale Bauer as it did to Harry Bertoia. This does not mean that Bertoia should not given any credit. Equally, it should not be forgotten that Bertoia must have learned a great deal from working with Charles and Ray. The origins of the idea aside, there are significant differences between the two wire chairs apart from their different sculptural forms. The Bertoia Diamond chairs used a diaper-pattern mesh which spread across the entire frame. The Eameses had experimented with a triangular mesh in a prototype, but for aesthetic and technical reasons they finally opted for a rectangular center panel composed of small squares, leaving the outer edges of the horizontal wires without cross-weaving. The Eames shell was lighter, less complex, and more economical to produce than its competitor (which was handmade), and it fitted the six bases already in production for the fiberglass group. It remained in production till 1967.

For those who wanted more comfort or more visual solidity, the Eames wire chair came partially or fully upholstered. But the early upholstery pads, manufactured by a tailoring firm, did not grip the frame satisfactorily. In the end the problem was solved, in a typically Eamesian way, by going back to basics and, in conjunction with the sewing department of the Santa Monica Technical School, developing new machines and techniques until the desired results were obtained. Charles recalled: "... we were at the point where the design and production of even the machinery for making the furniture was being done in our office. Jigs and fixtures for building up the upholstered pads were made and operated in the initial production stage by fellows in our office."[96]

The small low table (1950) and the larger elliptical one (1951) illustrate the elegance that could be achieved with legs of bent metal rod and with wood or laminate tops. The Eameses were not the only designers to combine these materials in small items such as tables and stools, but they were the first to see their work successfully mass produced. Although Florence Knoll claimed to have designed it as early as 1948,[97] her design for such a table was first manufactured in 1952—the year in which Isamu Noguchi designed a bent-wire-and-wood stool for her firm, Knoll Associates.[98] The minimalist structures of the Eameses' tables, which, at only 10 inches high, encourage Japanese-style seating, offered an elegance associated with Japanese aesthetics at a time when there was an increasing interest in all things Japanese in the United States. Christopher Wilk described the larger table, which consisted of two of the smaller frames supporting a surfboard-like elliptical top some 89 inches in length, as offering "a symbolic and literal meeting of East and West."[99] The bases were made out of two U-shaped rods on the short sides, with cross braces, for stability, on the other two sides. The top of the small table originally came in either black or white laminate or a natural wood veneer, but after a while only the white top was produced. The larger table was only ever made in black. Other, more exotic surfaces, including patterned laminates and gold and silver leaf impregnated with a protective coating, were tried but proved uneconomical.[100] That such decorative surfaces were experimented with illustrates that there were more varied tendencies within modernist design in the middle of the twentieth century than is often supposed. The patterned tops indicate that the Eameses were not solely interested in the undecorated aesthetic suggested

5.26 Elliptical Table Rod
Base (ETR), 1951, and
DCM lounge chair, 1946.
Eames Office.

by the pieces that went into production; in 1950 they saw nothing wrong with using decorative laminates in furniture. It is interesting to speculate whether, had they been produced, such tables would have sold as well as the plain-top ones, the smaller of which is still in production today. Probably not. As it was, decorative laminates for furniture were popular mainly in the cheaper ranges of furniture and were generally considered vulgar until they were rehabilitated and validated by the Italian designer Ettore Sottsass, Jr., and others as part of the 1980s' homage to the 1950s.

The next major development was the Aluminum Group (1958), manufactured a decade after the Eameses' first attempts at metal furniture and seven years after the bent-wire chair. Some furniture designers, most notably Marcel Breuer, had used aluminum before World War II; Breuer's first designs date from 1932, and there was an international competition for aluminum chairs held in Paris in the following year.[101] Although some aluminum furniture was made in the United States and Europe in the 1930s (such as Hans Coray's Landi chair of 1938, an example of which the Eameses are known to have owned by early 1950), aluminum was regarded as too expensive, inflexible, and brittle for domestic furniture.[102] But the war transformed the aluminum industry, increasing its production capacity by 600 percent, and after 1945 a great deal of time and money was spent promoting new uses for aluminum.[103] By the mid 1950s the three largest aluminum firms in the United States had established their own industrial design departments and hired designer/communicators whose job it was to facilitate product development rather than to produce actual designs.[104] In 1957 Alcoa set aside $3 million for the promotion of aluminum and commissioned several leading designers, including the Eameses, to design products that would showcase the material's potential. Alexander Girard designed aluminum shelving, Isamu Noguchi an aluminum table, and Jean Deoze an aluminum crepe ball gown.[105] The Eameses, asked to produce a toy, came up with the Solar Do-Nothing machine discussed in the preceding chapter.

The Aluminum Group (figure 5.27) marked a shift away from the shell forms of the 1950s while retaining their lightness, elegance, and minimalism. For the aluminum chair, which in profile recalled the high-backed Sofa Compact of 1954, the Eameses used a fabric sling to offer comfort without the bulk of the 1956 Lounge Chair. This furniture was the result of a request from Alexander Girard, who was unable to find

FURNITURE

suitable indoor and outdoor furniture for the Irwin Miller House in Columbus, Indiana (1953–1957, designed by Girard with Eero Saarinen). Charles described the initial design process as follows: "You start on a close human scale. Here is a friend who has done something. He needs something for it and you become involved. As we were trying to analyze the reasons why there was nothing available on the market to suit him, why we were of course starting to write a program for designing the object to fill this void. That's how it started."[106] Aluminum was chosen for its lightness and its resistance to corrosion. Thinking about relaxing led the Eameses to consider a hammock and then a sling. Sling chairs were popular in the 1950s (the Hardoy or "Butterfly" Chair of 1938 had been widely copied), but the Eameses wanted something that was easier to get into and out of. They and their team suspended a specially developed sling seat between the top and bottom parts of a standard-height frame, the sides of which act as a flange into which the sling is fastened and terminate at top and bottom in cylinders around which the ends of the sling are wrapped. An "antler" joins the side pieces to a stem and base; a similar one acts as a brace on the rear of the seat frame as well as forming a convenient carrying handle. These functional elements also add visual interest to the side and rear views. The original sling was made of a fibrous plastic developed by Girard; a later one, produced by ultrasonically welding together two layers of fabric and a vinyl filling, offered even more comfort and durability and came in a range of colors.[107] The tension between the skeletal frame and the "flesh" of the sling contributed greatly to the chair's visual impact, as did the elegant, flowing forms.

The aluminum chair was the most complex of the Eameses' chairs to manufacture, not least because of what Don Albinson calls "the complicated engineering" of the sand-casting process and the degree of hand finishing involved.[108] The technology came first, but, as Charles explained, it allowed a considerable degree of artistic freedom: ". . . when you've committed yourself to casting, you've committed yourself to a plastic material and the kind of freedom that can really give you the willies. . . . In casting there are times where the definition of the problem is pretty vague. At that moment you find yourself face to face with sculpture and it can scare the pants off you."[109] If it was scary it was also stimulating—especially to Ray, who loved dealing with sculptural form and who was willing to spend almost any amount of time to achieve a satisfactory result.

The Aluminum Group consisted of large and small lounge chairs, a dining chair, an ottoman, and dining and coffee tables with tops of slate, clear glass, or Botticino marble. The marble—an unusually luxurious choice for the Eameses—proved both attractive and utilitarian. "Engineered to withstand poolside or patio wear and weathering, yet styled to harmonize with the plushest contemporary interiors,"[110] the aluminum furniture was popular with the more "artistic" strata of the wealthy professional classes, but it was rarely bought for outdoor use; it was simply too expensive for that. The Eameses acknowledged the problem early on: "We've been using one [chair] for a test outside our house for the past six months. But it's also an indoor chair—probably a high budget outdoor chair, a low budget indoor chair."[111] Never cheap, the Aluminum Group furniture ended up in offices. To better meet office requirements, two swivel chairs were introduced in the mid 1960s. In 1969 the frame was used for the Soft Pad Group (figure 5.28), the separate cushions of which were somewhat reminiscent of the 1956 Lounge Chair.[112]

5.29 Time-Life chair and
walnut stool, 1960. Eames
Office.

5.30 Chaise, 1968. Eames
Office.

After the Aluminum Group was launched, in 1958, Don
Albinson left the Eames Office. His 13-year tenure and his contribution
to such "classics" of modern furniture as the Lounge Chair and Ottoman
and the Aluminum Group should be fully acknowledged. However, the
assertion that the Eames Office never produced an original furniture design after Albinson left—which implies that the originality of the earlier
designs is attributable to him[113]—is rather harsh, particularly in view of
the Eameses' innovative work in design and product development during
the early 1940s, before Albinson came to work for them, in view of their
creative output in areas with which Albinson was not greatly or regularly
associated, and in view of some of their later designs (such as the walnut
stool shown in figure 5.29 and the chaise shown in figure 5.30).

The chair and the walnut stool in figure 5.29 were produced in
1960 for use in three lobbies designed by the Eames Office for the Time-
Life Building in New York. The chair was a smaller version of the 1956
Lounge Chair with aluminum side frames and with the plywood shell con-
cealed. Although originally designed for the Time-Life Building, this luxurious button-upholstered chair filled a gap in the contract market for an
armchair-*cum*-office chair suitable for executive suites and conference
rooms, and swivel and tilt-swivel versions were retailed by the Herman
Miller Furniture Company as part of the Eames Executive Seating range.
The chair soon became identified as a status symbol in the business
world, and it achieved "cult" status when it was used during the 1972
world chess tournament at Reykjavik.[114] The combination of a metal-
and-leather modernist chair and a wooden ethnic-style stool may at first
seem strange; however, much of the Eameses' work in interior and exhibition design and in multi-media presentation was based on the juxtaposing of seemingly disparate objects or images. The stool also related to a
broader movement in design: the use of "ethnic" objects (particularly African, South American, and Native American ones), which not only showed
that the owner had "good taste" but also came to signify the up-to-date
"modern" interior. Although the former looked distinctly more hand-
crafted than the latter, both the stool and the chair were mass produced
by machine. Each was the result of careful thinking around the brief and
going back to fundamentals. Once Charles and Ray discerned the need
for a small seat that could double as a resting place for coffee cups and
magazines, it was but a short step to Ray's idea of basing the new piece

on the African stool they had at home, which they used as a "percher," a table, and a plant stand.[115]

The Time-Life stool is usually attributed to Ray. She played an important part in conceiving it and in determining its final form, yet she felt that to credit it entirely to her would have been to deny her role in other joint work with Charles and to deny his role in this project.[116] The stool is usually chalked up to Ray's interest in "crafts" and in other cultures and to her whimsicality. Those who emphasize Charles's concern with the technological aspects of furniture design while viewing Ray as having concerned herself with decorative and craft-inspired pieces (such as the stool) fail to acknowledge the importance of Ray's contribution to other Eames furniture. They also miss the fact that the turned stools were just as much machine products and modernist forms as the chair—indeed, their stark geometric forms recall early modernist "machine aesthetic" art and design. Yet, even though they were no less functional than the chair, the stools were regarded as less significant because they did not obviously make use of "new" materials or industrial techniques. A final irony is that, although Ray is rarely given any credit for the more "serious" Time-Life chair, Richard Donges recalls that she spent a great deal of time working with him on its development.[117]

A major Eames project of the late 1950s and the early 1960s was Tandem Sling Seating (1962), which was aimed at a perceived need for durable, comfortable, attractive, and relatively inexpensive airport seating. Airports were an increasingly important part of the contract furniture market in the late 1950s and the early 1960s. Air travel was becoming more popular, and new terminals were built to serve the increasing traffic and to update the image of airports, many of which had been constructed during the 1930s and reflected the era of the New Deal rather than the jet age.[118] By 1961 there was a takeoff every 85 seconds at Chicago's O'Hare Airport. This, together with an estimate that 10 million passengers would pass through O'Hare in the coming year, led the authorities responsible for the airport to embark on a program of expansion. By the time the architects specifying the furniture (C. F. Murphy Associates) contacted the Herman Miller Furniture Company, the Eameses had already been asked by their friend Eero Saarinen to design some furniture for Washington's Dulles Airport. The Aluminum Chair was too expensive to be adapted to this purpose, but use was made of the work on aluminum casting and on heat sealing that had been done for that project. Separate seat and back pads, which were easier to replace, took the place of a one-piece sling. The triangular and trapezoidal patterns impressed into the pads reflected a trend toward more geometric forms in the early 1960s and gave extra solidity and shape to the seat.[119] The prototypes were subjected to the most rigorous tests then available in the furniture industry at the Herman Miller Technical Center in Zeeland—testing much more stringent than anything the Eames Office had hitherto been involved with and a far cry from the testing of plywood prototypes that Charles and Ray had done in their own home. Tandem Sling Seating, used at Tampa International Airport (1972) and at Phoenix's Sky Harbor Airport (1984) as well as at O'Hare, is widely considered to be among the best seating of its kind.

Those who dismiss the furniture designed by the Eameses after 1958 should consider The Chaise (1968). Inspired by Billy Wilder's desire for an office couch on which he could nap yet which would not look like a "casting couch,"[120] the 17-inch-wide chaise (figure 5.30) is taut, elegant, slim, and strong. The design paid homage to the famous modernist chaise designed by Charlotte Perriand, Le Corbusier, and Pierre Jeanneret in 1928–29, yet it was subtler in profile. It showed some similarities to experimental forms developed by the Eameses in the 1940s and also to the Aluminum Chair of 1958, and the base was a variant of one developed for a sofa in 1951. Fabric stretched over the narrow frame supported six foam-filled leather cushions held together by zippers and attached to the frame at the head and the foot,[121] and additional small cushions offered extra head or limb support. The dark frame blended with the black upholstery, rather than contrasting with it as chromium steel tubing would. This high-quality piece was priced at $636 in 1968 and almost $3500 in 1993—"miserably expensive," in the Eameses' opinion.[122] Though it was marketed with a view to domestic as well as business use, its high cost meant that it was mainly found in executives' offices.

The Chaise was considered striking in "a severe, neo-Bauhaus way."[123] In the 1960s, when such styles enjoyed something of a revival, the Eames Office also produced other metal furniture that was less organic in style and more in keeping with a geometric modernist aesthetic than most of their work. In the Segmented Base Table system of 1964, modular bases similar to those of the La Fonda chair and table were used to support round, rectangular, and "super-ellipse" table tops up to 22 feet in length, which were offered in veneered hardwood, plastic laminates, or white Italian marble.[124] The Intermediate Desk Chair of 1968 was more angular than earlier Eames chairs.[125] After 1971, however, the Eames Office showed a renewed interest in organic forms. The Two-Piece Plastic Chair of 1971 reproduced the elegant forms of the plywood and metal DCM, by then established as a "classic."[126]

SOFAS

Sofas were a logical extension of single-seat furniture, but the Eameses did not successfully translate a sofa design into a mass-produced piece until 1954. The Sofa Compact (figure 5.31), the last piece of Eames furniture specifically designed to be low in cost,[127] is still in production today, selling at very un-low prices: $3000 in fabric and nearly $4000 in leather. Based on the alcove sectional seating of the Eames House (1949) and using ideas developed in 1951 for a fold-up wire sofa, this high-backed piece with thin upholstery and slim metal legs was altogether more elegant than either of those designs. The three horizontal foam pads that made up the back and the seat were available in leather, vinyl, or fabric and in a variety of colors. The back folded down for easy transportation and storage; this is one reason why the Sofa Compact is the least sculptural of the Eameses' metal furniture pieces.

The 3473 sofa (1964) was similar to the Sofa Compact but had a one-piece back. The plywood shell looked back to earlier pieces, but the cast aluminum legs and supporting frame were new.[128] Its fine detailing made the 3473 sofa too expensive to produce; however, it eventually led to the Teak and Leather (or Soft Pad) Sofa—a comfortable and luxurious piece developed in 1967, shelved until the mid 1970s (when Charles found a new enthusiasm for it), and first manufactured 6 years after Charles's death.[129] A wood frame gave this sofa a touch of distinction and luxury reminiscent of the Lounge Chair and Ottoman. Fabric-reinforced rubber webbing supported comfortable padded seat cushions designed to complement the Chaise and the Soft Pad Group. Cost-effective mass production may have remained a goal of the Eameses, but the high price of this sofa (over $3500) ensured that it was available only at the top end of the contract market or to very rich individuals.

5.31 Sofa Compact, metal
frame, 1954. Eames Office.

5.32 Eames Teak and
Leather Sofa (a.k.a. Soft
Pad Sofa), 1984. Eames
Office.

STORAGE UNITS

Although the Eames Office specialized in seat furniture, other types were not ignored. Prototypes of a wooden modular "case goods" system were developed in 1945–46 and shown in 1946 at the Museum of Modern Art. This system was based on some 1940 Eames-Saarinen designs for interchangeable cabinets resting on low benches that could also be used as tables, seats, or plant stands.[130]

The first Eames cabinet pieces to be mass produced were the modular steel-framed Eames Storage Units of 1950. As with the 1940 and 1946 designs, the emphasis was on standardization, with variety to be achieved through interchangeability. The ESUs were developed from steel shelving designed by the Eameses for the 1949 Design For Living exhibition but the inspiration for both lay in "knockdown" steel shelving.[131] The Eames House was being completed while this project was in progress, and similar "machine aesthetic" and Japanese influences can be seen in both, as can the idea of a steel frame with colorful infills. Chrome-plated steel uprights finished in either bright zinc or black supported plywood shelves, while lacquered Masonite and perforated aluminum panels acted as decorative shelf backs. Drawers were offered in plywood faced with birch or walnut and in black plastic laminate, doors in dimpled wood and white glass cloth. Infill panels came in eight colors, including bright yellow, red, and blue. The units came in two widths and three heights and offered a variety of options for the arrangement of shelves, sliding panel doors, and drawers. The components could also be combined to create desks. The colors included grey, tan, red, yellow, blue, black, and white. Aimed at both the home and contract markets, the ESU system found popularity in neither. The original version required assembly; however, this proved none too simple, and pre-assembled units were soon offered. When the completed structure proved somewhat fragile for transportation, modifications were made—the most significant being the setting in of the supporting legs. But the technical problems alone do not account for the lack of success of the ESU. Admired by other designers, copied by some,[132] and today sought after by collectors, the units did not prove very popular with domestic consumers, and they were not well suited for the office market. They were withdrawn from production in 1955.

5.33 Eames Storage Units,
1950. Eames Office.

In 1954 the Eames Office developed a prototype of a less traditional looking "knockdown" storage system of lightweight composition board with two bays of shelving or railings and a "starlight" mirror, all of which could be hidden behind a folding door.[133] Referred to as the Sears Compact Storage unit (the plan was to have it mass marketed by Sears, Roebuck), it was designed to cope with storage needs in the smaller postwar house. This project never came to fruition.

The Eameses' next storage system, the ECS (Eames Contract Storage) system of 1961, was specifically aimed at a particular sector of the contract market where, it was hoped, very large orders would help keep prices down: student dormitories.[134] The system comprised three dressing units, a study unit, and a bed unit. The units were sold separately and could be combined in a number of ways. Cost reductions could be realized by planning dormitories around the system, but it was expensive to install in existing buildings. Once again, an Eames-designed product of undoubted quality proved too expensive for its market niche. The ECS unit was not commercially successful, despite the educational expansion that was going on. It was the Eameses last venture into storage units.

By 1978, when Charles Eames died, he and Ray had moved a long way from their early ideals of designing relatively low-priced mass-produced domestic furniture. They had enjoyed enormous success at the cheaper end of the mass market, particularly with the DCM (1946) and the plastic chairs (1950), but most of their later furniture ended up in corporate offices or in the homes of the design-conscious and/or the wealthy. In the 1960s and the 1970s their office, airport, and stadium furniture was used by millions of ordinary people, but such people rarely bought Eames furniture for their homes. At first sight the Eameses' increased concern with the contract market would appear to reflect the increased importance of that market for the Herman Miller Furniture Company; however, it should be remembered that few of the designs started off being aimed specifically at that market.

After the early 1950s the Eameses were concerned less with low-cost furniture as such than with solving particular problems: making a comfortable lounge chair, or a chair that could be used indoors and out, or storage units for students' rooms. Their design work was not market-driven; they did not selfconsciously or cynically set out to design for the lucrative contract market. They genuinely deplored the high production

5.34 Eames Contract
Storage, 1961. Eames
Office.

5.35 Woman sitting in
Aluminum Group Chair
and Ottoman (1958) and
man in Lounge Chair and
Ottoman (1956), c. 1960.
Herman Miller publicity
photograph.

costs of their designs, but their priority was always the thorough resolution of each brief, whatever it might be. They aimed to resolve each problem to the best of their abilities and the abilities of their impressive staff, and enormous amounts of time and money were spent on furniture research and development, with Don Albinson responsible for coordinating most of it during the 1950s and Richard Donges thereafter. This obsessive striving after perfection is the common denominator in their work. It paid handsome dividends. In just over thirty years they produced some of the most successful American furniture of the twentieth century—successful in terms of style, technology, and the marketplace—and that is no mean achievement.

It is not surprising that people as interested in communicating ideas and visual delights as the Eameses turned their attentions to the design of exhibitions, beginning in 1950 with Good Design at the Chicago Merchandise Mart and the Museum of Modern Art and continuing into the mid 1970s with their work for IBM. Always beautifully produced, the Eameses' exhibitions were, as Robert Venturi has noted, similar to their interiors in having "varied and rich content."[1]

The exhibitions were similar to the Eameses' films and their multiple-image presentations in the use of "information overload," bombarding the consciousness with a rich superabundance of information in visually interesting ways, but with the exhibitions there was less control over the viewing process. Recognizing the limits of human attention spans, Charles and Ray aimed to create an intensity of feeling and "fun" in their major exhibitions in order to maximize the impact of what they were trying to convey.[2] They generally managed to achieve this, although some of the later exhibitions were criticized as too dense and too demanding.

Above all, the exhibitions were educational—learning experiences in the very best sense of the term. Each exhibition was rigorously researched by staff members (including Jehane Burns and Jeannine Oppewall), and outside experts (Raymond Redheffer, a professor of mathematics at UCLA, and Owen Gingerich, a professor of astronomy and the history of science at Harvard University) were consulted regularly. Despite the fact that the exhibitions were packed with information, artifacts, and images, a great deal of care was taken to make them accessible. This was done not by diluting or oversimplifying the content but by making learning interesting and "fun." Photographic images were used to great effect, as were short films, fascinating objects, and interactive games. "Human interest" was introduced wherever possible. For instance, A Computer Perspective (1971) offered details of the friendship between Charles Babbage and Ada Augusta, Countess of Lovelace, and also a handwritten letter from Alan Turing to his mother.[3] In Nehru: His Life and

His India (1965), a mockup of a jail cell with some of Nehru's prison writings pinned to the walls evoked the Indian leader's experience of imprisonment.

Charles's education provides a clue to the Eameses' use of interactive games and other "mechanical" devices to delight an audience while explaining complex ideas. In a paper presented to the American Academy of Arts and Sciences in 1974, he noted:

> I was raised in a nineteenth-century mode, where my first experiences with science involved minor physics experiments done almost as parlor tricks, mathematics through magic squares and electricity by way of a "shocking machine" which was reputed to have some therapeutic value. All this had an aura of magic about it; by the time I became an architect I was not at all surprised that our understanding of electricity grew out of toying around with pith balls, or that pneumatics and hydraulics were first used to impress the populace by magically opening doors and raising fountains. Joseph Needham says in his book, *Science and Civilization of China:* "Perhaps the passage of jugglers and acrobats to and fro merits more attention in the history of science than it has yet received, particularly when we remember how much of the early mechanics of such men as Nero of Alexandria and also of their Chinese counterparts were occupied with mechanical toys for palace entertainments—devices of illusion, stage play, machinery and the like. . . . For ancient and medieval people there was not much difference between jugglers, alchemists, mechanicians, star clerks and all dealers in magic and glamour."[4]

The Eameses fused their ideas about learning, illusion, toys, mathematics, science, technology, and new ways of seeing to produce exhibitions that offered some of the "magic and glamor" of ancient entertainment and some of the earnestness of nineteenth-century learning. The interactive games they produced for the Mathematica exhibition (see below) are more obviously "fun" than certain other aspects of the exhibition. However, such devices were never added extras; they were an essential part of the pleasurable but serious business of learning.

6.1 Mathematica: A
World of Numbers . . .
And Beyond, California
Museum of Science and
Industry, 1961 to present.
Interactive multiplication
cube (center) and Moebius
band (left). Eames Office.

The much-copied idea of using a "time line" or "history wall" to contextualize a subject originated in the Eames Office. In the exhibition celebrating the five-hundredth anniversary of the birth of Copernicus and featuring his contribution to astronomy, each "discovery" was related to developments in other fields of science and the arts; in the Nehru exhibition, the politician's life was depicted against a background of Indian and world history. These charts helped viewers lock the subject matter of the exhibition into their own (often impressionistic) knowledge of history by means of well-known events and images, which triggered all sorts of connections in the brain.

These various attempts to engage the visitor's interest added up to a distinctive exhibition style—a "vision of complexity."[5] The Eames Office, and Ray in particular, had the knack of finding appropriate objects to illustrate particular points. The illustrations were always of excellent quality, and the Eameses never shied away from text. Viewers were expected to negotiate the material themselves and make their own connections. An Eames exhibition was a multi-faceted experience; from a rigorously organized and systematic outline, it was built up, layer upon layer, using text, illustrations, and objects. The best of the exhibitions were exciting experiences; in the worst there was just too much of everything.[6] Some visitors enjoyed being inundated with material and free to make their own route through it; to others, certain exhibitions seemed cluttered if not overwhelming.

Beginning in the mid 1930s, exhibition design in the United States underwent considerable changes. This happened partly in response to the argument, put forward by European modernist designers, that an exhibition should be more than an eclectic collection of objects and that care and consideration should be given to the space as well as to the display of objects within it. Less appreciated today, but influential then, were the efforts of American designers—particularly Walter Dorwin Teague, Norman Bel Geddes, and Raymond Loewy—to introduce dramatic spectacle into hitherto dull but worthy business exhibitions. Eames exhibitions were later to synthesize aspects of these two major developments.

In the infant USSR, debates abounded as to the most effective ways of communicating ideas to large numbers of people, and the Constructivists—El Lissitzky in particular—became noted for a multi-media

approach to exhibition design, for an emphasis on new materials (such as
cellophane), and for riotous mixes of message and image.[7] This exuberant
avant-gardism encouraged Bauhaus designers in their crusade against the
"superficial beautification and historical eclecticism" of what they regarded as the cluttered and confused trade and industrial shows that had
proliferated in Germany in the early 1920s.[8] Herbert Bayer, the Austrian
who taught at the Bauhaus and became one of the leading exhibition designers in Germany, was greatly influenced by Lissitzky's work, particularly the huge photomurals and the innovative display features he saw at
the Pressa Ausstellung at Cologne in 1927.[9] He was also influenced by
the new notions of architectural space associated with the Dutch-based
De Stijl. The freedom to break the plane informed one of Bayer's most important contributions to modernist exhibition design: the recognition
that the line of vision was not limited to the horizontal plane, which led

to images' being placed at all sorts of unusual angles and heights as Bayer utilized the mobility of the human eye.[10] The Bauhaus became a powerhouse of new ideas about exhibition design. László Moholy-Nagy stressed the use of new materials, demonstrations, light projectors, slogans, and moveable partitions. He, Bayer, Walter Gropius, and Marcel Breuer each designed a part of the Deutsche Werkbund's 1930 display of German products in the Salon des Artistes Decorateurs Français at the Grand Palais in Paris. Bayer's use of blown-up photographs set at unusual angles and chairs hung on a wall anticipates the Eameses' exhibitions.[11] Lilly Reich, Ludwig Mies Van der Rohe, and others were also involved in innovative exhibition design in Germany in the late 1920s and the early 1930s.[12] By 1936, however, Max Bill's Swiss Pavilion at the Milan Exhibition was hailed as the most brilliant example of the integration of structure and exhibits,[13] and Herbert Bayer himself noted the importance of new ideas from Austria, Italy, and Sweden.[14]

6.3 Room 5, Deutsche Werkbund, Section Allemande, Salon des Artistes Décorateurs Français, Paris, 1930. Herbert Bayer.

CHAPTER 6

6.4 Faculty exhibition, Cranbrook Academy of Art, 1939. Charles Eames and Eero Saarinen.

Europe's influence on American exhibition design increased in the late 1930s, particularly after Bayer emigrated to the United States and was commissioned by the Museum of Modern Art to design several exhibitions, including *Bauhaus 1919–1928* (1938), *Road To Victory* (1942), and *Airways To Peace* (1943). Bayer's application of De Stijl spatial concepts and his use of ropes, screens, and poles as well as the objects themselves to define the space of an exhibition influenced Charles Eames and Eero Saarinen, whose design for the Cranbrook faculty exhibition of 1939 (a year after Bayer's first MoMA exhibition) reveals a debt to Bayer in the use of the tension lines and display platforms (figure 6.4). In later years the Eameses also drew on Bayer's use of panels to spell out themes as well as to partition space, on his strategy of showing familiar material in unfamiliar ways, on his emphasis on the "field of vision" rather than a predetermined hanging height for illustrations or objects, and on his ingenious methods of defining space.[15]

Although Eames and Saarinen drew on Alvar Aalto's organic forms in their molded-plywood designs of 1940 (see chapter 5 above), they eschewed the use of such forms for their exhibition despite their acquaintance with the exciting and strongly organic French, Swiss, and Finnish exhibits (the latter designed by Aalto) and with the Focal Food Stand (by the American Russel Wright) at the 1939 New York World's Fair.[16] Nevertheless, the influence of Aalto's Finnish exhibit (figure 6.5) can be seen in later Eames designs. Aalto's use of four levels of blown-up photographs, stretching from ceiling to floor (52 feet) and depicting the country, the people, work, and products (in that order) worked rather like the Eameses' later history wall. Both used the technique, so beloved of Eliel Saarinen, of relating one idea or process to one immediately preceding or following it. Furthermore, the Finnish exhibit housed an abundance of products. This was a far cry from the minimalism of most European modernist exhibitions, and Aalto expressly intended that it be so:

> An exhibition should be what in the early days it used to be: a general store, in which all possible objects are grouped together in a dense display—whether it be fish, cloth or cheese. Therefore in this pavilion I have attempted to provide the densest possible concentration of display, a space filled with wares, next to and above and beneath each other, agricultural and industrial products often just a few inches apart. It was no easy work—composing the individual elements into one symphony.[17]

A symphony composed from a superabundance of objects and information is a good description of an Aalto or an Eames exhibition at its best.

The more spectacular strand of exhibition design referred to earlier, also unacknowledged as a source of Eames design, developed as a response to and then became a reason for the increasing popularity of state, national, and world's fairs in the United States in the second half of the 1930s.[18] It can also be traced to corporations' and manufacturers' efforts to promote their images while somewhat paternalistically educating the common man. Between Walter Dorwin Teague's 1934 exhibition designs for Ford and the opening of the New York World's Fair in 1939, a host of new, exciting, and aesthetically varied ways of communicating informa-

6.5 Finnish pavilion, New
York World's Fair, 1939.
Alvar Aalto.

tion in exhibitions about products and processes—photomurals, photomontages, animated murals, dioramas, full-size working models, playlets, puppet shows, live dance performances, and specially commissioned films—were developed and delivered to delighted audiences. Accessibility of information was a key factor; however, some of the designers (Teague and Bel Geddes in particular) were willing to offer spectacle and visitor participation for the less lofty reasons of sheer pleasure and enjoyment.

It is not just because these exhibits influenced the later work of Charles and Ray Eames that I emphasize their importance. They were important cultural events, and they deserve recognition as such. Roland Marchand has recently rescued them from the dustbin of history, where they were dumped because pro-modernist design critics and historians had no use for them.[19] For example, Gwen Finkel Chanzit states in her study of Herbert Bayer that before the major migration of European modernists to the United States in the late 1930s American "methods of display were outmoded and uninspired"[20]—but this was not the case. Outside the Bauhaus-blinkered world of high culture, vibrant and dynamic developments were taking place, and these developments are just as important in the history of exhibition design as MoMA exhibits or the attempts by museum curators from the early 1930s to "scientifically" establish optimum exhibition and viewing conditions.[21]

The first time Charles and Ray Eames designed an exhibition, it was to display the furniture they had jointly developed since 1941. Ironically, the exhibition, held at the Museum of Modern Art in 1946, was titled New Furniture Designed by Charles Eames. Charles and Ray decided to show some of the furniture in conventional groupings that would help viewers imagine it in their own homes or offices. They also hung some chairs and tables on walls, as Bayer had done in 1930. In addition, they decided to illustrate the processes of manufacture[22] by means of stroboscopic and still photographs and three-dimensional objects (figure 6.7). Neither the use of a mirrored wall nor the hanging of furniture was new. The display of the furniture was unexceptional though extremely competent, but the demonstration exhibits, the panels, and the photographs gave a foretaste of the visually exciting displays the Eameses were to mount from 1949 on.

6.6 View of New
Furniture Designed by
Charles Eames, Museum of
Modern Art, New York,
1946.

6.7 Panel explaining the
process of molding
plywood, New Furniture
Designed by Charles
Eames, Museum of Modern
Art, New York, 1946.
Herbert Matter for Eames
Office.

Four years after the New Furniture show the Eameses were involved in the Good Design exhibition, a joint venture between the Museum of Modern Art and the Chicago Merchandise Mart that opened in
Chicago in January 1950.[23] In November 1950 a similar but smaller exhibition was installed at the Museum of Modern Art. Both illustrate the
ways in which the Eameses personalized, and thereby humanized, modernist interiors. The Chicago exhibition was austere and "functionalist" in
that the pipes and ducts were left exposed and the walls and ceiling were
stark white, but the effect was softened by the use of plants, shrubs,
blinds, and screens of ropes, chain, and string to break up the 5300
square feet of space into separate "pavilions," each denoted by a different
color scheme. Some 150 objects, including such things as food whisks,
coat hangers, glassware, and plastic furniture, were displayed, some on
open shelves and some in showcases; other objects were represented in
wall-mounted photographs, some blown up large and others greatly reduced, fragmented, and/or juxtaposed in unusual ways. Some of the photographic images were juxtaposed in unusual ways. Figure 6.8 shows a
photographic panel that derived its dramatic impact from changes in
scale and suggested that certain everyday functional objects un-self-
consciously represented "good design." This panel incorporated a Thonet
bentwood chair (one of the most commercially successful mass-produced
furniture pieces of the late nineteenth and the early twentieth centuries,
and one that became an icon of modernism when Le Corbusier and others
chose it to grace their avant-garde interiors in the late 1920s), an American Windsor chair (another well-known piece of furniture produced on a
large scale), tableware, and scissor handles. Glassware was displayed on
open shelves (to emphasize its public availability) and was placed near a
huge sofa in a section of the exhibition that doubled as a rest area. There
were also Kandinsky paintings and other "art" objects (on loan from the
Art Institute of Chicago), potted plants and shrubs, and desert weeds.
The latter, new to modernist iconography, puzzled many designers, some
of whom thought that the Californian sun had made the Eameses a little
crazy.[24] The weeds, which brought what the Smithsons, 16 years later,
would call "extra-cultural surprise,"[25] were in fact indigenous to the
United States, though sufficiently outside the dominant design discourse
for their presence to disconcert. For New York the Eameses created a
slightly more varied and colorful exhibition, using many of the same ob-

6.8 Good Design,
Chicago, 1950.

jects; *Interiors* complimented them on "providing a much needed service in returning to favor the clashing color combinations that have been banned by the advocates of color harmony."[26]

The idea of showing furniture in settings that suggested rather than recreated domestic interiors gained popularity in the United States in the late 1940s. Besides the Eameses and those museums that promoted "good design," department stores and manufacturers played an important part in persuading the American public of the desirability of contemporary design. Only four months before the Good Design exhibition opened in Chicago, the Eameses designed and furnished a "room" in An Exhibition For Modern Living, planned and designed by Alexander Girard, sponsored by the J. L. Hudson Company, and held at the Detroit Institute of Arts.[27] Girard invited the Eameses and six other prominent designers—Alvar Aalto, George Nelson, Bruno Mathsson, Jens Risom, Eero Saarinen, and Florence Knoll—to display objects they had designed. George Nelson described the Eames room (figure 6.9) as "not so much a literal presentation of a room as the expression of an attitude, conveyed through the use of a special personal vocabulary."[28] Nelson considered the key element of this expression, apart from the furniture itself, to be a wall studded with pegs on which a miscellaneous assortment of objects were hung, and he commented that this suggested not only the possibility but the desirability of endlessly arranging and rearranging the contents.[29] This was "functioning decoration" as it had developed before the Eameses designed the interior of their own home. It was apparently lighthearted, joyous, and a riot of color.

A collage approach to design was also apparent in the Eameses' 1950 window display for Carson Pirie Scott (figure 6.10).[30] This well-known Chicago store had also invited George Nelson, Edward Wormley, and Eero Saarinen to design displays of their most recent furniture. The Eames display, which featured plywood furniture jointly designed by Charles and Ray set against a dramatic backdrop of blown-up paper shadows of the abstract furniture forms, was a collaborative effort. Ray's working drawings suggest a considerable input from her and have all the signs of her method of shifting pieces of paper around until she came up with a satisfactory collage. The Herman Miller logo and some photographs of Charles completed the display, emphasizing the importance of both manufacture and design. That the Saarinen display (designed by Herbert

6.9 Room design, An
Exhibition for Modern
Living, 1949. Eames
Office.

6.10 Window design
displaying furniture
manufactured by Herman
Miller Furniture Company,
Carson Pirie Scott store,
Chicago, 1950. Eames
Office.

Matter and Florence Knoll along with Saarinen himself) also treated the windows as "semi abstract three-dimensional compositions"[31] and used the furniture forms as decorative shapes indicates just how closely the ideas of the Eameses coincided at that date with those of two former Cranbrook colleagues and a former employee. The idea of promoting and selling modern furniture through a store display continued in 1951 with a four-room display of Herman Miller furniture designed by George Nelson and the Eameses at the Chicago Macy's store and a similar display in Herman Miller's Grand Rapids showroom.[32]

As the Eameses' interest in communicating ideas developed in the 1950s, they moved away from producing settings for the display of designed objects and began to tackle larger thematic exhibitions. In this they were greatly influenced by Alexander Girard, the architect, exhibition and environmental designer, colorist, pattern maker, and folk art collector whose work was mentioned in chapter 4.[33] In 1955 Charles and Ray visited New York to help mount the Textiles and Ornamental Arts of India exhibition at the Museum of Modern Art. This stylish and interesting exhibition had been designed by Girard, who knew a great deal about Indian handicrafts and who had superb visual skills. Charles and Ray's major contribution to this project was to make a short film of the exhibition, but they were also involved in the arrangement of objects. Thus began their "love affair" with India.

Textiles and Ornamental Arts of India, which was planned to coincide with the world premiere of Satyajit Ray's film *Pather Panchali* (1955), triggered an exchange of design ideas and designers between India and the United States.[34] Shortly after the Girard exhibition, a MoMA exhibition toured India, arousing considerable interest and debate among manufacturers, government officials, and designers and leading the Indian government to consider establishing an institute of design. In the wake of the post-independence drive to create an industrial infrastructure for India, there was a strong movement among the artistic intelligentsia to find design solutions for the future that would look to modern technology but would also be cognizant of the past.[35]

Pupul Jayakar, a leading authority on Indian handicrafts who had known Mahatma Gandhi well, was one of the most vigorous Indian proponents of the Eameses' vision of design. She first met Charles and

6.11 Sequence from
*Textiles and Ornamental Arts
of India.*

Ray in 1955, when she represented the Indian Ministry of Commerce and
Industry as an adviser to the Girard exhibition and the related Eames
film. Fascinated by Indian myths, symbols, and the "unexplored rural psyche which was the cradle of the mind of India's past" and dedicated to the
survival of rural handicrafts and small industries,[36] Jayakar recognized in
the Eameses a combination that was rare in Western designers: an ability
to deal with the symbolic as well as the rational, the fantastic as well as
the functional.[37] She had gotten to know Charles first and had come to regard this man with "the deeply penetrating eyes of the seer" as something
of a guru:

We met and for hours talked of India, of its craftsmen and the traditions that sustained them; he questioned me on the land, the people, the poverty and the affluence, the values, the philosophy, the environment that had sustained an ancient culture and the impact of the new technologies, the revolution in communications. He was eager to know what was happening to the psyche of a nation suddenly thrust into the turmoil of twentieth century technology and its by-products. He wanted me to suggest books he should read to understand the traditional background and culture of India and I gave him a list amongst which were Isherwood's translation of the Bhagwad Gita, books by Coomaraswamy and Zimmer, Gandhiji's *Experiments with Truth* and Jawaharlal Nehru's *Discovery of India.*[38]

Then she met Ray, whose sense of fantasy and visual discipline impressed her enormously.[39] She recognized Charles and Ray's interdependence, but she especially valued Charles's ability to comprehend modern science, technology, and mass communications and still keep human beings and "the seemingly non-essential, the fantasy" at the center of his vision.[40]

It was largely through Pupul Jayakar and through Gautam and Gira Sarabhai, sibling heirs to a textile fortune who were interested in many areas of the arts, that Charles Eames (Ray was not officially included) was commissioned to report on design in India. Charles accepted on behalf of himself and Ray, and in 1958 they spent five months exploring "the actuality of India" and familiarizing themselves with Indian design traditions, especially those related to everyday objects. They met a host of people, officially and unofficially, involved in education, handicrafts, industry, design, architecture, science, philosophy, sociology, and literature. Jayakar notes that they "traveled through India visiting shoe factories and potters' huts, observing the landscape, the people—the hennaed foot of a woman riding a gaily decorated bullock cart—entered the magical village groves of magnificent clay horses and bulls, observed the way women and men worked in the fields—their economy of movement, their use of hands, the drape of a cloth, the rural capacity for attention, their skills and the intensity of their minds."[41]

In the Eames Report (often called the India Report in the United States and Europe, and referred to by Charles as a "position paper") Charles and Ray recommended for India a broad training that would draw on disciplines other than design and architecture and emphasized the importance of a problem-solving approach to design. They argued for a self-conscious articulation of India's centuries-old design tradition. The conscious awareness of the processes of an unconscious tradition could, they argued, be extrapolated from thinking about all the facts involved in the design and the design evolution of the Lota (figure 6.12)—a "simple vessel of everyday use" which the Eameses admired greatly and which they used as an example of considering a design brief from every possible angle: "optimum amount of liquid to be fetched . . . size and strength and gender of the hands (if hands) that would manipulate it . . . fluid dynamics . . . opening . . . cleaning . . . texture . . . heat transfer . . . feel, eyes closed eyes open . . . sound and materials and how it felt to possess it, to sell it, to give it."[42] Here they were advocating their own methods: going back to fundamentals, conducting thorough research, and never forgetting the human factor. They proposed the establishment of an institute of design, commenting: "The hope for and the reason for such an institute as we describe is that it will hasten the production of the 'Lotas' of our time. By this we mean a hope that an attitude be generated that

6.12 A lota photographed in India by Charles Eames.

will appraise and solve the problems of our coming times with the same tremendous service, dignity and love that the Lota served its time."[43]

Despite the huge problems thrown up by India's urbanization and industrialization, the Eameses saw some ground for optimism in the fact that the main problems of food, shelter, distribution, and population were so clearly defined and the needs so great that there should be little temptation to innovate for its own sake—the latter being, in their opinion, a flaw of Western design traditions. They also saw as an advantage the fact that within Indian culture there was a philosophical outlook "familiar with creative destruction" (a concept that probably held little comfort for those Indians suffering most from social, economic and cultural disruption). The Eameses' recommendation was to use the latest tools of communications technology to help solve problems and to change attitudes toward new developments brought about (according to them) by the new systems of worldwide communication in the first place. Drawing on Buckminster Fuller's belief that one of the great advantages of education is that it can bring about "security in change," they argued for the comprehensive use of education, particularly exhibitions, films, and information services.[44] This, to me, is the crux of the matter. Although the Eameses recognized that security would be forthcoming only if change was beneficial, they failed to grasp the magnitude of the problems facing the vast majority of Indians during a period of massive upheaval, and they underestimated the drive for profit and disregard for quality among some of India's manufacturers, the depth of divisions within Indian society, and the complexities involved in the supply of food and shelter (let alone the "control" of population growth). This said, I suspect that, even given a less optimistic and more complex view of Indian affairs, the Eameses' solution would have remained a two-pronged one of education and a "problem-solving" approach.

It would have been presumptuous to offer detailed solutions to India's problems, and that was certainly not the Eameses' style. The Eames Report suggested issues for clarification, including the need to decide exactly what values and qualities were deemed part of a "good life," and recommended that matters of quality and the environment be taken extremely seriously:

In the face of the inevitable destruction of many cultural values—in the face of the immediate need of the nation to feed and shelter itself—a drive for *quality* takes on a real meaning. It is not a self-conscious effort to develop an aesthetic—it is a relentless search for quality that must be maintained if this new Republic is to survive.[45]

Having stated an objective for the national design institute ("to create an alert and impatient national conscience—a conscience concerned with the quality and ultimate values of the environment") and established its functions (research, training, and service), the Eameses turned to recommendations for the institute's size ("small starting with perhaps a dozen students—but with a faculty that would more than complement them in number"), they suggested a program of exhibitions, films, literature, and other forms of information). In the main, however, the report dealt in generalities.

The Indian government minister responsible for the report (a graduate of MIT) and the representative of the Ford Foundation, which had funded the project, were dismayed at the lack of specificity about technology and product development and about how the design institute might liaise with small industries. Pupul Jayakar, who was present at the formal presentation of the report, described the scene as "an utter chaos of communications," with Charles Eames quoting extensively from the Bhagavad Gita, the Sanskrit eulogy to the importance of work for its own sake rather than its fruits.[46] Here was a member of the team that had designed the world's most commercially successful mass-produced furniture, and he was talking philosophy! In the end, Gautam Sarabhai's business acumen, Pupul Jayakar's reputation as a realist as well as a defender of India's heritage, and their joint insistence that behind the generalities lay a commitment to "hard" technology won the day and plans for what was to become the National Institute of Design (NID) went ahead. Thus it was that the Eameses' vision of a design training appropriate to India played a part in India's "Second Industrial Revolution," which began in the early 1960s and which recognized small-scale production as central to the country's economic development and its cultural identity.[47]

Indira Gandhi, daughter of Jawaharlal Nehru, met the Eameses in 1958 through her close friend Pupul Jayakar and was so impressed that she arranged for them to screen two of their films for her and her father. *Tocatta For Toy Trains* and an early version of *Tops* were shown, but Nehru (a hero of Charles's since his student days) was as bewildered by the Eamesian world of toys as his minister had been by the Eames Report. According to Jayakar, "Charles strode up and down the aisle, trying in broken sentences to explain the reason and the relevance of the films. A tired, bewildered prime minister, half asleep after a long day, could not understand what it was all about; what tops had to do with designing objects. Indira, sitting next to her father, kept assuring Eames that everything was crystal clear."[48]

After Nehru's death, in 1964, Jayakar suggested that the Eameses, in conjunction with the recently established NID, should organize the proposed memorial exhibition. They received the commission, and Ray Eames, Deborah Sussman, Robert Staples, and Bob Anderson spent three months in India working on the project at the NID, joined from time to time by Glen Fleck and Charles Eames.[49]

The exhibition, Nehru: His Life and His India (1965), was planned as a biography from the start, but, since Nehru's life was related so intimately to 50 years of Indian history and politics, it also became a history of India in that period. According to Charles, he, Ray, and their team had "thought long and hard on how you treat the life of such a great man conceptually." "First," he continued," we developed a photographic exhibit in an effort to show as many humanistic aspects as possible—little things to show what makes a man like Nehru great. We tried to show his stand on all crucial questions. Then we built a physical structure by using a number of elements such as photographs, fabrics, art objects and sound."[50]

Experts in Indian studies were consulted. The research was coordinated by Sharada Prasad of the Indian Ministry of Information and Broadcasting. Most of the 25,000 words in the text were Nehru's own.[51] More than 200,000 photographs were scrutinized before 1200 were finally chosen. A decision was made not to use blown-up photos—as Charles put it, "large photographs and words had ceased to have meaning, the eye of the viewer passed over them, without registering; human beings were losing the beauty of the small and the capacity to relate to the written word. . . ."[52] Family and newspaper photos were used to create a mood of intimacy, and aerial shots were used to emphasize the importance of land in Indian culture.

6.13 Indian fabrics, Nehru:
His Life and His India,
1965. Eames Office and
National Institute of
Design, India.

6.14 British Army
uniforms, Nehru: His Life
and His India, 1965.

CHAPTER 6

In addition to a history wall, there was a stand devoted to documents, photographs, and newspaper clippings. Besides being an effective vehicle for displaying interesting items, this stand encapsulated the contrasts between traditional India and the contemporary West. The large free-standing display panels were made from Formica-covered plywood, but their visible backs were covered with a variety of beautiful Indian textiles. Indian textiles were also used to cover the sandbags that stabilized the history wall and the document stands. Teak, an indigenous wood, was used to illustrate Indian woodworking skills and traditions. The Eameses hoped that this, together with the brass detailing, would suggest the craft-based nature of many Indian manufactures.

Great emphasis was placed on authenticity. Alexander Girard was brought in to augment Ray's skill at finding appropriate and visually stunning articles. He "scoured bazaars and village fairs, and went into the very mud-huts of craftsmen to get fabrics and rural handicrafts of rare design to give the exhibition the authentic Indian touch."[53] The stultifying oppression of the British Raj was conveyed by a display of uniforms and military paraphernalia, and Gandhi's ideas by means of a minimalist pavilion draped with khadi, the homespun Indian cloth with which he was associated. The latter pavilion was set slightly apart from the other sections of the exhibition and took on something of the atmosphere of a shrine.

The National Institute of Design, then temporarily housed in the Corbusier-designed civic art gallery at Ahmedabad, made all the structural parts of the exhibition, printed the text on handmade paper, and processed most of the black-and-white photographs. Sharada Prasad recalled that "working in the austere cement box had its thrills and its problems. It seemed to make monks of us all; and the pigeons, which could fly in and out of the great Corbusier grilles, were evidently fond of perching on and marking pictures. There was yet another handicap in working in Ahmedabad—the distance from Delhi, the source of all material, and of authority. The two cities are only 600 miles apart, but that is a long way in a country with underdeveloped communications."[54]

Last-minute work was completed in the United States, where the exhibition was to premiere. The Indian members of the team were amazed at the speed at which text written in New York and telephoned to Los Angeles could be printed in California and then flown back overnight to New York.[55] At last everything was ready for the New York opening in February 1965. The exhibition proved a resounding success in New York; it was seen by as many as 90,000 people (estimates vary) before traveling to London, Washington, and Los Angeles. It fulfilled its objectives of bringing the period "alive" and produce a "feel" of India so well that some considered "exhibition" an inadequate term for such a "ravishing experience . . . a memorial so alive with breath and feeling."[56] It was transferred to India in 1966, and parts of it are still on display at the Pragati Maidan in New Delhi and in the Discovery of India exhibit (designed by an NID team) at the Nehru Centre in Bombay.[57]

Besides presenting a picture of an important part of Indian history, conveying something of the rich visual splendors of Indian material culture, and validating the products of a handicraft system, the Nehru exhibition also conveyed socio-political ideas in which the Eameses believed. The British MP Tony Benn, a longtime friend of Charles, saw it as the work of a "committed Internationalist . . . capable of seeing mankind as a whole and understanding its purpose and its problems" who had "thought himself into the whole history of the Indian Liberation Struggle and presented it to us."[58] Some in Britain saw it as a visually spectacular human interest story; others reveled in self-congratulation about the greatness of Britain "giving India its freedom."[59] In India, where it was enormously popular, the exhibition was read as a celebration of the Indian heritage, the heroic struggle for national independence, and the efforts to build a homogeneous, unified, and modernized "new India" as well as a moving affirmation of the vision of a free India and a tribute to the efforts of one man. While radicals abroad praised the exhibition's anti-imperialism, some in India thought it glossed over issues of difference and dissent.[60] Others remarked on its candor—Ashoke Chatterjee noted that it was remarkable for such an exhibition to avoid eulogizing and to depict failures and contradictions as well as victories.[61]

The charge of eulogizing was directed against another Eames exhibition: The World of Franklin and Jefferson (1975–1977), which toured Europe before opening in the United States in the bicentennial year. The original brief, which came from the U.S. Information Agency in 1972, was for an exhibition on Thomas Jefferson. Partly because Jefferson had been something of a childhood hero to both Charles and Ray, they approached the project with caution, and at their suggestion the brief was expanded to include the circle of people and ideas around Benjamin

6.15 The World of
Franklin and Jefferson,
1975. Eames Office.

6.16 Detail of time line in
The World of Franklin and
Jefferson.

6.17 The World of
Franklin and Jefferson.

Franklin and Jefferson in order to avoid a "great heroes" approach toward history: "When we looked for an idea for the exhibition we decided if we were to do an exhibition exclusively on Jefferson, it would turn out to be a kind of hero show and we felt 1975 is not the ideal time for such events. We thought it would be much more helpful to prepare an exhibition about two people—completely different in many ways but whose ultimate goal was much the same."[62] That they chose to concentrate on the ways in which ideas of the European Enlightenment were received and translated into political action in America rather than other aspects of the fight for independence is no surprise; the Eameses were steeped in the liberal, humanist, rationalist, "enlightened" tradition in American thought which dates back to that time.

The exhibition, which dominated the activities of the Eames Office for about five years, was divided into four main sections, each with a separate theme and layout.[63] The first section, "Friends and Acquaintances," introduced the circles of people around Franklin and Jefferson. Photographs and text explaining the ideas and achievements of George Washington, Thomas Paine, Paul Revere, and others were mounted on four display stands of plastic laminated plywood while perspex cases contained related objects (beautifully arranged, of course), including silver, ceramics, toys, and musical and scientific instruments. The second section, "Contrast and Continuity," presented the life stories of Franklin and Jefferson; it featured vertical and horizontal display panels, as did the third section, "Three Documents," which looked at the roles played by the two men in the creation of the Declaration of Independence, the Constitution, and the Bill of Rights. The final section, "Jefferson and the West," dealt with westward expansion.[64]

This, the most extensive exhibition designed by the Eames Office and the last major project to be undertaken before Charles's death, was a huge success abroad. It opened in Paris in 1975, where in two months it was seen by 50,000 people. According to Charles Eames, the French mostly "perceived it as a celebration of that time when the eighteenth century European Enlightenment was meeting up with American immediacy."[65] In Poland, as in Paris, visitors showed considerable interest in national figures of their own who had been involved in the American Revolution.[66] Some 1500 visitors per day saw it at Warsaw's National Museum, and 1000 per day in Britain (whose role as the oppressing power was underplayed considerably).[67]

Although the exhibition had been specially designed for convenient transportation, such a degree of use brought considerable wear and tear. Given a complete overhaul after each venue,[68] it was shown at New York's Metropolitan Museum of Art, at the Art Institute of Chicago, and at the Los Angeles County Museum of Art before traveling to the National Museum of Anthropology in Mexico City in April 1977. The exhibition was specially adapted to suit each venue while retaining all its main elements, including the almost statutory white walls, a special grid for overhead lighting, high-quality carpeting, and a full-scale model of a Neo-Classical doorway (which gave an air of sanctity to the setting and formed an impressive entrance to the "Three Documents" section). For each venue, texts were translated into the appropriate language and objects related to the country or the museum in which the exhibition was being shown were added.[69]

Despite its tremendous popularity abroad, the exhibition had a mixed reception at home. The favorable American reactions included "witty . . . efficient . . . intelligent" and "a magnificent learning experience"; the negative responses included "overcrowded," "overwhelms by its richness, abundance and fragmentation," "a wealth of information but not an argued development," "strangely unevocative of the period," and "like a coffee table book."[70] Some critics took the stuffed bison (figure 6.18) as an indication that the Eameses had finally gone too far; others saw it as signifying that serious learning need not be dull and applauded their showmanship. Since the intention behind most of the Eameses' exhibitions was "information overload," the charge of superabundance did not unduly worry them; they believed that viewers were sufficiently intelligent, discriminating, and skilled to take from an exhibition what they wanted. What some saw as confusing in its inclusiveness could, they thought, be approached in many different ways and negotiated by many different routes.

Whereas they had found a debate with some French curators about "high information content in a museum setting" interesting and fruitful, the Eameses were dismayed at what they saw as the hostility of New York art critics and museum curators to an exhibition which, although it included works of art, was not primarily about them and which was clearly both pedagogic and celebratory in tone.[71] They defended themselves by pointing out that The World of Franklin and Jefferson was

6.18 View of "Jefferson
and the West" area of The
World of Franklin and
Jefferson, 1975.

advertised as a "citizens' exhibition" rather than as one for historians or connoisseurs—as "more like a colored walk-through tabloid" than an art exhibition.[72] The charge of "information overload" was parried with arguments that they had used a lot of captions and text because the exhibition was about particular problems and circumstances, that if they had been dealing with accomplishments they "could have done it in very few words," that they had always "thought of the Met as a cultural history establishment, at least as much as an art museum," and that they took literally and seriously the museum's "commitment to offer information not just to confront the visitor with objects."[73]

The World of Franklin and Jefferson was also seen as an unwelcome intrusion by a sponsor into the "neutral" museum world—perhaps more so than in the case of sponsorship of an art exhibition, because this particular exhibition involved history and, by implication, politics. "Maybe they felt," said Charles Eames, "that because there was a story and IBM had paid for it, it must somehow be IBM talking—which was not at all the case."[74]

This "citizens' exhibition" was seen by some as "shallow—garish and jingoist," "undifferentiated patriotism,"[75] and "a Turkish bazaar of *American Heritage Magazine*-like images and disconnected bits of information. It is not an art exhibition; nor is it, as some have suggested, educational. Rather, it is propaganda designed to overwhelm rather than convince. Its excesses are stunning—banners, memorabilia machines and artifacts."[76]

The banners bearing quotations from Franklin and Jefferson were read by some as embarrassingly naive, particularly Jefferson's dictum that "where the press is free, and every man able to read, all is safe." Such smugness and complacency about a fledgling United States with a supposedly free press and mass literacy was seen by some critics as inappropriate if not as part of an establishment campaign to whitewash both historical events and contemporary problems. In a country increasingly aware of the history and politics of oppression, it seemed ironic that this major exhibition could celebrate the ideas of freedom and equality yet omit any reference to Jefferson's belief that black people were inferior to whites or to the Indian Removal Policy.[77]

Unfortunately, this neatly packaged and (at many levels) tremendously well informed and informative exhibition presented westward expansion within a framework of the inevitability of unproblematic progress. Numerous artifacts were shown to illustrate the richness of Native American cultures, but Native American peoples were given no voice. The Eameses had a serious interest in Native American material culture, and were seen as "progressive" because of this, but neither they nor this exhibition offered a critique of the dominant culture's version of the past—indeed, this sanitized show could easily be read as a eulogy to that vision.[78] The Eameses had fallen into the very trap they had hoped to avoid—and, to a degree, they recognized the fact: "It is true that we set out originally to be quite critical and hard about the main characters, but as we went on, we were so impressed by how much someone like James Madison was able to pull off time and again that we came out pretty much all admiration."[79]

Anxieties about the degree of propaganda in The World of Franklin and Jefferson were fueled by misgivings about the USIA's role in the commissioning and funding of the exhibition.[80] Although it had in fact been the USIA that had first approached the Eames Office about the exhibition, The World of Franklin and Jefferson was actually produced for the American Revolution Bicentennial Administration in collaboration with the Metropolitan Museum of Art and IBM. The latter provided $500,000 toward the cost of the exhibition and related publications, but the Eameses appear to have been given a free hand to tell the story as they saw it. However, because the USIA dealt with the foreign transportation of the exhibition as well as the initial payments to the Eames Office, questions were raised about the legitimacy of holding such an exhibition in the United States when regulations stipulated that USIA money could be used only outside the country. In the end, because the exhibition had received most of its money from other organizations (particularly IBM), it was allowed to tour at home.[81]

During the 1960s and the early 1970s the Eameses designed for IBM a series of exhibitions centered on scientific and mathematical themes and on famous individuals within those fields. Charles had a lifelong interest in all aspects of science, and he was one of the first laymen to recognize the importance of the computer. Indeed, his fascination approached passion. Ray was less passionate about computers, but she shared Charles's belief in their importance and used her talents to make them understandable and acceptable to ordinary people. As communica-

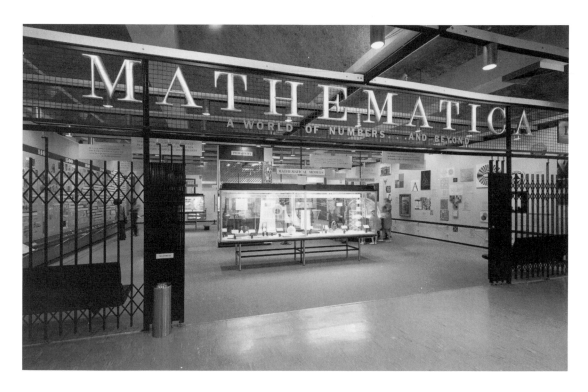

6.19 Marhematica: history
wall or time line on left,
image wall on right.

tors, the Eameses saw the interesting and intelligible presentation of science and technology as an exciting challenge.

The IBM Corporation, having been asked by the California Museum of Science and Industry to contribute a display to its new wing, to be opened in 1961, commissioned the Eameses, who had already made several films for IBM but had not yet undertaken a major exhibition. The result was Mathematica: A World of Numbers and Beyond, the basic idea behind which was to present mathematical concepts in a pleasurable way. Charles argued that the exhibition "should be of interest to a bright student and not embarrass the most knowledgeable." He continued:

> One of the best kept secrets in science is how unpompous scientists are at their science, and the amount of honest fun that for them is part of it. In doing an exhibition, as in Mathematica, one deliberately tries to let the fun out of the bag. The catch is that it can't be any old fun but it must be a very special brand. The excitement, or joke, must be a working part of the idea. The fun must follow all of the rules of the concept involved.[82]

An enormous amount of detailed research went into this, the Eameses' first concept exhibition. Ray Redheffer, Professor of Mathematics at UCLA, served as a consultant. There was a comprehensive history wall (the first time such a thing was used) and an image wall, but the main fun was in the nine mechanical interactive demonstrations of mathematical concepts. For example, when the visitor activated the "Probability Machine," 30,000 plastic balls fell through a maze of 200 pegs, forming a classic bell curve and thus illustrating that probability is "nothing more than good sense confirmed by calculation."[83] In the "Peep Shows," one could watch any or all of five two-minute animated films about mathematical concepts.

The development of the history wall or time line is an excellent example of how things got done in the Eames Office. This idea originated, not with Charles or Ray, but in discussions involving John Neuhart and two assistants, one of whom, Dick Bungay, suggested the idea of a wall devoted to the tools of mathematics (such as compasses and scales)—a "landscape of mathematics." Charles thought this "pretty boring" and suggested that they add some other things, particularly graphics. When he asked who used the tools, the focus shifted to the lives of

6.20 Peepshows,

Mathematica.

the mathematicians, and eventually to a time line that would display the main developments in mathematics within the life spans of the mathematicians associated with them.[84] As has already been noted, this early example of the Eameses' penchant for using personal stories to tell a wider story is related to Alvar Aalto's approach to exhibition design.

Charles and Ray Eames insisted on quality at every level of the exhibition. They battled fiercely to get the entire floor area covered with high-quality carpet rather than with something that could be hosed down for easy cleaning. The attention to detail paid off. Mathematica was such a success that a duplicate was installed at the Chicago Museum of Science and Industry, remaining there until it was moved to the Boston Museum of Science in 1980. The original Los Angeles exhibition remains *in situ,* and to see it well used thirty years after its installation is a delight. That it continues to stimulate and educate in a pleasurable manner is a tribute to the Eames Office and, in particular, to Charles's pioneering approach to scientific education.

Mathematica's success gave the Eameses the confidence to continue to use exhibitions to explore complex themes, and the prestige it brought IBM led that corporation to commission a pavilion and an exhibition for the New York World's Fair of 1964. The Eameses immediately entered into discussions on this project with Eero Saarinen. After Saarinen's death in September 1961, the joint project was continued by the Eames Office and Saarinen's former firm, Roche Dinkeloo and Associates.[85] The result was a 1¼-acre site divided into several distinct exhibition areas, each covered with an enormous translucent plastic canopy held up by steel "trees." On top of the canopies was a spectacular ovoid theater housing one of the Eameses' most elaborate multi-media presentations, Think, which drew directly on Herbert Bayer's technique of placing multiple images (in this case as many as 22) at various angles and heights. The aim of Think was to demystify the computer and demonstrate that the methods

6.21 Scale model of screen layout, Think, Ovoid Theater, IBM Corporation Pavilion, New York World's Fair, 1964. Eames Office.

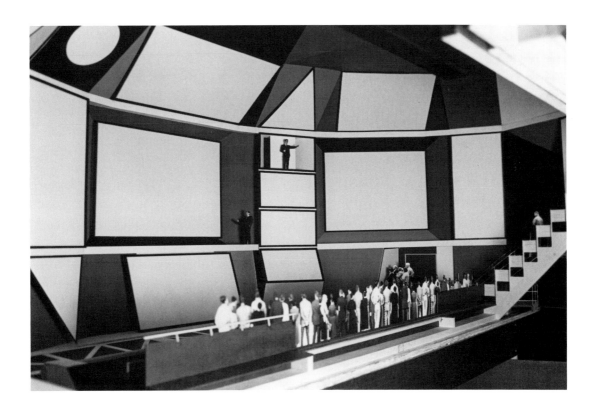

used to solve complex problems were simply elaborations of basic methods used to solve everyday ones. Smaller exhibits included computer-operated puppet shows, a display of "antique" computers, a "typewriter bar" where visitors could play with the latest IBM machines, the "probability machine" discussed above, and a "scholar's walk" for those who wanted additional information. While the exhibits showed the latest in computer technology and the larger structures reflected the latest trends in exhibition architecture, the lower exhibition area, with its small pavilions and kiosks, had some of the flavor of earlier world's fairs, drawing on the iconography of the fairground, Americana, and commonplace nineteenth-century graphics to produce a "popular" atmosphere, at once celebratory and nostalgic, in which people might relax, enjoy themselves, and shed their inhibitions about learning. Musicians entertained those waiting for the giant "People Wall," which lifted up to 400 fairgoers at a time into the egg-shaped theater for the multi-screen presentation (figure 6.22). Before that ascent the show's master of ceremonies descended to greet his new audience, "appearing before you high on a platform let down from the egg—like a jolly young god, triumphant over gravity. . . . In this punctual deus ex machina the designers have hit a Dionysian button, calling up emotions of awe, terror, recognition and joy. . . ."[86] Some people, mainly designers and design critics, considered it all somewhat excessive and vulgar and felt that the Eameses had gone too far in their popularizing of science and technology and of the "modern."[87] The general public, however, appears to have loved it.[88]

In 1968, IBM allocated some space in its new headquarters in Armonk, N.Y., to a permanent exhibition gallery that was to house a collection of books, antique calculators, and computers belonging to founder Thomas Watson.[89] Roche Dinkeloo and Associates designed the gallery, and the Eames Office produced a 10-minute color "study film," written by Glen Fleck and Charles Eames, illustrating its role as a resource center for IBM employees. The project was not realized; however, IBM did commission a smaller exhibition space for its Washington office which incorporated some of the ideas developed in the earlier proposal, including graphic displays of old and new computers and desks where visitors could use IBM machines.[90]

The Eameses' promotion of computers climaxed with the 1971 exhibition A Computer Perspective.[91] The thesis behind this exhibition

6.22 People Wall ready for
ascent to Think, 1964.
Eames Office in association
with Roche Dinkeloo and
Associates.

was that the modern computer had emerged from three distinct sources—logical automata (including mechanical toys, an Eames passion), statistical handling devices (such as census card sorters), and adding machines—and that "an exhibit on the origins and development of the computer demanded 'bold new techniques of communication.'"[92] The exhibition included a number of machines, including one designed and built by Herman Hollerith to record the census of 1890 and one installed in 1949 to keep records of reservations for American Airlines. One key feature was the largest and most comprehensive of the history walls, made up of six floor-to-ceiling panels, each 8 feet wide and 3 feet deep and each representing a decade (figure 6.23). For the first time, actual objects were fastened to the panels, and documents and photographs were mounted at varying distances from the wall in overlapping layers. The glass that covered the entire history wall was overlaid with text and with lines and arrows designed to help viewers wend their way through the mass of material in a coherent manner.[93] The idea was that "a visitor moving from one place to another in front of the History Wall would find that certain objects, graphics and comments would disappear from view while others would appear, providing a fluid or constantly shifting kaleidoscope effect, a kinetic equivalent of the actual passage of time correlated with the viewer's movement. In this way the exhibit technique reproduced the complexity and interaction of the forces and creative impulses that had produced the computer."[94] Unfortunately, some found the display very difficult to follow, because of its density and because objects, text, and images seemed to appear and disappear without reason.[95] In general, however, the exhibition was considered a success, and it remained at IBM's Corporate Exhibit Center in New York until 1975.

During the early 1970s the Eames Office also produced for IBM a series of small, easily transportable exhibitions on topics related to mathematics and astronomy. The corporation had initially requested small seasonal exhibits that would attract the attention of pedestrians passing the Corporate Exhibit Center.[96] Characteristically, the Eameses transformed the brief into something more far-reaching and educational, using scientific notions related to the seasons. For example, Fibonacci: Growth and Form (1972) illustrated how the Fibonacci numerical sequence related to growing things by means of a series of panels, each consisting of one blown-up photograph of a flower or plant or as many as 36 smaller photographs.[97]

6.23 A Computer
Perspective, IBM
Corporate Exhibit Center,
New York, 1971. History
wall or time line. Eames
Office.

The larger Copernicus exhibition (1972) utilized rectangular glass and laminate panels attached to an overhead grid as a backdrop against which aspects of Copernicus's life and work were told through photographs, charts, and text (figure 6.24).[98] As in every Eames exhibition, the attention to detail was all important. The Eames Office consulted both a professor of astronomy and a professor of history at Harvard University. Charles made a photographic trip to Poland, where Copernicus had lived and worked, and when the exhibition opened in December 1972 the windows of the Corporate Exhibit Center were adorned with Polish Christmas decorations—"functioning decoration" brought into the public world of exhibitions. In 1973 the Eames Office produced another festive display for the exhibition Isaac Newton; Physics for a Moving Earth. This time Charles and Ray supplemented their own collection of Christmas decorations with items from Girard's collection of English Yuletide ones, decked the exhibition hall with holly and mistletoe, and placed plum puddings and mince pies on classical columns as though they were precious works of art. As ever with an Eames exhibition, the project was thoroughly researched. The Christmas "decorations" amounted to a mini-exhibition in themselves because they were used to illustrate the ways in which the Christmas period was observed in seventeenth- and eighteenth-century England.[99] Some thought it too much on top of the existing exhibition, but most enjoyed its mix of scholarship and festivity, the joyful insistence that objects as simple and transient as mince pies were as worthy of attention as a bust of a "great master" or a fragment of ancient pottery, and the implicit assertion that "serious" exhibitions should be allowed their Christmas decorations just as much as a department store, an office, or a private home.[100]

The Eameses moved into exhibition design because they were passionately interested in ideas and in communicating those ideas to others. Their outstanding contribution was to fuse pleasing designs and new approaches (including the use of films, slide shows, and interactive games) with older concepts to produce exhibitions that were arenas for viewing and learning about a multitude of objects. Elevating a few select objects into "works of art" by placing them in splendid isolation in a plain unadorned exhibition space was not for them. Indeed, their distinctive style was additive and visually complex. Their exhibitions became as crammed with objects as those of the nineteenth century, which curators and designers had been so desperately trying to get away from.

6.24 Copernicus, IBM
Corporate Exhibit Center,
New York, 1972. Eames
Office.

6.25 Window display of
Polish Christmas
decorations. Copernicus,
IBM Corporate Exhibit
Center, New York, 1972.
Eames Office.

Overcrowded the exhibitions may have been, but objects were never presented in isolation. The Eameses were fanatical contextualizers and often gave viewers a great deal of text to read. Some thought that this particular aspect of "information overload" was better suited to books than to exhibitions and that some of the later Eames exhibitions privileged written text over the total "experience"[101]; others regarded well-researched text as just one of the many pleasures of Eames exhibitions. National differences in attitudes toward large amounts of text also need to be taken into consideration here; for example, the written material in The World of Franklin and Jefferson was better received in Europe than in the United States.[102] But there are as many readings of an exhibition (or a film, or any text, for that matter) as there are viewers, and the Eameses' denser exhibitions actively encouraged multifarious readings and experiences. Furthermore, as Marilyn and John Neuhart point out, precursors of "hypermedia" can be found in the later exhibitions.[103]

That the Eameses' presentations marked a significant shift in exhibition design was noted by the mid 1960s, when they were welcomed by some as an antidote to contemporary exhibitions that sacrificed meaning to appearance and which, at worst, were "little more than repetitive clichés, too often unrelated to the material displayed."[104] The Eameses were seen as "responsible for turning what might have been routine displays into meaningful experiences."[105]

Interior of St. Mary's,
Helena, Arkansas. (Eames
Demetrios)

Meyer House, Huntleigh
Village, Missouri. (Laurent
Jean Torno Jr.)

Ray Eames with panel
detailing the work of the
Eames Office, 1957. (Lucia
Eames Demetrios d.b.a.
Eames Office)

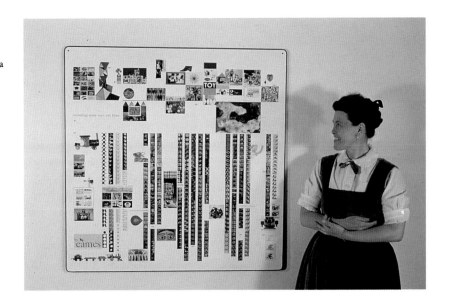

Crosspatch (fabric design),
1945. Ray Eames. (Lucia
Eames Demetrios d.b.a.
Eames Office)

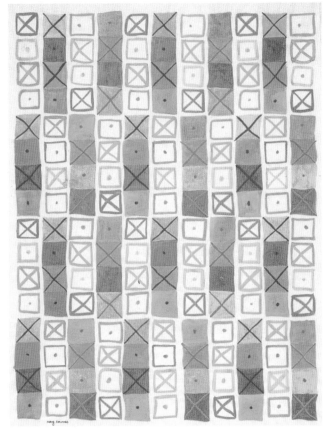

Room design, An
Exhibition for Modern
Living, 1949. Ray Eames
for Eames Office. (Lucia
Eames Demetrios d.b.a.
Eames Office)

Pattern deck of House of
Cards, 1952. (Lucia Eames
Demetrios d.b.a. Eames
Office)

Picture deck of House of
Cards, 1953. Eames Office.
(Lucia Eames Demetrios
d.b.a. Eames Office)

Plastic and metal shell chairs with assorted bases. Eames Office. (Herman Miller Furniture Co.)

Lounge Chair and Ottoman, 1956. Eames Office. (Herman Miller Furniture Co.)

Tandem Sling Seating, 1962. Eames Office. Photographed at John Wayne Airport, Orange County, California, 1993. (Herman Miller Furniture Co.)

EAMES® LOUNGE AND OTTOMAN   herman miller

Tandem Shell Seating,
1963. Eames Office.
(Herman Miller Furniture
Co.)

Chaise, 1968.

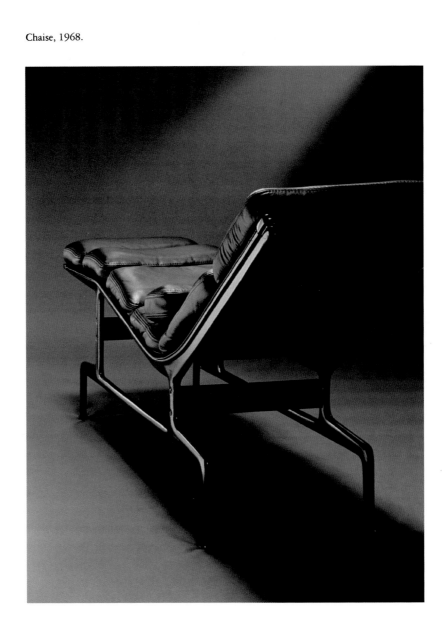

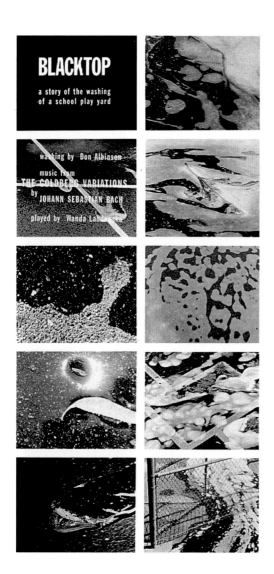

Blacktop, 1952. (Lucia
Eames Demetrios d.b.a.
Eames Office)

*Textiles and Ornamental Arts
of India,* 1955.

Toccata for Toy Trains, 1957.

Tops, 1969. (Lucia Eames Demetrios d.b.a. Eames Office)

Copernicus exhibition, IBM Corporate Exhibition Center, New York, 1972.

Eames House, Pacific
Palisades, 1945–1949.
Charles and Ray Eames.
(Lucia Eames Demetrios
d.b.a. Eames Office)

Breakfast at the Eames
House, c. 1951: table set
by Ray Eames. (Lucia
Eames Demetrios d.b.a.
Eames Office)

The living room of the
Eames House, 1992. (Lucia
Eames Demetrios and
Shelley Mills)

Charles and Ray Eames won international acclaim as independent filmmakers with their very first films to be shown in public. Two years after
their release, and only four years after the Eameses' first attempt at filmmaking, *Parade, or Here They Come Down Our Street* and *Blacktop* won
awards at the 1954 Edinburgh International Film Festival. By 1978 the
Eameses had made more than eighty short films, many of which had been
praised for their visual beauty and intellectual stimulation; however, they
still found it difficult to view themselves as filmmakers, because, in the
main, they made films as a means of communicating ideas rather than for
entertainment or creative expression.

Most of the Eameses' films were made about issues or objects
that had long concerned them, as teaching tools, as records of exhibitions,
or as parts of presentations. The Eameses approached filmmaking much as
they approached their design work, putting the same depth of research,
insistence on quality, and attention to detail into the shortest of films as
into any other project. The film medium appealed to their preference for
working in a disciplined manner within tight constraints and offered
them an outlet for exploring relationships between scripts and visual
material.

Falling partly into but largely between the categories of "experimental" and "business" films, Eames films do not fit neatly into any one
category or genre. Postwar America witnessed a veritable boom in independent and commercially sponsored filmmaking, as well as the begin-
nings of the fascination with multi-media projects that came to
symbolize the free experimental spirit of the 1960s.[1] Charles and Ray
Eames were not only part of these important cultural developments; their
work influenced these developments. During World War II the American
public, already well versed in watching and "reading" Hollywood feature
films, became increasingly familiar with shorter propagandistic, documentary, educational, and training films, many of which were sponsored by
government agencies and private corporations and intended to inspire
workers and management to even greater efforts. Beginning in the early

7.1 Page from A Sampling
of Eames Films Available
From Pyramid (Pyramid
Films, Santa Monica,
California, c. 1974).

1950s, television further extended Americans' familiarity with visual imagery and the language of film and photography. At the same time, still and movie cameras became increasingly popular as prices dropped throughout the decade. It was against this background that Charles and Ray Eames began to make films and became involved in multi-media and multiple-image presentations.

Both Charles and Ray had long been interested in film and photography. Ray had been a film enthusiast since her student days, and Charles had been fascinated by photography since his boyhood. From 1942 on Charles had spent a great deal of time documenting objects in photographs. Yet, as Ray later put it, "Charles would never take a shot simply as a record . . . just to document a piece. He would only take it if he got the photograph looking right, looking as he wanted it."[2] Charles became fascinated with color film (developed in Europe in 1936 and commercially available from 1938[3])—especially transparencies, which he used to explore objects in great detail. Within the partnership he was very definitely the one in charge of photography, although the actual images often owed a great deal to Ray. From 1945 they were both involved in using fast-changing color transparencies (some of which included "found" objects, such as a daisy, a feather, or insect wings, placed between the two glass sections of the slide) in visually spectacular "slide carnivals."[4] They both learned a tremendous amount from Herbert Matter, who joined their team in 1943[5]; he taught Charles how to use a 35-millimeter camera with technical virtuosity, particularly for close-ups, and he encouraged Ray to try new ways of composing images. To describe the Eameses' interest in images and photography as an obsession is not an exaggeration; the Library of Congress now holds approximately 750,000 images (mainly slides) from the Eames Office. Friends and colleagues love to tell how, when hearing an interesting or amusing story, Charles, who was rarely without a camera, would always ask "Did you get a picture?"[6]

It was as photographers and designers interested in how as well as what the eye saw, and also in recording images, that the Eameses came to filmmaking. They did not try to engage in mainstream Hollywood movie making, although they knew that world well. Living in Los Angeles and moving in "artistic" circles, they knew many people in the motion picture industry. Charles had worked as a set designer in MGM's art department between 1941 and 1942, under art directors such as

Vincente Minnelli, Randell Duell, Lyle Wheeler, George Davis, and Gabriel Scanamillo, and Charles and Ray were introduced to the director Billy Wilder—thereafter to become one of their best friends—by an MGM scriptwriter.[7] Wilder had been a champion of modernist art and design, particularly paintings and furniture.[8] In the Eameses he found a couple who not only were at the forefront of furniture design but also shared his love of painting and sculpture. Like Charles, Billy Wilder enjoyed photography. Audrey Wilder, who thought Charles "a fantastic photographer," recalls how in 1948, on her honeymoon (a short trip to Nevada with the Eameses), her new husband and Charles Eames spent a great deal of time together photographing rock formations and trees.[9] She also recalls "feeling something of a fraud because the other three were so good with cameras and artistic too," and saying so. Charles thereupon decided to teach her how to use a camera, much as in the films made for the Polaroid Corporation more than twenty years later.[10]

The Eameses' only direct connection with the Hollywood film industry after 1942 came when Charles worked on Wilder's film *The Spirit of St. Louis* (Warner Brothers, 1957), a bio-pic (and a box-office flop) about one of Charles's childhood heroes, the St. Louis native Charles Lindbergh. Ray Eames felt that Charles's enthusiasm for Lindbergh played at least a small part in Wilder's decision to make this film. Appointed "photographic consultant," Charles was in charge of the second unit. He indulged in such exploits as taking aerial photographs from a plane flown by a stunt pilot.[11] He was also involved with the design and construction of the Lindbergh plane, and with the scenes related to its production—which are linked by superb montage sequences, for which Charles receives credit in the opening title sequence. Designed in collaboration with Ray, the montages feature beautifully shot details of the design and manufacturing processes, including pieces of paper being moved around on a drawing board (just as in the Eames Office), plans, instruments, tools, and the construction of the plane itself. Grids and circular shapes help to unify the separate elements. A "hands on" approach to design is emphasized, again just as in the Eames Office. These sequences are a joy to behold and deserve more attention than they have been given, ranking with the Saul Bass–Alfred Hitchcock scenes in *Psycho* as an example of collaboration between a designer and a film director at its best. In 1960 this film's producer, Leland Hayward, contacted Charles when he was producing a CBS television program, "The Fabulous Fifties"; the result was six short film sequences for which Charles and Ray each won an Emmy.[12]

Although the Eameses made it clear that they were not trying to reach a mass audience with their films, they were delighted that some of the later ones were seen by many thousands of people.[13] In general, their films had more in common with experimental filmmaking than with Hollywood feature films; however, they insisted that these were not experimental films in the accepted sense of that term. "They're not experimental films," Charles said. "they're not really films. They're just attempts to get across an idea."[14] Had a better medium for presenting ideas and objects to a larger audience been available then they would have grasped it: "You must be committed to the subject, to the discipline of the concept involved, not to the medium. In the process you may make a good film."[15]

EXPERIMENTAL FILMS

From the 1920s on there was a significant, if minority, interest in experimental filmmaking in America, influenced mainly by German, French, and Russian cinema.[16] The production of *Manahatta* in 1921 by the painter Charles Sheeler and the photographer Paul Strand, who together created stunning visual patterns out of the real world of New York, is usually seen as the beginning of this movement. In the late 1920s, when the influence of German Expressionist art forms was being felt,[17] interest grew rapidly: "Young artists, photographers, poets, novelists, dancers, architects, eager to explore the rich terrain of movie expression, learned how to handle a camera and with the most meager resources attempted to produce pictures of their own."[18] Many of these low-cost independent films were extremely inventive, varying in technique from montage and abstract photography to realism. In the 1930s the Museum of Modern Art actively promoted the cause of experimental film, which it saw as part and parcel of the new modernism in the arts.[19] During World War II, "experimental" and non-commercial techniques were used in documentary and training films, and audiences became used to seeing on screen things that looked "different."

All these factors, together with the increasing currency of modernism in the United States, led to an upsurge in independent filmmaking after 1945. Films by Maya Deren, Kenneth Anger, Curtis Harrington, Oskar Fischinger, James and John Whitney, Hans Richter, and others offered a wide variety of form and content—modern dance, movement, and metamorphosis; abstraction of form; a more open concern with sexuality; an almost obsessive portrayal of psychological disturbances—and helped the movement drop its "amateur" tag.

California was one of the main centers of postwar experimental cinema, with a great deal of creative activity and viewing taking place in San Francisco and in Los Angeles.[20] John Entenza, who for a time in the 1930s had worked in an experimental film unit at MGM, was extremely interested in avant-garde film. His "salon" brought together filmmakers, dancers, architects, painters, and other members of Los Angeles's artistic and bohemian fringe,[21] and through him the Eameses met the people responsible for establishing avant-garde film culture in California immediately after the war, including Oskar Fischinger (the German filmmaker whose reputation for special effects, animation, and other technical developments was such that Paramount had "headhunted" him in 1936),[22] the Whitney brothers, James Broughton, Sidney Peterson, Kenneth Anger, Curtis Harrington, and Harry Smith. The Eameses became part of this coterie in the 1950s.[23] In 1956 John Whitney joined their staff,[24] and in 1957 they joined Fischinger, Harrington, the Whitneys, and Wallace Berman as founding members of a distribution and exhibition service for independent films.[25] However, the Eameses remained somewhat separate from this Californian film clique. They were less intensely and selfconsciously "artistic" about their work, of which film was only one part, than many whose main life work was to be in film.

It is difficult to pinpoint particular stylistic influences in the Eameses' films. Unlike many other architects and designers, they did not simply use the camera to explore space; indeed, even when looking at architecture, their films are remarkably unconcerned with space. They knew the "classic" German, Russian, and French avant-garde films,[26] and some touches of Fischinger appear in their work. There are echoes of Fischinger's *An American March* (1940) in *Parade* (1952) (both make use of Sousa's "Stars and Stripes Forever"), and *Blacktop* (1952) draws on Fischinger's experiments with capturing abstract motion and sound on film.[27] Norman McLaren was more of an influence than Fischinger. He knew the Eameses, and he admired their work (as they did his).[28] An artist turned filmmaker, McLaren was fascinated by animation, by giving visual form to "thoughts," by the relationship of sound and visual form, by the play of light and shade, and by the use of the traveling zoom and multiple optics.[29] The Eameses' *Introduction to Feedback,* finished in 1960 but begun in the mid 1950s, includes a scene of two men fighting which is reminiscent of scenes in McLaren's *Neighbours* (1952). *Eames Lounge Chair* (1956), which uses fast-cut footage to create the illusion of movement and which ends with a body stretched out on the ground, is also reminiscent of *Neighbours,* but the question of influence is problematic: certain still images of the Eameses themselves taken in 1949 (figure 2.5) may have influenced McLaren. McLaren's *Chairy Tale* (1957) almost certainly influenced the dancing-chair sequence in the Eameses' *Kaleidoscope Jazz Chair* (1960), and McLaren's *Chalk River Valley* (1967), which features repeating atoms in space, predates the Eameses' *Powers of Ten* by a year, although both projects had very long gestations and were influenced by similar scientific developments. Other features of the Eameses' work that are reminiscent of McLaren's include similar "looks" achieved through lighting and film quality, varied animation techniques mixed with other forms of filmmaking, and the use of nonprofessional actors to give a stylized feel to certain scenes. Otherwise, however, the similarities between McLaren's films and the Eameses' are loose rather than specific and appear to have arisen out of thinking and working along similar lines under similar influences. From the late 1940s on the Eameses and McLaren shared a liberal bourgeois internationalist outlook which found expression in some of their films, and McLaren too spent time in India in the 1950s. Other shared interests included the relationship of visuals to sound, the conveying of thought by means of film, the zoom lens, and multiple optics. However, McLaren's work was more firmly within "mainstream" experimental filmmaking and took many more of its references from the fine arts.

The Eameses' films owed at least as much to their own aesthetic sensibilities—particularly Ray's collage and decorating skills, Charles's ability to handle ideas as well as a camera, and their mutual concerns with structure, images, and connections between images and ideas—as to experimental or mainstream filmmaking. They saw themselves as artisans as much as artists, though the latter word was one they often used to describe architects, philosophers, and scientists as well as painters, designers, and filmmakers. They were "Renaissance" people, and their films reflect their broad range of interests and their wealth of creative ideas.

SPONSORED FILMS

Besides being members of an independent filmmaking fraternity, Charles and Ray Eames made sponsored (otherwise known as business, commercial, or industrial) films. The sponsors were sometimes educational or cultural institutions, but the majority of clients were from big business or industry.[30]

The genre of the sponsored film dates back to Robert Flaherty's *Nanook of the North* (1922), which was sponsored by the Revillon Fréres fur company,[31] but it was not until after World War II that this sector boomed. After 1945 many firms reappraised their training and marketing techniques so as to better secure the large and lucrative markets for new products and materials. Seduced by the prospect of "1,000,000, new customers . . . from one little reel,"[32] many firms became convinced that films which directly advertised their products, obliquely referred to their company, or even simply associated their company with a seemingly worthy or progressive cause were good for business—and very often they were. By the 1960s, sponsored films formed a substantial part of American filmmaking, particularly in terms of the numbers of films made and viewed. Today it is easy to forget just what a remarkable commercial, and sometimes artistic, phenomenon this was.

Large corporations, smaller family firms, museums, charitable foundations, and the federal government all turned to film, whether to communicate the attractions of a product or the essence of an ideology. In 1959, when 223 feature films were made in the United States, 5400 sponsored films were made, at a total cost of $280 million.[33] A periodical called *Business Screen* promoted the new phenomenon, as did books such as *The Dollars and Sense of Business Films,* which assured investors of good returns on high capital outlays. The Society of Motion Picture and Television Engineers published a report entitled The Scope and Nature of Non-Theatrical Films.[34] The larger producers of what were also called "information films," such as Jam Handy of Detroit and Wilding Inc. of

Chicago, employed as many as 500 people in 1960, producing between 125 and 200 pictures per year. By 1960 few of the filmmaking firms went by the old rule of thumb of $1000 per minute for black-and-white film without special effects; one firm made 10-minute films for as little as $7000 and as much as $70,000.[35] The topics of sponsored films ranged from the virtues of particular products to "the loftiest reaches of disinterested public service."[36]

A company which accepted that "selling" involved more subtle and sophisticated mechanisms than mere product promotion and acknowledged its own lack of expertise would often give a filmmaker a remarkably free hand and a considerable amount of capital. This was certainly the case when IBM approached the Eameses in the early 1950s with the idea of making a film about computers. The initiative came from Eliot Noyes, IBM's design director, who had known Charles and Ray well since the early 1940s and who admired their work greatly. The Eameses had not yet made a sponsored film, but their award-winning work included *A Communications Primer* (1953)—perhaps the first film to extol the virtues of the computer. They went on to develop this theme for IBM in *The Information Machine: Creative Man and the Data Processor* (1957), which was shown at the 1958 World's Fair in Brussels (as was a shorter Eames film made for the Herman Miller Furniture Company).

It was the chance to develop a project related to computers that convinced the Eameses that the IBM commission was worthy of their attention. They never accepted commissions of which they did not wholeheartedly approve, and they always demanded the right to work in their own way, often plowing substantial amounts of their own money into an over-budget project. In addition to further work for both Herman Miller and IBM, they went on to produce films for Westinghouse, ABC, Boeing, and Polaroid.

MULTI-MEDIA AND MULTIPLE-SCREEN PRESENTATIONS

After George Nelson was approached by the Fine Art Department of the University of Georgia to discuss educational policy, he contacted Charles Eames. The result was the first public multi-media presentation in the United States, delivered in 1953 as A Rough Sketch for a Sample Lesson for a Hypothetical Course.[37] Ray and Charles collaborated on the film sequences produced in their office, and Ray and Alexander Girard assisted with the planning and presentation of the project, but the ideas behind the presentation seem to have come mostly from George Nelson and Charles Eames. The aim was to replace the conventional lecture with new teaching techniques, including three concurrent slide images, film, a narrator, a large board of printed visual information, sound, and complementary smells piped through the ventilation system. Charles Eames later remembered:

> We used a lot of sound, sometimes carried to a very high volume so you would actually feel the vibrations. . . . We did it because we wanted to heighten awareness. . . . The smells were quite effective. They did two things: they came on cue, and they heightened the illusion. It was quite interesting because in some scenes that didn't have smell cues, but only smell suggestions in the script, a few people felt they had smelled things—for example, the oil in the machinery.[38]

Nelson and Eames had reconsidered the whole approach to teaching and learning in the department, and they suggested a move away from the delivery of detailed factual information in favor of developing the students' creative capacity and their ability to understand ideas. They hoped to break down compartmentalization by helping the students make links and cross-references between subject areas. Charles, for once, seemed unable to find much to praise in traditional methods, or to appreciate the complexities of the teacher-student relationship at its most stimulating and intimate, although he did acknowledge that certain exceptional teachers were able to convey knowledge well in lectures. In their scheme to redistribute the large amounts of money spent on staff, Nelson and Eames proposed retaining only a few "gifted" teachers and supplementing reading with new teaching aids utilizing the latest technology. They were optimistic that students would understand their "own" subjects more quickly and that the money saved could be used to broaden their then stultifyingly narrow education. This proved of little consolation to those staff members who, understandably, feared for their jobs and for the loss of valued and time-honored approaches to their work.

7.2 Presentation of A
Rough Sketch for a Sample
Lesson for a Hypothetical
Course, UCLA, 1953.
George Nelson, Charles
and Ray Eames, and
Alexander Girard.

Because their ideas on the most effective ways to teach and communicate course material were not well received by the staff (to say the least), Eames and Nelson decided to produce an example of what they were talking about. The result was A Rough Sketch for a Sample Lesson for a Hypothetical Course (figure 7.2). Funded by the Rockefeller Foundation, it included two films by Nelson and two by the Eameses, two slide sequences by Nelson, and some film extracts. The Eameses' sections, Communications Process and Communications Methods, were based on the belief that what an individual receives from a particular message or image depends on what the individual brings to the experience of receiving—an idea commonplace enough now but not so in 1953. The sample lesson played to packed lecture theaters and made some converts among the staff, but as a system it was too costly to implement. Researching, producing, and staging such a presentation took enormous sums of money. The technologically complex sample lesson, for instance, required the services of up to eight people, and the cost of filming alone was astronomical by academic standards.[39] Significantly, it was the world of commerce that sponsored the Eameses' most exciting educational films, multi-media presentations, and exhibitions.

For an occasion of sufficient importance, the U.S. government was also prepared to spend lavishly. Such was the case with Glimpses of the USA. This, the most famous of the Eameses' multi-screen presentations,[40] was commissioned by the U.S. Department of State for a major exhibition to be held in Moscow in 1959 as part of a "cultural exchange." Once again, the commission came indirectly via George Nelson, the designer of the exhibition, who flew to California to persuade the Eameses to prepare a film about "a day in the life of the United States."[41] They accepted, and they also offered ideas about the exhibition as a whole. Nelson later recalled that his three days of intensive discussions with the Eameses culminated when the three of them, plus Billy Wilder and Jack Macey, the U.S. Information Agency's coordinator of design and construction, spent an evening at the Eames House, during which "all the basic decisions of the fair were made."[42]

The Eameses were given a virtually free hand with the presentation, not only by Nelson but also by the U.S. government. "Dressed like a boy scout and girl scout," Charles and Ray arrived in Moscow the night before the premiere, having personally transported the precious cans of

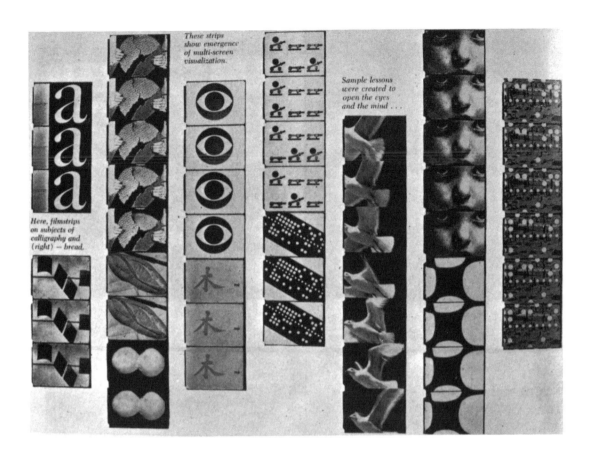

7.3 Page from *Business Screen* 23, no. 7 (1962) referring to Sample Lesson.

7.4 Glimpses of the USA.
Multi-screen presentation,
Moscow, 1959. Eames
Office.

film.[43] Nobody saw the presentation before its public viewing. Nelson and a host of government officials were anxious, but they need not have worried; the "totally new type of presentation" went off flawlessly.[44]

The presentation was envisaged as a message from one urban community to another at a time when both had had their fill of words but, the Eameses hoped, could still respond to visual images. There was a 12-minute film presentation of 2200 rapidly changing images (most of them still but some moving), accompanied by music composed by Elmer Bernstein. The images, projected onto seven 32-feet screens enclosed in a wonderful geodesic dome designed by Buckminster Fuller, emphasized everyday life. Image by image and screen by screen, the Eameses offered what Fuller described as "a universal language of the everyday life of human beings"[45] and took the audience on a coast-to-coast tour of the United States. Fuller expressed amazement that anyone could orchestrate so many colors, images, and sounds in such a "masterful" way and claimed to have been extremely moved by the presentation—as, apparently, were the 1500 people (including Premier Nikita Khrushchev) who saw it with him when it opened. Peter Blake later recalled that "everyone [had] tears in their eyes as they came out."[46] Ray Eames always spoke of the show as a very "affective" experience. It clearly meant a great deal to her, and the remembering of it in a television interview years later brought tears to her eyes and a comforting gesture from Charles.[47]

The Moscow show illustrated the ability of images and music to touch the heart as well as the intellect. It preached that the world was (or should be) not about great nation-states but about human beings who all shared the same planet, and that similarities should be considered as important as differences. One particularly noteworthy example of this is the use of a short film clip of Marilyn Monroe. Charles Eames had asked Billy Wilder for a short piece of film to use in the middle of the presentation, and Wilder had suggested a close-up sequence from *Some Like It Hot* in which Monroe breaks into a big smile and winks.[48] This proved an inspired choice. That Marilyn Monroe was not known in Russia at the time did not matter; the ovation each time the clip was shown came from the recognition of an attractive woman caught by the camera in a basic but powerful human act of communication. Here was the friendly face of America.

The final stroke of genius came from Ray. There was some debate as to how to end the presentation. One idea was to end with a dynamically angled shot of a jet airliner taking off, to symbolize progress and the drawing together of different peoples in the "global village" that some saw as the inevitable result of high-speed air travel and other modern technologies. A usually reliable source attributes this idea to Charles[49]; however, in a televised interview in 1975 Charles emphasized that the idea finally used came from Ray, simply noting that the "official idea" involved jet planes and a fanfare.[50] Ray wanted to end the show on a more human and intimate note. The last few images were of people saying goodnight. This produced a strong sense of closure but had less finality than a formal goodbye. Hoping to generate feelings associated with caring and friendship, the Eameses used as the final image a close-up of a bowl of flowers. Forget-me-nots were chosen because of their connotations of remembrance, constancy, and simplicity. As it turned out, this was a fortunate choice: not only do these flowers symbolize love, friendship, and remembrance in Russia, but their Russian name—*nezabutki*—translates literally as "forget-me-not." It was this word that could be heard over and over again as visitors left the presentation.[51] Three million Soviet citizens saw this show; the floor had to be resurfaced three or four times during the six-week exhibit. [52]

The Eameses learned a great deal about the effects of multiple images when they were preparing the Moscow show. They wanted to make a powerful impact, but they had to be careful not to overwhelm:

> We wanted to have a credible number of images, but not so many that they couldn't be scanned in the time allotted. At the same time, the number of images had to be large enough so that people wouldn't be exactly sure how many things they had seen. We arrived at the number seven. With four images, you always knew there were four, but by the time you got up to eight images you weren't quite sure. They were very big images—the width across four of them was half the length of a football field. . . . We tried out various tricks and rhythms in changing the images. We discovered that if you had seven images and changed one of them, this put an enormously wasteful, noninformative burden on the brain, because with every change the eye had to check every image to see which one had changed. When you're busy checking you don't absorb information.[53]

What they learned was soon put to use in a project wherein the multiple images were used to convey simultaneity.

The resounding success of the Moscow presentation led the U.S. government to commission another multi-screen presentation, The House of Science, for the 1962 Seattle World's Fair.[54] As visitors sat on the floor of a pavilion designed by Minoru Yamasaka, slide transparencies were projected onto the 34-feet concave walls to set the mood for the presentation film, which used six rectangular screens arranged so as to form a larger rectangle (figure 7.5). Animation (drawn by Glen Fleck), still images, and live action were used to depict the history of science as an architectural allegory, to review the current state of science, and to outline future possibilities.

The most elaborate example of the Eameses' multi-screen work was Think, prepared for the IBM pavilion at the 1964–65 New York World's Fair to illustrate the relationships between modern data-processing technology and the problem-solving methods used in everyday life.[55] This project was visually spectacular, with 22 separate screens (fourteen large and eight smaller)—squares, triangles, and circles as well as the usual rectangles—showing a rapidly cut sequence of still and moving images, including some animation (figure 7.6).

Esquire called this "the thinking man's pavilion," but Ralph Caplan argues that its message about problem-solving processes was not generally comprehended and most visitors read it as an attempt to explain how computers worked.[56] Mina Hamilton asked whether the media did not detract from the message and whether the excess of technology did not obscure what the Eameses were trying to convey:

> At first, the technique seems eminently suited to the conceptual statement, but the quick succession of images thrown on screens placed widely apart is occasionally confusing, more often frustrating—particularly because of the beauty and precision of each individual still or "take". . . .
>
> The pace of the show . . . is so fast that a person does not have enough time (as he does in a static exhibit) to weed out what he wants to see or not see so the different sets of information are completely haphazard. In a sense, what Eames has done to the film in the IBM show is to present it as a symphony or ballet: a succession of images and sounds move so rapidly across

7.5 The House of Science.

Multi-screen presentation,

Seattle World's Fair, 1962.

Eames Office.

7.6 Think. Multi-screen
presentation, IBM
Corporation Pavilion, New
York World's Fair,
1964–65. Eames Office.

time and space that they cannot be isolated, recognized, or re-membered as individual events but they are interwoven to form a total impression. The kaleidoscope-like result is overwhelming and "spectacular" but too fragmented to be entirely successful.[57]

What the Eameses thought of this particular criticism is not known. Hamilton herself admitted that the Eameses did not expect everybody to see everything and hoped that each person would take away different experiences and information. Ray regarded the multi-media shows at Montreal's Expo 67 as "rather frivolous,"[58] and she and Charles came to accept that a multiplicity of images or action on a single screen can have at least as much impact as a multi-screen presentation. For whatever reason, the Eameses moved away from multi-screen presentations to concentrate on film, design, and exhibition work.

The pioneering nature of the multi-media work has been widely acknowledged. As I have noted, A Rough Sketch for a Sample Lesson for a Hypothetical Course (1953) was the first public presentation anywhere in the world of what came to be a well-used art form. Although the filmmaker Abel Gance had used multiple images and rapid cutting in the 1920s,[59] the techniques had been largely forgotten, and the Eameses developed them in new ways. Jordon Belson and other contemporaries expanded on their work and developed multi-media events into "sublimi-nal" experiences,[60] but the Eameses' work was crucial in both pioneering and popularizing multi-media and multi-image shows. Some of their work in this area now seems dated, but there is no doubt that in its time it was extremely innovative. Belson and the Eameses were part of a move-ment to free film from the orthodox use of standard lenses, projection equipment, and screens, and multi-media shows became an exciting part of American and West European cultural practice in the 1960s.[61] The Eameses were central to these developments, although they kept a slight distance from the selfconscious avant-gardism, the psychedelia, and the "happenings" of the 1960s.

FILMMAKING

At the same time they were producing multi-image presentations, the Eameses were using many of the same techniques in films.[62] The use of multiple images and the rapid cutting of still images transferred to motion-picture footage were two of their major contributions to filmmaking. Another major contribution was the related concept of information overload, which was also related to some of their exhibitions. Other Eames techniques included using animation to simplify complex data and ideas and to present images of periods, people, products, and concepts for which there were few (if any) established frameworks of representation; splitting the screen between animation and live action; fracturing images with a kaleidoscope lens; and zooming toward and away from particular images. Charles and Ray's tightly structured approach to filmmaking reflected the discipline imposed by the shortness of a reel, a keen sense of visual and musical form, the same fascination with "object integrity" and eye for detail that their design work showed, a sensitivity to color, and an increasing desire to communicate ideas—to inform.

The Eameses preferred their films to have original musical scores. Many of these were composed by Elmer Bernstein, who was fascinated by the relationship between visual and musical forms. The Eameses met Bernstein through a mutual friend. Because he was interested in both film and mathematics, they asked him to work on *A Communications Primer* (1953).[63] Before this date they had not used original compositions. Their first film, *Traveling Boy* (1950), had simply been cut to the music, and so had *Blacktop*.[64] Wanting greater control over the musical accompaniment, they used bar charts to dovetail action with music in *Parade*. When there was obviously appropriate music for a certain film, they used it: for example, Baroque organ music in *Two Baroque Churches in Germany* (1955), and a raga played by Ali Akbar Khan and Chatur Lal in *Textile and Ornamental Arts of India* (1955). However, in 1955 the Eameses chose to have Bernstein score the film of their own house, and his lyrical piece adds greatly to the feeling of that film. In 1956 he was called upon to improvise music for a two-minute film made when Charles and Ray were invited to appear on a television show to discuss the launch of the Eames lounge chair.[65] Bernstein went on to compose the music for many other Eames films, including *The Information Machine* (1957), *A Computer Glossary or Coming to Terms with the Data Processing Machine* (1968), and *A Computer Perspective* (1972).[66] Other composers were occasionally used: Laurindo Almeida composed and played the guitar music for *Day of the Dead* (1957) and *Two Laws of Algebra* (1973); the jazz composer Buddy Collette provided scores for two Herman Miller films, *Eames Contract Storage* (1961) and *Fiberglass Chairs* (1970), and for the widely acclaimed

National Fisheries Center and Aquarium (1967); and Don Specht composed and conducted the musical accompaniment to *Something about Photography* (1976).

In filmmaking, as in design, the Eameses considered the discipline of the brief and the constraints it imposed a challenge. Film was, for them, an excellent medium through which to clarify concepts.[67] A film has to be viewed in a certain way; the viewer cannot jump ahead, skip an image or two, set it aside for a while, or go through it at random (as one can with, say, an exhibition or a book). For the Eameses, part of the excitement of film lay in the fact that "you can make statements on film that you just can't make in any other way. Certainly not in designing a product, and not even in writing a book. You have certain elements of control—over the image, the content, the timing—that you can't have in other media."[68]

"Object" Films and "Ideas" Films

The Eameses' films, all but one of which were made either in the small studio at the Eames House or in the Venice workshop, can be classified into two main types: "ideas" films and "object" films.[69]

The Eameses' fascination with objects was discussed in detail in chapter 4. "Object integrity" was central to much of their design work and also to some of their films, including *House: After Five Years of Living* (1955), *Two Baroque Churches,* and *Day of the Dead.* The early "object" films featured toys, partly because they lent themselves to work on a small scale. In *Traveling Boy,* a mechanical boy leads the viewer through a world of toys against a background of Saul Steinberg drawings and circus posters. *Traveling Boy* was made when Charles and Ray, who had been lent a 16-mm editing machine by the screenwriter Philip Dunne (who was away on location), decided to rent a camera and make their own film.[70] Charles improvised cardboard extension rings for the lens and a wooden device to hold the reels for cutting and editing. The film was shot at nights and weekends in the Eames House studio, with friends and colleagues volunteering their services. Lacking a main title, a narration, and a musical score, and having three different endings, *Traveling Boy* was a joy to view in the Eames Office. It was never shown publicly.

Two years later *Parade* elaborated the theme of toys as visual spectacle.[71] It was "filmed entirely with mechanical toys as actors moving

against a background of children's drawings of a city street. Band music, Sousa's 'Stars and Stripes Forever,' accompanies the toy elephants and tigers and horses while brilliant Japanese paper flowers and balloons burst in the air over their heads."[72] This description of the film, written by the Eameses themselves, does not begin to capture the excitement of the pageant of toys moving in time to the fast music (Sousa's "Radetsky March" and "March of the Gladiators" are also used) against a background of toy buildings and drawings by Sansi Girard, Alexander and Susan's five-year-old daughter. Nor does it suggest the *jouissance,* visual pleasures and nostalgia to come. *Parade* is at once a riot and a symphony of color. Oranges, yellows, golds, reds, and pinks contrast with bright clear blues and greens. A white Japanese doll adds a touch of serenity and a grey elephant a touch of solemnity. A large brown robot and a giant multi-colored bull evoke childhood fears and uncertainties, but in a relatively light way. Whereas Jan Svankmajor and the Brothers Quay rendered toys strange, sinister, and surreal by presenting them out of context, the Eameses presented them closely and accurately against backgrounds that kept them in context. Indeed, they insisted that they were fascinated by objects as they actually were and how they were made,[73] although in *Parade* and in some of the other films some toys (especially those used to represent human beings) act out a range of emotional responses. *Parade*'s quick pace, its vibrant colors, its loud, stirring music, and its movement induce an almost hypnotic sensation, or at least a heady feeling. John Neuhart has pronounced this film "pure Ray."[74]

Textiles and Ornamental Arts of India, made in 1955 as a record of an exhibition of the same name and therefore not readily thought of as a "toy" film, is reminiscent of *Parade* in the emphasis on objects, the use of close-ups, and the use of colors (lots of red, ochre, and yellow). Toys were among the Indian objects chosen for detailed study—there are several close-ups of the faces of painted dolls, for example—but a great deal of attention was also paid to textiles and to jewelry. The pieces are so beautifully arranged in the film that one almost automatically attributes this to the hand (and eye) of Ray; however, Alexander Girard, the exhibition's organizer, probably also played a part in this, as did Charles. There is a tremendous concentration in the film on heads, and in particular on eyes. The film ends with a visual feast of eyes in rapid succession accompanied by a dramatic musical crescendo, ending with a sustained shot of a single eye. The message that one has witnessed a vision of another culture makes this film more than a mere record of an exhibition.

Toccata for Toy Trains (1957), a celebration of "great old toys from the world of trains," is the third in the trilogy of "toy" films. The Eameses hoped that this close study of toys moving to music would encourage viewers to think about the qualities of design and production that they regarded as basic to healthy creativity.[75] This film, with its details of railway stations, trains, and other toys shot against a much more elaborate set than that used in *Parade,* offers not only visual and nostalgic pleasures but also a sense of how things move and of the pleasures of moving mechanisms such as pistons and wheels. Like *Parade,* it offers an almost physical pleasure in the speed of travel.

Charles Eames loved toys and all the paraphernalia that went with them. He also had a passion for toy boats. Among the many other toys the Eameses collected were marionettes, Native American dolls, tin musicians, puppets, and baby dolls, which proved less temperamental and less expensive to employ than their human counterparts (although the wind-up toys often wound down at crucial moments during filming, causing expensive footage to be wasted). Toy humans, in one form or another, not only conjured up the pleasures of childhood but could also depict adults acting in the free and playful way of children. Thus, besides the many visual pleasures they provide, the "toy" films evoke a lost age that is at once childhood and the pre-twentieth-century world—an age of simplicity, joy, and lack of selfconsciousness, factors the Eameses felt should play a much larger part in everyday life.[76]

Parade and *Toccata for Toy Trains* both won international awards, the former at the Edinburgh Film Festival in 1954 and the latter at Edinburgh in 1957, Melbourne in 1958, and the American Film Festival in 1959. It is *Tops* (1969), however, that is regarded as their best "toy" film. Although the Eameses would have contended that *Toccata for Toy Trains,* made a dozen years earlier, had already done so, *Tops* extended the genre from observing toys, opening up the world of childhood, and presenting visual spectacles to conveying an understanding of the *principles* behind toys—principles the Eameses often mentioned but tantalizingly, infrequently, and inadequately explained in words.

Paul Schrader classified *Tops* as a "toy" film, but it can just as easily be labeled an "ideas" film—indeed, Schrader has written about the

7.9 Charles and Ray Eames in studio of Eames House in 1957, surrounded by items used in *Toccata for Toy Trains*. Boats and other objects collected by them can also be seen, as can some of the drawings and specifications for the Lounge Chair and Ottoman (1956).

7.10 *Tops*.

ideas it conveys. Tony Benn observed that it "shows mankind of all races, and from all over the world, and every culture, playing with a single simple toy. The unity of humanity comes through in a way that is utterly pleasurable and absolutely unforgettable."[77] It well illustrates the point that in the later films ideas and objects were increasingly fused in an ongoing dialectic. The "cast" comprises 123 tops from countries all over the world. In their varied forms and colors, they provide a rich visual spectacle. A sense of equality between objects of different sizes was obtained by photographically controlling the relative size of objects, something Charles had done in other toy films. Not only were small tops made to seem as important as large ones, but cheap ones were given as much attention as rare and beautiful hand-carved ones. Many of the shots include fingers and hands, and these work to humanize the tops (which are also used to explain complicated scientific ideas). What most transforms this film from an "object" film into an "ideas" film is a wonderful moment of comprehension when a simple tack, thrown onto a drawing board, spins and is suddenly seen as a top. As Schrader puts it, "This is a moment of object-integrity: all the complexity and variation of tops have resolved into the basic form of two planes, one of them suspended by the balanced forces of gravity and gyroscopic momentum. The unaware viewer realizes that he has never really understood even an insignificant creation like a top, never accepted it on its own terms, never *enjoyed* it."[78]

Tops epitomizes the Eameses' ability to convey complex ideas— in this case, ideas about the physics of motion and the universal nature of tops. The MIT physics professor Philip Morrison felt that it illustrated his own astronomical theory about spinning objects in the galaxy and was fond of showing it to demonstrate this theory as well as the applicability of science to all aspects of life.[79] Through the Eameses (Charles in particular), Morrison became increasingly interested in scientific education. He used Tops to illustrate how, through play, children learn an understanding of scientific laws that can be built upon in later years.

But not all the "object" films are about toys. The Eameses saw many of the qualities of toys in simple objects, such as loaves of bread, and in simple processes, such as soapy water running over a school yard. Their 1952 film *Blacktop,* which sets out to illustrate the uncommon beauty of common things, is a series of stunning images of moving water choreographed to music. It shows the same remarkable eye for detail as the early color slides and the "toy" films, and it reveals the Eameses' abil-

7.11 *Blacktop.*

ity to see ordinary things afresh—to offer a new vision of an everyday object or event. The Neuharts point out that *Blacktop* was "a live-action extension of the [still photographic] studies of the seashore Charles made in his first years in California . . . to record close-ups of tide pools and the natural textures of the water and the sand."[80] At first Charles used 4 × 5 film for his still images; after 1945 he used 35-millimeter. Although he was used to adjusting for parallax when taking still photographs, it was no mean feat for an amateur to do so continuously with the hand-held 16-millimeter Cine-Special camera he used to shoot *Blacktop*. Using home-made and hand-made editing equipment, Charles produced beautiful dissolves.[81] It is difficult to believe that this was only his and Ray's second essay in the medium.

Of all the films, *Blacktop* is the one most orthodoxly in the mode of the short "art film." Its main appeal lies in the rare visual poetry of abstract patterns changing in time to Bach's Goldberg Variations. The Eameses stated that their aim in making it was "to see what happens when you put one variation over another, visual form over musical ones,"[82] and the result was quite extraordinary. The abstract nature of the images gave the film a very "arty" and "modern" feel. In 1957 it was used in the television program "Stars of Jazz," with the improvising hands of Oscar Peterson superimposed upon it.[83] That fusion of sound and image was so successful that the producers commissioned a follow-up, a short black-and-white film that turned out to be a forerunner of *Tops*.

Despite the popularity of *Blacktop,* the Eameses made no other films in that vein. Perhaps they felt that *Blacktop* was too obviously concerned with art for art's sake or that too many independent filmmakers were taking that road.

Among the Eameses' more "experimental" films are two in which they used kaleidoscopic images: *Kaleidoscope Shop* (1959) and *Kaleidoscope Jazz Chair* (1960). *Kaleidoscope Shop* was prepared for a lecture to be given by Charles at London's Royal College of Art. He had been asked to bring some illustrations of the Eames Office so that students might see how the famous workshop functioned. Charles thought this too boring and decided to make a short film that would capture the experimental nature and excitement of the work. Next to nothing was recognizable when broken down into fragments and viewed through a kaleidoscope lens, but the film showed the Eameses to be at the forefront of new ways of looking and seeing. Former Royal College students recall that the event felt more like the beginning of the "swinging sixties" than a presentation by the world's most "serious" industrial designer.[84] The images were obtained by means of mirrors attached to a movie camera. This method, developed by Charles Eames, Parke Meek, and Jeremy Lepard, was also used in making *Kaleidoscope Jazz Chair.*[85] Each of the kaleidoscope films opens with a view of the Eames Office lobby, but in the second the music changes to a jazz beat. Beautiful patterns form from chairs and their bases, from fabrics, and from lanterns. Images change as they move toward and away from the viewer, and in one pixilated sequence plastic chairs seem to dance.

After *Blacktop* the Eameses reverted from moving images to still ones in their "object" films. The next films of this kind, made in 1955, were devoted to objects of greater complexity, including their own home (*House: After Five Years of Living*) and a couple of churches (*Two Baroque Churches in Germany*). They did not regard still images as better than continuous motion, but they thought still images could more easily be used to create the "mood" they wanted. They also felt that they could convey much more information by using a multiplicity of stills. Two Eames films of the 1950s which have been categorized as "object" films but which are more properly about "events" are *Day of the Dead* (1957), made with the assistance of Deborah Sussman and Susan and Alexander Girard, and *De Gaulle Sketch* (1958), a compilation of press images relating to the Algerian uprising. What these four films had in common was the fast cutting of a large number of images so that the viewer was left with an overall impression rather than one or two dominant images. The Eameses consid-

7.12 *Kaleidoscope Shop.*

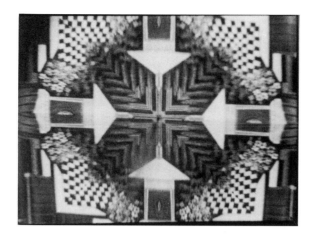

7.13 *Kaleidoscope Shop.*

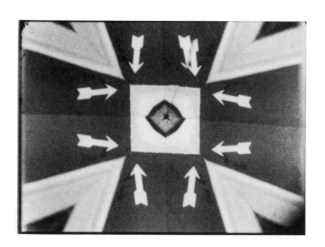

7.14 *Day of the Dead.*

7.15 *Day of the Dead.*

ered fast cutting a particularly productive way of looking at things because of the interesting juxtapositions it offered as well as the large numbers of images and amounts of information conveyed. This technique, similar to the "information overload" of the exhibitions, was also used in the sequences for the TV show "The Fabulous Fifties" and in three sequences (one made up entirely of still images, one using stills and animation, and one combining still and live-action photography) made for use in "The Good Years," a 1962 CBS program about turn-of-the-century America.

House began the experiment with fast-cut stills. The Eameses already had hundreds of photographs of their house when they decided to document it on film, and they used these, together with new photos, to make a loving and personal view of their home. Offered as fragments of architecture and design rather than a tour through architectural space, the film offers an impression of what it is like to experience different aspects of the house. The images are partly arranged according to broad categories (color, materials, flowers, location), and contrasts are drawn between indoors and out, the domestic space and the studio, seasonal changes, and, in the final sequence, day and night. Aficionados of the Eames House are divided on the question of whether a film of this type is better than a more orthodox room-by-room exploration as a way of seeing and experiencing the house for those unable to visit it. The film does convey the Eameses' aesthetic approach to the viewing and grouping of objects (crockery in a bowl in the sink is as aesthetically arranged as the furniture), and it details the way the house was personalized by the objects within and surrounding it and thereby transformed into a home. Some feel, however, that this is a curiously abstracted and detached way of depicting a home—and, in particular, that the beautiful visuals and Elmer Bernstein's evocative score produce a sense of poetic wonder at a rare art object rather than a "lived in" residence.[86]

Two Baroque Churches also uses fast-cut stills, but despite some superb individual images and color tones it is not as successful as *House.* This is partly because the fast and even rate of change of 296 images (roughly one every two seconds)[87] is somewhat wearing and slightly monotonous despite the beauty of the individual images and partly because two buildings cannot easily encapsulate the complexity and richness of the Baroque. The Eameses (who researched the topic well, spending some time in Germany when Charles was awarded a cultural-exchange fellowship by the West German State Department) decided not to try to explain the Baroque in architectural terms but rather to convey a feeling of the style.

Two Baroque Churches was not the only film from which the Eameses hoped the viewer would extract a wider cultural understanding. *Tops* and *Toccata for Toy Trains,* which have the same intent, probably succeed better because they focus on more specific and less historical topics and because their live-action footage seems to affect the viewer more directly.

That leading modernists such as Charles and Ray Eames should make a film about the Baroque came as a surprise to many who shared their interest in modernism. "Cultured" Americans of the 1950s could accommodate the Eameses fascination with those aspects of "primitive" or "folk" art that were acceptable within the broad aesthetic parameters of modernism and abstract form; however, the Baroque was the antithesis of minimalist modernism—it was decoration and mannerism run wild. Yet here were the Eameses encouraging them to look at it anew and seducing them with their beautiful images. What Eames devotees drew from *Two Baroque Churches* was a smattering of knowledge and a validation of a relatively unfamiliar decorative style—a style that they then used in tiny doses to humanize and personalize their own domestic or working environments, as did Charles and Ray. The Baroque became "exotic," like "primitive" art, and was plundered in the same way to add "color" and interest to modernist interiors. *Two Baroque Churches* offered a cache of images to be raided by individuals who were interested in visual forms but who lacked an understanding of the society that had produced them. Whereas some of the Eameses' films and many of their exhibitions determinedly and relentlessly contextualized the subject matter, *Two Baroque Churches* and *House,* fall more clearly into the part of the Eameses' work that celebrated bricolage and visual eclecticism.

Paul Schrader has argued that the superabundance of images and data in the Eameses' fast-cut or multiple-image films was never superfluous, because it related directly to the central theme of the particular piece. Michael Brawne regarded the impressionistic nature of the total viewing experience of an Eames film as corresponding "surprisingly closely with the way in which the brain normally records the images it receives."[88] Schrader noted that

Eames's innovation . . . is a hypothesis about audience perception which, so far, is only proved by the effectiveness of his films. His films pursue an Idea (Time, Space, Symmetry, Topology) which in the final accounting must stand alone, apart from any psychological, social, or moral implications. The viewer must rapidly sort out and prune the superabundant data if he is to follow the swift progression of thought. This process of elimination continues until the viewer has pruned away everything but the disembodied Idea. By giving the viewer more information than he can assimilate, information-overload short-circuits the normal conduits of inductive reasoning. The classic movie staple is the chase, and Eames's films present a new kind of chase, a chase through a set of information in search of an Idea.[89]

Paul Schrader also argued that the Eameses' film aesthetic introduced "a new way of perceiving ideas into a medium which has been surprisingly anti-intellectual" and brought "innovation to an art which in the area of ideas is only spinning its wheels."[90] Some of the early films were concerned with the basic principles of how to communicate ideas as such; later ones were visually creative essays conveying complex notions of time, space, and symmetry. The latter group, Schrader argued, returned to film "in a limited and exploratory manner what Cubism took from it in the early 1900s." Schrader continued: "What Sypher wrote of the cubist art of Cézanne, Eliot, Pirandello, and Gide is now true of Eames's films—Have we not been misled by the nineteenth-century romantic belief that the imagination means either emotional power or the concrete image, the metaphor alone. We have not supposed there is a poetry of ideas."[91]

The films that represent the Eameses' "ideas" films at their best are *Powers of Ten* and *National Fisheries Center and Aquarium.* The latter developed out of a report commissioned in 1965 by the U.S. Department of the Interior, but after two years of intensive research the Eames Office decided against presenting a conventional printed report (which would have run to several volumes). Wanting to convey to Congress the idea of a national aquarium and the importance of conservation, they presented a 10-minute film and an illustrated pamphlet which argued that "the greatest souvenirs of the Aquarium may be the beauty and intellectual stimula-

tion it holds. The principal goal is . . . to give the visitor some understanding of the natural world. If the National Aquarium is as good as it
can be, it will do just that." According to Paul Schrader, "to extrapolate
an environmental aesthetic from a ten-minute sponsored film like *National Fisheries Center and Aquarium* may seem like the height of critical
mannerism to some," yet Schrader was genuinely excited by the "radical,
wonderful" aquarium and the ecologically safe and pleasant environment
constructed in the film.[92] What Charles Eames called a "fiction of reality"
existed only in the film, but after the film it became fixed in people's
minds and had its own reality.

"Educational" Films

Although it could be argued that all Eames films were educational, some
were more directly so than others. These fall into four categories (which
are by no means exclusive): films made to present proposals or works in
progress to clients "just as you would use architectural models"[93]; films
that presented computers as having a "human face"; films that explained
concepts, usually from mathematics or science, that non-specialists considered to be beyond their understanding; and films that recorded exhibitions or recast them in cinematic terms. The Eameses were never ashamed
to describe themselves as teachers. Like all good teachers, they remained
perpetual students and felt compelled to convey their beliefs and enthusi-
asms to others.

   The Expanding Airport (1958), like several other Eames products,
came about as the result of a request or suggestion from a friend. In this
case the presentation concerned Eero Saarinen's design for the new international airport for Washington, D.C. Saarinen had a vast amount of material to communicate to his clients,[94] He decided that a short film would
be the most effective way to do so—and who better to ask make it than
Charles and Ray Eames? They agreed because they held similar views on
planning and design. Any project that analyzed the way a building was
conceived, planned, built, used, and misused, and then went on to pro-
pose a viable alternative, immediately appealed to them. Charles and Ray
spent an intensive weekend locked away with Saarinen to familiarize
themselves with all the necessary details before producing the film
(within three weeks).[95] As with the Moscow presentation, they worked on
it until the very last minute; Saarinen had a momentary panic when he

thought it would have to be shown without his even previewing it. As it turned out, he managed to run it through once before presenting it to his clients.

Unlike *National Fisheries Center and Aquarium, The Expanding Airport* focused on communicating facts rather than poeticizing an idea. It is a catalog of problems ending with a solution. Although Dulles Airport is highly original in aesthetic form, the Eameses chose not to "sell" the project on the basis of its design but rather to concentrate on communicating the basic concepts involved in Saarinen's proposal. Although originally intended only for use by Saarinen, the film had so much general appeal (largely to educational institutions and designers) that 300 prints were made.[96] Part of its success derived from the animation (drawn by Glen Fleck), which helped simplify the basic concepts of Saarinen's scheme. This was accomplished not only by means of diagrams but also by simulating the experience of using the existing and proposed schemes. Here and elsewhere the Eameses used this familiar mode to increase the accessibility of ideas and projects, particularly those related to the past or future, that lacked working visual or conceptual references.

The first time the Eameses used a film to present one of their own projects was in relation to the IBM exhibit for the 1964 World's

7.17 *IBM Fair Presentation # 1*, 1962–63, dir. Charles and Ray Eames.

Fair.[97] Still photography and animation were used to outline the overall concept, the architecture, and the content for the benefit of IBM senior executives, but the sequence that simulated the elaborate multi-image production—the most "avant-garde" aspect of the exhibit and the one most likely to frighten senior executives—was entirely animated. The soundtrack for this highly polished five-minute presentation was "A Nice Day," performed by the Chico Hamilton Quintet.

The most obviously educational of the Eameses' films relate to mathematics, science, and technology. Mathematics and science came to take up more and more of Charles's time, but it was as a result of thinking about the wider questions of architecture and city planning that he first became involved with what today would be called communications theory, a subject then in its infancy and largely developed by the mathematicians Claude Shannon and Warren Weaver.[98] Charles realized that to arrive at optimum solutions on questions of major importance to large cities and the environment in general one had to "master" data across a wide range of disciplines, including demography, sociology, and economics—a task that daunted most architects. Charles's research revealed a lack of suitable material on communications—from the Bell Laboratories, he recounted (exaggerating for humorous effect), all one could get were "pictures of a man with a beard and somebody says, 'You will invent the telephone,' or something."[99] However, Shannon and Weaver were employed at Bell Labs, and their work on identifying the processes involved in even the simplest acts of communication was to be the focus of much of the Eameses' early work in this area—work that eventually focused on the computer.[100]

Charles and Ray Eames were the first people to popularize the computer through film. Philip Morrison believed that it was Charles's interest in theoretical structures and a belief that "you could take apart everything that had meaning and form and could show it as a simple combination of yes-no binary choices" that made him so enthusiastic about this new machine.[101] Charles and Ray understood that people were intimidated by huge amounts of information and wanted them to feel at home with the computer. Realizing that computers, the "vernacular of tomorrow," would have to be made "user friendly," the Eameses devoted themselves to explaining their forms and language to non-specialists.[102] As in their architectural and design work, they attempted to humanize the modern.

One of the ways in which the Eameses helped change attitudes toward these alien machines was by associating them with human feelings. In *A Communications Primer* they used "I love you" as an example of communicating a thought; the accompanying graphics included a couple and a red heart. The latter symbol was also chosen to end two of the major "computer films," *The Information Machine: Creative Man and the Data Processor* and *Introduction to Feedback,* in an effort to break down the notion that computers had nothing to do with human feelings. Hand drawing and lettering in the apparently artless style then popular in American graphics were used to lend childlike simplicity to the world of high technology,[103] as were cartoon-style single images and animation (usually drawn by Dolores Cannata or Glen Fleck, often after sketches by Charles).

The Information Machine was the first completely animated film produced by the Eames Office in its attempt to convey the general prin-

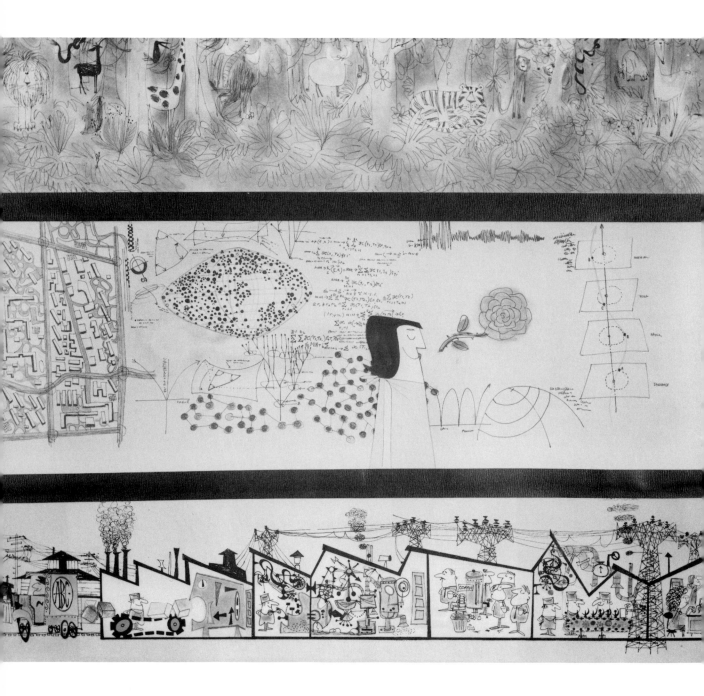

CHAPTER 7

7.18 *The Information Machine: Creative Man and the Data Processor.*

7.19 *Introduction to Feedback.*

ciples of the computer and the uses to which it could be put. Commissioned by IBM for the Brussels World's Fair of 1958, it was based on ideas that went back to *A Communications Primer*. *The Information Machine* emphasized that the use of computers should always be dictated by "creative man"—a point of view that was reiterated in two film versions of electronically controlled puppet shows developed to dispel "the bogeyman which some see lurking behind every computer."[104] In *Sherlock Holmes and the Singular Case of the Plural Green Mustache* (1965), Holmes solves a mystery using his familiar method of deduction and also by means of a computer utilizing Boolean algebra. *Computer Day at Midvale* (1965) depicts the effects of the installation of the first computer on an imaginary town, pokes fun at the old-fashioned mayor's fear that computers will make decisions for humans, and emphasizes the role of human imagination and creativity. *Computer Glossary, or Coming to Terms with the Data Processing Machine* (1968) uses some animation to explain the specialist vocabulary associated with computers. *Computer Perspective* (1972) examines the ideas and inventions that led to the computer, using both fast-cut still images and live-action footage.

Nothing less than the entire development of science was the subject of *The House of Science* (1962), originally produced as a multi-screen performance for the United States pavilion at the Seattle World's Fair.

The Eameses' attempts to explain mathematical concepts to non-specialists began in 1961 with the two-minute "peep show" films made to accompany the Mathematica exhibition. In 1968 came a much more ambitious project: *A Rough Sketch for a Proposed Film Dealing with the Powers of Ten and the Relative Size of the Universe,* an eight-minute film illustrating what it means when things increase at an exponential rate. This "sketch," inspired by Kees Boeke's 1957 book *Cosmic View: The Universe in Forty Jumps*[105] and originally commissioned to be shown at a conference of 1000 American physicists, presented "a linear view of our universe from the human scale to the sea of galaxies, then directly down to the nucleus of a carbon atom. With an animated image, a narration and a dashboard, it gives a clue to the relative size of things and what it means to add another zero to any number."[106]

Powers of Ten (1968) was used as a teaching aid in many American schools and science museums.[107] Meant to appeal to an interested ten-year-old as well as to a specialist, this film had to convey a complex, theo-

7.20 *Sherlock Holmes in the*
Singular Case of the Plural
Green Mustache.

7.21 *Powers of Ten: A Rough Sketch for a Proposed Film Dealing with the Powers of Ten and the Relative Size of the Universe.*

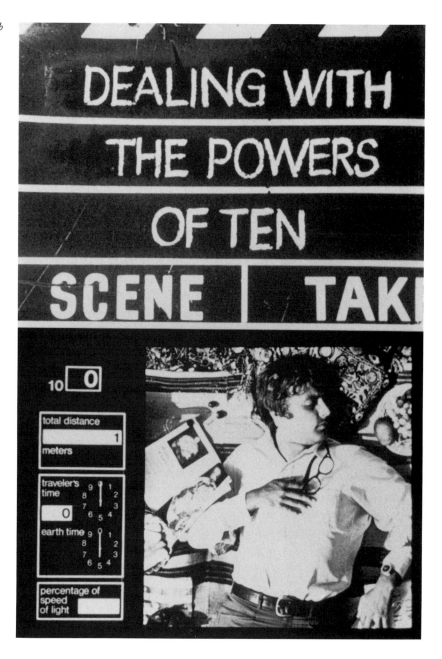

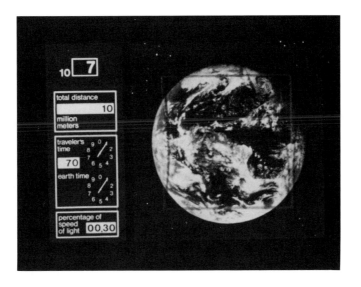

retical way of viewing the world in a very simple manner. The aim was to convey a "gut feeling" about the "new physics," and particularly about relative dimensions in time and space.[108] One comes away from *Powers of Ten* feeling as if one has had a physical as well as an intellectual experience. Using a continuous zoom, the film takes the viewer out from Earth to the farthest known point in space and then back to the nucleus of a carbon atom while chronometers on a split screen register distance traveled at the rate of one power of ten every ten seconds. The dashboard of clocks gives the film "a strong but not imposing theoretical framework" by which viewers can orient themselves and see how fast they are going— Philip Morrison likened the sensation to being "like a driver in a space ship."[109] The strangeness of the experience is accentuated by an Elmer Bernstein score played on a Japanese synthesizer; the human connection is emphasized through the atom's being part of the wrist of a man we see lying on the ground. We, the viewers, comprehend the time travel in terms of our own size and realize our relativity.

Powers of Ten is clearly much more than an introduction to science. Philip Morrison thought it "beautifully visualized." The architect Craig Hodgett called it "a clear exposition and a poem, too" and said that it "communicates an ethical view of the world."[110] Paul Schrader waxed lyrical:

The interstellar roller-coaster ride of *Powers of Ten* does what the analogous sequence in *2001: A Space Odyssey* should have: it gives the full impact—instinctual as well as cerebral—of contemporary scientific theories. . . . It popularizes (in the best sense of the word), post-Einsteinian thought the way the telescope popularized Copernicus; and the effect is almost as upsetting. The spectator is in perspectiveless space; there is no one place where he can objectively judge another place . . . the time-space traveler of *Powers of Ten* thinks of himself as a citizen of the universe, an unbounded territory. . . . *Powers of Ten* . . . concretizes a concept of the universe true to contemporary experience. And that Idea is covetable.[111]

In 1977 *Powers of Ten* was remade with the assistance of Philip Morrison, who incorporated new scientific knowledge and wrote and narrated the text. In the remake, the presentation of the scientific information and the visuals are more confident than in the earlier version and the removal of the "dashboard" makes the film less obviously a teaching aid. But, although it includes more beautiful imagery, it is not so existential as the 1968 version. There is less of the sense of being alone out in space, less sense of the viewer as driver. On the plus side, the expanding and diminishing point that takes us from beneath the surface of a human hand to outer space is now directly in the center of the frame.

So successful was the original *Powers of Ten* that the Eameses considered exploring other concepts by means of a time-clock sequence. In 1976 they produced *Atlas: A Sketch of the Rise and Fall of the Roman Empire,* in which the viewer is taken from ancient Carthage to the end of the Roman Empire and back at a rate of eight years per second. The animated graphics depicting the changing boundaries are clear and simple, and this underrated film is a great help in teaching the chronology and the geography of the empire.

One of the many experts the Eameses brought in to advise them was Raymond Redheffer, a professor of mathematics at UCLA, who served as a consultant on projects concerning mathematics through the 1960s and who became a close friend. By the early 1970s Redheffer had become so fascinated with the Eames Office's method of using aesthetically pleasing animated color films to explore mathematical and scientific

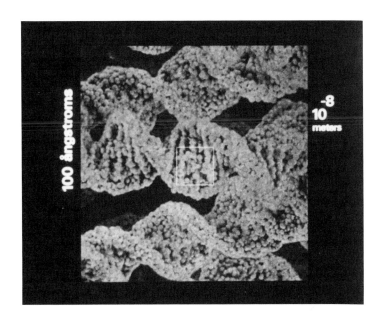

concepts that he decided to try making some of his own. Working at and in full collaboration with the Eames Office, he produced *Alpha* (1972), *Exponents: A Study in Generalization* (1973), and *Two Laws of Algebra: Distributive and Associative* (1973). Pleased with the results, Charles and Ray used the techniques developed by their staff in conjunction with Redheffer to animate numerals in *Newton's Methods,* produced in 1974 to accompany an exhibition. For *Copernicus* (1973) they used quite a different technique, transferring slides to film in order to outline and contextualize the work of the famous astronomer. The latter two films bring us to another category of Eames "educational" films: those made for or about exhibitions.

The first exhibition which the Eameses were inspired to record on film was *Textiles and Ornamental Arts of India,* designed by Alexander Girard and held in 1955 at the Museum of Modern Art. The fascinating film of the same title, accompanied by Indian music and narrated by Pupul Jayakar and Edgar Kaufmann jr., offers a beautiful pictorial record of the objects in the exhibition (and more). But it was 14 years before the Eameses recorded another exhibition. That exhibition, held at the Smithsonian Institution in 1968, was Photography and the City: The Evolution of an Art and a Science, which illustrated photography's role in urban planning. Charles thought that the exhibition had failed to convey the chaos of the cities and the urgency of the problems facing them, partly because certain stunning blown-up images had detracted from the overall message. He hoped that the film, made a year later under the more succinct title *Image of the City,* might succeed where the exhibition had not.[112]

The American bicentennial year, 1976, brought three Eames films based on exhibitions. *The World of Franklin and Jefferson,* narrated by Nina Foch and Orson Welles, retold the "story" of the exhibition. The shorter film *The World of Franklin and Jefferson: The Opening of an Exhibition* focused on the periods immediately before and after the show opened in Paris. *The Look of America 1750–1800* was commissioned for the Yale University Art Department by Charles Montgomery, director of Yale's Garvan Collection of furniture at the university. Montgomery, whose energy, enthusiasm, charm, and charisma were much like Charles Eames's and who like Charles regarded himself as self-taught, had long admired the Eameses' furniture and their exhibitions and films, and jumped at the chance to commission a film by them to accompany an exhibition he was curating. *The Look of America,* prepared to be shown at Yale and also at London's Victoria and Albert Museum, concentrated on the second half of the eighteenth century and focused on industrialization, a topic that interested Montgomery as much as it did the Eameses.[113] The film helped to transform the exhibition from a large display of very beautiful objects to something much more informative. Intended to illustrate (unfortunately from the colonists' and settlers' point of view) various strands of American history, particularly the movement from a rural society to one that "would carry America into a new wilderness of commerce and production,"[114] this film did nothing to placate those who felt that the "bicentennial fever" of idealizing America had affected the Eameses. However, after 1976, almost as if they sensed the danger of their being incorporated into the establishment,[115] the Eameses turned to smaller and less contentious subjects.

Some of the films the Eameses made in the 1970s were continuations of earlier work. For example, Charles had been taking circus photographs since as early as 1942, yet it was not until 1971 that he and Ray made a film about circus life. *Clown Face* was made in response to a request from a client with whom the Eameses had enjoyed a close relationship for thirty years: the famous Ringling Brothers Barnum and Bailey clown college, of which Charles was a trustee. *Clown Face* was made as a training film to illustrate the art of classical clown makeup to student clowns, but like all Eames films it went beyond the narrow educational brief.[116] It is a discourse on symmetry, using the human face and traditional clown makeup to explore symmetry, transformation, and disguise.

Four films were made for the Polaroid Corporation. The first, *SX-70* (1972), introduced a new "instant camera." Four years later, *Something about Photography* demonstrated how excellent results could be obtained with the SX-70; it also gave Charles a chance to expound his views about the camera as a vital recorder of images and events, the many choices involved in taking a photograph, the added significance of photos shot in a series, and photography as a truly democratic "art" open to all. *Polavision* (1977) used six two-and-a-half-minute episodes to demonstrate a new instant movie camera. Besides showing what excellent results could be obtained, this film demonstrated how amateur filmmakers could expand their technical repertoire with animation and stop-motion camera work. *Sonar One-Step* (1978) demonstrated yet another new camera, in this case one with a sonar-based automatic focusing system.

In 1978 (the year of Charles's death) a project was undertaken to prepare for IBM two videodisk programs exploring the potential of that then-new technology. One was to be based on historical topics, the other on Impressionist and Post-Impressionist paintings.[117]

Daumier: Paris and the Spectator (1977) was made in conjunction with Judith Wechsler, an art historian at MIT, and was based on her study of Honoré Daumier and other nineteenth-century French caricaturists and illustrators. Wechsler, herself now a maker of films about art, had written a report on how to present art on film as part of an Eames Office proposal for an orientation center at the Metropolitan Museum of Art. Although the project fell through, the idea of presenting art on film intrigued Charles and he asked Wechsler to collaborate. She introduced the film and drew some conclusions at the end, but the body of the film consisted mainly of lively camera moves on the caricatures and illustrations themselves.[118] A sound stage was used, with set decor by Ray.

Judith Wechsler learned a great deal during the making of the Daumier film, but she was to learn much more (particularly about how to design camera moves) from the making of *Cézanne: The Late Work* (1978). Charles wanted to make a film of the exhibition of Cézanne's late work

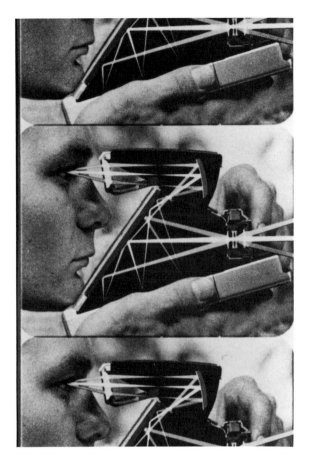

7.24 *SX-70.*

7.25 *Something about Photography.*

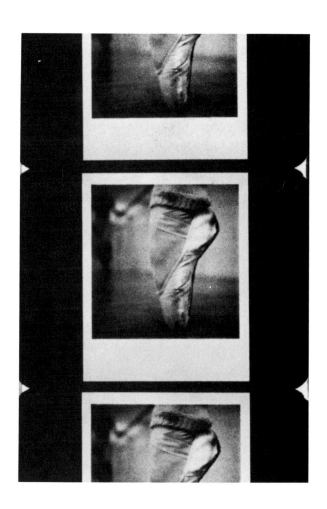

held in 1977 in Paris and New York, but in the low light only still photography was possible. This problem was overcome with a computerized animation camera, specially developed by Eames Office employee Bill Tondreau, which had been used for *Powers of Ten* and could pan across or zoom into a slide transparency.[119] Wechsler, who originated and developed the storyboard for the Cézanne film, had written a dissertation and a book on the artist, but making a film on him was another matter. Encouraged by Charles, she produced a first script only to be told "Throw it out—it isn't a film. It is based on words and you need to figure out how to make it work visually."[120] In the end she decided to restrict the text to quotations from Cézanne's letters and reminiscences; most of the film's impact comes from the way details of the artist's work are built up to convey an overall sense of composition and form.

At the time of Charles's death, *Degas in the Metropolitan* was in preparation.[121] For this film (based on an exhibition held at the Metropolitan Museum of Art), Judith Wechsler and Eames Office staffers transferred 35-millimeter transparencies to film using Bill Tondreau's computerized control system. The script was prepared by Jehane Burns and Charles Moffett, the curator of the exhibition. Moffett did the narration, and Ray Eames worked on the sets.[122]

7.26 *Goods*, 1982. This 33-image slide show, which Ray transferred to film after Charles's death with sponsorship from the Herman Miller Furniture Company, was compiled by Charles and Ray Eames in 1971.

In 1982 Ray, with assistance from Alex Funke and other staff members, completed *Atlas,* which had been made quickly in 1976 and never given a narration or a musical score. She also transferred to film a slide show, *Goods,* of which she and Charles had been particularly fond. *Goods* featured ordinary objects not normally regarded as visually interesting. It was Ray's personal tribute to Charles. Together they had created a formidable number of slide shows, multi-screen presentations, and films, mainly as a means of communicating information, enthusiasm, and ideas. Without selfconsciously aiming to do so, they had given filmmaking a strong visual emphasis at a time when Saul Bass and others were complaining that film had lost its sense of the visual.[123] Paul Schrader felt it had also lost a feel for ideas—something the Eameses never shied away from.[124]

Combining clear exposition and engaging visuals, the Eameses' films and presentations added up to something more than the sum of the parts. Sometimes serious issues prevailed; at other times, visual delights, as simple as they were rich, were the *raison d'etre.* Yet, as I have said, all the multi-image shows and films were constructed with as much attention to detail and structure as any of Charles and Ray's design projects. More than one critic described them as "poetic."[125]

CONCLUSION

Much of the Eameses' work stands in the best tradition of the design reform movement (which argued for making high-quality everyday objects
available at reasonable prices), and also in the best tradition of modernism (which, from the 1920s on, offered a vision of harnessing new technologies, industrial production, and relevant design to the service of
humankind). Charles and Ray Eames belonged to a generation of designers who, before, during, and immediately after World War II, were determined to make the world a better place in which to live but were not
wedded to a narrow or solely stylistic definition of modernism. Without
ever losing sight of their serious objectives, the Eameses brought to their
products a lightness of spirit that, to a degree, disguised their commitment and dedication. Their furniture, their films, and their exhibitions delighted the eye, the mind, and the spirit; they also worked well.

The Eameses' work was often innovative, although they always
insisted that designers should innovate only as a last resort.[1] They reveled
in the particular constraints of specific briefs and in the rationalistic
search for the best possible solution to the problem at hand, yet they produced work that has been described as poetic. If, as Frank Lloyd Wright
said, the poetry of architecture is that which touches the heart,[2] then it is
not difficult to understand why Paul Schrader and others have referred to
the work of the Eameses in that way.[3] It was not simply their liberal use
of hearts and flowers, their direct appeal to what they perceived as universal truths and the inner humanity of people the world over, or even the
power of their ideas and the exquisiteness and affectivity of their compositions and imagery that made many of their products so memorable; as
in a symphony, the whole was much more than the sum of the parts.

In their passion to convey their enthusiasm to others, the
Eameses "shaped not only things but the way people think about
things."[4] Their films, exhibitions, and multi-screen presentations show
them to have been at the forefront of new thinking about the most effective and pleasurable ways of communicating knowledge to large numbers
of people. Their exhibitions and multiple-image shows, in particular,
reached large and largely appreciative audiences. Their design work was

respected by the cognoscenti and, at the same time, popular in the sense of being seen, used, enjoyed, and admired by many. In this they achieved the modernist designer's dream of enriching the lives of ordinary people with quality objects produced by means of the most up-to-date technology.

The multifarious influences on the Eameses' work, including ideas drawn from the Arts and Crafts movement, from Frank Lloyd Wright, from European modernism, from Japanese architecture and design, from "primitivism," from contemporary fine art, from the "Romantic" interior, from Californian modernism, and from a belief in the pleasures of work, have been traced. No matter what the sources, the end result was invariably distinctive and informed by a concern with structure; for the Eameses, designing a chair, an exhibition, a film, or the front page of a newspaper was as much about structure as was designing a building. Despite this, there was not a single aesthetic formula that related to every area of their work; the architecture, for instance, favored the geometric forms of International Style modernism, whereas a great deal of the furniture was more plastic in form. Their buildings and many of their furniture pieces were minimalist, yet their films, multi-screen presentations, exhibitions, toys, and decorative arrangements of objects drew on addition, juxtaposition, fragmentation, cross-cultural and extra-cultural reference, repetition, and excess. However, as Esther McCoy has pointed out, the interaction between the minimalist frames of the Eameses' buildings and their "varied and rich" contents was similar to that between the structure and the content of their films and exhibitions.[5]

Eames products were part of a shift in postwar American taste toward favoring organic over geometric forms, and they found success at a time when modernist design was broadening from a movement with aspirations toward the monolithic to a pluralism in which alternative aesthetics coexisted more or less happily. The Eameses eschewed exclusive insistence on a machine aesthetic, which they used only when and where it suited them. The Cranbrook experience was crucial to their joint work; it validated the eclecticism inherent in Charles's earlier designs while extending his knowledge and understanding of International Style architecture and design, and it tempered Ray's more purist modernism.

In Eero Saarinen and in Ray, Charles Eames found empathetic and immensely talented collaborators. The furniture he designed with

Saarinen certainly proved seminal to the later work of the Eames Office, but it was with Ray that Charles produced some of the most visually interesting and technologically adventurous furniture of the mid twentieth century.

For every designer who was influenced by the Eameses in terms of style, there were others who drew strength from their commitments to design as a problem-solving exercise, to quality at every level, and to engagement with a wide range of activities, issues, and commercial contexts. They became well known as designers and communicators in the United States, in Western Europe, in Japan, and in India. After World War II Japan paid great attention to American design, and from the early 1950s on the Eameses' work was publicized there by Torao ("Tiger") Saito of *Japan Today*.[6] In India they became near-celebrities after the release of the Eames Report, which considered the question of design in modern India in relation to small industries and the "rapid deterioration in the design and quality of consumer goods."[7] Insofar as this report led to the establishment of the National Institute of Design, the Eameses had a direct impact on design education in India.[8] Their indirect influence was felt in many other countries through design teachers who took them and their methods as models.

The furniture was particularly influential. Beginning in 1950, the plywood and plastic pieces received considerable publicity in leading Western European design magazines, such as *Domus* and *Bauen und Wohnen,* and department stores.[9] It inspired many designers, particularly in Italy, West Germany, France, Britain, the Netherlands, and Scandinavia.[10]

Eames furniture was manufactured and distributed by the Herman Miller Furniture Company, or by firms under license to it, all over the world. The management of Herman Miller was horrified at the first imitations of the molded plastic shell furniture but soon realized that this did not stop the upward sweep of the sales curve of the originals. More than 5 million of the chairs were sold in the 25 years after they were first produced.[11] All over the world people experienced these chairs and other pieces of Eames furniture in offices, schools, colleges, and homes.

The Eames House (their only widely known architectural work) was celebrated in Europe as proving that the purist, rationalist aesthetic of the International Style could produce habitable buildings.[12] The influ-

C.1 Charles Eames talks to
staff and students, NID,
Ahmedabad, 1978.

CONCLUSION

C.2 Ray Eames presents
the first Charles Eames
Award to Kamaladevi
Chattopadhyaya, pioneer of
India's craft revival, NID,
Ahmedabad, 1987. NID
Director Vinay Jha is on
the right; designer S.
Sethuraman is in the
center.

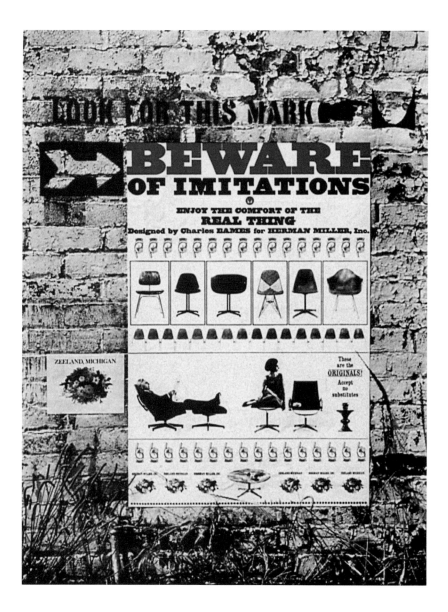

ence of the Eames House on modernist and "high-tech" architects (particularly Norman and Wendy Foster and Richard and Su Rogers) is widely
acknowledged, not least by those architects themselves. They, Michael
and Patti Hopkins, and others have paid homage to the work of the
Eameses, not only in the concepts and structures of their buildings but
also in their use of Eames furniture.[13]

Their exhibitions, films, and multi-media presentations, particularly those prepared for World's Fairs, were seen by great numbers of people. Several generations of Americans were introduced to scientific and mathematical concepts through them—particularly the exhibitions. Charles's "deep understanding of the processes of science and technology" greatly impressed some of the top experts in those fields.[14] This and the role he and Ray played in demystifying and popularizing the computer deserve greater recognition than they have so far been given.

The exhibitions that were most criticized in their time for being overloaded with text, objects, and ideas suggest that, had they been working in the 1990s, the Eameses would have been fascinated with interactive media and "hyperreality." It seems more than likely, for example, that they would have been involved in developing the communications and educational potential of interactive video, which allows for the differential exploration of images and information.

In their day the Eameses' films had many admirers, some of whom worked in a similar manner.[15] Today some of the techniques once hailed as sophisticated[16] seem somewhat passé and some of the ideas naive, but the films have aged better than many other short films of the period (both "artistic" and "informational" ones) because they have a strong aesthetic framework as well as offering intellectual and emotional stimulation. Paul Schrader recognized their significance in 1970, by which time the early "toy" and partially animated films were already becoming unfashionable; he argued that they personalized "assembly-line art," gave "greater power to the consumer," and permitted "individual integrity within a humanist collective"[17]—points I have made about other areas of the Eameses' work. For Schrader, at that time, the Eameses had more to offer in terms of returning a cerebral sensibility to cinema than Godard, Rohmer, and Resnais. I would not go quite so far, but I feel that the Eameses' films still have something to say to filmmakers—particularly about the relationship between the visual and ideas. The films deserve greater appreciation.[18] Had they been more readily categorizable as either "mainstream" or "avant-garde" or "experimental," they would have received more attention from filmmakers and historians. Those that were screened at the 1992 Sundance Institute Festival were well received. I hope that more people will now study the entire range of Eames films, including the sponsored ones, without prejudice, and will judge and enjoy them on their own terms and their own merits.

Charles and Ray visited Britain more regularly than other countries and had a dedicated following there. The September 1966 issue of *Architectural Design* revealed the extent of the Eameses' influence on British design (particularly on the Independent Group, which in turn influenced Pop Art[19]), articulated a new understanding of their work as offering an additive dimension to a minimalist movement and claimed for it a wit rare in architecture and design and an extensive influence.[20] The authors writing in that journal saw the wonderful melange of the ordinary, the old, and the exotic represented and rearranged by Peter Blake and others in Britain during the 1960s as a result of the Eameses' liberating aesthetic, which validated "the extravagance of the new purchase," gave "courage to make sense of anything that attracted," and led to interiors decorated with "fresh, pretty, colorful ephemera."[21] The decorative and apparently lighthearted presentation of serious objects and ideas was characteristic not only of "functioning decoration" but also of the Eameses' exhibitions, films, multi-media presentations, toys, furniture, and buildings; if anything unifies their work, it is this, rather than a single aesthetic.

Certain features of the Eameses' work, such as "functioning decoration" and the more general use of juxtaposition, addition, and eclecticism, are not antagonistic to some of those defined as postmodern, and it can be argued that in certain ways these features prefigured some postmodern notions and practices. This is not to say that the Eameses can or should be claimed as postmodernists—although I now better understand Deborah Sussman's comment that it has taken a long time for her to analyze and voice her feeling that Ray, joint head of a design office claimed to epitomize the best in rational design, "was not really a modernist, or at least she was doing things I didn't and don't think of as 'modernist.'"[22] However, if one accepts that there was much more flexibility within modernism than the narrow and until recently dominant definitions allow, and that many modernisms flourished in the quarter-century after World War II, one can accept both Charles and Ray as modernists. The "prettiness," the information overload, and the decoration overload evident in much of their work alarmed many purists, but at the end of the day the Eameses were undoubtedly modernists. They were optimists who believed in progress and in a coherent, unified, and rational world, the problems of which were soluble though admittedly immense.

Their work allayed fears that machine-made or machine-age products were "inhuman" and "impersonal"; however, they considered themselves "functionalists" to the end, believing that there were certain basic rational principles that explained the workings of such seemingly disparate objects as the wing structure of an airplane and the body structure of a jellyfish.[23] Their words and writings generally privileged technology, structure, materials, and function over aesthetics, but from time to time they acknowledged that their work was a complex dialogue between these elements—as when Charles parried the question of whether function or beauty was more important by asking "Which do you consider more important—a man's heart or a man's head?"[24] They never doubted the basic premises of modernism, yet they added significantly to its vocabulary and its terms of reference. Their certainty about their position, their dedication to rigorous research, and their reputation as the people who had finally made low-cost mass-produced modernist furniture widely available enabled them to introduce "prettiness" in the form of flowers, toys, paper kites, and other seemingly frivolous items to a movement that had been known for its overriding seriousness. They combined the seriousness of Enlightenment thought and modernist design principles with the fun of popular entertainment; in the process, they personalized, humanized, popularized, and reshaped modernism.

The Eameses championed the machine in their aim "to get the most of the best to the most for the least" and insisted that it be subservient to human control.[25] They wanted their products to reach as many people as possible, but (like William Morris) they were never willing to sacrifice quality for cheapness. They fulfilled their early aim of reaching a mass market with relatively inexpensive furniture, though it sometimes proved impossible to retail their goods at the prices they wished.[26] Moreover, as modernist architecture and design in the United States gradually shifted from being concerned with social ideals to providing vehicles for the "American dream" lifestyle, the Eameses shifted from a preoccupation with relatively low-priced mass-produced objects for everyday use to a reluctant acceptance that some of their furniture was expensive and was destined for the offices of large corporations and institutions and the homes of the wealthy. But, as I have argued, this was not a cynical move influenced by market trends; the Eameses were too idealistic and too intensely engaged with each particular project for that. If working through a problem and obtaining a solution fitted in with consumer demand, they were delighted; however, the problem-solving process was what interested them most.

Designers who compromised their design ideals by pandering to what they read as public taste took little pleasure in the fact that it was the Eameses who broke down the barriers to popular acceptance of mass-produced modernist furniture in the United States, and even less pleasure in the irony that, in the process, they made a considerable amount of money. In that they always put design ethics before money or fame, the Eameses were role models for many younger designers. (For example, their refusal of a commission to redesign the Budweiser logo because they liked the existing one became legendary in design circles.[27]) In the opportunistic years of the postwar boom in America, the Eameses offered an alternative to the rather crude money-making ethos of certain sections of the design professions and of the business community. During the 1960s and the 1970s, however, many radical younger designers were disappointed that Charles and Ray distanced themselves from the "alternative" design movement of those years, finding it too overtly political.[28] Although they held strong liberal views on many issues, they never aligned themselves with any group or movement—artistic, social, or political. Their approach to design never challenged capitalism; indeed, they were held up as proof that it was possible for designers to retain integrity and also be commercially successful. However, they did, to a certain degree, cut against the grain of the mainstream ideology of postwar America, fitting in better with older paternalist and populist views than with the consumerist and competitive ethos of the postwar years or the new radicalism of the late 1960s and the 1970s.

The Eameses were lucky in that they managed the rare feat of surviving economically without ever having to resort to "bread-and-butter" commissions. There is little doubt that without the manufacturing and marketing experience of the Herman Miller Furniture Company the Eameses would not have found commercial success on such a scale or quite so quickly. Their collaboration with that paternalistic company was particularly successful because the company's management, which belonged to the Dutch Calvinist Reformed tradition, shared the Eameses' high-minded ideals about quality in design and production. The world of the De Prees in Zeeland and that of the Eameses in Venice were many miles apart in ideology as well as in geography, but the Eameses (Charles in particular) straddled the gap with consummate ease.[29] The Eames-Herman Miller relationship remains a model for management consultants. Once they had entered into a "gentleman's" business relationship with Herman Miller (it was never set down on paper), the Eameses never designed for any other furniture producer.

Also crucial to the success of the Eameses was George Nelson, who shared their liberal humanist outlook on life and their passion for design and who consistently championed them. It was Nelson who recommended Charles and Ray to the Herman Miller Furniture Company, who gave them the opportunity to be part of the first multi-media presentation in the United States, and who invited them to produce what was to become Glimpses of the USA (Moscow, 1959).

In IBM they were fortunate to find another "ideal" client. Once again, as with Herman Miller, they joined forces with a well-established and paternalistic company, and they never did any similar work for a competitor. Once again, the company was already sure of the importance of design. And, just as the Eameses had been introduced to the Miller firm by a fellow designer (George Nelson), it was IBM's first director of design, Eliot Noyes, who commissioned their work for that company. In both cases, therefore, someone in the design community was responsible for the Eameses' getting the commissions; it was not that the firm contacted them directly or vice versa.

IBM gave Charles and Ray generous budgets and enormous freedom[30] (though at the end of the day each exhibit, presentation, or film had to meet with the IBM's approval) and gained, in exchange, the image of a company interested in the pursuit of knowledge and progress and conscious of the importance of human beings in the new machine age. In other words, the image the Eameses gave IBM reflected their own humanist concerns with education, mathematics, science, technology, and history—indeed, they accepted the work for IBM in the first place only because they considered the proper promotion of computers a worthwhile cause.

The Eameses never disappointed Eliot Noyes (who had ultimate control over IBM's design policy) or the accountants, and they had a very cordial relationship with the management. However, more than a few middle managers wished Noyes had chosen less exacting people with whom to work.[31] Especially when it came to the exhibitions, they demanded a great deal of IBM 's staff. Every object, potted plant, screen, display stand, color, and texture had to be just right. To the Eameses there was no other way to operate; perfection was the goal. They always insisted on quality; it was their watchword. They set standards not only in the furniture and exhibition trades but also in sponsored filmmaking.

Contemporaries greatly admired their breadth of vision. Besides working in a variety of media and being interested in a wide range of topics, they cared about ideas as well as visuals. Paul Schrader saw the Eames Office as a Renaissance workshop; others used similar terms. Charles was, and is, often described as a "Renaissance man" and likened to Leonardo da Vinci.[32] Buckminster Fuller touched on both the Eameses' belief in the parallels between science and art and their particular and unique ways of seeing things when he noted that "a really great scientist is an artist. Charles is an artist-scientist. He has a beautiful lens."[33]

Fuller was correct, but his viewpoint was partial. The Eameses' special way of designing and looking at things—their lens, if you like—came from Ray as much as from Charles. At the end of the day it was often her "special touch" that determined the final visual form of a chair, an exhibition, a film set, or an arrangement of objects. In the words of the Neuharts, it was Ray who so often made the difference between "good, very good" and "Eames."[34] There is no doubt that some people, at the time and since, undervalued Ray's contribution to the partnership. Few were as crudely sexist as the British Society of Industrial Artists and Designers, which, when it awarded Charles its design medal in 1967, presented Ray with a red rose. Ernestine Carter of London's *Sunday Times* protested "the Englishman's innate prejudice against women" and asked "Why fob off the female half of the partnership with a sentimental gesture?"[35] She was correct about the prejudice (although it is by no means restricted to English men), but she did not realize that both Charles and Ray preferred sentimental gestures and roses to more formal tributes.

I have put considerable emphasis on Ray's contribution to the partnership in the preceding chapters not to distract readers from the achievements of Charles (once characterized as a "one-man think tank, whose restless unconfined brain sheds ideas with dazzling brilliance")[36] but to give Ray due credit and to indicate something of her many talents, including what Billy Wilder called her "absolutely perfect taste,"[37] what Esther McCoy referred to as her "rich and audacious imagery,"[38] and what former staff members spoke of as her brilliant and exceptional eye. In order to investigate the working relationship of Charles and Ray I have drawn on ideas and issues raised by feminist scholarship, such as the degree to which women have been marginalized within design and within history, gender stereotyping, mutual respect and support, domestic arrangements, autonomy, "public" and "private" spheres, individual competition, imitation, male "genius," and "creative couples."[39] The evidence unearthed over the last few years about this particular couple has taken me in various directions, some different from those I originally envisaged but most revealing more mutuality, richness, and complexity in the collaboration between Charles and Ray than I at first suspected.

Ray's role was always far more than a silent partner who "mothered the mind," provided inspiration, and helped create an atmosphere in which her partner could flourish.[40] Nevertheless, although she was a working designer who received some public recognition, she also did her share of "mothering the mind" of Charles, as I have shown in chapter 2. However, Charles also gave Ray a great deal of support and encouragement, as she was always at pains to point out, and was protective toward and "parenting" of her.[41] Neither Ray nor Charles made any radical breaks from the dominant codes of masculinity and femininity, but it should be remembered that Ray's choice (for whatever reasons) to work full-time and not have children was not the typical one for an American middle-class woman in the postwar years.

The binary oppositions of public/private and male/female around which so much feminist analysis has centered in the last twenty years call for some qualification in the case of the Eameses. Ray did not remain at home and Charles in the office. Instead she shared the life of a thriving design firm with her creative and sexual partner. However, to the extent that the Eames Office became their "second home," one could argue that they shared a space that was part domestic, part work; part private, part public. They occupied and negotiated that space in different ways, as has been detailed in chapters 2–7, but the point I wish to emphasize here is that Ray shared it with Charles. She relinquished the autonomy of the housewife for a share in running and working in a design office and spending her working day with Charles—a choice that brought her great satisfaction as well as some frustration. Charles, by contrast, not only shared the experience of building and sustaining a design office and working on some extremely rewarding projects with Ray but also enjoyed an autonomous field of activities related to clients, commissions, finance, public engagements, and the "outside world" in general. Ironically, by choosing not to have children, not to be a housewife, and to work full-time in conjunction with Charles, Ray ended up with no autonomous sphere. I am not arguing that this was necessarily a "bad" thing for her or that she did not gain by the tradeoff, but a tradeoff there was. Ray was much less self-centered than Charles, and most of her time was subsumed in matters that also involved him. To a large degree, however, the same was true of him. By and large, they both seem to have negotiated living and working together over a long period of time remarkably well.

Ray's relinquishing fine art and graphics and working collaboratively with Charles meant that they avoided a competitive situation of two individual "artists" living together and having to negotiate individual, and sometimes fluctuating, reputations based on their personal creations.[42] Within the design collaboration of Charles and Ray, the differences in their training and areas of expertise at least meant that there was never the possibility of her being considered a pale imitator of her husband, as was the case with her friend Lee Krasner (some of whose work Ray owned) and Jackson Pollock.[43] As it was, Ray had to contend with the fact that her contributions to joint projects sometimes went unrecognized. She may not have felt competitive with Charles—she adored him and never wished him less glory than he had—but from time to time she expressed some frustration at her lack of recognition, although we do not know whether she expressed it to him (and, if she did, how).[44] Charles's high public profile (partly the result of Ray's extreme shyness in the public sphere, his reputation before they met, and the attribution of their early work to him alone and thereafter to the Eames Office) worked against the building of a public reputation for Ray; however, according to close friends, colleagues, and family, she found compensation in Charles's public acknowledgment of her contribution and insistence on equal credit, in the admiration of her creative abilities by many people, including Charles, and in the work itself.[45] Had Ray remained a painter she would have had a separate existence as an artist, but she would have missed out on what most people who have done it agree was a rewarding and often adrenaline-producing experience: working with Charles Eames. Like many modernist painters, including Sonia Delaunay, Ray did not believe paint on canvas to be more important than more obviously utilitarian items—"I liked painting but, because I was so interested in structure, the design work seemed very similar. . . . What we were doing in California in the early days with the plywood furniture project was very exciting and very important too"[46]—and did not view the transfer of her attention from one area to the other as a sacrifice. Rather, she saw it as an opportunity to be grasped with all of her not-inconsiderable energies.[47]

In many ways Ray suffered from being the partner of someone to whom his peers gave the accolade of genius. While this tells us a great deal about the tremendous abilities of Charles, abilities which Ray always wanted recognized and from which it is not my intention to detract, it led to assumptions that anyone working with him was *less* than him and, probably worse for Ray, that every brilliant idea or image must have originated with him. The myth of the (male) genius works to the detriment of women,[48] and Ray was no exception. This is not to argue for her as a genius but simply to point out that she lived in the shadow of a man thought to be one by many people with whom he came into contact in a variety of different fields. Charles was undoubtedly an exceptionally talented individual, but I hope to have shown in the preceding chapters that, in different ways, so too was Ray, and that in some areas of their joint work her talents were greater or made such a significant contribution to the end product that it would be difficult to imagine it without her input or to imagine Charles's producing something of such quality without her.

In general, their partnership was an easy one. Charles was used with working in partnerships; indeed he seemed to flourish in them—as did Ray in her partnership with him. Ray was always the first to give Charles credit, and vice versa. Each had enormous admiration for the other's abilities. Trained as an abstract artist, Ray approached design largely in terms of form, composition, color, and structure; Charles, the architect, saw the design process mainly in terms of structure, technology, and the rational solving of problems. But it was not just in relation to structure that their concerns and abilities overlapped. In terms of interests, it was simple; they had many in common, and what were not Ray's at first soon became hers also. Matters such as the fundamental question of how one sees and understands things interested them both when they met in 1940 and remained a concern throughout their lives, forming one of the main themes of the lectures delivered by Charles at Harvard in 1971.[49] They both insisted on perfection, as has been evident in every chapter of this book; the young St. Louis architect who so impressed the builder of one of his churches in the 1930s was only slightly less manic in his search for perfection than the woman with whom he lived for nearly forty years.

If in the search for perfection they were similar (although Charles knew when to finally say "enough"), in practical workshop skills they were very different—in fact, they were polar opposites. Charles was outstanding, but Ray was almost completely devoid of such skills. Although she had very much a "hands-on" approach to design, which partly came from her work as a sculptor, and was acutely aware of her lack of technical skills, she chose not to remedy the situation. Many members of the staff had exceptional technical abilities, so Ray did not need them, but the regret that she had not had a more practical training remained with her all her life, and this was one area of women's education that she thought should receive more attention.[50] She also regretted that she had not received a better grounding in mathematics, science, history, and philosophy, subjects to which she said Charles "opened [her] eyes."[51] This was another area in which Charles was clearly more able and talented than Ray. Like the question of practical skills, it raises few problems in trying to unravel their relative contributions to the partnership, because the issue is clear cut. The question of individual contributions becomes more difficult in those areas where, in my opinion, Ray's abilities were sometimes greater than those of Charles, namely a sense of composition and the ability to shape form and image, not least because Charles was by no means lacking in such talents himself.

It is difficult to make any statement in relation to the areas where they worked closely together without wanting to immediately qualify it, so close and complex was their relationship—as I hope the preceding chapters have shown. Although Charles and Ray may have had different and differential inputs into various projects, the interweaving of their personal and professional lives was so close that most of the time the "join could not be seen."[52] Philip Morrison, who worked on the scientific films with them, suggested that "Ray makes a surround around Charles, and Charles makes a direction for Ray,"[53] and thus it was that they supported and enabled each other. Whatever particular qualities or insights each brought to the work of the partnership, I hope to have shown that, together, Charles and Ray Eames designed some remarkable furniture, exhibitions, and buildings and also opened people's eyes not only to new images, new juxtapositions of images, and new ways of communicating ideas but also to new values, meanings, and delights in objects.

The most cursory glance at a chronology of their work indicates just how far the Eameses' interests and output changed over the years. In the mid to late 1950s there was a shift from a firm mainly but not exclusively concerned with furniture to one mainly but not exclusively concerned with films, multi-screen presentations, and exhibitions. Charles, in particular, became increasingly fascinated by ideas and communication and increasingly committed to communicating ideas. But there was more to the shift than the excitement and mental stimulation of unexplored territory and an impulse to educate, although they account for much of it. Both Charles and Ray commented on a degree of disillusionment at that time—particularly during and after their trip to India and in regard to the United States exhibition in Moscow in 1959, which they felt showed more than a glimpse of a country consumed by consumption: "We had pancake mixers there and TV dinners and toasters that jumped up and buttered themselves . . . and you went out and looked at people who had problems of their own and were facing them in their own way, and it wasn't this way."[54] The Eameses had always stood aside from conspicuous consumption, but seeing the harsh realities of life in India and the USSR focused their conviction that design should be about more than profit and novelty. They worried about the social responsibility of the designer, especially in the light of revelations in the 1950s of the polluting effect of many products, and they began to think that the main question facing designers would soon be "should rather than how we do it."[55]

Despite their dislike of many contemporary design practices, the Eameses never turned their backs on modern technology. As their knowledge of past and contemporary handicrafts grew, so too did their conviction that the way to solve the problems of the modern world was with the very latest technology. They saw salvation in more-sophisticated technology, especially that related to mass communications. However, they never applauded new technology or new materials for their own sake, and they were always conscious of the appropriateness to the job at hand of the materials and techniques they were using.

Like all good teachers, the Eameses remained perpetual students. They had an underlying philosophy relating to contemporary solutions to the problems of the modern world, and they were never afraid to enter into new areas of investigation. They had the ability to push forward on more than one front at a time, and in each case there was a complex dialectic between past work and present interests. Never concerned with innovation for its own sake, they were interested in solving problems. Because they valued the past (particularly its objects and ideas) for what it could teach us about the present, because they never produced anything without expending an enormous amount of time and energy on research and development, they were the antithesis of the throwaway "Kleenex culture" prevalent in certain aspects of American life in the 1950s and the 1960s. They were prepared to stick to their guns even when their ideas seemed to go against the grain of fashionable thought.

The Eameses seemed little changed by wealth and fame. In 1965 Charles was given an entry in *Current Biography* (between Bob Dylan and T. S. Eliot), and Ray enjoyed a certain recognition as his partner in work and marriage. *Fortune* magazine estimated that in 1974 they received $15,000 per month in royalties from furniture sales alone and that the Eames Office grossed $750,000.[56] However, a great deal of what might have been profit was spent when projects went over budget, and actual profits were often plowed back into research and development on new projects. Perhaps their success was one reason why the Eameses stuck so close to the patterns of their early life together. In the 1970s they lived much as they had thirty years earlier, in studied simplicity. Designer simplicity it certainly was, but nevertheless it was a type of simplicity. More than most contemporary middle-class Americans, they resisted the massive consumption of lifestyle-related products—but it should be remembered that many of the products they designed were associated with the consumer lifestyle. They would have been horrified at the late 1980s' cult of "designer" objects; however, if that phenomenon was a result of the concern with the salability of manufactured objects through appearance—a concern that, though as old as capitalism, became much stronger after World War II, when the Eameses were at the forefront of promoting design for a new lifestyle—then they must be seen as part of the process that led to it.

As designers and filmmakers the Eameses grew in stature over the years, learning not only from their own experiences but also from other individuals and other cultures about how people thought, worked, lived, played, and designed. They remained as enthusiastic about everything they did in later life as in their early years, and they continued to open their home and office to students and admirers. They never ceased to care about quality, design, education, and life, believing "the capacity for really caring" to be the mark of the good individual artist, designer, scientist, poet, or teacher.[57] Their caring manifested itself at many levels in their work, from the enormous drive for perfection in everything they did down to the smallest detail. They insisted on trying to keep human concerns central in a world that was becoming increasingly focused on high technology. Hard work and commitment kept them young; it seemed they would never grow old, so enthusiastic were they about everything they did.

Above all, the Eameses were educators and communicators. This was why films, exhibitions, and multi-media presentations interested them so much. They believed that most people had talents and gifts within them which would flourish if nurtured. In contrast with the idea of a "gifted few," they believed "just in people doing things they are really interested in doing."[58] They were critical of the American educational system, which encouraged early specialization and failed to produce rounded individuals. In their time, they were the American designers most committed to education in the broadest sense of the word—to a continuous, continuing, pleasurable process of learning—and the ones best able to present serious educational material in apparently unserious ways. Suzanne Muchnic commented on some of these qualities in a tribute published shortly before Charles died: "The couple's commitment to education as a joyful sensuous process is inspiring, and their spirit of boundless creative energy is contagious."[59] Their boundless energy, their spirit of independent inquiry, their joy in life, and their commitments to education and quality in all things and to exploring the possibilities of new ways of seeing and experiencing life were, and remain, inspiring.

C.4 Charles Eames
thinking before answering
a question about design in
the contemporary world.
NID, Ahmedabad, 1978.

C.5 Ray Eames on Chaise
(1968) with Xander, great-
grandson of Charles Eames
and son of Shelley Mills
and Eames Demetrios.

CHRONOLOGY

RAY EAMES (NÉE KAISER)

1912
Born December 15, Sacramento

1931
Graduates from high school, Sacramento

1933
Art Students League, New York

1933–1939
Hans Hofmann School, New York

1936
Founding member, American Abstract Artists

1937
Exhibited at first AAA show

1940
Studies at Cranbrook Academy of Art (4 months)

1941
Marries Charles Eames, moves to Los Angeles

CHARLES EAMES

1907
Born June 17, St. Louis

1920
Takes up photography

1925

Graduates from high school, St. Louis

Designs lighting fixtures for Edwin F. Guth Fixture Co.

1925–1928

Studies architecture, Washington University, St. Louis

Works part-time for Trueblood & Graf, architects

1928–1930

Works for Trueblood & Graf

1929

Marries Catherine Dewey Woermann

Visits Europe

1930–1933

Gray & Eames, architects, West Pine Boulevard, St. Louis (later Gray, Eames & Pauley)

1931

Sweetser House, 7147 Lindell Avenue, University City, St. Louis

1933

Restoration and some design work, Pilgrim Congregational Church, St. Louis

1933–34

Visits Mexico

Historic American Buildings Survey

1934–1938

Eames & Walsh, architects, Olive Street, St. Louis

Plan: "Ideal St. Louis home"

1935

Dean House, 101 Mason Avenue, Webster Groves, Missouri

1936

Dinsmoor House, 335 Bristol Road, Webster Groves, Missouri

Meyer House, 4 Deacon Drive, Huntleigh Village, Missouri

Two churches in Arkansas

1938

Fellowship at Cranbrook Academy of Art

Assists Carl Milles with *Meeting of the Waters* fountain (St. Louis)

1939–40

Instructor of Design, Cranbrook Academy of Art

Works in Saarinen Office and assists with seating for Klienhans Music Hall, Buffalo

Exhibition design with Eero Saarinen

Visits California, New Bauhaus (Chicago), and Grand Rapids

Designs for Organic Design in Home Furnishings competition (MoMA) with Eero Saarinen (first prize)

1941

Divorced

Marries Ray Kaiser

Moves to Los Angeles

1941–42

Art Department, MGM

CHARLES AND RAY EAMES

1941–1945

Plywood splint and litter

1942

Arts & Architecture covers (Ray)

1943

Plywood aircraft parts

City Hall project (Charles)

Arts & Architecture covers (Ray)

Packing label for splint (Ray)

"For C in Limited Palette" (Ray)

Cut-paper collage (Ray)

Plywood sculpture (Ray)

1944
Arts & Architecture covers (Ray)

"Composition in Yellow" (Ray)

1945
Plywood children's furniture

Plywood animals

Case Study Houses 8 and 9 (1945–1949)

Lecture 1 (slide show)

Fabric Designs (Ray)

1945–46
Plywood furniture, including DCM and DCW

1946
Lounge Chair

Screen

Tables

Case goods

New Furniture Designed by Charles Eames (exhibition)

Radio cases

1947
Folding tables

Jefferson Memorial competition

Arts & Architecture covers (Ray)

Fabric design (Ray)

1948
International Competition for Low-Cost Furniture Design (MoMA): stamped-metal furniture and Chaise

Herman Miller advertising

1949
Exhibition room in An Exhibition for Modern Living

Herman Miller showroom

1950
Eames Storage Units

Plastic Armchair

Plastic Side Chair

LTR Table

Good Design (exhibition)

Carson Pirie Scott window display

Wilder House

Traveling Boy (film; 12 minutes, color)

Masks

Herman Miller showroom interior

Herman Miller advertising

1951
ETR Table

Wire Mesh Chair

Wire Sofa

Kwikset House

The Toy

Macy room display

Herman Miller advertising

1952

The Little Toy

House of Cards

Philip Dunne Office, Twentieth Century Fox

Herman Miller showroom interior

Blacktop (11 minutes, color)

Parade, or Here They Come Down Our Street (6 minutes, color)

1953

Giant House of Cards

Hang-It-All

Herman Miller advertising

Railroad, Seascape, Townscape (slide shows)

Bread (7 minutes, color)

A Communications Primer (22 minutes, color)

A Rough Sketch for a Sample Lesson for a Hypothetical Course (multi-media presentation)

1954

Sears Compact Storage

De Pree House

Sofa Compact

Stadium Seating

Herman Miller advertising

S-73 (11 minutes, color)

1955

Stacking Chair

The Coloring Toy

Konditorei (slide show)

House: After Five Years of Living (11 minutes, color)

Textiles and Ornamental Arts of India (11 minutes, color)

Two Baroque Churches in Germany (11 minutes, color)

1956

Lounge Chair and Ottoman

Stephens Speaker

Eames Lounge Chair (2 minutes, black and white)

1957

Film montage for *The Spirit of St. Louis*

Griffith Park Railroad

Alcoa Solar Do-Nothing Machine

Stars of Jazz (3 minutes, black and white)

Day of the Dead (15 minutes, color)

Toccata for Toy Trains (14 minutes, color)

The Information Machine: Creative Man and the Data Processor (10 minutes, color)

1958

Aluminum Group

Eames Report

Herman Miller at the Brussels World's Fair (5 minutes, color)

The Expanding Airport (10 minutes, color)

De Gaulle Sketch (2 minutes, black and white)

1959

Revell Toy House

Kaleidoscope Shop (4 minutes, color)

Time & Life Building International Lobby (3 minutes, color)

Glimpses of the USA (multi-screen presentation)

Herman Miller showroom interior

1960

Lobbies, Time-Life Building

Time-Life Chair and Stool

"The Fabulous Fifties" (six film segments)

Kaleidoscope Jazz Chair (7 minutes, color)

Introduction to Feedback (11 minutes, color)

1961
La Fonda Chair

Eames Contract Storage

Herman Miller showroom interior

Mathematica: A World of Numbers . . . and Beyond (exhibition)

Mathematica Peep Shows (five films, each 2 minutes; color)

ECS (11 minutes, color)

Tivoli (slide show)

1962
Tandem Sling Seating

"The Good Years" (three film segments; two 5 minutes and one 2 minutes; black and white)

The House of Science (multi-screen presentation)

Before the Fair (7 minutes, color)

IBM Fair Presentation #1 (5 minutes, color)

IBM Fair Presentation #2 (5 minutes, color)

1963
Tandem Shell Seating

Herman Miller showroom interior

1964
School Seating

3473 Sofa

Segmented Base Tables

IBM Pavilion, New York World's Fair

Think (multi-screen presentation)

The House of Science (14 minutes, color)

1965

Nehru: His Life and His India (exhibition)

Westinghouse in Alphabetical Order (12 minutes, color)

The Smithsonian Institution (21 minutes, color)

Computer Day at Midvale (9 minutes, color)

Sherlock Holmes and the Singular Case of the Plural Green Mustache (9 minutes, color)

IBM at the Fair (8 minutes, color)

1966

Smithsonian Carousel

View from the People Wall (13 minutes, color)

The Leading Edge (11 minutes, color)

Herman Miller showroom interior

1967

National Fisheries Center and Aquarium (11 minutes, color)

The Scheutz Machine (5 minutes, color)

Herman Miller International, G.E.M., Picasso (slide shows)

1968

Chaise

Intermediate Desk Chair

Washington Presentation Center

Photography & the City (exhibition)

A Computer Glossary, or Coming to Terms with the Data Processing Machine (11 minutes, color)

Babbage's Calculating Machine or Difference Engine (4 minutes, black and white)

The Lick Observatory (8 minutes, color)

IBM Museum (10 minutes, color)

Powers of Ten: A Rough Sketch for a Proposed Film Dealing with the Powers of Ten and the Relative Size of the Universe (8 minutes, color)

1969
Soft Pad Group

National Fisheries Center and Aquarium (book)

Room in What Is Design exhibition

Image of the City (15 minutes, color)

Tops (7 minutes, color)

1970
Drafting Chair

Charles Eliot Norton Lectures, Harvard University

Computer House of Cards

Soft Pad (4 minutes, color)

The Fiberglass Chairs: Something of How They Get the Way They Are (9 minutes, color)

The Black Ships: The Story of Commodore Perry's Expedition to Japan Told with Japanese Pictures of the Time (8 minutes, color)

A Small Hydromedusan: Polyorchis haplus (3 minutes, color)

Circus, Louvre, Cemeteries (slide show)

1971
Charles Eliot Norton lectures, Harvard University

Two-Piece Plastic chair

Secretarial Chair

Loose Cushion Armchair

A Computer Perspective (exhibition)

Computer Landscape (10 minutes, color)

Clown Face (16 minutes, color)

Sets, Timgad, Goods, Baptistery, Lota, Eero Saarinen, India, Tanks (slide shows)

1972
Copernicus (exhibition)

Wallace J. Eckert: Celestial Mechanic (exhibition)

Fibonacci: Growth and Form (exhibition)

Computer Perspective (8 minutes, color)

Sumo Wrestler (unfinished)

Cable: The Immediate Future (10 minutes, color)

Banana Leaf: Something about Transformations and Rediscovery (2 minutes, color)

SX-70 (11 minutes, color)

Design Q&A (5 minutes, color)

1973
A Computer Perspective (book)

On the Shoulders of Giants (exhibition)

Movable Feasts and Changing Calendars (exhibition)

Isaac Newton: Physics for a Moving Earth (exhibition)

Franklin and Jefferson: Authors of Independence and Architects of the American Experiment (13 minutes, color)

Copernicus (10 minutes, color)

1974
Newton Cards

Philosophical Gardens (exhibition)

Newton's Method (3 minutes, color)

Kepler's Laws (3 minutes, color)

Callot (3 minutes, color)

1975
The World of Franklin and Jefferson (exhibition)

Metropolitan Overview (9 minutes, color)

1976
Images of Early America (exhibition)

Images of Early America (book)

The World of Franklin and Jefferson (book)

The World of Franklin and Jefferson (28 minutes, color)

The World of Franklin and Jefferson: The Opening of an Exhibition (Paris Opening)
(8 minutes, color)

Atlas: A Sketch of the Rise and Fall of the Roman Empire (3 minutes, color;
unfinished)

Something about Photography (9 minutes, color)

The Look of America 1750–1800 (26 minutes, color)

Tall Ships (slide show)

1977
IBM Corporate Exhibit Center proposal

Daumier: Paris and the Spectator (18 minutes, color)

*Powers of Ten: A Film Dealing with the Relative Size of Things in the Universe, and the
Effect of Adding Another Zero* (9 minutes, color)

Polavision (15 minutes, color)

1978
Sonar One-Step (8 minutes, color)

Art Game (12 minutes, color)

Merlin and the Time Mobile (3 minutes, color)

Cézanne: The Late Work (10 minutes, color)

Degas in the Metropolitan (10 minutes, color)

1979
A Report on the IBM Exhibition Center (12 minutes, color)

1982
Atlas (3 minutes, color)

Goods (6 minutes, color)

1984
Eames Leather and Teak Sofa

SELECT BIBLIOGRAPHY

Abercrombie, Stanley. *George Nelson: The Design of Modern Design.* Cambridge, Mass., 1995.

Architectural Design. Eames Celebration (special issue). September 1966, pp. 432–471.

Banham, Reyner. *Los Angeles: The Architecture of Four Ecologies.* London, 1971.

Black, Misha. *Exhibition Design.* London, 1950.

Caplan, Ralph. *By Design.* New York, 1982.

Caplan, Ralph. "Experiencing Eames." *Industrial Design,* January–February 1990, pp. 63–69.

Caplan, Ralph. *The Design of Herman Miller Pioneered by Eames, Girard, Nelson, Propst, Rohde.* New York, 1976.

Caplan, Ralph. "The messages of industry on the screen." *Industrial Design,* April 1960, pp. 50–65.

Caplan, Ralph, John Neuhart, and Marilyn Neuhart. *Connections; The Work of Charles and Ray Eames.* Los Angeles, 1976.

Carpenter, Edward K. "A tribute to Charles Eames." *Industrial Design 25th Annual Design Review,* 1979.

Chadwick, Whitney, and Isabelle de Courtivron, eds. *Significant Others: Creativity and Intimate Partnership.* London, 1993.

Clark, Robert J., et al., eds. *Design in America: The Cranbrook Vision 1925–1950.* Detroit and New York, 1983.

Cumming, Elizabeth, and Wendy Kaplan. *The Arts and Crafts Movement.* London, 1991.

Curtis, David. *Experimental Cinema: A Fifty-Year Evolution.* London, 1971.

Davis, Mike. *City of Quartz: Excavating the Future in Los Angeles.* New York, 1990.

De Pree, Hugh. *Business as Unusual.* Zeeland, Mich., 1986.

Design Quarterly. "Eames films on urban communications." No. 80, 1971, pp. 19–22.

Drexler, Arthur. *Charles Eames: Furniture from the Design Collection.* New York, 1973.

Eames, Charles. "Language of vision: The nuts and bolts." *Bulletin of the American Academy of Arts,* October 1974, pp. 13–25.

Eames, Charles, and Ray Eames. Eames Report. Los Angeles, 1958.

Eidelberg, Martin, ed. *Design 1935–1965: What Modern Was.* New York, 1991.

Fairbanks, Jonathan L., and Elizabeth Bidwell Bates. *American Furniture: 1620 to the Present.* New York, 1981.

Foy, Jessica, and Thomas J. Schlereth, eds. *American Home Life, 1880–1930: A Social History of Spaces and Services.* Knoxville, 1992.

Gebhard, David, and Robert Winter. *Architecture in Los Angeles: A Complete Guide.* Salt Lake City, 1985.

Gingerich, Owen. "A conversation with Charles Eames." *American Scholar* 46, part 3, 1977, pp. 326–337.

Girard, Alexander, and W. D. Laurie Jr. *An Exhibition for Modern Living.* Detroit, 1949.

Glickman, Michael. "Ray Eames." *Architects Journal,* September 7 1988, pp. 26–27.

Goldstein, Barbara. *Arts & Architecture: The Entenza Years.* Cambridge, Mass., 1990.

Greenhalgh, Paul, ed. *Modernism in Design.* London, 1990.

Grief, Martin. *Depression Modern: The Thirties Style in America.* New York, 1975.

Hamilton, Mina. "Films at the Fair II." *Industrial Design,* May 1964, pp. 37–41.

Hanks, David A. *Innovative Furniture in America from 1800 to the Present.* New York, 1981.

Heskett, John. *Industrial Design.* New York, 1980.

Hiesinger, Kathryn B., and George H. Marcus, eds. *Design since 1945.* Philadelphia, 1983.

Horn, Richard. *Fifties Style: Then and Now.* New York, 1985.

Jayakar, Pupul. "Charles Eames 1907–1978: A personal tribute." *Designfolio* (Ahmedabad) 2, January 1979, pp. 1–6.

Kaplan, Wendy, ed. *The Art That Is Life: The Arts and Crafts Movement in America, 1875–1920.* Boston, 1987.

Kaufmann, Edgar jr. *Prize Designs for Modern Furniture from the International Competition for Low-Cost Furniture Design.* New York, 1950.

Kaufmann, Edgar jr. *What Is Modern Design?* New York, 1950.

Kirkham, Pat. "Introducing Ray Eames (1912–1988)." *Furniture History* 26, 1990, pp. 132–141.

Lacey, Bill N. "Warehouse full of ideas." *Horizon,* September 1980, pp. 21–27.

Larabee, Eric, and Massimo Vignelli. *Knoll Design.* New York, 1981.

McCoy, Esther. "An affection for objects." *Progressive Architecture,* August 1973, pp. 64–67.

McCoy, Esther. "Charles and Ray Eames." *Design Quarterly* no. 98/99, 1974–75, pp. 20–29.

McCoy, Esther. "On attaining a certain age: Eames House, Santa Monica, California." *Progressive Architecture,* October 1977, pp. 80–83.

McQuade, Walter. "Charles Eames isn't resting on his chair." *Fortune,* February 1975, pp. 96–100, 144–145.

Meikle, Jeffrey. *Twentieth Century Limited: Industrial Design in America 1925–1939.* Philadelphia, 1979.

Morgan, Annie Lee, and Colin Naylor, eds. *Contemporary Architects.* Chicago, 1987.

Morrison, Philip, Phylis Morrison, and the Office of Charles and Ray Eames. *Powers of Ten: About the Relative Size of Things in the Universe.* San Francisco, 1982.

Naylor, Colin, ed. *Contemporary Designers.* Chicago, 1990.

Naylor, Gillian. *The Arts and Crafts Movement: A Study of Its Sources, Ideals and Influences on Design Theory.* London, 1971.

Nelson, George. *Display.* New York, 1953.

Nelson, George. *Problems of Design.* New York, 1957.

Nelson, George. "The furniture industry: Its geography, anatomy, physiognomy, product." *Fortune,* January 1947, pp. 106–111, 171–181.

Nelson, George. Foreword to *The Herman Miller Collection. Furniture Designed by George Nelson, Charles Eames, Isamu Noguchi, Paul Laszlo.* Zeeland, Michigan, 1948.

Neuhart, John, Marilyn Neuhart, and Ray Eames. *Eames Design: The Work of the Office of Charles and Ray Eames.* New York, 1989.

Noyes, Eliot. "Charles Eames." *Arts & Architecture,* September 1946, pp. 26–45.

Noyes, Eliot. *Organic Design in Home Furnishings.* New York, 1941.

Office of Charles and Ray Eames. *A Computer Perspective: Background to the Computer Age.* Cambridge, Mass., 1990.

Ostergard, Derek E., ed. *Bentwood and Metal Furniture 1850–1940.* New York, 1987.

Pulos, Arthur J. *American Design Ethic: A History of Industrial Design to 1940.* Cambridge, Mass., 1983.

Sandler, Irving. *Abstract Expressionism: The Triumph of American Painting.* New York, 1971.

Santa Barbara Museum of Art, *Turning the Tide: Early Los Angeles Modernism 1920–1956* (catalog), 1991.

Schrader, Paul. "Poetry of ideas: The films of Charles Eames." *Film Quarterly,* spring 1970, pp. 2–19.

Singer, M., ed. *A History of the American Avant-Garde Cinema.* New York, 1976.

Smith, Elizabeth A. T., ed. *Blueprints For Modern Living: History and Legacy of the Case Study Houses.* Cambridge, Mass., 1990.

Starr, Kevin. *Inventing the Dream: California through the Progressive Era.* Oxford, 1985.

Temko, Allan. *Eero Saarinen.* New York, 1962.

Torre, Susana, ed. *Women in American Architecture: A Historic and Contemporary Perspective.* New York, 1977.

Wallance, Don. *Shaping America's Products.* New York, 1956.

CREDITS

I would like to thank all those who helped with and gave permission to reproduce illustrations, particularly the Herman Miller Furniture Company, Andrew Raimist, Laurent Jean Torno Jr., Ashoke Chatterjee of the National Institute of Design (India), Julius Shulman, Marilyn and John Neuhart, David Travers of *Arts & Architecture,* Alice Gerdine, Martha Deese, Lucia Eames Demetrios d.b.a. Eames Office, Deborah Sussman, the Museum of Modern Art (New York), the Cranbrook Academy of Art, the University of California at Berkeley, the Gamble House, and the Photography Department of De Montfort University.

PERMISSIONS TO REPRODUCE AND COPYRIGHTS

Arts & Architecture: 1.19–1.23, 1.25–1.26, 3.3 (images © *Arts & Architecture*)

Cranbrook Academy of Art Museum: 1.12 (image © Cranbrook Academy of Arts Museum)

Eames Demetrios: 1.4, 1.5 (images © Eames Demetrios, Eames Office)

Deese Archive: 5.4

Photography Department, De Montfort University: 5.1

Lucia Eames Demetrios d.b.a. Eames Office: frontispiece, 1.1, 1.14–1.16, 2.1, 2.3–2.7, 3.2, 3.4–3.6, 3.8, 3.9, 3.17–3.22, 4.1, 4.2, 4.4–4.13, 4.15–4.23, 4.25, 4.30, 4.31, 5.6, 5.9, 5.11, 5.18, 5.24, 5.33, 6.1, 6.2, 6.4, 6.6–6.25, 7.2, 7.4–7.26 (images © Lucia Eames Demetrios d.b.a. Eames Office)

Gamble House: 1.27 (images © Gamble House)

Alice Gerdine: 1.11 (images © Alice Gerdine)

Herman Miller Furniture Company: 3.15, 3.16, 4.32, 4.33, 5.14, 5.15–5.17, 5.20–5.23, 5.26, 5.27, 5.29–5.32, 5.34, 5.35, C.3 (images © Herman Miller Furniture Co.)

Pat Kirkham: 2.2, 4.3, 4.24, 4.27–4.29, 5.7, 5.10, 5.12, 5.19, 5.28, 7.1 (images © Pat Kirkham)

Museum of Modern Art, New York: 1.18, 3.7, 5.2, 5.3, 5.5, 5.8, 5.13 (images ©
Museum of Modern Art)

National Institute of Design, India: 2.8–2.11, C.1, C.2, C.4 (images © NID)

Neuhart Donges Neuhart: 4.2, 6.2, 6.4, 6.11, 7.8, 7.10–7.20, 7.22–7.26 (N.B.:
Lucia Eames Demetrios d.b.a. Eames Office holds copyrights to all the Eames
films)

Andrew Raimist: 1.6–1.10, 1.13 (images © A. Raimist)

Julius Shulman: 1.28, 3.10–3.14, 4.26 (images © J. Shulman)

Sussman Archive: 4.14 (images © D. Sussman)

Laurent Jean Torno Jr.: 1.2, 1.3 (images © L. J. Torno Jr.)

University Art Museum, University of California, Berkeley: 1.17 (images © University Art Museum, University of California, Berkeley)

Vitra: C.5 (images © Vitra)

PHOTOGRAPHIC CREDITS

Eames Demetrios: 1.4, 1.5

Bruce Hudson: 5.1

Pat Kirkham: 2.2, 4.3, 4.24, 4.27–4.29, 5.7, 5.10, 5.12, 5.19, 5.28, 7.1

Shelley Mills: 4.24

John Neuhart: 4.2, 6.2, 6.4, 6.11, 7.8, 7.10–7.20, 7.22–7.26 (N.B.: Lucia
Eames Demetrios d.b.a. Eames Office holds copyrights to all the Eames films)

Andrew Raimist: 1.6–1.10, 1.13

Marvin Rand: 1.27

Julius Shulman: 1.28, 3.10–3.14, 4.26

Laurent Jean Torno Jr.: 1.2, 1.3

NOTES

INTRODUCTION

1. Charles D. Gandy and Susan Zimmermann-Stidham, *Contemporary Classics: Furniture of the Masters* (New York, 1981), list Charles Eames as one of eight selected "masters," the others being Thonet, Breuer, Mies, Le Corbusier, Aalto, Wegner, and Eero Saarinen. (The article on "Charles Eames" refers to the Eameses and the Eames partnership.) See also *Contemporary Masterworks,* ed. C. Naylor (Chicago, 1991). As early as 1959 three Eames chairs were included in a list of "The 100 Best Design Products" compiled by the world's leading designers and released by the Institute of Design at the Illinois Institute of Technology; see entry for Charles Eames in *Current Biography* (New York, 1965). In 1982 *Interior Design* asked six curators of modern design to choose design "classics" that had "made major contributions to our understanding of important design of this and the last century"; in the seating section, the 1946 plywood chair was the first choice of all the curators (Robert Mehlman, "Antiques of the future," *Interior Design,* April 1982). In 1985 Charles Eames was given the enormous accolade of being voted (posthumously) the world's most influential designer at the World Design Conference. Ray collected the award on behalf of Charles—an award that, in reality, honored their joint work.

2. John Neuhart, Marilyn Neuhart, and Ray Eames, *Eames Design: The Work of the Office of Charles and Ray Eames* (New York, 1989).

3. Elaine Sewell Jones, interview with Pat Kirkham, 1993.

4. I saw a great deal of material in the Eames Archive before 1988, but between then and the time of this writing it has not been available for further study. I am therefore particularly grateful to Ford Peatross of the Library of Congress for his help with queries. In checking factual information I have been greatly helped by Eames Demetrios and by Marilyn and John Neuhart. (My copy of *Eames Design* is well worn.)

5. For an examination of the methodologies employed in this book see Pat Kirkham, "The personal, the professional and partner(ship): Exploring the husband/wife collaboration of Charles and Ray Eames, designers and film makers, USA, 1941–1978," in *Feminists Produce Cultural Theory,* ed. B. Skeggs (Manchester, 1995).

6. See *Women in American Architecture: A Historic and Contemporary Perspective,* ed. S. Torre (New York, 1977); Anthea Callen, *Angel In the Studio: Women in the Arts and Crafts Movement 1870–1914* (London, 1979); Rozsika Parker and Griselda Pollock, *Old Mistresses: Women, Art and Ideology* (London, 1981); Dolores Hayden, *The Grand Domestic Revolution: A History of Feminist Design for American Homes, Neighborhoods, and Cities* (Cambridge, Mass., 1981); *Women Architects: Their Work,* ed. L. Walker (London, 1984); Rozsika Parker, *The Subversive Stitch: Embroidery and the Making of the Feminine* (London, 1984); *A View From the Interior: Feminism, Women and Design,* ed. J. Attfield and P. Kirkham (London, 1989). The phrase "hidden from history" is taken from Sheila Rowbotham's seminal work of that title (London, 1973).

7. For an exposition of the postmodernist position see Frederic Jameson, "Postmodernism, or the cultural logic of late capitalism," *New Left Review* no. 146, July-August 1984.

8. See David Harvey, *The Condition of Postmodernity* (Oxford, 1989); Peter Wollen, *Raiding the Icebox: Reflections on Twentieth-Century Culture* (New York, 1993); Alex Callinicos, *Against Postmodernism: A Marxist Critique* (London, 1989); Beverley Skeggs, "Postmodernism: What is all the fuss about?" *British Journal of Sociology of Education* 12, no. 2 (1991), pp. 255–267.

9. DIA Archive (Lethaby), DIAP and PeH, Library of the Royal Institute of British Architects, London. See also Pat Kirkham, *Harry Peach: Dryad and the DIA* (London, 1986), pp. 67–69.

10. Paul Thompson, "Organic design," *Issue* no. 8 (1991), pp. 12–15.

11. See Michael Collins, *Towards Post-Modernism: Design since 1851* (London, 1987), pp. 86–100; Martin Eidelberg, "Biomorphic modernism," in *Design 1935–1965: What Modern Was,* ed. M. Eidelberg (New York, 1991), pp. 88–120; Lesley Jackson, *The New Look: Design in the Fifties* (London, 1991), pp. 35–44.

12. Thompson, "Organic design"; Malcolm Quantrill, *Alvar Aalto: A Critical Study* (London, 1983), pp. 241–242.

13. For a history and a critique of the concept and label "genius" see Christine Battersby, *Gender and Genius: Towards a Feminist Aesthetics* (London, 1989).

14. Edward K. Carpenter, "A tribute to Charles Eames," in 25th Annual Design Review, *Industrial Design* (1979), p. 10.

15. Paul Schrader and Richard Donges, respectively, interviews with Pat Kirkham, 1991.

CHAPTER 1

1. "An Eames Celebration: The Several Worlds of Charles and Ray Eames," WNET television, New York, February 3, 1975 (hereafter referred to as Eames Celebration).

2. *Eames Design* offers a chronology of the early years of Charles and Ray. It was compiled with Ray, but there are several inaccuracies-particularly with regard to Charles. During conversations (of which there are notes), Charles told Tony Benn that his father was 60 when he married, whereas he told Don Wallance that his father was 60 when he "sired" him. According to his death certificate, Charles Ormand Eames Senior was born in 1849 in Petersburg, Rensselaer County, New York, the son of Joseph Eames (born in New Jersey) and Lucina Emerson (born in Vermont), and died in St. Louis in 1921 at the age of 72, the age cited by Charles to Don Wallance. On that occasion, Charles gave his own age when his father died as 12 (rather than almost 14), but on some other occasions he stated that he was 10. Eames Senior married Celine A. Lambert on May 28 1901, with F. O. Fannon, pastor of the First Christian Church, officiating. On his mother's side Charles was descended from René Kiercereaux, one of St. Louis's first "settlers," who arrived in 1764, and related to the Aubuchons and the Chomeaus of the Florissant area. I am grateful to Esley Hamilton for this information.

3. Charles Eames, interview with Virginia Stith, 1977. I am grateful to Virginia Stith for sending me copies of the tapes. (This interview is hereafter referred to as "Eames/Stith"; other interviews are referred to in similar fashion.)

4. Eames/Stith.

5. Eames file, Don Wallance Collection, Cooper-Hewitt National Museum of Design, New York.

6. Carpenter, "Tribute to Charles Eames," p. 10.

7. *Eames Design,* p. 19.

8. Eames Celebration.

9. Eames/Stith.

10. John Neuhart, Marilyn Neuhart, and Deborah Sussman, interviews with Pat Kirkham, August 1991.

11. Eames Celebration.

12. Eames/Stith; *Eames Design,* p. 19.

13. It is commonly assumed that Charles Eames was related to the St. Louis architect William S. Eames, a partner in Eames and Young, an architectural practice responsible for a number of impressive buildings in the city, including the Renaissance Revival Lammert Building (1898) and some warehouses at the Cupple Railroad Station (1894–1914). (See "Examples of architecture in St. Louis," *Architectural Record,* May 1896, pp. 393–410; William Herbert, "Some business buildings in St. Louis," *Architectural Record* no. 23, 1908, pp. 391–396.) This information was given in Robert W. Duffy, "Designing a whole building is just too demanding," *St. Louis Post-Dispatch,* August 1, 1982. Victoria Stith did not ask Charles Eames directly about his relationship with William Eames, but she did ask him if he had received any assistance in building his career. Charles, who did not mention William Eames, answered that he had received no assistance.

14. Frank Lloyd Wright, *An Autobiography* (London, 1977), pp. 33–34.

15. Eames/Stith.

16. Ibid.

17. Ibid.

18. Ibid.

19. Ibid.

20. Patricia McCarron, "School class looks back on 50 years," *St. Louis Post-Dispatch,* June 16, 1975.

21. Ibid.

22. Eames/Stith; *Eames Design,* p. 20.

23. Ibid.

24. *Eames Design,* p. 20.

25. Eames Celebration. In 1958 Washington University bestowed an Alumni Award upon Charles Eames (*Eames Design,* p. 228), who used to joke that the only diploma he had was one designed and made for him by his friend Saul Steinberg.

26. Ray Eames/Kirkham, 1987.

27. Eames Celebration.

28. Eames/Stith.

29. Ibid.

30. Ibid.

31. Ibid.

32. Ibid. See also Eames file, Don Wallance Collection.

33. Eames/Stith.

34. Ibid.

35. In 1915 a group of female architecture students at Washington University formed an association. See Mary Otis Stevens, "Struggle for place: Women in architecture: 1920–1960," in *Women in American Architecture: A Historic and Contemporary Perspective,* ed. S. Torre (New York, 1977).

36. Eames/Stith.

37. Ibid.

38. I am grateful to Andrew Raimist for this information, which he was given by Joseph Pulitzer Jr.

39. *Eames Design,* pp. 20–21. His set designs were for the St. Louis municipal outdoor theater.

40. Eames Celebration.

41. In the interview with Virginia Stith, Charles commented on his poor memory with regard to his early architectural work, with the exception of the Meyer House and the church at Helena. In 1982 Ray told a reporter preparing an article on Charles's work in the St. Louis area that she knew only of the alterations and repairs to the Pilgrim Congregational Church (Duffy, "Designing a whole building is just too demanding"). She seemed slightly surprised that I was so interested in Charles's early buildings, describing them as less "interesting" than the work after 1941 (Eames/Kirkham, 1987).

42. *Eames Design,* p. 21.

43. Eames/Stith.

44. *St. Louis Globe-Democrat,* February 14, 1932; agreement between the Woermann Construction Company and E. O. Sweetser, Esq., August 31, 1931; Duffy, "Designing a whole building is just too demanding"; Public Utility Records, St. Louis, 1931.

45. Richard Guy Wilson, "American Arts and Crafts architecture: Radical though dedicated to the cause conservative," in *The Art That Is Life: The Arts and Crafts Movement in America 1875–1920,* ed. W. Kaplan (Boston, 1987).

46. Duffy, "Designing a whole building is just too demanding"; *Eames Design,* p. 22.

47. Eames/Stith.

48. David Handlin, *American Architecture* (London, 1985), p. 197.

49. Eames file, Don Wallance Collection.

50. Eames/Stith.

51. Eames file, Don Wallance Collection.

52. Eames/Stith.

53. "Personalities," *Progressive Architecture,* August 1960, p. 59; Judith Wechsler/ Kirkham, 1991.

54. "St. Louian's Mexican Diary in Watercolor," *St. Louis Post-Dispatch* Sunday magazine, July 29, 1934. (The date of the start of the Mexican trip is incorrectly given as 1934 in *Eames Design.*)

55. "St. Louian's Mexican Diary in Watercolor."

56. Ibid.

57. His Mexican paintings were exhibited at Norfolk, Virginia. A show was planned for New York.

58. *Eames Design,* p. 23.

59. "St. Louis art for Arkansas," *St. Louis Post-Dispatch* Sunday magazine, April 5, 1936. The statue on the front elevation was by Carolyn Risque, a St. Louis artist.

60. See James Stokoe, *Decorative and Ornamental Brickwork* (New York, 1982).

61. I am extremely grateful to Eames Demetrios (grandson of Charles Eames) for this information, which came from the children of the builder.

62. Eames/Stith.

63. *Architectural Forum,* January 1935, p. 9.

64. Thomas Tileston Waterman and John A. Barrows, *Domestic Colonial Architecture of Tidewater Virginia* (New York, 1932), pp. 99–104; Thomas Tileston Waterman, *The Mansions of Virginia 1706–1776* (New York, 1945), pp. 180–187.

65. This was probably the house referred to by Charles in Victoria Stith's interview. He could not remember the name of the clients on whose house "Bob [Walsh] did a lot of work," but he described it as "the closest to an International Style because [the clients] were intellectually orientated."

66. Duffy, "Designing a whole building is just too demanding." See also David G. De Long, "Eliel Saarinen and the Cranbrook tradition in architecture and urban design," R. Craig Miller, "Interior design and furniture," and Christa C.

Mayer Thurman, "Textiles," all in *Design in America: The Cranbrook Vision 1925–1950,* ed. R. J. Clark et al. (New York, 1983). Duffy and Miller quote from interviews with Alice Gerdine, formerly Alice Meyer, who, with her husband John Meyer, commissioned the house. Most of the information about the house presented in this chapter is taken from their articles.

67. Ibid.; Eames/Stith.

68. Duffy, "Designing a whole building is just too demanding."

69. Eames/Stith.

70. Duffy, "Designing a whole building is just too demanding."

71. Ibid.

72. See the sources acknowledged in note 66 above.

73. Miller, "Interior design and furniture (note 66 above), p. 109.

74. Ibid.; Duffy, "Designing a whole building is just too demanding,"

75. Miller, "Interior design and furniture," p. 109. Miller makes no mention of the carpet designed by Eames and made in the studio of Loja Saarinen, to which Thurman refers on pp. 189–190 of "Textiles." The source is a 1976 interview with Charles Eames, housed in the Cranbrook Archive, in which Charles Eames commented on his hesitation before asking her about making up his designs.

76. Caroline Risque, Josephine Johnson, and Charles Eames were among those who sculpted the bricks (Eames/Stith).

77. Hewson Jackson, interview with Eames Demetrios. I am grateful to Eames Demetrios for bringing this remark to my attention. In the interview with Virginia Stith, Charles stated, à propos the Meyer House, that he and Walsh "were doing some great things at that time."

78. Several sources state that Eames went to Cranbrook in 1937 (see, e.g., Ralph Caplan, "Nelson, Eames, Girard and Propst: The design process at Herman Miller," *Design Quarterly* 98/99 (1976), p. 58); however, he did not enroll officially until the autumn of 1938, the date also given in *Eames Design* (source: Cran-

brook Archive, Registrar's Office, Cranbrook Academy of Art). R. Craig Miller ("Interior design and furniture," p. 306, n. 80) notes that Jill Mitchell recalls Charles Eames telling her that he was in New York for part of 1937 working on stage designs.

79. Eames Celebration.

80. *Eames Design,* p. 18.

81. Ibid.

82. Deborah Sussman/Kirkham, 1991.

83. Ibid.

84. Ray Eames/Kirkham, 1983.

85. *Eames Design,* p. 21.

86. In my 1991 interviews, Marilyn Neuhart and Deborah Sussman each made the point about the "finishing school," and both thought that Charles considered Ray to have a lot of "class." Several people I interviewed mentioned that she had a private income, details of which she never disclosed.

87. See Cynthia Goodman, *Hofmann* (New York, 1986); Walter Bannard, *Hans Hofmann* (Houston, 1977); Sam Hunter, *Hans Hofmann* (New York, 1963), Barbara Rose, *Hans Hofmann: Drawings 1930–1944* (New York, 1978); Irving Sandler, *Hans Hofmann: The Years 1947–1952* (New York, 1976); William C. Seitz, *Hans Hofmann* (New York, 1972); John R. Lane and Susan C. Larsen, *Abstract Painting and Sculpture in America, 1927–1944* (New York, 1983).

88. Clement Greenberg, "Art," *The Nation,* April 21, 1945, p. 469.

89. Eames/Kirkham; Cynthia Goodman, *Hans Hofmann as Teacher: Drawings by His Students* (Provincetown, Mass., 1980).

90. Ibid., pp. 32–40.

91. Ibid., pp. 40–41; Seitz, *Hans Hofmann,* pp. 27–34; David Anfam, *Abstract Expressionism* (London, 1990), pp. 55–56.

92. Goodman, *Hans Hofmann as Teacher,* pp. 58–59.

93. S. Naith and S. G. White, *Jackson Pollock: An American Saga* (New York, 1989), p. 382.

94. McQuade, "Charles Eames isn't resting on his chair," *Fortune,* February 1975, p. 99.

95. Eames/Kirkham, 1983.

96. Lane and Larsen, *Abstract Painting and Sculpture in America, 1927–1944* p. 36; *The New Deal Art Projects: An Anthology of Memoirs,* ed. F. O'Connor (Washington, 1972), p. 228. Ray Eames was a founding member.

97. *New Deal Art Projects,* p. 239.

98. Irving Sandler, *Abstract Impressionism, The Triumph of American Painting* (New York, 1970), pp. 17–19.

99. *Eames Design,* p. 22.

100. Ibid., pp. 30–45.

101. "Ray Eames," *California Arts & Architecture,* September 1943; *Eames Design,* p. 45.

102. I am grateful to Ford Peatross of the Library of Congress for this information.

103. See Kathleen Burnett, "Typography in space: Herbert Bayer and exhibition design," *Journal of Design History,* forthcoming.

104. I am grateful to Ford Peatross of the Library of Congress for information about Ray's interest in cut-out fashion dolls in the late 1930s.

105. *Eames Design,* p. 86.

106. See *The Art That Is Life: The Arts and Crafts Movement in America 1875–1920,* ed. W. Kaplan (Boston, 1987), esp. part III. See also Elizabeth Cumming and Wendy Kaplan, *The Arts and Crafts Movement* (London, 1991), pp. 107–178;

Davira S. Taragin, "The history of the Cranbrook community," in *Design in America: The Cranbrook Vision 1925–1950,* ed. R. J. Clark et al. (New York, 1983), pp. 35–45.

107. Taragin, "History of the Cranbrook community," p. 35.

108. Pat Kirkham, *Harry Peach: Dryad and the DIA* (London, 1986), pp. 47–70; Noel Carrington, *Industrial Design in Britain* (London, 1976), pp. 21–28; John Heskett, *Design in Germany 1870–1918* (London, 1987), pp. 57–154; Gillian Naylor, *The Arts and Crafts Movement* (London, 1971), pp. 190, 193.

109. Ibid.

110. Cumming and Kaplan, pp. 206–207.

111. Eames Celebration; Don Albinson/Kirkham, 1991; *Eames Design,* p. 23.

112. Scandinavian design was popularized through a number of traveling exhibitions held in museums and department stores. One of the most important was Swedish Contemporary Decorative Arts, which was shown in New York, Chicago, and Detroit in 1927. See David McFadden, *Scandinavian Modern Design 1880–1980* (New York, 1981).

113. Taragin, "History of the Cranbrook community."

114. Ibid., p. 44. Aalto admired Saarinen's resistance to architectural fashions. Saarinen was influenced by the classicism of Aalto's 1920s style, which stressed asymmetry, the free grouping of volumes, and clearly marked divisions in wall surfaces; he also admired Aalto's adoption in the 1930s of the "new functionalism," with its strong emphasis on social concerns, but it was Aalto's insistence that rationalism and standardization should not mean the end of human imagination and creativity that most informed Saarinen's work as director of Cranbrook.

115. Alvar Aalto Synopsis, Papers of the Institute for History and Theory of Architecture at the Swiss Federal Institute of Technology (Zurich, 1980), pp. 19–24.

116. Ibid., pp. 15–20. See also *Alvar Aalto Sketches,* ed. G. Schildt (Cambridge, Mass., 1978); Goran Schildt, *Alvar Aalto: The Mature Years* (New York, 1991).

117. For biographical details about well-known designers associated with Cranbrook see *Design in America,* ed. R. J. Clark et al. (New York, 1983).

118. See "Stimulus range," *American Fabrics* 20 (1949), pp. 68–72; *Eames Design,* pp. 86–87.

119. Eames/Stith, 1977.

120. See "Nude nuptials; Milles' Aloe Plaza fountain," *Architectural Forum,* November 1937; "Milles's nude god stirs art war in St. Louis, wedding in doubt," *Art Digest* 12 (1937).

121. Taragin, "History of the Cranbrook community."

122. Eames Celebration.

123. *Eames Design* (p. 24) states that Charles was made head of the Department of Industrial Design but does not actually give him the title of Head of Department. That went to his successor. In 1940–41 Charles's title was Instructor of Design (Robert Judson Clark, "Cranbrook and the search for twentieth century form," in *Design in America,* ed. R. J. Clark et al. (New York, 1983). See also Eames/Stith, 1977; Eames Celebration; Eames file, Don Wallance Collection.

124. "3 chairs/3 records of the design process," *Interiors,* April 1957, p. 118.

125. Miller, "Interior design and furniture," p. 307, n. 96.

126. Eric Larrabee and Massimo Vignelli, *Knoll Design* (New York, 1990), p. 56.

127. Eames Celebration.

128. Quoted in Sherban Cantacuzino, *Great Modern Architecture* (London, 1966), p. 78.

129. Ibid. The Eameses put together a slide show on the work of Eero Saarinen in 1970–71 as part of one of Charles's Norton Lectures at Harvard University. Saarinen's work was used as a model of how a "systems" approach to design worked (*Eames Design,* p. 356).

130. Cantacuzino, *Great Modern Architecture,* p. 78.

131. Eames Celebration; Ray Eames, introduction to P. Morrison et al., *Powers of Ten: About the Relative Size of Things in the Universe* (San Francisco, 1982).

132. Allan Temko, *Eero Saarinen* (New York, 1962), p. 14.

133. See Arthur A. Cohen, *Herbert Bayer: The Complete Work* (Cambridge, Mass., 1984).

134. *Eames Design,* p. 24; Miller, "Interior design and furniture," pp. 104–105; Albert Christ-Janer, *Eliel Saarinen* (Chicago, 1948), pp. 82–87.

135. Miller, "Interior design and furniture," p. 105.

136. Eames file, Don Wallance Collection. Charles appears in a photo with what appears to be a prototype of the chair (Miller, "Interior design and furniture," p. 305, n. 59).

137. Grant Hildebrand, *Designing for Industry: The Architecture of Albert Kahn* (Cambridge, Mass., 1974).

138. Miller, "Interior design and furniture," p. 109.

139. George Nelson and Henry Wright, *Tomorrow's House: How to Plan Your Post-War Home Now* (New York, 1945).

140. Kirkham, *Harry Peach,* p. 57.

141. Eames Celebration; Ray Eames/Kirkham, 1983; Rose Slivka, *Peter Voulkos: A Dialogue with Clay* (New York, 1978).

142. Eames file, Don Wallance Collection.

143. Eames Celebration.

144. Mike Davis, *City of Quartz: Excavating the Future in Los Angeles* (New York, 1990).

145. Eames/Kirkham, 1983.

146. Davis, *City of Quartz,* p. 28.

147. See Randell L. Mackinson, *Greene and Greene: Architecture as Fine Art* (Layton, 1977).

148. See Robert Winter, *The California Bungalow* (Los Angeles, 1980).

149. John Entenza, introduction to K. Current, *Greene & Greene: Architecture in the Residential Style* (Fort Worth, 1974).

150. Davis, *City of Quartz,* pp. 24–30.

151. Wendy Kaplan, "Pioneer modernism on the American West Coast," in *Modernism in Design,* ed. P. Greenhalgh (London, 1990), p. 105.

152. Ibid., p. 108.

153. Reyner Banham, *Los Angeles: The Architecture of Four Ecologies* (London, 1971), p. 60.

154. Eames Celebration.

155. Ibid.

156. David Gebhard, *The Californian Architecture of Frank Lloyd Wright* (San Francisco, 1988), p. 3.

157. Eames Celebration.

158. Ibid.

159. Ibid.

160. Frank Lloyd Wright, *A Testament* (New York, 1957), quoted on p. 26 of Cantacuzino, *Great Modern Architecture.*

161. Wright, *An Autobiography,* pp. 424, 541. Wright at first regarded Saarinen, whom he called "the Finnish cosmopolite with the Norse accent," to have copied his work as well as that of other architects and designers. And Wright acknowledged that he was a little envious of how the foreigner's career had flourished, in contrast to his own. The two became friends in the 1930s.

162. Cantacuzino, *Great Modern Architecture,* p. 8. See also Frank Lloyd Wright, *Ausgeführte Bauten und Entwürfe* (Berlin, 1910) and *A Testament.*

163. David Gebhard, *Schindler* (London, 1971); A. Sarnitz, *R. M. Schindler Architect 1887–1953* (New York, 1986); Thomas S. Hines, *Richard Neutra and the Search for Modern Architecture* (New York, 1982); Arthur Drexler and Thomas Hines, *The Architecture of Richard Neutra* (New York, 1982).

164. Gebhard, *Schindler,* p. 51.

165. Ibid., pp. 114–116.

166. Ibid., p. 116

167. Kaplan, "Pioneer modernism on the American West Coast," p. 114.

168. Banham, *Los Angeles,* p. 189.

169. *Modern Architecture: International Exhibition* (exhibition catalog, Museum of Modern Art, 1932), pp. 166–167.

170. Ray Eames/Kirkham, 1983. In his book *Life and Human Habitat* (New York, 1956), Neutra noted "Charlie Eames once wrote to me touchingly after living full seven years in an apartment I had designed."

171. Thomas S. Hines, "Case Study trouvé: Sources and precedents, Southern California, 1920–1942," in *Blueprints for Modern Living: History and Legacy of the Case Study Houses,* ed. E. A. T. Smith (Cambridge, Mass., 1989), passim.

172. Gebhard and Winter, passim.

CHAPTER 2

1. Elaine Sewell Jones/Kirkham, 1991; Carpenter, "Tribute to Charles Eames," p. 12; Walter McQuade, "Charles Eames isn't resting on his chair," *Fortune,* February 1975, p. 99.

2. John and Marilyn Neuhart/Kirkham, 1991.

3. Audrey Wilder/Kirkham, 1993.

4. See Sally Buchanan Kinsey, "A more reasonable way to dress," in *The Art That Is Life: The Arts and Crafts Movement in America 1875–1920,* ed. W. Kaplan (Boston, 1987).

5. See *American Fashion,* ed. S. T. Lee (New York, 1975), pp. 221–267; Anthea Jarvis, "Fashion," in *The New Look: Design in the Fifties,* ed. L. Jackson (London, 1991), pp. 117–118.

6. I am grateful to Lou Taylor of Brighton University for discussing this and other issues of dress with me.

7. *Eames Design,* pp. 21–22.

8. "Report from Chicago: The Eames Design," Public Broadcasting Laboratory, April 6, 1969 (hereafter referred to as Report from Chicago).

9. Louisa May Alcott, *Little Men.*

10. *Eames Design,* pp. 21–22.

11. For a discussion of Rand and architects see Meryl Secrest, *Frank Lloyd Wright: A Biography* (London, 1992), p. 496. Rand worked in Kahn's office in order to learn about architecture.

12. Caplan/Kirkham, 1991; Marilyn Neuhart/Kirkham, 1991.

13. Carpenter, "Tribute to Charles Eames," p. 12; Don Albinson/Kirkham, 1991.

14. See *Significant Others. Creativity and Intimate Partnership,* ed. W. Chadwick and I. de Courtivron (London, 1993).

15. Alison Smithson/Kirkham, 1991.

16. *Eames Design,* pp. 45, 60, 80, 81, 85, 91, 97, 107, 131, 148. I am well aware that photographic representations are conscious "constructions" rather than simple reflections of reality and that those of Charles and Ray taken or composed by them should only be read as indicating how they wanted to represent themselves to the outside world and to themselves. However, this coziness is striking and consistent, and it corresponds to evidence from friends and colleagues about their relationship.

17. Michael Glickman, "Ray Eames," *Architects' Journal,* September 7, 1988, p. 27.

18. Many people discussed the personal relationship of Charles and Ray and its effect on their working relationship with me. For reasons of confidentiality, I am not referencing all these points. I touch upon this particular topic only to deal with the claims that, in some unspecified ways, Charles's sexual relationships with women other than Ray stand as proof of her marginality to the working partnership. I came across such assertions so frequently, in lectures and in informal discussions, that I felt obliged to address them. To have found Ray marginal to the partnership would not have offended my feminist or historical sensibilities—far from it. At the end of the day, however, those who wish to refute the evidence of Ray's creativity and input need to marshall evidence other than this. As far as I can gather, Charles tried not to let his affairs interfere with his personal relationship with Ray or with their working relationship. I have been informed by a close friend of Ray's that in the late 1950s she contemplated divorce. Part of her decision to stay with Charles almost certainly was a desire to remain in a close working partnership—as was his decision to stay within the marriage and that partnership. Charles and Ray may have been less close in the last few years of Charles's life; even if this was the case, there remained mutual interests and bonds of affection which sustained both their personal and working relationships. By that time, they had so influenced each other in terms of design that the ideas and the work of one were inevitably informed by those of the other—so much so as to make questions of authorship and influence far from simple.

19. Paul Schrader/Kirkham, 1991.

20. *Eames Design,* p. 8.

21. Pupul Jayakar, "Charles Eames 1907–1978: A personal tribute," in *Design-folio* (Ahmedabad) 2, January 1979.

22. See Gilles Deleuze, *Masochism* (New York, 1971).

23. Esther McCoy, "An affection for objects," *Progressive Architecture,* August 1973, p. 66.

24. Carpenter, "Tribute to Charles Eames," p. 12.

25. See Morton P. Shand, "Scenario for a human drama: The Glasgow interlude," *Architectural Review,* January 1935, pp. 23–26; Thomas Howarth, *Charles Rennie Mackintosh and the Modern Movement* (London, 1977), pp. 145–146. In recent years the work of Margaret Macdonald Mackintosh and other women artists and designers working in Glasgow at the turn of the century has been the subject of considerable study. See *The Glasgow Girls: Women in Art and Design 1880–1920,* ed. J. Burkhauser (Edinburgh, 1990).

26. See note 6 to the introduction.

27. Smithson/Kirkham, 1991.

28. I am grateful to Janice Helland for tracking down this often-used but never-referenced quote. It comes from the memoirs of a close friend of both Charles and Margaret Mackintosh who felt that her "decorative creativeness" complemented his talents. See Desmond Chapman-Huston, *The Lamp of Memory* (London, 1949), p. 127.

29. Howarth, *Charles Rennie Mackintosh and the Modern Movement,* pp. 145–146.

30. Bill N. Lacy, "Warehouse full of ideas," *Horizon,* September 1980, p. 22; presentation to 28th International Design Conference, 1978, Aspen, Colorado; *Current Biography,* 1965, p. 141, respectively.

31. "Report from Chicago: The Eames Design," Public Broadcasting Laboratory, April 6, 1969.

32. See *Women in American Architecture: A Historical and Contemporary Perspective,* ed. S. Torre (New York, 1977).

33. Ibid., pp. 91–96, 152–154.

34. Deborah Sussman and Marilyn Newhart, respective interviews with Pat Kirkham, 1991.

35. J. and M. Neuhart/Kirkham, 1991. When Jill Mills (later Mitchell), who knew Charles well at Cranbrook, told him she was going to marry a Cranbrook colleague, Charles told her that he thought Loja Saarinen the perfect wife because not only was she a talented artist/designer in her own right but she provided the perfect surroundings in which Eliel could work at his best (J. Neuhart/Kirkham, 1991).

36. See "Shock-proof furniture," *Architectural Forum,* April 1946, p. 10; Doris Saatchi, "All about Eames," *House and Garden,* February 1984, p. 129.

37. Alison Smithson, "And now Dhamas are dying out in Japan," *Architectural Design,* September 1966, p. 447.

38. J. and M. Neuhart/Kirkham, 1991.

39. Albinson/Kirkham, 1991.

40. Report from Chicago.

41. These are detailed in *Eames Design* (passim).

42. *Eames Design,* pp. 443–450.

43. Smithson/Kirkham, 1991; Report from Chicago.

44. Ken Garland, conversation and subsequent correspondence with Pat Kirkham, 1991.

45. Jayakar, "Charles Eames 1907–1978," p. 53.

46. Carpenter, "Tribute to Charles Eames," p. 12.

47. Sussman/Kirkham, 1993.

48. Jehane Burns/Kirkham, 1991.

49. *Eames Design,* p. 8.

50. Sussman/Kirkham, 1991. Deborah Sussman described Charles as "something of a control freak."

51. Kevin Jackson, *Schrader on Schrader & Other Writings* (London, 1990), p. 26.

52. Ibid.

53. Lacy, "Warehouse full of ideas," pp. 22, 25.

54. J. H. Kay, "The Eameses' modernism: Democratic yet still elite," *New York Times*, December 7, 1989.

55. Sussman/Kirkham, 1991; Richard Donges/Kirkham, 1991.

56. J. and M. Neuhart/Kirkham, 1991; Eames Demetrios/Kirkham, 1993.

57. Albinson/Kirkham, 1991.

58. Sussman/Kirkham, 1991.

59. Jeannine Oppewall/Kirkham, 1991.

60. Ibid.

61. Ibid. Charles was fond of quoting the physicist Richard Feynman ("You have to find a corner and pick away at it") on the question of not taking too broad a perspective. Paul Schrader, "Poetry of ideas: The films of Charles Eames," *Film Quarterly,* spring 1970, p. 4.

62. Demetrios/Kirkham, 1991; Dan McLoughlin/Kirkham, 1993.

63. Albinson/Kirkham, 1991.

64. Ibid.

65. Sussman/Kirkham, 1991.

66. Peter Smithson/Kirkham, 1991.

67. Jackson, *Schrader on Schrader,* p. 26.

68. Sussman/Kirkham, M. and J. Neuhart/Kirkham, and Oppewall/Kirkham, 1991, respectively.

69. *Eames Design,* pp. 69, 81; M. and J. Neuhart/Kirkham, Albinson/ Kirkham, and Donges/Kirkham, 1991. Ray was better at giving credit to staff members than Charles. When asked about her role in designing the lounge chair and ottoman, Ray stated "a million things [including]. . . to be able to look critically at the total form" and added "but that is the same for everyone in the office" ("Today" show, 1956).

70. Eames/Kirkham, 1987; Donges/Kirkham, 1991. (*Eames Design* remains the best source for attribution.)

71. Ray told me that the switching around of whose name came first was done to indicate equal credit.

72. *Eames Design,* p. 9.

73. Jackson, *Schrader on Schrader,* p. 26.

74. Paul Schrader/Kirkham, 1991.

75. M. and J. Neuhart/Kirkham, 1991.

76. *Eames Design,* p. 9.

77. Ralph Caplan/Kirkham, 1991.

78. Ibid.; A. Smithson, "And now Dhamas are dying out in Japan," p. 447.

79. Oppewall/Kirkham, 1991. Many other interviews and conversations about the Eameses confirm that Charles could be dictatorial.

80. Speech by the Rt. Hon. Tony Benn, MP, at American Embassy, London, November 8, 1978. I am grateful to Tony Benn, who was a friend of Charles Eames for more than 20 years, for sending me a copy.

81. Ibid.

82. Oppewall/Kirkham, 1991.

83. By the 1970s there were about as many women as men employed in the Eames Office, where the wages were at the mid to lower ends of the relevant scales. The growth of the firm, the nature of the output, and the gender of the workers are roughly correlated, but there were many fluctuations in the size of the firm and in the gender balance of the employees from year to year and from project to project. About one-fifth of the workforce was female in the mid 1940s, and just under one-third by the late 1950s. In the mid 1960s the fraction stood at one-third; it was almost one-half by the mid 1970s.

84. Former Eames Office employees, interviews with Pat Kirkham, 1991.

85. Ibid.

86. Ibid.

87. Charles and Ray Eames, Eames Report (Los Angeles, 1958). For some looser "quotations" see Carpenter, "Tribute to Charles Eames," p. 10.

CHAPTER 3

1. Gingerich, Owen. "A conversation with Charles Eames," *American Scholar* 46 (1977), p. 327.

2. Geoffrey Holroyd, "Retrospective statements," in *The Independent Group: Postwar Britain and the Aesthetics of Plenty,* ed. D. Robbins (Cambridge, Mass., 1990), pp. 189–190.

3. See *Blueprints for Modern Living: History and Legacy of the Case Study Houses,* ed. E. A. T. Smith (Cambridge, Mass., 1990).

4. Thomas Hine, "The search for the postwar house," in *Blueprints for Modern Living,* pp. 170–171, 176.

5. Ibid., p. 171; Dolores Hayden "Model houses for the millions; Architects' dreams, builders' boasts, residents' dilemmas," in ibid., p. 209.

6. Ibid.

7. Hayden, "Model houses," p. 203.

8. Arthur Drexler and Thomas S. Hines, *Richard Neutra: From International Style to California Modern* (New York, 1982), p. 7.

9. Between 1932 and 1934 the Public Works Administration built 43 housing projects in a variety of styles. See David Handlin, *American Architecture* (London, 1985) pp. 205–206.

10. Mike Davis, *City of Quartz: Excavating the Future in Los Angeles* (New York, 1990), pp. 9–10.

11. Drexler and Hines, *Richard Neutra,* p. 8.

12. Davis, *City of Quartz,* passim (esp. chapter 3).

13. David Gebhard and Robert Winter, *Architecture in Los Angeles: A Complete Guide* (Salt Lake City, 1984), p. 23; Kevin Starr, "The Case Study House program and the impending future: Some regional considerations," in *Blueprints for Modern Living,* p. 134.

14. See *Arts & Architecture: The Entenza Years,* ed. B. Goldstein (Cambridge, Mass., 1990). Most of the following information about the magazine is taken from this anthology of facsimile articles. See also Esther McCoy, "*Arts & Architecture* Case Study Houses," in *Blueprints for Modern Living,* pp. 15–16; Elizabeth A. T. Smith, "*Arts & Architecture* and the Los Angeles vanguard," ibid., p. 145.

15. John Neuhart, Marilyn Neuhart, and Ray Eames, *Eames Design: The Work of the Office of Charles and Ray Eames* (New York, 1989), p. 31. See also Charles Eames, "Design today," *California Arts & Architecture,* September 1941, pp. 18–19; Charles Eames, "Organic design," *California Arts & Architecture,* December 1941, pp. 16–17; Charles Eames, "Mies van der Rohe," *Arts & Architecture,* December 1947, pp. 24–27; Ray Eames, "Line and color define volume that volume can be tangible or not but the place between two tangible volumes is nevertheless a volume," *California Arts & Architecture,* September 1943.

16. *Arts & Architecture: The Entenza Years,*, pp. 8–12; *Blueprints for Modern Living,* p. 13. See also Dalton Trumbo, "Minorities and the screen," *Arts & Architecture,* February 1944; Jules Langsner, "Art summoned before the inquisition 1573–1951," *Arts & Architecture,* December 1951.

17. Davis, *City of Quartz,* chapter 1, esp. pp. 31–34; *Blueprints for Modern Living,* p. 147.

18. Frank Lloyd Wright, *An Autobiography* (London, 1977), p. 255. See also Kathryn Smith, "Frank Lloyd Wright, Hollyhock House and Olive Hill, 1914–1924," *Journal of the Society of Architectural Historians,* March 1979, pp. 15–33.

19. Davis, *City of Quartz,* p. 31.

20. David Gebhard, *Schindler* (London, 1971), pp. 47–52.

21. Davis, *City of Quartz,* p. 33.

22. Ibid., passim. See also *Turning the Tide: Early Los Angeles Modernism 1920–1956* (Santa Barbara, 1990), p. 15; *Blueprints for Modern Living,* p. 147.

23. Ray Eames/Kirkham, 1983. See also chapter 7 below.

24. *Blueprints,* p. 151.

25. Esther McCoy, "Remembering John Entenza," in *Arts & Architecture: The Entenza Years,* p. 8.

26. Ibid.

27. Sumner Spaulding, "Small homes of the West, fads, or quality," *California Arts & Architecture,* November 1938, p. 31.

28. "Designs for post war living: Announcing the winning designs in the architectural competition sponsored by *California Arts & Architecture,*" *California Arts & Architecture,* August 1943, p. 19.

29. John Entenza, "Announcement: the case study house program," *Arts & Architecture,* March 1945, p. 54.

30. Helen Searing, "Case Study Houses in the grand modern tradition," in *Blueprints,* p. 108.

31. "Case Study Houses 8 and 9 by Charles Eames and Eero Saarinen, Architects," *Arts & Architecture,* December 1945, p. 43.

32. For details of the individual houses see Amelia Jones and Elizabeth A. T. Smith, "The thirty six Case Study projects," in *Blueprints,* pp. 41–81.

33. Banham, Reyner "Klarheit, Ehrlichkeit, Einfachkeit . . . and wit too!: The Case Study houses in the world's eyes," in *Blueprints,* p. 189.

34. F. R. S. Yorke, *The Modern House* (Cheam, 1943), p. 212. Neutra's experimental timber houses cost $3500 each, including furniture. Frank Lloyd Wright had experimented with "ready cut" modern houses in 1915, and Marcel Breuer had designed a wooden prefabricated house in 1925.

35. Yorke, *The Modern House,* pp. 193, 203–204.

36. Ibid., pp. 29, 188–189, 198. The Columbian Steel Tank Company offered a three-room house with a porch for $600 and a four-room house with two terraces for $1900 (exclusive of plumbing, flooring, and foundations); houses offered by National Steel Homes varied in price from $495 to $1200.

37. Steel-panel houses were not greatly popular then. After World War II the general public rejected them in favor of the more traditional "ranch-style" homes and the avant-garde rejected them in favor of light steel frames.

38. Thomas S. Hines, "Case Study trouvé: Sources and precedents, Southern California, 1920–1942," in *Blueprints,* p. 111.

39. *Studio Year Book* (London, 1942), p. 74; Gilbert Herbert, *The Dream of the Factory-Made House: Walter Gropius and Konrad Wachsmann* (Cambridge, Mass., 1984), pp. 306–313; Robert B. Harmon, *The Search for Low-Cost Housing* (Monticello, Ill., 1981). Ain, who was awarded a Guggenheim Fellowship in 1940 to enable him to continue his research into low-cost housing, was only a year younger than Charles Eames. He had worked with Schindler (in 1932) and with Neutra (in 1932–1935) and, apart from Irving Gill, he was "the first architect in California to refine and dignify low-cost housing" (Esther McCoy, in *Contemporary Architects,* ed. A. L. Morgan and C. Naylor (Chicago, 1987), pp. 15–16).

40. Yorke, *The Modern House,*, pp. 190–192. Other architects included Maynard Lyndow and David Runnells, both of Detroit. The latter worked with Rapson.

41. "Steel shelf with a view," *Architectural Forum,* September 1950, p. 97–98.

42. Eames/Kirkham, 1983.

43. One suspects that Ray was more attracted to it than Charles at the time.

44. Eames/Kirkham, 1983; Charles Eames, Eames Celebration.

45. *Eames Design,* p. 107. The original design appeared in the December 1945 issue of *Arts & Architecture,* where it was credited to Charles Eames and Eero Saarinen.

46. See chapter 4 below.

47. Eames/Kirkham, 1983. See also Esther McCoy, "On attaining a certain age," *Progressive Architecture,* October 1977, p. 80.

48. "Case Study Houses 8 and 9," p. 43. Dolores Hayden (in *Blueprints,* p. 203) has pointed out that the Eames House differed from other Case Study houses in that it offered a "blueprint" of what life might be like for a professional couple as opposed to a family and did not reflect contemporary patriarchal attitudes and gender roles; it was a house designed for working equals.

49. See Jones and Smith, "The thirty six Case Study projects," in *Blueprints,* pp. 51, 53; David Spaeth, "Charles Eames (1907–78). Eames House, Pacific Palisades, California, 1945–49," in *Contemporary Masterworks,* ed. C. Naylor (Chicago, 1991), p. 335.

50. Jones and Smith, in *Blueprints,* p. 53, n. 2. The house referred to was almost certainly the Sam Bell house (c. 1941). See David G. De Long, "The Cranbrook tradition in architecture and urban design," in *Design in America: The Cranbrook Vision 1925–1950,* ed. R. J. Clark et al. (New York, 1983), p. 73.

51. The pavilions were featured in the 1947 Mies van der Rohe exhibition at the Museum of Modern Art, which was photographed by Charles Eames for *Arts & Architecture* (December 1947, pp. 24–27). See also *Eames Design,* p. 107. Charles Eames was also impressed by the two-story plan and exterior of a house designed by I. M. Pei and E. H. Duhart in 1943. See "Designs for post war living," *California Arts & Architecture,* August 1943, pp. 32–34.

52. Charles Eames. Eames Celebration. See also "Life in a Chinese kite: Standard industrial products assembled in a spacious wonderland," *Architectural Forum,* September 1950, p. 94.

53. Ibid., p. 94. Charles Eames claimed that a two-story steel structure similar to the Eames House would have cost $11.50 per square foot—about the same as a middle-class wood-frame Californian home. he argued (not very convincingly) that, because the usable square feet in about half the Eames House were "17 feet tall," the cost was reduced to only $1 per square foot. The Herman Miller Showroom (1949) was built for $6.50 per square foot as opposed to $11.00, the normal cost for that type of space (Michael Brawne, "The wit of technology," *Architectural Design,* September 1966, p. 449).

54. Charles Eames, Eames Celebration.

55. Eames/Kirkham, 1983.

56. "Life in a Chinese kite," p. 94.

57. Ibid., p. 90.

58. Edgardo Contini, quoted by Jones and Smith (*Blueprints,* p. 52).

59. Charles Eames, quoted in "Life in a Chinese kite," p. 94.

60. Eames/Kirkham, 1983.

61. See also Clay Lancaster, *The Japanese Influence in America* (New York, 1962). The interest of American architects and designers in Japan goes back to the Greene brothers and Wright and can also be seen in the work of Schindler and Neutra. George Nelson was one of the designers who most enthused about Japan and things Japanese in the 1950s; he and his friend Bernard Rudovsky both wrote books and articles on the subject. Eero Saarinen showed a predilection for the formality of Japanese gardens in the 1950s, the decade in which Isamu Noguchi designed Japanese gardens for Skidmore, Owings & Merrill (*Design in America: The Cranbrook Vision 1925–1950,* ed. Clark et al., p. 309, n. 130). Sam Fuller and other North American film makers made movies with Japanese themes, including *House of Bamboo* (Fuller, 1955), *The Crimson Kimono* (Fuller, 1959), *Teahouse of the August Moon* (Daniel Mann, 1956), and *Sayonara* (Joshua Logan, 1957).

62. See *Eames Design,* pp. 154, 170, 375. Isamu Noguchi and Charlie Chaplin were both present at one such ceremony.

63. "Life in a Chinese kite," pp. 90–96.

64. Ibid., p. 95. Charles always claimed that wood was used simply to have "something to nail into."

65. "Case Study Houses 8 and 9," p. 44.

66. Eames/Kirkham, 1983.

67. Ibid.

68. "Case Study Houses 8 and 9," p. 44.

69. Most of the equipment still works well today; only the refrigerator has been replaced (Eames/Kirkham, 1983; Eames Demetrios/Kirkham, 1991).

70. Molly Noyes, correspondence with Pat Kirkham, January 1991.

71. Esther McCoy, "Remembering John Entenza," in *Arts & Architecture: The Entenza Years,* p. 13; David Gebhard and Robert Winter, *Architecture in Los Angeles: A Complete Guide* (Salt Lake City, 1984), p. 45.

72. "Case Study Houses 8 and 9," p. 46.

73. "The castle-cabana of John Entenza: Eames and Saarinen design a machine for expansive living," *Interiors,* December 1950, p. 92.

74. Eames/Kirkham, 1987.

75. "Designs for post war living," pp. 24–28.

76. "The castle-cabana of John Entenza," p. 92.

77. "Steel shelf with a view," *Architectural Forum,* September 1950, p. 92.

78. McCoy, "Remembering John Entenza," p. 13.

79. Ibid., p. 10.

80. "Showroom: Los Angeles, California, Charles Eames, designer," *Progressive Architecture,* August 1950, p. 49.

81. Ibid.; "Furniture Showroom," *Arts & Architecture,* October 1949, pp. 26–29.

82. *Eames Design,* p. 189.

83. Ibid.

84. Ibid.

85. Ibid., pp. 218–219; Eames/Kirkham, 1983; M. and J. Neuhart/Kirkham, 1991; Deborah Sussman/Kirkham, 1991.

86. A. and P. Smithson/Kirkham, 1991.

87. *Eames Design,* p. 37.

88. "Probably no other project in the issue was prepared under as adverse circumstances as this city hall by Mr. Eames. As the result of a misunderstanding, Mr. Eames was left blissfully unaware of the program until a few days before closing time, when he finally received an urgent wire from THE FORUM. Despite preoccupation with important Government work, he submitted these brilliant sketches for the design of a city hall. . . ." ("City Hall: Charles Eames, Los Angeles, Calif.," *Architectural Forum*, p. 89)

89. Ibid.; John Neuhart, A Rough Sketch About a Lot of Work (lecture at "Charles and Ray Eames: Quintessential Twentieth Century American Designers" conference, Cooper-Hewitt National Museum of Design, New York, 1989). When I spoke to her in 1983, Ray Eames suggested that the Getty Museum would be best developed as an "information center."

90. "City Hall: Charles Eames, Los Angeles, Calif.," p. 89.

91. *Eames Design,* p. 85

92. Axel Madsen, *Billy Wilder* (London, 1968), p. 9.

93. Maurice Zolotow, *Billy Wilder in Hollywood* (London, 1977), p. 101. Zolotow notes that Wilder at first wanted a house for himself, his first wife Judith (who was interested in interior design), and their daughter Vicki, but his marriage was falling apart. *Eames Design* dates the Wilder commission to late 1949, by which date he had married Audrey Young, and includes a photograph of the couple in 1950 with a model of the house designed by Charles and Ray. See also *Eames Design*, pp. 136–137.

94. Madsen, *Billy Wilder,* p. 9. Wilder's art collection included pieces by Klee, Picasso, Miró, Magritte, Chagall, Dufy, and Calder.

95. The material relating to the Wilder House that I saw at the Eames Office is now in the Library of Congress. I am grateful to Ford Peatross for his comments on this project.

96. R. Craig Miller, "Interior design and furniture," in *Design in America,* ed. Clark et al., pp. 122, 310.

97. David DeLong, "Eliel Saarinen and the Cranbrook tradition in architecture and urban design," in *Design in America,* p. 75.

98. Miller, "Interior design and furniture," p. 122.

99. Ibid., p. 122. Ray Eames told me that the Wilder House was not built because it would have been too great an undertaking in terms of time and energy for someone as busy as Billy Wilder (Eames/Kirkham, 1987)—a view corroborated by Wilder in conversations with Ford Peatross, David De Long, Eames Demetrios, and Pat Kirkham.

100. *Eames Design,* p. 155.

101. Thomas B. Sherman, "Ex-St. Louisan who made Eames chairs," *St. Louis Post-Dispatch,* October 22, 1951.

102. Hines, in *Blueprints for Modern Living,* p. 94.

103. On Ain see note 39 to the present chapter. On Albinson see p, 55 of *Eames Design* and "House in 'industry,' a system for the manufacture of industrialized building elements by Konrad Wachsmann and Walter Gropius," *Arts & Architecture,* November 1947.

104. *Eames Design,* p. 155.

105. Ibid., p. 235.

106. Ibid., pp. 20, 243. This was probably more traditional than the "ultra-modern" bandstand and park pavilion Charles designed in 1928 as a student.

107. Ibid., p. 308.

CHAPTER 4

1. Quoted in Bill N. Lacy, "Warehouse full of ideas," *Horizon,* September 1980, p. 22.

2. Peter Smithson, "Just a few chairs and a house: An essay on the Eames-aesthetic," *Architectural Design,* September 1966, p. 443.

3., Esther McCoy "An affection for objects," *Progressive Architecture,* August 1973. Billy Wilder told me that to grasp the breadth of Charles's interests one had to "envisage a man who could not only talk about architecture, design, science, philosophy and a host of other things obviously related to creative and intellectual life but also to others less obviously so. He could talk for an hour or more on how beautifully made was a particular piece of food—a cake, for example—and the processes used in the particular bakery which made it." (Billy Wilder/Kirkham, 1993) It was at the suggestion of Wilder and another friend, Frank Perles, that the Eameses visited the famous Kreutzmann Konditorei in Munich in 1954, photographing almost every aspect of the food preparation as well as the details of the shop and its contents. A three-screen slide show, Konditorei (1955), was the result. (See *Eames Design,* p. 203.) In "Just a few chairs and a house," Peter Smithson used the term "object-integrity" to convey something of the seriousness with which the Eameses endowed their concern and respect for objects; he defined this as "a kind of reverence for the object's integrity."

4. Paper delivered by Charles Eames at a conference in Aspen, Colorado, 1951, to which the Container Corporation of America had invited 200 business executives, product designers and graphic designers to consider the role of design in business. See "Design, designer and industry," *Magazine of Art* 44, December 1951, pp. 320–321.

5. In his introduction to the 1957 film *Toccata for Toy Trains* Charles argued that "real toys" (as opposed to scale models) were as made as unselfconsciously they were used and that they revealed pride in workmanship and respect for materials and manufacture: "What is wood is wood, what is tin is tin, and what is cast is beautifully cast." A quarter-century later, Ray reiterated the same points: "Toys, particularly old toys, get you back to basic principles. Materials were used sensitively for what they were, i.e. tin or steel, not *mis-used.* Toys have *essences.* Charles always maintained that there was a big difference between models and toys. Toys were made by people who cared and put a great deal of care into making them. Even in early wind-ups springs are used well. Mostly it was all kept *simple* and toys are examples of the *use of principles.*" (Ray Eames/Kirkham, 1983)

6. Ray Eames/Kirkham, 1983.

7. *Eames Design,* p. 145; Eames/Kirkham, 1983.

8. I have argued this in "The inter-war handicrafts revival," in *A View from the Interior: Feminism, Women and Design,* ed. J. Attfield and P. Kirkham (London, 1989). See also David Hounshell, *From the American System to Mass Production, 1930–1932* (Baltimore, 1984); Wendy Kaplan, "Spreading the crafts: The role of the schools," in *The Art That Is Life: The Arts and Crafts Movement in America, 1875–1920,* ed. W. Kaplan (Boston, 1987); Pat Kirkham, *Harry Peach, Dryad and the DIA* (London, 1986).

9. Kirkham, *Harry Peach,* p. 73; Kaplan, "Spreading the crafts," p. 301.

10. Kaplan, "Spreading the crafts," pp. 70, 302.

11. Frank Lloyd Wright, *An Autobiography* (London, 1977), pp. 33–34; Charles Eames/Virginia Stith, 1977.

12. Kirkham, *Harry Peach,* pp. 70–72. See also Francesca M. Wilson, *Professor Cizek Takes His Class: An Authoritative Account of an Actual Lesson* (Dryad leaflet no. 6, Leicester, 1921); Franz Cizek, *Children's Coloured Paperwork* (Vienna, 1927), and W. Viola, *Child Art and Frans Cizek* (Vienna, 1936).

13. On Lethaby see Kirkham, *Harry Peach,* pp. 2–3, 89–91; Gillian Naylor, *The Arts and Crafts Movement* (London, 1971), pp. 179–184; Elizabeth Cumming and Wendy Kaplan, *The Arts and Crafts Movement* (New York, 1991), pp. 38–39, 84, 96–98; Sylvia Backemeyer and Theresa Gronberg, *W. R. Lethaby 1857–1931: Architecture, Design and Education* (London, 1984); Godfrey Rubens, *William Richard Lethaby: His Life and Work 1957–1931* (London, 1986), esp. chapter IX: Richard Guy Wilson notes that Lethaby influenced some Americans seeking a new organic basis for architecture ("American Arts and Crafts architecture: Radical though dedicated to the cause conservative," in *The Art That Is Life,* p. 113).

14. Geoffrey Holroyd, "Architecture creating relaxed intensity," *Architectural Design,* September 1966, p. 458. See also John Dewey, *The School and Society* (New York, 1900).

15. Eames/Kirkham, 1987; *Eames Design,* p. 91.

16. Saul Pett, "Charles Eames: Imagination unlimited," *St. Louis Post-Dispatch,* July 27, 1971, p. 3. Their joining a circus would have been a great loss to the world of design, but I confess to wondering just what the world of performance missed!

17. Notes included in The Coloring Toy.

18. The modernist interest in masks dates back to the early twentieth century. Gordon Craig, who edited the magazine *The Mask,* greatly admired Chinese masks, as did Bertolt Brecht. See Brecht, "Alienation effects in Chinese acting," in *Brecht on Theatre,* ed. J. Willett (London, 1964).

19. *Eames Design,* pp. 372–373. Bill Ballantine, director of the Clown College of Ringling Brothers Barnum and Bailey, first met the Eameses when they photographed the circus in Los Angeles in 1948, and Charles eventually became a trustee of the Clown College (Eames/Kirkham, 1983). One of the examples in the film *Introduction to Feedback* is of a clown juggling.

20. Deborah Sussman/Kirkham, 1993. In 1953 Deborah Sussman and some friends threw a Halloween party in Santa Monica Canyon. To everyone's astonishment, Ray and Charles (who hardly ever went to parties) attended.

21. *Eames Design* (p. 125) states that the "galaxy" light fixture was designed by Don Albinson and, although much copied, never commercially produced. This may have been because it resembled a lamp designed by Gino Sarfatti of Milan—so much so that Richard Lohse wrongly attributed the one in the Eames display to "D. Sarfatti" in his book *New Designs and Exhibitions* (Zurich, 1953).

22. I am grateful to Deborah Sussman for the following note about Ray's mask: "A black Japanese oshibori dyed fabric-classic, highest quality-used probably for the only time in oshibori history as a mask. Probably silk. Used in Japan as obi-aki worn under obi. Certainly improvised during the hour that preceded the invention."

23. Sussman/Kirkham, 1991. Most Eames activities, even the most apparently casual, were carefully planned in advance. Carpenter ("Tribute to Charles Eames," p. 12) quotes John Neuhart and Don Albinson as stating that the apparent casualness within the Eames House was anything but.

24. Eames/Kirkham, 1983. In view of the comments of Deborah Sussman and others, it is difficult to imagine any event at the Eames House being of that nature.

25. Eames/Kirkham, 1987.

26. I am grateful to Ford Peatross for information about Ray's designing cut-out dolls prior to her studying at Cranbrook.

27. *Eames Design,* pp. 156–157; Michael Haber, "Designed for play," *Graphics* no. 14 (March 1958), pp. 129–130.

28. *Eames Design,* p. 128.

29. Ibid., p. 161.

30. Holroyd, "Architecture creating relaxed intensity," p. 469. See also *Eames Design,* pp. 169–175, 181; Haber, "Designed for play," pp. 127–129 The asterisks on the second standard set were grey-green.

31. *Eames Design,* p. 181.

32. Ibid., p. 184; Eames/Kirkham, 1987.

33. See Thomas Hine, *Populuxe* (London, 1990), pp. 108, 132–134. The centerpiece of the 1958 World's Fair in Brussels was a huge "atomic model."

34. *Eames Design,* p. 205.

35. "Alcoa ventures a forecast," *Industrial Design,* July 1957, p. 74; Olga Gueft, "For Alcoa's forecast program Eames creates a sun machine that accomplishes nothing?" *Interiors,* April 1958, p. 123.

36. See Dennis Doordan, "Promoting aluminum: Designers and the American aluminum industry," *Design Issues* 9, no. 2 (1993), pp. 44–50.

37. Eames Demetrios/Kirkham, 1991.

38. Allan Temko, *Eero Saarinen* (New York, 1962), p. 11.

39. Alison Smithson, "And now Dhamas are dying out in Japan," *Architectural Design,* September 1966, p. 447.

40. Introduction to "Eames Celebration," *Architectural Design,* September 1966, p. 432.

41. Wright, *An Autobiography,* pp. 169, 373.

42. *Display,* ed. G. Nelson (New York, 1953), p. 65.

43. Ibid., p. 68; *Eames Design,* p. 132.

44. Esther McCoy, "Charles and Ray Eames," *Design Quarterly* 98/99 (1975), p. 25.

45. Ibid., p. 25. See figures 5.23 and 5.35 in the present volume.

46. P. Smithson, "Just a few chairs and a house," p. 443.

47. Ibid.

48. Quoted in Esther McCoy, "An affection for objects," *Progressive Architecture,* August 1973, p. 67.

49. Accretion and proliferation are elements of postmodernism noted by Dick Hebdige on p. 191 of *Hiding in the Light* (London, 1988).

50. Quoted in McCoy, "An affection for objects," p. 67. Venturi was greatly influenced by Aalto, whose buildings he considered to be imbued with "humanity and meaning." See Robert Maxwell, "The Venturi effect," in *Venturi and Rauch: The Public Buildings* (London, 1978).

51. See Clive Wainwright, *The Romantic Interior: The British Collector at Home, 1750–1850* (New Haven, 1989); see also my review (*Journal of Design History* 3, no.4 (1990), pp. 235–238) and Stefan Muthesius, "Why do we buy old furniture? Aspects of the antique in Britain 1870–1910," *Art History* 11, no. 2 (1988).

52. Wainwright, *The Romantic Interior,* pp. 217–218.

53. Ibid., p. 36. (Dickens's *Old Curiosity Shop* was published in 1840.)

54. Ibid., pp. 196–197, 213, 296.

55. Ibid., p. 213.

56. Candace M. Volz, "The modern look of the early twentieth century home: A mirror of changing lifestyles," in *American Home Life, 1880–1930,* ed. J. Foy and T. J. Schlereth (Knoxville, 1992), p. 41.

57. Ibid., pp. 35, 41; Pauline Metcalf, *Ogden Codman and the Decoration of Houses* (Boston, 1988). Wharton and Codman devoted a whole chapter to bric-a-brac in their 1897 book *The Decoration of Houses,*; I am grateful to Clive Wainwright for bringing this to my attention.

58. Katherine C. Grier, "The decline of the memory palace: the parlor after 1890," in *American Home Life, 1880–1930,* p. 59.

59. Ibid., p. 54.

60. Ibid., p. 62.

61. Ibid., p. 56.

62. Eileen Boris, "Dreams of brotherhood and beauty: The social ideas of the Arts and Crafts movement," in *The Art That Is Life,* p. 211.

63. Ibid., p. 220.

64. Cheryl Robertson, "House and home in the Arts and Crafts era: Reforms for simpler living," in *The Art That Is Life,* p. 353.

65. See note 15 to the present chapter; see also W. R. Lethaby, "Art and workmanship," *The Imprint* (1913), reprinted in *Form in Civilization: Collected Papers on Art and Labour* (1922). See also "Town Tidying" in the latter volume.

66. Ibid., esp. *Form in Civilization.*

67. Boris, "Dreams of brotherhood and beauty," p. 220.

68. Robertson, "House and home in the Arts and Crafts era," pp. 349–350.

69. Ibid., p. 338; Boris, "Dreams," p. 217.

70. See "Indian blankets, baskets and bowls: The product of the original craftworkers of this continent," *Craftsman* no. 17 (February 1910), p. 588. This article argued that the work of Native American women was "the only real handicraft this country knows" (Boris, "Dreams," p. 217). By 1902 Navajo blankets were so popular that at least one manufacturer was making a "close reproduction of the real Indian product" (*Upholstery Dealer and Decorative Furnisher* 1 (January 1902), p. 64, quoted in *The Art That Is Life* (pp. 384–385, n. 1).

71. Cumming and Kaplan, *The Arts and Crafts Movement,* pp. 148–149.

72. See Kirkham, *Harry Peach,* pp. 77, 84–87. Peach corresponded with curators at the Boston Museum and at Chicago's Field Museum of Natural History and

with M. B. Cummings, manager of the Indian Arts Shop in Tucson, from whom he obtained examples of Pima work (p. 126, n. 71). The Eames film *The World of Franklin and Jefferson* makes the point that Jefferson set a precedent for the scholarly recording of the languages and cultures of Native Americans.

73. For discussions of this important paralleling of the "primitive" and the "child" see Gordon Sutton, *Artisan or Artist?* (London, 1967), pp. 261–262; Stuart MacDonald, *The History and Philosophy of Art Education* (London, 1970), pp. 329–330. See also *Primitivism in Twentieth Century Art,* ed. W. Rubin (New York, 1984) and James Clifford's critique in *The Predicament of Culture: Twentieth Century Ethnography, Literature and Art* (Cambridge, Mass., 1988).

74. See Jack Lenor Larsen, "Alexander Girard," *Design Quarterly* 98/99 (1976), pp. 31–39; Robert Carleton Hobbs and Gail Levin, *Abstract Expressionism: The Formative Years* (Ithaca, 1978), pp. 14–15.

75. Larsen, "Alexander Girard," p. 39.

76. Edward Said (*Orientalism* (New York, 1978)) argues that Western representations of the "Orient" helped the West dominate the East and catalogues the discounting of what non-Westerners said about themselves. See also M. Ames, *Museums, the Public and Anthropology* (Vancouver, 1986).

77. Boris, "Dreams of brotherhood and beauty," p. 211. Mike Davis (*City of Quartz,* pp. 20, 24–30) is much harsher on Lummis. See also Kevin Starr, *Inventing the Dream: California through the Progressive Era* (New York, 1985), pp. 107–124: Carey McWilliams, *Southern California: An Island on the Land* (Salt Lake City, 1990), pp. 77–83; Robert Winter, "The Arroyo Culture," in *California Design 1910,* ed. T. J. Anderson et al. (Pasadena, 1974).

78. See Clifford's discussion of this shift and the collecting of "art and culture" in *The Predicament of Culture* (especially his critique of Rubin). For a discussion of the issues involved in the display of objects from other cultures see I. Karp and S. D. Lavine, *Exhibiting Cultures: The Poetics and Politics of Museum Display* (Washington, 1991).

79. Eames/Kirkham, 1987. At a 1987 design symposium at the Cooper-Hewitt National Museum of Design, Ray Eames used this phrase in relation to herself and also in relation to opinions held by Charles.

80. Kirkham, *Harry Peach,* pp. 84–88.

81. Ibid., pp. 84–88.

82. Davis, *City of Quartz,* p. 27.

83. McWilliams, *Southern California.,* p. 80; Boris, "Dreams of brotherhood and beauty," p. 211.

84. Davis, *City of Quartz,* p. 26

85. Ibid, pp. 26–27; McWilliams, *Southern California.,* pp. 80–83; Wilson, "American Arts and Crafts architecture," in *The Art That Is Life,* pp. 123–124.

86. For a broad discussion of authenticity, appropriation, and re-appropriation see Clifford, *The Predicament of Culture,* esp. "On collecting art and culture."

87. Kay F. Turner, "The cultural semiotics of religious icons: La Virgen de San Juan de los Lagos," *Semiotica* no. 47 (1983), pp. 1–4; see also Turner's unpublished thesis, Mexican American Women's Home Altars: The Art of Relationship (University of Texas, Austin, 1990). I am grateful to Jennifer González for drawing these to my attention and for sending me copies of her then-unpublished papers "Autotopographies" (since published in *Prosthetic Territories,* ed. G. Brahm and M. Driscoll (Boulder, 1994) and "Rhetoric of the object: Material memory and the artwork of Amalia Mesa-Bains" (*Visual Anthropology Review* 9, no. 1 (1993), pp. 82–92).

88. Melissa Meyer and Miriam Schapiro, "Waste not/want not: Femmage," *Heresies* no. 4 (1978), pp. 66–69; Norma Broude, "Miriam Schapiro and 'Femmage': Reflections on the conflict between decoration and abstraction in twentieth-century art," in *Feminism and Art History: Questioning the Litany,* ed. N. Broude and M. D. Garrard (New York, 1982), pp. 315–329.

89. Quoted in Broude, "Miriam Schapiro and 'Femmage,'" p. 320.

90. González, "Autotopographies," p. 22.

91. Ibid., p. 13.

92. Hobbs and Levin, *Abstract Expressionism,* p. 39.

93. Ibid., p. 15.

94. Ibid., p. 14.

95. Eames/Kirkham, 1987.

96. Rosa Maria Malet, "Joan Miró 1893–1993, a Centenary Exhibition," *Catalonia* no. 34 (1993), p. 9.

97. Ibid., pp. 10–11.

98. *Eames Design,* pp. 70–71. See the entry on Matter in *Contemporary Designers,* ed. C. Naylor (Chicago, 1990).

99. See Clifford, *The Predicament of Culture,* esp. "On collecting art and culture."

100. Lacy, "Warehouse full of ideas," p. 27.

101. Larsen, "Alexander Girard," p. 31. On Liebes see *Dorothy Liebes* (New York, 1970).

102. It should be noted that by the time they first worked together, in 1949, the basic elements of their "functioning decoration" were already established.

103. Some of these appeared in Ray's original color plan, which also included a structure anticipating The Toy, a starfish, a small propeller, an oriental figure, a hat, and a scarf.

104. The Eameses assisted Girard with the 1955 exhibition; in 1965, Girard assisted them.

105. *Eames Design,* pp. 212–213. Deborah Sussman researched the story and many of the objects. The Mexican "folk" art she acquired on that trip was to influence her work thereafter (Sussman/Kirkham, 1991). The Girard collection is now housed in a special wing of the Museum of International Folk Art in Santa Fe. On the Girards see Gueft, Olga "Scientific sell, with sight gags: Nelson, Eames, and Girard collaborate on a new Herman Miller showroom in New York," *Interiors,* September 1966, pp. 134–137; Charles Lockwood, "A perfectionist at play," *Connoisseur* 213, January 1983, pp. 92–99; Jack Lenor Larsen, "Alexander Girard," *Design Quarterly* 98/99 (1976), pp. 31–39, "The Girard story," *House Beautiful,* February 1953, pp. 66–87; "House of many colors," *Architectural*

Forum, February 1957, pp. 132–139; "Alexander Girard invites you to dine at The Compound," *Architectural Forum,* June 1967, pp. 60–63.

106. Larsen, Larsen, "Alexander Girard," illustrations on p. 32. The house was remodeled in 1953.

107. Sussman/Kirkham, 1991; M. and J. Neuhart/Kirkham, 1991.

108. Davis, *City of Quartz,* pp. 65–66. See also Andrew Morland, *Street Machines: '49 and on Custom Cars* (London, 1984); Mike Key, *Street USA* (London, 1990).

109. However, the Eameses loved Saul Steinberg's drawings of "La Chaise" and the fiberglass chair (figure 5.19).

110. Holroyd, "Architecture creating relaxed intensity," p. 466.

111. Ibid., p. 466.

112. "Case Study Houses 8 and 9, by Charles Eames and Eero Saarinen, Architects," *Arts & Architecture,* December 1945.

113. "Today," 1956.

114. Carpenter, "Tribute to Charles Eames," p. 13.

115. Eames/Kirkham, 1987.

116. Billy Wilder/Kirkham, 1993. An illustration of the stabile in *Architectural Review* 6, no. 632 (1949) also includes an Eames plywood chair and table-erroneously attributed to Eliel Saarinen.

117. Sussman/Kirkham, 1991; J. Neuhart/Kirkham, 1991; Demetrios/Kirkham, 1991.

118. Audrey Wilder/Kirkham, 1991.

119. Carpenter, "Tribute to Charles Eames," p. 12.

120. Holroyd, "Architecture creating relaxed intensity," p. 469.

121. Ibid., pp. 446, 469.

122. Ibid., pp. 446.

123. P. Smithson, "Just a few chairs and a house," p. 445.

124. Peter Blake, *Mies van der Rohe: Architecture and Structure* (London, 1960), pp. 83–89; Philip C. Johnson, *Mies van der Rohe* (London, 1978), pp. 154, 167.

125. Holroyd, "Architecture creating relaxed intensity," p. 446.

126. "Furniture show room, designed by Charles Eames," *Arts & Architecture,* October 1949, p. 99; Billy Wilder/Kirkham, 1993.

127. "Furniture show room, designed by Charles Eames," *Arts & Architecture,* October 1949, p. 99.

128. *Eames Design,* p. 166.

129. Photographs of the recently completed room show a bouquet of daisies, which Ray loved. When I went to visit Ray at 901 Washington Boulevard in 1983 I took a bunch of daisies. Obtaining them had made me slightly late, and I was apprehensive, but luck was on my side: only a few minutes before I arrived, she had announced that what the lobby needed was some daisies. My bringing them was interpreted as providential, if not psychic. I thought of taking them because, when I had worked on an exhibition of Ray Hille furniture a couple of years earlier, daisies had been used to give an "Eames feel" to the room and office arrangements. Ray Hille, Rosamind Julius, and Cherill Scheer, all of whom knew Ray Eames, had told me how much she liked those particular flowers.

130. "Eames Celebration," *Architectural Design,* September 1966, p. 462.

131. *Eames Design,* p. 243.

132. Ibid., p. 279.

133. Originally designed in 1961 for the restaurant La Fonda del Sol (see figure 5.23).

134. Gueft "Scientific sell, with sight gags," p. 134.

135. Ibid., p. 134.

136. Ibid., p. 138.

137. Mrs. Harris Armstrong, quoted in "Eames: A man who did what he wanted," *St. Louis Post Dispatch,* August 27, 1978.

138. Eames/Kirkham, 1983; Doris Saatchi, "All about Eames," *House and Garden,* February 1984, p. 129.

139. M. and J. Neuhart/Kirkham, 1991.

140. Don Albinson, Deborah Sussman, Julius Shulman, Audrey Wilder, and Billy Wilder, interviews with Pat Kirkham, 1991, 1991, 1993, 1993, and 1993 respectively.

CHAPTER 5

1. Vincent, Clare "John Henry Belter's patent parlour furniture," Furniture *History* 111 (1967), pp. 92–99; Elizabeth Bidwell Bates and Jonathan L. Fairbanks, *American Furniture: 1620 to the Present* (New York, 1981), p. 395; Derek E. Ostergard, "Before industrialization: Bent wood and bent metal in the hands of the craftsman," in *Bent Wood and Metal Furniture: 1850–1946,* ed. D. E. Ostergard (Washington, 1987), pp. 25–30, 219–221.

2. On Cole see Ostergard, "Before industrialization," p. 309. On the Gardner Company see Christopher Wilk, Eames Furniture: Antecedents and Progeny, lecture at "Charles and Ray Eames: Quintessential American Designers" conference, Cooper-Hewitt National Museum of Design, New York, 1989; Graham Dry, "The development of the bent-wood furniture industry, 1869–1914," in *Bent Wood and Metal Furniture: 1850–1946,* ed. Ostergard, pp. 69–70 and n. 104.

3. Alessandro Alvera, "Michael Thonet and the development of bent-wood furniture: from workshop to factory production," in *Bent Wood and Metal Furniture: 1850–1946,* ed. Ostergard, p. 50; David A. Hanks, *Innovative Furniture in America from 1800 to the Present* (New York, 1981), pp. 47–73.

4. Wilk, Christopher "Furnishing the future: Bent wood and metal furniture 1925–1946," in *Bent Wood and Metal Furniture: 1850–1946,* ed. Ostergard, p.

147. On the Luther Company see J. Stewart Johnson, *Alvar Aalto: Furniture and Glass* (New York, 1987), p. 3. Aalto visited the factory to study the manufacture of these seats.

5. These had been produced since the late nineteenth century by the Luther company of Estonia, the world's largest plywood manufacturer. See Wilk, Eames Furniture: Antecedents and Progeny.

6. Schmidt, a founding member of the Deutsche Werkbund, is the only one of these men known to have worked in plywood. He established a factory to produce plywood panels in Rehtelde, near Berlin, in 1902. See Paul Overy, "Carpentering the classic: A very peculiar practice," *Journal of Design History* 4, no. 3 (1991), pp. 148–149.

7. See A. S. Levetus, "Modern Austrian wicker furniture," *Studio,* January 1904, pp. 323–328; Christopher Wilk, *Thonet: 150 Years of Furniture* (New York, 1980); Eva B. Ottilinger, *Korbmöbel* (Salzburg, 1990); Pat Kirkham, "Willow and cane furniture in America, Germany and England c. 1900–14," *Furniture History* 21 (1985), pp. 127–131.

8. Otakar Macel and Marijke Kuper, "The chairs of Heinz Rasch," *Journal of Design History* 6, no. 1 (1993), p. 35.

9. Overy, "Carpentering the classic," pp. 148–149.

10. Wilk, "Furnishing the future," pp. 148–149; Gillian Naylor, *The Bauhaus: Sources and Design Theory* (London, 1985), p. 152.

11. Quoted in *Alvar Aalto Sketches,* ed. G. Schildt (Cambridge, Mass., 1978), p. 77.

12. R. Craig Miller, "Interior design and furniture," in *Design in America*, ed. Clark et al., p. 103.

13. Wilk, "Furnishing the future," p. 160; John McAndrews, preface to *Aalto, Architecture and Furniture* (New York, 1938).

14. Wilk, Eames Furniture. The furniture sold at one of the U.S. outlets was manufactured illegally.

15. Wilk, "Furnishing the future," p. 159.

16. Ibid. Also see Miller, "Interior design and furniture," p. 104.

17. Wilk, "Furnishing the future," pp. 161–163,312–313.

18. Martha Deese, "Gerald Summers and makers of simple furniture," *Journal of Design History* 5, no. 3 (1992), pp. 183–205.

19. This drew on the work of Aalto and Rohde. See Miller, "Interior design and furniture," pp. 105, 305.

20. Eliot Noyes, *Organic Design in Home Furnishings* (New York, 1941), pp. 10–17 and 26–29; "Organic design: Winning furniture designs by Saarinen and Eames from the Museum of Modern Art competition," *California Arts & Architecture,* December 1941, pp. 16–17. Aalto and Breuer were among the judges.

21. Wilk, "Furnishing the future," pp. 168–169.

22. Eames file, Don Wallance Collection.

23. Ibid.

24. Arthur Drexler, *Charles Eames: Furniture from the Design Collection* (New York, 1973), p. 12.

25. Richard Donges/Kirkham 1991. See also *Eames Design,* pp. 60–61; Don Wallance, *Shaping America's Products* (New York, 1956), pp. 178–179.

26. Don Albinson/Kirkham, 1991; Wallance, *Shaping America's Products,* pp. 178–179.

27. Miller, "Interior design and furniture," p. 307, n. 96.

28. Such a view is consonant with my argument that Charles, in his collaboration with Ray, drew on her exceptional aesthetic sensibility.

29. Eliot Noyes, "Charles Eames," *Arts & Architecture,* September, 1946, p. 38; Wallance, *Shaping America's Products,* p. 179.

30. *Eames Design,* p. 27.

31. Ibid., p. 29.

32. See W. Scott and C. Eames, "A new emergency splint of plyformed wood," *U.S. Naval Bulletin* 41, no. 5 (1943), pp. 1423–1428; *Eames Design,* pp. 28–29, 32–33.

33. Their other employees were Griswald Raetze and Margaret Harris, both of whom had worked with Charles at MGM (*Eames Design,* p. 29). On Ain see *Studio Year Book* (London, 1942), p. 74; D. Gebhard, H. Von Breton, and L. Weiss, *The Architecture of Gregory Ain: The Play Between the Rational and High Art* (Santa Barbara, 1980), pp. 9–24.

34. George Nelson, "The furniture industry: Its geography, anatomy, physiognomy, product," *Fortune,* January 1947, p. 178; Ralph Caplan, *The Design of Herman Miller: Pioneered by Eames, Girard, Nelson, Propst, Rohde* (New York, 1976), pp. 43–44.

35. Eames file, Don Wallance Collection.

36. *Eames Design,* p. 42. Some of the technical advances of the early 1940s were covered by patents that also related to the early chairs (the latter were cited by way of illustrating the technical developments); see Owen Gingerich, "A conversation with Charles Eames," *American Scholar* 46 (1977), pp. 327–328. About 2500 parts for aircraft were produced (Eames file, Don Wallance Collection).

37. Serge Chermayeff and Rene D'Harnoncourt, "Design for use," in *Art in Progress* (New York, 1944), p. 200. The sculptural form illustrated is sometimes attributed to Ray alone and sometimes to her and Charles. *Eames Design* (p. 40) attributes it to Charles and Ray; Elizabeth A. T. Smith cites it as by Ray ("*Arts & Architecture* and the Los Angeles Vanguard," in *Blueprints for Modern Living,* p. 148). Most of the plywood sculpture in the mid 1940s was by Ray, and the label on the piece in the Design for Use exhibition credited that particular sculpture to her.

38. Eames file, Don Wallance Collection.

39. *Eames Design,* pp. 66–67, 76–77. (See figure 5.13.) In 1956 the Eames Office designed a hi-fi speaker (*Eames Design,* p. 209).

40. *Eames Design,* p. 55.

41. See Christopher Wilk, *Marcel Breuer: Furniture and Interiors* (New York, 1981), pp. 132–35.

42. Ray Eames/Kirkham, 1987. There is no reference to these chairs in Drexler's 1973 catalog (note 24 above).

43. Ray Eames/Kirkham, 1987.

44. *Eames Design,* p. 55; Eames/Kirkham, 1987.

45. Eames/Kirkham. 1987.

46. Noyes, "Charles Eames," p. 66. In a later conversation with Owen Gingerich, Charles commented that the DCM was "probably the only chair we ever did that got the amount of attention from us, that it deserved" (Gingerich, "A conversation with Charles Eames," p. 328). In 1946 Eero Saarinen telegraphed Aalto to inform him that Charles Eames wanted to meet and show him some "most interesting molded plywood furniture developed by him." However, despite continued attempts to arouse Aalto's interest, the Finn remained convinced that such plastic forms did not speak "the language of wood fibers" (Goran Schildt, *Alvar Aalto: The Mature Years* (New York, 1991), p. 115). The telegram cited is in the Aalto Archive.

47. The Eameses had some reservations about showing in the museum because of what they perceived as pressure to theorize about their designs when they were still beset by seemingly endless technical problems (Eames file, Don Wallance Collection).

48. Caplan, *The Design of Herman Miller:;* Stanley Abercrombie, "The company that design built. 1927–1941," *American Institute of Architects Journal,* February 1981, pp. 54–57.

49. Nelson, "The furniture industry," pp. 107–108.

50. Ibid., p. 110.

51. "Herman Miller," *Industrial Design,* June 1974, p. 36; Ralph Caplan/ Kirkham, 1991.

52. Caplan, *The Design of Herman Miller,* pp. 21–23.

53. The last of the period items did not disappear until 1945. See "Herman Miller," *Industrial Design,* June 1974, p. 36; Ralph Caplan/Kirkham, 1991.

54. "Herman Miller," *Industrial Design,* June 1974, p. 38; Derek Ostergard and David S. Hanks, "Gilbert Rohde and the evolution of modern design: 1927–1941," *Arts Magazine,* October 1981, pp. 98–107.

55. Caplan, *The Design of Herman Miller,* p. 28; Wallance, *Shaping America's Products,* p. 110.

56. Ibid., p. 37; "Herman Miller," *Industrial Design,* p. 38.

57. Stanley Abercrombie, *George Nelson: The Design of Modern Design* (Cambridge, Mass., 1995), p. 103.

58. In addition to collaborating on furniture designs, Ray Eames produced graphics and advertising for Herman Miller. Her long and fruitful relationship with the firm continued after Charles's death.

59. Caplan, *The Design of Herman Miller,* p. 43; *Eames Design,* pp. 70–71.

60. Florence Bassett (formerly Knoll), interview with Simon Thackway, 1987, cited in Thackway's unpublished BA thesis on Florence Knoll (De Montfort University, Leicester, England, 1988).

61. I am grateful to Linda Folland, archivist of the Herman Miller Furniture Company, for supplying the "net" prices (i.e., wholesale or volume discount prices, which are lower than retail list prices and higher than dealer net prices) that follow: lounge chair (metal $19.20, wood $21), a dining chair (metal $19, wood $20.65), a round-top coffee table (wood $24.15, metal $22.85), an oblong-top coffee table (in two sizes, one $19 and one $24), a folding screen ($43), and a dining table (in two sizes, one $48 and one $37). (The estimated cost for the Eames-Saarinen side chairs in 1940 was $75 (Drexler, *Charles Eames,* p. 12).)

62. R. Craig Miller, Form, Technology and Ornament: A Commentary on the Work of Charles and Ray Eames, lecture at conference on "Charles and Ray Eames: Quintessential American Designers."

63. Eames/Kirkham, 1987. A Christmas card to the Eameses from Lee Krasner and Jackson Pollock is illustrated on p. 42 of *Eames Design.*

64. See Irving Sandler, *Abstract Expressionism: The Triumph of American Painting* (New York, 1970), p. 24. This "push and pull" element can be seen in Hofmann's work a decade before the DCM, although it was mainly manifested in his paintings of the mid to late 1940s, by which time the DCM was in the process of design and production (see *Eames Design,* pp. 30–31, 38–39, 44–45).

65. Drexler, *Charles Eames,* p. 24.

66. Wilk, "Furnishing the future," p. 168. Two or more organic shapes joined together by thin connectors feature in certain Miró pieces (see, e.g., figure 1.18), suggesting both human and animal forms.

67. "Dining Table," *Arts & Architecture,* February 1948, p. 33; *Eames Design,* pp. 80–81.

68. *Eames Design,* pp. 78–79. The others involved in establishing Artek were Aino Aalto, Marie Gullichsen, and Nils Gustav. See Wilk, "Furnishing the future," p. 155.

69. *Eames Design,* pp. 206–207.

70. *Eames Design,* p. 207. Since 1990 the chair has not been available in rosewood. Had the current debates about ecological issues relating to the use of hardwoods in furniture making taken place in the 1950s, the Eameses probably would not have used that wood.

71. *Eames Design,* pp. 98–99.

72. G. Dunne, A. Gregor, and D. G. Meldrum, "Reinforced plastics," *Industrial Design,* May 1958, p. 40.

73. Abercrombie, *George Nelson,* p. 103.

74. See Philip Johnson, *Mies van der Rohe* (New York, 1947), pp. 172–173; Arthur Drexler, *Ludwig Mies van der Rohe* (New York, 1960), figure 30; L. Glaesser, *Ludwig Mies van der Rohe* (New York, 1977), pp. 16, 76–85; "Modern doesn't pay, or does it ?" *Interiors,* March 1946, pp. 66–74.

75. Eames/Kirkham, 1987.

76. *Eames Design,* p. 139.

77. The name came from a play on the term "chaise longue" and the surname of sculptor Gaston Lachaise, whose floating figure sculptures could, the Eameses joked, just about fit this piece of furniture.

78. These details are noted in the specifications illustrated on p. 97 of *Eames Design.*

79. *Eames Design,* p. 97.

80. Drexler, *Charles Eames,* pp. 36–37.

81. Caplan, *The Design of Herman Miller,* p. 57. See also Edgar Kaufmann jr., *Prize Designs for Modern Furniture from the International Competition for Low-Cost Furniture* Design (New York, 1950), pp. 19–23; *Eames Design,* pp. 138–143.

82. Ralph Randall, letter to *Architectural Review,* June 1951, pp. 398–400.

83. Eames/Kirkham, 1987.

84. *Eames Design,* pp. 140–143.

85. "Report from Chicago: The Eames Design," Public Broadcast Laboratory, April 6, 1969.

86. Robin Day/Kirkham, 1980. See also Pat Kirkham, *Hille: Profile of a British Furniture Company 1906–1982* (exhibition catalog, Leicester, 1982).

87. On the Loose Cushion Armchair see *Eames Design,* p. 371. On the La Fonda chair see *Eames Design,* p. 252; "Eames Chairs," *Architectural Forum,* February 1962.

88. On Bertoia see Eric Larrabee and Massimo Vignelli, *Knoll Design* (New York, 1981), pp. 68–69. On Sol Bloom see Cara Greenberg, *Mid-Century Modern* (New York, 1985), p. 116.

89. Designed by Antonio Bonet, Juan Kurchan, and Jorge Ferrari-Hardoy, it is sometimes known as the BKF chair. It is reputedly based on an anonymous Argentinian design of the 1930s which was, in turn, derived from a design pat-

ented in Britain in 1877 and British officers' chairs of World War I. See Greenberg, *Mid-Century Modern,* p. 76; Cheri Fehrman and Kenneth Fehrman, *Postwar Interior Design, 1945–1960* (New York, 1987), pp. 148–149.

90. "3 Chairs/3 Records of the design process," *Interiors,* April 1958, p. 119.

91. Olga Gueft, "Eames chairs of molded metal mesh," *Interiors,* April 1952, p. 109.

92. The details of the patent dispute are outlined in a letter, dated February 1, 1961, from Peter Price of Price and Heneveld, Patent Counsel, of Grand Rapids, to Vernon Poest of the Herman Miller Furniture Company (Herman Miller Archive). See also *Eames Design,* p. 151.

93. A. and P. Smithson/Kirkham, 1991.

94. See note 92 above.

95. Larrabee and Vignelli, *Knoll Design,* pp. 68–69.

96. "3 Chairs/3 Records of the design process," p. 119.

97. Bassett/Thackway, 1987.

98. "The new seat with a neater teeter," *Life,* February 6, 1956, pp. 122–123, 125.

99. Christopher Wilk, "Charles and Ray Eames," in *Design 1935–1965: What Modern Was,* ed. M. Eidelberg (New York, 1991), p. 213.

100. *Eames Design,* p. 148.

101. Wilk, *Marcel Breuer,* pp. 116–118.

102. Ibid.

103. Dennis Doorman, "Designing an aluminum world: Industrial Designers and the American aluminum industry," paper presented at conference on "Industry and Anti-Industry," Design History Society, Victoria and Albert Museum, London, 1990.

104. Ibid.

105. Ibid.

106. "3 Chairs/ 3 Records of the design process," p. 120.

107. *Eames Design,* pp. 227–228. Polished aluminum arms, optional on both the recliner and the lounge version, were thought by some to reduce the coherence of the design.

108. *Eames Design,* pp. 227–228; Albinson/Kirkham, 1991. Most of the development work was carried out by Don Albinson, Dale Bauer, and Bob Staples; modifications were later undertaken by Peter Pearce.

109. "3 Chairs/ 3 Records of the design process," p. 120.

110. "Eames aluminum chair styled for indoors or out," *Architectural Forum,* May 1958, p. 143.

111. "3 Chairs/ 3 Records of the design process," p. 120. Whether the chair could ever have been seriously considered a "low budget indoor chair" is another matter; with the small lounge version selling originally at $168 and the large one at $252, it was never cheap.

112. *Eames Design,* p. 342.

113. Carpenter, "Tribute to Charles Eames," pp. 18–19.

114. *Eames Design,* p. 249.

115. Finding inspiration in an African stool was not as original as was once thought. Stools similar to the one owned by the Eameses were in the African "art" collections of many American artists, designers, and intellectuals of the day. The photographer Eliot Elisofon had one, and his sculptor-furniture designer friend Isamu Noguchi took inspiration from it. (See "The new seat with a neater teeter," pp. 122–123, 125.) Noguchi's rocking "Teeter Seat" stool, designed in 1952 and manufactured in 1954 by Knoll Associates, must have been known to the Eameses. Noguchi's stool may well have been influenced by the Eameses' wire tables and metal bases. Noguchi retained something of the "dumbbell" shape but broke radically from the form of his friend's African stool, whereas the

Time-Life stool (which came in four variations-concave, convex, zigzag concave, and zigzag convex) retained the African form but gave it modern expression.

116. Eames/Kirkham, 1983.

117. Donges/Kirkham, 1991.

118. "Evolution of a design," *Interior Design Data,* November 1962, p. 140. The late 1950s saw the introduction of civilian jet aircraft, including the DC8 and the 707, which required longer runways and larger passenger terminals. See Henry Goddard and Gordon Brown, "Design for air travel," *Architectural Review* 105 (1949).

119. *Eames Design,* p. 275; Donges/Kirkham, 1991.

120. Eames/Kirkham, 1987. "A man of my reputation," Wilder said, "simply can't afford to have something that looks like a casting couch. It's too obvious a symbol of lechery." ("The anti casting couch," *Time,* January 5 1970, p. 37) The challenge was to update the traditional wood-and-leather couch so that it would lose its connotations. A great deal of the development work was done by Richard Donges.

121. *Eames Design,* p. 339.

122. Charles Eames, in "An Eames Celebration."

123. "The anti casting couch," p. 37.

124. *Eames Design,* p. 293.

125. This chair represented a fusion of several designs, including the Time-Life Chair (1960) and Eames Executive Seating (1961). Expected to be less expensive than much of the other Eames contract furniture, it proved too expensive for its niche. It remained in production for only 5 years (*Eames Design,* p. 343).

126. Ibid., p. 363.

127. Ibid., p. 191.

128. Ibid., p. 283. The 3473 sofa was developed by Dale Bauer, Peter Pearce, and Richard Donges.

129. Ibid., p. 451; J. Smith, "Modern classic comes to the market," *The Scotsman*, March 31, 1983.

130. *Eames Design*, pp. 66–67.

131. Ibid., pp. 126–129.

132. See figure 225 of *Holland in Vorm*, ed. G. Staal and H. Wolters (Haarlem, 1987), which shows Wim Rietveld's 1950 metal storage unit.

133. *Eames Design*, p. 188.

134. "Dormitory in a nutshell: ECS," *Interiors*, November, 1961, pp. 144–145; "Eames designs contract line for dorms," *Progressive Architecture*, February 1961, p. 73.

CHAPTER 6

1. Robert Venturi, quoted in Esther McCoy, "An affection for objects," *Progressive Architecture*, August 1973, p. 647.

2. Charles Eames, in "Report from Chicago: The Eames Design," PBL, April 6 1975. It was for similar reasons that the Eameses admired Disneyland—see Christopher Finch, *The Art of Walt Disney* (New York, 1973), p. 425.

3. The Office of Charles and Ray Eames, *A Computer Perspective: Background to the Computer Age* (Cambridge, Mass., 1990).

4. Charles Eames, "Language of vision: The nuts and bolts," *Bulletin of the American Academy of Arts and Sciences*, October 1974, pp. 18–19.

5. Ibid., p. 67.

6. In the case of The World of Franklin and Jefferson (1975–1977), for example, it seemed to some that the Eameses did not know when to stop the additive process.

7. Arthur A. Cohen, *Herbert Bayer: The Complete Work* (Cambridge, Mass., 1984), p. 283; Gwen Finkel Chanzit, *Herbert Bayer and Modernist Design in America* (Ann Arbor, 1987), pp. 115–118.

8. Cohen, *Herbert Bayer,* p. 284.

9. Ibid., p. 289.

10. Ibid., p. 288–289.

11. Other designers used blown-up photographs in modernist interiors in the United States before the Eameses. See, for example, Abel Faidy's interior design for the Hedrich-Blessing studio (1936) in Martin Grief, *Depression Modern: The Thirties Style In America* (New York, 1975), p. 66.

12. Franz Schulze, *Mies Van der Rohe: A Critical Biography* (Chicago, 1985), pp. 141–143. In 1927 the industry and craft exhibits designed by Lilly Reich for the Weissenhof Siedlung and by Reich and Ludwig Mies van der Rohe for the Exposition de la Mode, with their bold use of color and drapes, had also signaled an advance in German exhibition design.

13. *Exhibition Design,* ed. M. Black (London, 1950), p. 15.

14. Chanzit, *Herbert Bayer and Modernist Design in America,* p. 144.

15. *Display,* ed. G. Nelson (New York, 1953), pp. 110–116. Frederick Kiesler, a Viennese artist living in New York, used similar small platforms connected by wires to display paintings and sculpture at the Peggy Guggenheim Gallery in the 1940s.

16. See *Dawn of a New Day: The New York World's Fair, 1939/40,* ed. H. Harrison (New York, 1980).

17. Quoted in *Alvar Aalto,* ed. K. Flieg (London, 1975), p. 60.

18. Roland Marchand, "The designers go to the fair: Walter Dorwin Teague and the professionalization of corporate industrial exhibits, 1933–1940," *Design Issues* 7, no. 2 (1991), pp. 63–75; "Part II—The designers go to the fair: Norman Bel Geddes, the General Motors 'Futurama,' and the visit-to-the-factory transformed," *Design Issues* 8, no. 2 (1992), pp. 23–40.

19. Ibid.

20. Chanzit, *Herbert Bayer and Modernist Design in America,* p. 144.

21. Ibid.; Arthur W. Melton, "Problems of installation in museums of art," *Studies in Museum Education* no. 14 (1935).

22. Eliot Noyes, "Charles Eames," *Arts & Architecture,* September 1946, pp. 26–45.

23. Richard P. Lohse, *New Design in Exhibitions* (Zurich, 1953), pp. 110–113.

24. Marilyn Neuhart and John Neuhart, "The Los Angeles Legacy of Charles and Ray Eames," lecture, National Conference, Society of Environmental Graphic Designers, Pasadena, 1991.

25. Peter Smithson, "Just a few chairs and a house: An essay on the Eames-aesthetic," *Architectural Design* 36, September 1966, p. 443.

26. "Eames, weeds and colored paper," *Interiors,* January 1951, p. 10.

27. *Display,* ed. Nelson, pp. 64–65, Lohse, *New Design in Exhibitions,* pp. 104–107; *Eames Design,* p. 125.

28. *Display,* ed. Nelson, p. 68.

29. Ibid. Also quoted in *Eames Design,* p. 125.

30. *Eames Design,* p. 132.

31. *Display,* ed. Nelson, p. 68.

32. *Eames Design,* p. 160. Developed by Charles Kratka and Fred Usher of the Eames Office, the display had settings representing a living room, a dining room, a bedroom, and a children's room arranged in a cross pattern.

33. Jack Lenor Larsen, "Alexander Girard," *Design Quarterly* 98/99 (1976), p. 31. See also chapter 4 above.

34. Pupul Jayakar, "Charles Eames 1907–1978: A personal tribute," *Designfolio* (Ahmedabad) 2, January 1979.

35. Ibid.; Pupul Jayakar, *Indira Gandhi* (New Delhi, 1992), pp. 150–151; Ashoke Chatterjee, "Design in developing societies: Problems of relevance,"

Designfolio 2, January 1979; S. Balaram, "Product symbolism of Gandhi and its connection with Indian mythology," *Design Issues* 2, no. 2 (1989), pp. 60–86; Kumar H. Vyas, "The designer and the socio-technology of small production," *Journal of Design History* 4, no. 3 (1991), pp. 187–210.

36. Jayakar, *Indira Gandhi,* p. 150.

37. Ibid., pp. 150–151.

38. Jayakar, "Charles Eames." ("Something of a design guru" was how Peter Reyner Banham described Charles Eames shortly after first meeting him. I am grateful to Mary Banham for this information.)

39. Ibid.

40. Ibid.

41. Jayakar, *Indira Gandhi,* p. 150.

42. Eames Report, April 1958, reprinted in *Design Issues* 2, no. 2 (1989).

43. Ibid.

44. "Design, designer and industry," *Magazine of Art,* December 1951, p. 326.

45. Eames Report.

46. Jayakar, *Indira Gandhi* and "Charles Eames."

47. Vyas, "The designer and the socio-technology of small production," p. 194.

48. Jayakar, *Indira Gandhi,* p. 151.

49. *Eames Design,* pp. 294–299. I am grateful to Deborah Sussman and Ashoke Chatterjee for discussing matters related to the Eameses, the NID, and the Nehru exhibition with me.

50. "Nehru exhibit," *SPAN,* May 1965, p. 7.

51. Sharada Prasad, "The Nehru memorial exhibition," *Architectural Design,* October 1965, p. 489.

52. Jayakar, "Charles Eames."

53. Prasad, "The Nehru memorial exhibition," p. 488.

54. Ibid.

55. Ibid.

56. Ashoke Chatterjee, "The Nehru memorial exhibition," *Illustrated Weekly of India,* May 29 1965.

57. I am grateful to Ashoke Chatterjee and J. A. Panchall for this information.

58. "A tribute to Charles Eames," speech by Rt. Hon. Tony Benn, M.P., at U.S. Embassy, London, 1978.

59. Tony Benn, *Out of the Wilderness* (London, 1987), pp. 268–269, 272.

60. I am grateful to Darshana Bogilal for this information.

61. Chatterjee, "The Nehru memorial exhibition."

62. Marek Suchowiak, "Franklin and Jefferson's circle," *Poland*, January 1975, pp. 18–19. I am grateful to Stanton Stephens for this reference.

63. *Eames Design,* pp. 416–425.

64. Larry Rosing, "Bison-tennial show: The bazaar world of Franklin & Jefferson," *New Age Examiner,* summer 1976.

65. Patricia Rice, "Franklin and Jefferson visit the enemy camp," *St. Louis Post-Dispatch,* October 20, 1975; Owen Gingerich, "A conversation with Charles Eames," *American Scholar* 46 (1977), p. 335.

66. Ibid. In France the heroes were La Fayette and Rochambeau; in Poland, Kosciuszko and Pulaski.

67. Ibid. It was shown at the British Museum in London.

68. *Eames Design,* p. 422; Marilyn Neuhart, John Neuhart, Deborah Sussman, Richard Donges, Jehane Burns, and Jeanine Oppewell, respective interviews

with Pat Kirkham, 1991. That the exhibition looked as good as it did was due largely to the efforts of Richard Donges, Jehane Burns, Jeannine Oppewall, and Michael Russell, who looked after it with great care.

69. For example, a vacuum pump built in England for Franklin was included in the British exhibition (Rice, "Franklin and Jefferson visit the enemy camp," p. 21).

70. Thomas B. Hess, "From 'bisontennial' beasts to Cornell boxes," *New York,* March 22, 1976; Rosing, "Bison-tennial show"; Rice, "Franklin and Jefferson visit the enemy camp; Franchesca Stanfel, "At the Met: The World of Franklin & Jefferson," *Women's Wear Daily,* March 4, 1976.

71. Gingerich, "A conversation with Charles Eames," pp. 334–337.

72. Ibid.

73. Ibid.

74. Ibid., p. 336. It should be remembered that if anyone insisted on doing their own thing and working to their own briefs it was the Eameses.

75. Hess, "From 'bisontennial' beasts to Cornell boxes," p. 59; Rosing, "Bison-tennial show."

76. Rosing, "Bison-tennial show."

77. Ibid.

78. For Thomas Hess ("From 'bisontennial' beasts to Cornell boxes"), the world it presented was so cozy and perfect, such a nostalgic and partial representation of the past, that it made him "long for the dark side of America."

79. Gingerich, "A conversation with Charles Eames," p. 335.

80. Rosing, "Bison-tennial show."

81. Ibid.

82. Charles Eames, "Language of vision," p. 17.

83. Information panel, Mathematica, California Museum of Science and Industry, Los Angeles. The quotation was attributed to Laplace and dated 1796.

84. Neuharts, lecture, 1991; Neuharts/Kirkham 1991.

85. *Eames Design,* pp. 284–291.

86. Vincent Scully, quoted in Rosemarie Haag Bletter, "The 'laissez-fair', good taste, and money trees: Architecture at the fair," in *Remembering the Future* (New York, 1989), p. 112.

87. A. and P. Smithson/Kirkham, 1991. They felt it contrasted poorly with the images in and the presentation of the multi-media show itself.

88. Bletter, "The 'laissez-fair,'" p. 112.

89. *Eames Design,* p. 392.

90. Ibid., p. 335.

91. Ibid., pp. 364–369. See also *A Computer Perspective* (Cambridge, Mass., 1973); *A Computer Perspective: Background to the Computer Age* (Cambridge, Mass., 1990).

92. I. Bernard Cohen introduction to *A Computer Perspective* (1990), p. 5.

93. *Eames Design,* p. 366.

94. *A Computer Perspective,* p. 5.

95. Ibid.

96. *Eames Design,* p. 379. The exhibitions were Wallace J. Eckert: Celestial Mechanic (1972), Fibonacci: Growth and Form (1972), Copernicus (1972), Moveable Feasts and Changing Calendars (1973), On the Shoulders of Giants (1973), Isaac Newton (1973), and Philosophical Gardens (1974).

97. *Eames Design,* p. 379.

98. Ibid., pp. 384–387.

99. Ibid., p. 407.

100. Marilyn and John Neuhart, Jeannine Oppewall, Ralph Caplan, and Deborah Sussman, respective interviews with Pat Kirkham, 1991.

101. Suzanne Muchnic, " A tribute to Charles and Ray Eames," *Artweek,* January 15, 1977; Smithsons/Kirkham, 1991.

102. Marilyn and John Neuhart, Jeannine Oppewall, Ralph Caplan, and Deborah Sussman, respective interviews with Pat Kirkham, 1991.

103. In a 1991 lecture, the Neuharts compared The World of Franklin and Jefferson to "a circuit board that you could walk through."

104. Katherine Kuh, quoted in Chatterjee, "The Nehru memorial exhibition."

105. Ibid.

CHAPTER 7

1. David Curtis, *Experimental Cinema: A Fifty Year Evolution* (London, 1971), pp. 49–133; *A History of the American Avant-Garde Cinema* (New York, 1976), pp. 19–132; Sheldon Renan, *The Underground Film: An Introduction to Its Development in America* (New York, 1967), pp. 93–105; Lewis Jacobs, *The Rise of the American Film* (New York, 1968), pp. 563–582.

2. Ray Eames/Kirkham, 1983. On p. 24 of *Eames Design* there is a picture of Charles with a movie camera at Cranbrook.

3. *Eames Design,* p. 51.

4. Ibid.; Geoffrey Holroyd, "Retrospective statements," in *The Independent Group: Postwar Britain and the Aesthetics of Plenty,* ed. D. Robbins (Cambridge, Mass., 1990), p. 189.

5. *Eames Design,* p. 45 and passim.

6. John Neuhart/Kirkham, 1991.

7. *Eames Design,* pp. 27–28; Eames/Kirkham, 1983. The art department was then run by Cedric Gibbons. The movies Charles worked on included *Johnny Eager* (1941, dir. Mervyn Leroy), *I Married an Angel* (1942, dir. W. S. Van Dyke), *Ran-*

dom Harvest (1942, dir. Mervyn Leroy), and *Mrs. Miniver* (1942, dir. Sidney Franklin)—none of which Ray found "particularly interesting" or "important."

8. He had been forced to leave behind a chair designed by Mies (bought soon after the Weissenhof Siedlung exhibition of 1927) when he left Germany for the United States in 1933 (Eames/Kirkham, 1983). Ray Eames told me that Wilder "had a good sense of quality. Early on he bought a monumental Picasso head, also a Magritte. He also had a beautiful Miró." See also Zolotow, *Billy Wilder in Hollywood;* Madsen, *Billy Wilder.*

9. Audrey Wilder/Kirkham, 1993; Zolotow, *Billy Wilder,* p. 215. When the happy couple finally found a justice of the peace to marry them, Ray went out into the backyard of the building and made a beautiful wedding bouquet for Audrey out of the simple wildflowers and ferns growing there. On p. 109 of *Eames Design* there is a photograph taken by Charles of the Wilders on the Nevada trip.

10. Audrey Wilder/Kirkham, 1993. On the Polaroid films see the end of this chapter.

11. *Eames Design,* p. 210.

12. Billy Wilder/Kirkham, 1993. See also *Eames Design,* p. 244.

13. Eames/Kirkham, 1987.

14. Paul Schrader, "Poetry of ideas: The films of Charles Eames," *Film Quarterly,* spring 1970, pp. 2–19.

15. Patricia Deneger, "The visual image is the Charles Eames message," *St. Louis Post-Dispatch,* April 13, 1975.

16. Curtis, *Experimental Cinema;* Renan, *The Underground Film;* Jacobs, *The Rise of the American Film*; *A History of the American Avant-Garde Cinema* (see note 1 to the present chapter).

17. Jacobs, p. 546; Curtis, pp. 25–30, 38–48.

18. Jacobs, pp. 544–554.

19. Charles and Ray were both aware of this new art form—Charles because of his long-standing interest in photography and in general artistic matters, Ray through her involvement in avant-garde circles in New York.

20. Jacobs, p. 563–570; Curtis, pp. 52–54.

21. Barbara Goldstein, *Arts & Architecture: The Entenza Years* (Cambridge, Mass., 1990), pp. 8, 13–26.

22. Curtis, *Experimental Cinema,* pp. 30, 53–54.

23. Ibid., pp. 52–58.

24. Whitney stayed for four years, working on the 1959 Moscow multi-screen presentation, among other things.

25. Curtis, *Experimental Cinema,* p. 134. It was established in 1957 by Bob Pike as a service run by and for filmmakers.

26. Saul Pett, "Charles Eames: Imagination unlimited," *St. Louis Post-Dispatch,* July, 27 1971; Eames/Kirkham, 1983.

27. Jacobs, p. 562. Curtis (p. 53) suggests that Fischinger's technique (developed for a cigarette commercial in the 1930s) of parading lines of cigarettes like soldiers was used and developed by the Eameses in *Toccata for Toy Trains.* Despite wishing this to be the case (partly because it would place the Eameses more squarely in the "experimental" cinema camp), I am afraid that I do not agree.

28. Elaine Sewell Jones/Kirkham, 1993.

29. On McLaren see David Curtis, "Where does one put Norman McLaren?" in *Norman McLaren: Exhibitions and Films* (London, 1975), pp. 47–53.

30. Charles and Ray Eames were not the only designers to enter this area of filmmaking; their most notable contemporaries included Saul and Elaine Bass and Morton and Mildred Goldscholl. These three couples, together with Francis Thompson and Alexander Hammid, set lofty visual and technical standards. See Ralph Caplan, "The messages of industry on the screen," *Industrial Design,* April 1960, p. 50; Mina Hamilton, "Films at the fair," *Industrial Design,* April 1964, pp. 36–42.

31. R. J. Flaherty, *My Eskimo Friends: "Nanook of the North"* (London, 1924); F. H. Flaherty, *The Odyssey of a Film Maker; Robert Flaherty's Story* (Urbana, Ill., 1960).

32. Victor Animatograph Corporation, advertisement in *Business Screen* 1, no. 3 (1945). This journal is a mine of information about this underresearched area of film history; volume 19, no. 1 (1958), for instance, includes some Robert Searle drawings used in *Energetically Yours.* See also Peter Spooner, *Business Films: How to Make and Use Them* (London, 1959) and *Business, Industry and Film,* an undated pamphlet produced by Wilbur Streech Productions of New York. For a general discussion of industrial and business films see Caplan, "Messages of Industry on the Screen," pp. 50–65.

33. Caplan, "Messages of Industry on the Screen," p. 50.

34. Ibid..

35. Ibid.

36. Ibid.

37. Ibid., p. 177; *Business Screen* 23, no. 7 (1962), p. 36; George Nelson, "Art X—The Georgia Experiment," *Industrial Design,* October 1954.

38. Owen Gingerich, "A conversation with Charles Eames," *American Scholar* 46 (1977), p. 331.

39. To make a 100-minute presentation in a commercial studio utilizing 16-mm color film with sound cost approximately $1500 per minute in the early 1950s (Nelson, "Art X"). Nelson estimated that one complete course would cost $1,000,000.

40. In general, the Eameses concentrated on multiple-image presentations rather than multi-media events. Multi-screen projection, described by Charles Eames as an "ideal outlet for a picture taking maniac"(Eames Celebration), offered the opportunity to show more images in a short space of time than ever before and was perfect for people as obsessive about images as he and Ray.

41. "American National Exhibition in Moscow," *Industrial Design,* March 1959, pp. 47–51; Eames Celebration.

42. Stanley Abercrombie, *George Nelson: The Design of Modern Design*. Wilder recalled meeting Nelson that night but could not remember such important decisions being made (Wilder/Kirkham, 1993).

43. Peter Blake, Eames Celebration.

44. Ibid.; Eames/Kirkham 1983.

45. Buckminster Fuller, Eames Celebration.

46. Peter Blake, Eames Celebration.

47. Eames/Kirkham, 1983; Ray Eames, Eames Celebration.

48. Wilder/Kirkham, 1993.

49. Carpenter, "Tribute to Charles Eames," p. 32. Carpenter stated that the idea for a jet came from Charles and the idea for flowers from Ray. Abercrombie (via Jacqueline Nelson) attributes the idea of ending "with love" to George Nelson. I do not doubt that Ray might have discussed the ending with Nelson, and I can accept that he may have advised the often-indecisive Ray to follow her inclination to end with a warm human touch. I am a little skeptical, however, about the idea of the ending originating with Nelson—not least because both Charles and Ray separately always credited this to Ray and because the element of "love" played a greater part in Ray's aesthetic practice than in Nelson's.

50. Charles Eames, Eames Celebration.

51. Buckminster Fuller, Eames Celebration.

52. Wilder/Kirkham, 1993.

53. Gingerich, "Conversation with Charles Eames," pp. 333-334.

54. *Eames Design,* pp. 270–273 (presentation) and p. 292 (film).

55. Ibid., pp. 284–291.

56. Ralph Caplan, "Experiencing Eames," *Industrial Design,* January-February 1990, p. 66.

57. Mina Hamilton, "Films at the fair 2," *Industrial Design,* May 1964, pp. 36–38.

58. Schrader, "Poetry of ideas," p. 10.

59. Curtis, *Experimental Cinema,* pp. 14–15.

60. Ibid., pp. 57–59.

61. Ibid., pp. 49–135.

62. Many of the multi-media presentations included motion-picture footage.

63. Eames/Kirkham, 1983.

64. Ibid.; Ray Eames, Eames Celebration.

65. Ibid.

66. *A Computer Perspective* also featured jazz percussion improvisation by Shelley Manne.

67. Carpenter, "Tribute to Charles Eames," p. 31. See also Schrader, "Poetry of ideas," p. 14.

68. Caplan, "Industry on the Screen," p. 50. Later they were to modify these views and acknowledge that even film was far from a perfectly controlled or controllable medium. See Schrader, p. 14.

69. Schrader (p. 8) classifies them as "toy" and "ideas" films and McCoy as "object" and "informational" ones. See Esther McCoy, "Charles and Ray Eames," *Design Quarterly* 98/99 (1975), p. 29. It is important to remember that the former feature objects, that many of the latter convey important ideas.

70. Eames/Kirkham, 1983.

71. This is the only Eames film listed in John G. Hanhardt's "Chronology 1943–1972," in *American Avant Garde Cinema.*

72. A Sampling of Eames Films Available from Pyramid (undated publicity leaflet. Pyramid Films, Santa Monica).

73. Eames/Kirkham, 1983. See also chapter 4 of the present volume.

74. John Neuhart (in joint lecture session with Marilyn Neuhart), "A Rough Sketch About a Lot of Work: Eames Office Films and Exhibitions," at conference on Charles and Ray Eames : Quintessential American Designers, Cooper-Hewitt National Museum of Design, New York, 1989.

75. Opening narration, *Toccata for Toy Trains,* 1957. See also chapter 4 above.

76. This philosophy probably owed more to Arts and Crafts ideas and to Romanticism than to modernism.

77. A Tribute to Charles Eames, speech made by Rt. Hon. Tony Benn, M.P., U.S. Embassy, London, 1978.

78. Schrader, "Poetry of ideas," p. 9.

79. Philip Morrison, Eames Celebration.

80. *Eames Design,* p. 163.

81. Charles Eames, Eames Celebration, 1975. Charles stated that for the first two or three films there was no synchronizer and no rewinds—"just scissors and glue" and guidance from his friend Tom Fogelman at Consolidated Film Industries.

82. Charles Eames, Eames Celebration, 1975.

83. *Eames Design,* p. 163.

84. The excitement of the event is testified to by several former students who kindly discussed it with me. John Neuhart and Richard Donges recall that "for some reason or other" Charles and Ray considered the request for illustrations of their workshop to be an intrusion of their privacy (respective interviews with Pat Kirkham, 1991).

85. *Eames Design,* pp. 236, 250.

86. I am grateful to Steve McIntyre for raising this point, and to him, David Curtis, Jim Cook, Peter Smithson, and the late Alison Smithson for discussing and viewing this and other Eames films with me.

87. Schrader, "Poetry of ideas," p. 10.

88. Michael Brawne, "The wit of technology," *Architectural Design,* September 1966, p. 452.

89. Schrader, "Poetry of ideas," p. 7.

90. Ibid., pp. 13–14.

91. Ibid., p. 14.

92. Ibid., p. 13.

93. Charles Eames/Virginia Stith, 1977. 94. "Report from Chicago: The Eames Design," PBL, April 6, 1969.

95. Ibid.; Eames/Kirkham, 1983.

96. David Wainwright, *Guardian,* August 20, 1963.

97. The Eameses' other presentation films made were for the prestigious World of Franklin and Jefferson exhibition, for an information center at the Metropolitan Museum of Art in New York (1975, and for an IBM exhibition center (1979). These films combined animation, live action, and still photography.

98. See C. Shannon and W. Weaver, *The Mathematical Theory of Communications* (1949).

99. Schrader, "Poetry of ideas," p. 9.

100. Their first film in this area, *A Communications Primer* (1953), resulted from the work done with George Nelson on communications and education, discussed above.

101. Philip Morrison, Eames Celebration.

102. Report from Chicago.

103. See Richard Horn, *Fifties Style: Then and Now* (New York, 1985), pp. 52–53.

104. Report from Chicago.

105. Kees Boeke, *Cosmic View: The Universe in Forty Jumps* (Haarlem, 1957). Stanley Kubrick, who later directed *2001: A Space Odyssey,* was also inspired by this book.

106. A Sampling of Eames Films.

107. Eames/Kirkham, 1987.

108. Schrader, "Poetry of ideas," pp. 10–11.

109. Philip Morrison, Eames Celebration.

110. Quoted in Esther McCoy, "An affection for objects," *Progressive Architecture,* August 1973, p. 67.

111. Schrader, "Poetry of ideas," p. 11.

112. Report from Chicago.

113. I first met Charles Montgomery in 1967 and thereafter spent many hours with him discussing a variety of issues, including eighteenth- and nineteenth-century furniture making (particularly labor relations and mechanization), education, art and design, and, last, but by no means least, the Eameses.

114. Narration, *The Look of America 1750–1800* (1976).

115. Another reason that they "scaled back" is that the Franklin and Jefferson project had proved extremely tiring (Eames/Kirkham, 1983).

116. *Eames Design,* pp. 372–373.

117. Ibid., pp. 444–445.

118. Judith Wechsler, interview and subsequent correspondence with Pat Kirkham, 1991–1994.

119. Ibid.; *Eames Design,* p. 448.

120. Wechsler/Kirkham, 1991.

121. Ibid. There were plans to make a film on Monet. She and Charles Eames were in St. Louis to photograph Monet paintings at the time of Charles's death.

122. Ray was considerably less involved in the three films made with Judith Wechsler than in many of the others,

123. Caplan, "Industry on the Screen," p. 63.

124. Schrader, "Poetry of ideas," p. 14.

125. Ibid.; Hodgett, quoted in McCoy, p. 67.

CONCLUSION

1. Charles Eames/Virginia Stith, 1977.

2. Frank Lloyd Wright, *An Autobiography* (London, 1977), p. 362.

3. Paul Schrader, "Poetry of ideas," *Film Quarterly,* spring 1970, p. 10. See also *Blueprints for Modern Living,* p. 52.

4. Walter McQuade, "Charles Eames isn't resting on his chair," *Fortune,* February 1975, p. 98.

5. Esther McCoy, "Charles and Ray Eames," *Design Quarterly* 98/99 (1974–75), p. 29. There is also a direct link between the design process of looking at a problem from the scale above and the scale below (a process Charles Eames learned from Eliel Saarinen) and the film *Powers of Ten.*

6. Ray Eames and Elaine Sewell Jones, interviews with Pat Kirkham, 1983 and 1991 respectively.

7. Eames Report, 1958.

8. Charles last visited India in January 1978, shortly before his death, and spoke to staff and students at the NID. Ray last visited the NID in December 1987, when she presented the first Charles Eames Award.

9. Reyner Banham, "Klarheit, Ehrlichkeit, Einfachkeit . . . and wit too!" in *Blueprints,* pp. 184–187.

10. See *Holland in Vorm,* ed. G. Staal and H. Wolters (Haarlem, 1987), which illustrates furniture very derivative of that of the Eameses by W. Rietveld, U. Gispen, F. Kramer, and C. Braakman. See also Gingerich, "Conversation with Charles Eames," p. 329; Wilk, "Eames Furniture: Antecedents and Progeny," and Guy Julier, "Radical modernism in contemporary Spanish design" in Modernism in Design, ed. P. Greenhalgh (London, 1990), p. 222.

11. Gingerich, "Conversation with Charles Eames," p. 328.

12. Banham, "Klarheit," pp. 184–187.

13. For example, the Hopkins House, in London (Michael and Patti Hopkins, 1975) and the Sainsbury Centre, in Norwich (Norman and Wendy Foster, 1974–1978).

14. See Bernard I. Cohen, "Introduction to the Office of Charles and Ray Eames," in *A Computer Perspective* (Cambridge, Mass., 1990), p. 5.

15. Schrader ("Poetry of ideas," p. 10) cites Wheaton Galentine's *Treadle and Bobbin* (1954) and Don Levy's *Time Is* (1964) as directly influenced by Eames films. *Powers of Ten* has directly influenced a range of films and advertisements, including Peter Greenaway's *Dante* (1988) and a British Telecom television commercial (1989).

16. National Film Theatre, London, November 1975. The program notes referred to Eames films as "sophisticated in technique, dazzling to watch." Charles Eames spoke at the NFT on November 10, 1975.

17. Schrader, "Poetry of ideas," p. 13.

18. Some are still in distribution and/or available on video (Pyramid Films and Home Video, Santa Monica).

19. "Eames Celebration," *Architectural Design,* September 1966, pp. 432–471.) See also *The Independent Group,* ed. D. Robbins (Cambridge, Mass., 1990)' Banham, "Klarheit"; and, particularly for the Pop Art influence, Alison Smithson, "And now Dhamas are dying out in Japan," *Architectural Design,* September 1966, pp. 447–448.

20. Michael Brawne, "The wit of technology," *Architectural Design,* September 1966, pp. 449–457.

21. Peter Smithson, "Just a few chairs and a house," *Architectural Design,* September 1966, p. 443.

22. Deborah Sussman/Kirkham, 1991.

23. McQuade, "Charles Eames isn't resting on his chair," p. 98.

24. Thomas B. Sherman, "Ex-St. Louisan who made 'Eames Chair,'" *St. Louis Post-Dispatch,* October 22, 1951.

25. Schrader, "Poetry of ideas," p. 6; *Current Biography,* 1965, p. 139.

26. Charles Eames, Eames Celebration, 1975.

27. *Eames Design,* p. 149.

28. When Ken Garland eagerly showed Charles Eames one of his radical manifestos about the purpose of design, he was surprised and somewhat dismayed when Charles told him not to focus on such "useless things" (Ken Garland, conversation and subsequent correspondence with Pat Kirkham, 1991).

29. Ralph Caplan/Kirkham, 1991.

30. Ibid. I am grateful to Michael Large for discussing with me the relationship of IBM, Noyes, and the Eameses and for putting me in touch with Molly Noyes.

31. Ralph Caplan/Kirkham, 1991.

32. Eames Celebration; Julius Shulman/Kirkham, 1993. Shulman told me that he thought Charles Eames to be one of the greatest minds ever—possibly as great as Leonardo da Vinci, a biography of whom he was currently reading. He stated that as he read he was constantly reminded of Charles Eames and his extraordinary breadth of vision.

33. Buckminster Fuller, Eames Celebration.

34. *Eames Design,* p. 10

35. Ernestine Carter, "Imports and exports," *Sunday Times* (London), October 1, 1967.

36. *Washington Post,* quoted in NFT program notes, London, November 10, 1975.

37. On Wilder see Carpenter, "Tribute to Charles Eames," p. 12.

38. McCoy, "Charles and Ray Eames," p. 21.

39. See also *Significant Others. Creativity and Intimate Partnership,* ed. W. Chadwick and I. De Courtivron (London, 1993). There is no doubt that dominant social stereotypes about masculinity and femininity affected how Charles and Ray saw themselves, how they were (and are) seen by friends and by those with and for whom they worked, and how they are seen by critics and historians; however, the nuances and qualifications to those stereotypes that are evident in their joint story have also been central to my concerns.

40. See *Mothering the Mind: Twelve Studies of Writers and Their Silent Partners,* ed. R. Perry and M. W. Brownley (New York, 1984).

41. Ray Eames/Kirkham, 1983 and 1987.

42. *Significant Others,* pp. 9–10.

43. Ibid., p. 10; Anne M. Wagner, "Fictions: Krasner's presence, Pollock's absence," pp. 223–243, in the same anthology.

44. Alison Smithson, Jeannine Oppewall, Deborah Sussman and Marilyn Neuhart, respective interviews with Pat Kirkham, 1991.

45. Deborah Sussman, Eames Demetrios, John Neuhart, Marilyn Neuhart, Jehane Burns, and Elaine Sewell Jones, respective interviews with Pat Kirkham, 1991.

46. Eames/Kirkham, 1983.

47. Ibid.

48. *Significant Others,* p. 10. See also Christine Battersby, *Gender and Genius: Towards a Feminist Aesthetics* (London, 1989).

49. *Eames Design,* pp. 355–362.

50. Ray Eames, in "Report from Chicago"; Eames/Kirkham, 1983.

51. Eames/Kirkham, 1983.

52. Michael Glickman, "Ray Eames," *Architects' Journal,* September 7, 1988, p. 26.

53. Carpenter, "Tribute to Charles Eames," p. 12.

54. *Current Biography,* 1965, p. 141; Eames/Kirkham, 1987.

55. Eames/Kirkham, 1987.

56. With $400,000 coming from IBM for the World of Franklin and Jefferson exhibition, and the rest from fees and royalties (McQuade, "Charles Eames isn't resting on his chair," p. 99).

57. Eames/Kirkham, 1987.

58. Lacy, "Warehouse full of ideas," p. 27.

59. Suzanne Muchnic, "A tribute to Charles and Ray Eames," *Art Week,* January 15, 1977, p. 5.

INDEX

Numbers of pages containing illustrations are italicized. Titles of films, books, and periodicals are italicized. Titles of exhibitions and presentations are set in Roman with initial capitals.

DATE DUE

SEP 2 0 1995	
OCT - 8 1995	
DEC 1 5 1995	
JAN 2 0 1996	
MAR - 2 1996	
OCT 9 1996	
DEC 2 7 1999	
AUG 2 2 2002	
SEP 1 6 2002	
DEC 1 9 2004	
GAYLORD	PRINTED IN U.S.A.